THE OLD TESTAMENT

IN THE

JEWISH CHURCH

TWELVE LECTURES ON BIBLICAL CRITICISM

By W. ROBERTSON SMITH, M.A.

SIETE VOI ACCORTI,
CHE QUEL DI RETRO MUOVE CIÒ CHE TOCCA?
COSÌ NON SOGLION FARE I PIÈ DE' MORTI.

Wipf & Stock
PUBLISHERS
Eugene, Oregon

Wipf and Stock Publishers
199 W 8th Ave, Suite 3
Eugene, OR 97401

The Old Testament in the Jewish Church
Twelve Lectures on Biblical Criticism
By Smith, W. Robertson
ISBN: 1-59752-642-8
Publication date 6/14/2006
Previously published by Adam and Charles Black, 1881

PREFACE.

THE Twelve Lectures now laid before the public had their origin in a temporary victory of the opponents of progressive Biblical Science in Scotland, which has withdrawn me during the past winter from the ordinary work of my Chair in Aberdeen, and in the invitation of some six hundred prominent Free Churchmen in Edinburgh and Glasgow, who deemed it better that the Scottish public should have an opportunity of understanding the position of the newer Criticism than that they should condemn it unheard. The Lectures were delivered in Edinburgh and Glasgow during the first three months of the present year, and the average attendance on the course in the two cities was not less than eighteen hundred. The sustained interest with which this large audience followed the attempt to lay before them an outline of the problems, the methods, and the results of Old Testament Criticism is sufficient proof that they did not find modern Biblical Science the repulsive and unreal thing which it is often represented to be. The Lectures are printed mainly from shorthand reports taken in Glasgow, and as nearly as possible in the form in which they were delivered in Edinburgh after final revision. I have striven to make my exposition essentially popular in the legitimate sense of that word—that is, to present a continuous argument, resting at every point on valid historical evidence, and so framed that it can be followed by the ordinary English reader who is familiar with the Bible and accustomed to consecutive thought. There are some critical processes which cannot be explained without constant use of the Hebrew Text; but I have tried to make all the main parts of the discussion independent of reference to these. Of course it is not possible for any sound argument to adopt in every case the renderings of the English Version. In important passages I have indicated the necessary corrections; but in general it is to be understood that, while I cite all texts by the English chapters and verses, I argue from the Hebrew.

The appended notes are designed to complete and illustrate the details of the argument, and to make the book more useful to students by supplying hints for further study. I have made no attempt to give complete references to the modern literature of the subject. Indeed, as the Lectures have been written, delivered, and printed in three months, it was impossible for me to reconsult all the books which have influenced my views, and acknowledge my indebtedness to each. My effort has been to give a lucid view of the critical argument as it stands in my own mind, and to support it in every part from the text of Scripture or other original sources. It is of the first importance that the reader should realise that Biblical Criticism is not the invention of modern scholars, but the legitimate interpretation of historical facts. I have tried therefore to keep the facts always in the foreground, and, where they are derived from ancient books not in every one's hands, I have either given full citations, or made careful reference to the original authorities.

The great value of historical criticism is that it makes the Old Testament more real to us. Christianity can never separate itself from its historical basis on the Religion of Israel; the revelation of God in Christ cannot be divorced from the earlier revelation on which our Lord built. In all true religion the new rests upon the old. No one, then, to whom Christianity is a reality can safely acquiesce in an unreal conception of the Old Testament history; and in an age when all are interested in historical research, no apologetic can prevent thoughtful minds from drifting away from faith if the historical study of the Old Covenant is condemned by the Church and left in the hands of unbelievers.

The current treatment of the Old Testament has produced a widespread uneasy suspicion that this history cannot bear to be tested like other ancient histories. The old method of explaining difficulties and reconciling apparent contradictions would no longer be tolerated in dealing with other books, and men ask themselves whether our Christian faith, the most precious gift of truth which God has given us, can safely base its defence on arguments that bring no sense of reality to the mind. Yet the history of Israel, when rightly studied, is the most real and vivid of all histories, and the proofs of God's working among His people of old may still be made, what they were in time past, one of the strongest evidences of Christianity. It was no blind chance, and no mere human wisdom, that shaped the growth of Israel's religion, and finally stamped it in these forms, now so strange to us, which preserved the living seed of the Divine word till the fulness of the time when He was manifested who transformed the religion of Israel into a religion for all mankind.

The increasing influence of critical views among earnest students of the Bible is not to be explained on the Manichæan theory that new views commend themselves to mankind in proportion as they ignore God. The living God is as present in the critical construction of the history as in that to which tradition has wedded us. Criticism is a reality and a force because it unfolds a living and consistent picture of the Old Dispensation; it is itself a living thing, which plants its foot upon realities, and, like Dante among the shades, proves its life by moving what it touches.

"Così non soglion fare i piè de' morti."

W. ROBERTSON SMITH.

ABERDEEN, *April* 4, 1881.

CONTENTS.

LECTURE I.
CRITICISM AND THE THEOLOGY OF THE REFORMATION . 1

LECTURE II.
CHRISTIAN INTERPRETATION AND JEWISH TRADITION . 30

LECTURE III.
THE SCRIBES 55

LECTURE IV.
THE SEPTUAGINT 84

LECTURE V.
THE SEPTUAGINT (*continued*)—THE CANON . . 118

LECTURE VI.
THE HISTORY OF THE CANON 149

LECTURE VII.
THE PSALTER 176

LECTURE VIII.

The Traditional Theory of the Old Testament History 208

LECTURE IX.

The Law and the History of Israel before the Exile 241

LECTURE X.

The Prophets 268

LECTURE XI.

The Pentateuch; The First Legislation . . 305

LECTURE XII.

The Deuteronomic Code and Levitical Law . . 343

Notes and Illustrations 389

Index 443

LECTURE I.

CRITICISM AND THE THEOLOGY OF THE REFORMATION.

I HAVE undertaken to deliver a course of lectures to you, not with a polemical purpose, but in answer to a request for information. I am not here to defend my private opinion on any disputed question, but to expound as well as I can the elements of a well-established department of historical study. Biblical criticism is a branch of historical science; and I hope to convince you as we proceed that it is a legitimate and necessary science, which must continue to draw the attention of all who go deep into the Bible and the religion of the Bible, if there is any Biblical science at all.

It would be affectation to ignore the fact that in saying so much I at once enter upon ground of controversy. The science of Biblical Criticism has not escaped the fate of every science which takes topics of general human interest for its subject matter, and advances theories destructive of current views upon things with which every one is familiar and in which every one has some practical concern. You remember the early struggles of the astronomy of Galileo and Newton. The evidence for the discoveries of these great philosophers was the clearest that has ever been offered in support of a new truth. But the resistance which they elicited had nothing to do with the clearness of the evidence. It gained its strength from the fact that the astronomers dealt with very familiar phenomena, with such things as the rise of the sun and the immovableness of the earth, which form part of every man's daily experience. About these phenomena they gave a theory inconsistent with all current ideas, with the idioms of human speech, and even, as it seemed, with the daily observations of sound common sense. They seemed to destroy the very conditions of human life. If the sun did not rise morning by morning, if the earth, instead of being stable under men's feet, was never in the same place when you opened your eyes in the morning as you had left it in when you went to bed, a gigantic element of uncertainty appeared to be introduced into the most valuable and practical convictions of mankind. Views so radical seemed to be necessarily irreligious. Not only the Church of Rome, but respected Puritans like John Owen (*Works*, vol. xix. p. 310), were convinced that the Newtonian philosophy was "built on fallible phenomena and advanced by many arbitrary presumptions against evident testimonies of Scripture."

We are not so much wiser than our forefathers, and our theologians are not so much superior to John Owen, that we should think it impossible for suspicions equally unfounded to attack a new science in our days, especially a science like that of Biblical Criticism, which comes far closer than anything in astronomy to the familiar and cherished opinions of lovers of the Bible. It would argue indifference rather than enlightenment, if the great mass of Bible-readers, to whom scientific points of view for the study of Scripture are wholly unfamiliar, could adjust themselves to a new line of investigation into the history of the Bible without passing through a crisis of anxious thought not far removed from distress and alarm.

The deepest practical convictions of our lives are seldom formulated with precision. They have been learned by experience rather than by logic, and we are content if we can give them an expression accurate enough to meet our daily wants. And so when we have to bring these convictions to bear on some new question, the formula which has sufficed us hitherto is very apt to lead us astray. For in rough practical formulas, in the working rules, if I may so call them, of our daily spiritual life, the essential is constantly mixed up with what is unimportant or even incorrect. We store our treasures of conviction in earthen vessels, and the broken pipkin of an obsolete formula often acquires for us the value of the treasure which it enshrines. To return for a moment to the astronomical analogy: the fundamental physical truth of the alternation of night and day was embodied in the formula of the sun's daily journey round our globe. Accurate enough for the ordinary affairs of human toil, this formula was thoroughly false for the purposes of astronomy. This did not prevent outraged common sense from rising to condemn the astronomers for challenging a truth which had its evidence in every man's experience. And yet as a matter of fact the evidence of experience, when taken as a whole, bore out the Newtonian astronomy, and did not agree with the old view.

The persuasion that in the Bible God Himself speaks words of love and life to the soul is the essence of the Christian's conviction as to the truth and authority of Scripture. This persuasion is not, and cannot be, derived from external testimony. No tradition as to the worth of Scripture, no assurance transmitted from our fathers, or from any who in past time heard God's revealing voice, can make the revelation to which they bear witness a personal voice of God to us. The element of personal conviction, which lifts faith out of the region of probable evidence into the sphere of divine certainty, is given only by the Holy Spirit still bearing witness in and with the Word. But then the Word to which this spiritual testimony applies is a written word, which has a history, which has to be read and explained like other ancient books. How we read and explain the Bible depends in great measure on human teaching. The Bible itself is God's book, but the Bible as read and understood by any man or school of men is God's book *plus* a very large element of human interpretation. In our ordinary Bible-reading these two things, the divine book and the human understanding of the book, are not kept sharply apart. We are aware that some passages are obscure, and we do not claim divine certitude for the interpretation that we put on them. But we are apt to forget that the influence of human and traditional interpretation goes much further than a few obscure passages. Our general views of the Bible history, our way of looking, not merely at passages, but at whole books, are coloured by things which we have learned from men, and which have no claim to rest on the self-evidencing divine Word. This we forget, and so, taking God's witness to His Word to be a witness to our whole conception of the Word, we claim a divine certainty for opinions which lie within the sphere of ordinary reason, and which can be proved or disproved by the ordinary laws of historical evidence. We assume that, because our reading of Scripture is sufficiently correct to allow us to find in it the God of redemption speaking words of grace to our soul, those who seek some other view of the historical aspects of Scripture are trying to eliminate the God of grace from His own book.

A large part of Bible-readers never come through the mental discipline which is necessary to cure prejudices of this kind, or, in other words, have never been forced by the necessities of their life to distinguish between the accidental and the essential, the human conjectures and the divine truth, which are wrapped up together in current interpretations of Scripture. But those who are called in providence to make systematic and scholarly study of the Bible the work of their lives inevitably come face to face with facts which force them to draw those distinctions which, to a practical reader, may seem superfluous.

Consider what systematic and scholarly study involves in contradistinction to the ordinary practical use of the Bible. Ordinary Bible-reading is eclectic and devotional. A detached passage is taken up, and attention is concentrated on the immediate edification which can be derived from it. Very often the profit which the Bible-reader derives from his morning or evening portion lies mainly in a single word of divine love coming straight home to the heart. And in general the real fruit of such Bible-reading lies less in any addition to one's store of systematic knowledge than in the privilege of withdrawing for a moment from the thoughts and cares of the world, to enter into a pure and holy atmosphere, where the God of love and redemption reveals Himself to the heart, and where the simplest believer can place himself by the side of the psalmist, the prophet, or the apostle, in that inner sanctuary where no sound is heard but the gracious accents of divine promise and the sweet response of assured and humble faith. Far be it from me to undervalue such use of Scripture. It is by this power of touching the heart and lifting the soul into converse with heaven that the Bible approves itself the pure and perfect Word of God, a lamp unto the feet and a light unto the path of every Christian. But, on the other hand, a study which is exclusively practical and devotional is necessarily imperfect. There are many things in Scripture which do not lend themselves to an immediate practical purpose, and which in fact are as good as shut out from the circle of ordinary Bible-reading. I know that good people often try to hide this fact from themselves by hooking on some sort of lesson to passages which they do not understand, or which do not directly touch any spiritual chord. There is very respectable precedent for this course, which in fact is nothing else than the method of tropical exegesis that reigned supreme in the Old Catholic and Mediæval Church. The ancient fathers laid down the principle that everything in Scripture which, taken in its natural sense, appears unedifying must be made edifying by some method of typical or figurative application.[1] In principle this is no longer admitted in the Protestant Churches (unless perhaps for the Song of Solomon), but in practice we still get over many difficulties by tacking on a lesson which is not really taken out of the difficult passage, but read into it from some other part of Scripture. People satisfy themselves in this way, but they do not solve the difficulty. Let us be frank with ourselves, and admit that there are many things in Scripture in which unsystematic and merely devotional reading finds no profit. Such parts of the Bible as the genealogies in Chronicles, the description of Solomon's temple, a considerable portion of Ezekiel, and not a few of the details of ritual in the

Pentateuch do not serve an immediate devotional purpose, and are really blank pages to any other than systematical and critical study. And for a different reason the same thing is true of many passages of the prophetical and poetical books, where the language is so obscure, and the train of thought so difficult to grasp, that even the best scholars, with every help which philology can offer, will not venture to affirm that they possess a certain interpretation. Difficulties of this sort are not confined to a few corners of the Bible. They run through the whole volume, and force themselves on the attention of every one who desires to understand any book of the Bible as a whole.

And so we are brought to this issue. We may, if we please, confine our study of Scripture to what is immediately edifying, skimming lightly over all pages which do not serve a direct purpose of devotion, and ignoring every difficulty which does not yield to the faculty of practical insight, to the power of spiritual sympathy with the mind of the Spirit, which the thoughtful Christian necessarily acquires in the habitual exercise of bringing Scripture to bear on the daily needs of his own life. This use of Scripture is full of personal profit, and raises no intellectual difficulties. But it does not do justice to the whole Word of God. It cannot exhaust the whole mind of the Spirit. It is limited for every individual by the limitations of his own spiritual experience. Reading the Bible in this way, a man comes to a very personal appreciation of so much of God's truth as is in immediate contact with the range of his own life. But he is sure to miss many truths which belong to another range of experience, and to read into the inspired page things from his own experience which involve human error. In this way he becomes narrow, and full of prejudices, which prevent him from seeing that the Bible is larger than his knowledge of it, and that other men whose needs are different from his may be quite in the right in getting things out of Scripture which he does not know, does not need, and is inclined to call false or dangerous. Of course, in proportion as a man's spiritual experience widens, and his Christian life becomes more deep, he will rise superior to such prejudices. But no man's spiritual life is so large, so perfectly developed, in a word, so normal, that it can be used as a measure of the fulness of the Bible. The absolute value of the Bible as the manual of the spiritual life lies in the fact that it is the mirror of all normal religious experience. In other words, the inspired writers were so led by the Spirit that they perfectly understood, and perfectly recorded, every word which God spoke to their hearts. But the ripest Christian appropriates the perfect record in an imperfect way, and with a certain admixture of positive error, which comes out as soon as he attempts to express in his own words the truths he has learned from Scripture. The Church, therefore, which aims at an all-sided and catholic view, cannot be content with so much of truth as has practically approved itself to one man, or any number of men, all fallible and imperfect. What she desires to obtain is the sum of all those normal views of divine truth which are embodied in the experience of the inspired writers. She must try to get the whole meaning of every prophet, psalmist, or apostle,—not by the rough and ready method of culling from a chapter as many truths as at once commend themselves to a Christian heart, but by taking up each piece of Biblical authorship as a whole, realising the position of the writer, and following out in its minutest details the progress of his thought. And in this process the Church, or the trained theologian labouring in the service of the Church, must not be discouraged by finding much that seems strange, foreign to current experience, or, at first sight, positively unedifying. It will not do to make our notions the measure of God's dealings with His people of old. The systematic student must first, and above all, do justice to his text. When he has done this, the practical use will follow of itself.

I am anxious that you should at the very outset form a clear conception of the purpose and utility of this kind of study. Observe that the exhaustive and all-sided knowledge of the meaning of the Bible which we are now contemplating is something quite distinct from a complete knowledge of the system of theological doctrine. Systematic theology, the sort of theology of which the Westminster Confession and the Thirty-nine Articles are compends, may be called the abstract theory of the truths of religion. It tries to refer the facts and experiences of the religious life, and the whole method of revelation and redemption, to general principles, and to explain all details under these principles in a philosophical and logical sequence. In doing this systematic theology goes beyond the Bible, although it builds upon it. The abstract terms which it uses, the philosophical notions which it develops, are often not Biblical. The Bible did not need them, because, for the most part, it abstains from systematic and philosophic discussions, and treats of the relations of God to man and of the work of redemption in a directly experimental manner. For example, you will not find in the Bible any exposition of the doctrine of the Trinity, any definition of person and substance and essence, and all the other terms of which the chapter about the Trinity in every theological system is full. Nor will you find any discussion as to the theory of the Person of Christ, or any of those definitions as to the two natures, the two wills, the *communicatio idiomatum*, and all the other points which arise when we attempt to give a theory of the Person of our Lord. In place of such abstract and theoretical discussion, the Bible sets before us the living Christ in experimental manifestation, as He actually lived and taught, suffered and rose again; it sets before us the Father, Son, and Spirit as revealed in the actual work of redemption, and in that multiplicity of relations to man which forms the experimental basis of all dogmatic speculation on the Divine Being.

Now up to the time of the Reformation the only

kind of theological study which was thought worthy of serious attention was the study of dogma. People's daily spiritual life was supposed to be nourished, not by Scripture, but by the Sacraments. The experimental use of Scripture, so dear to Protestants, was not recognised as one of the main purposes for which God has given us the Bible. The use of the Bible was to furnish proof texts for the theologians of the Church, and the doctrines of the Church as expressed in the Creeds were the necessary and sufficient object of faith. The believer had indeed need of Christ as well as of a creed, but Christ was held forth to him, not in the Bible, but in the Mass. The Bible was the source of theological knowledge as to the mysterious doctrines of Revelation, but the Sacraments were the means of grace.

The Reformation changed all this, and brought the Bible to the front as a living means of grace. How did it do so? Not, as is sometimes superficially imagined, by placing the infallible Bible in the room of the infallible Church, but by a change in the whole conception of faith, of the plan and purpose of Revelation, and of the operation of the means of grace.

Saving faith, says Luther, is not an intellectual assent to a system of doctrine superior to reason, but a personal trust on God in Christ, appropriation of God's personal word and promise of redeeming love. God's grace is just the manifestation of His redeeming love, and the means of grace are the means which He adopts to bring His word of love to our ears and to our hearts.

All means of grace, all sacraments, have value only in so far as they bring to us a personal Word, that Word which is contained in the gospel and incarnate in our Lord. The supreme value of the Bible does not lie in the fact that it is the ultimate source of theology, but in the fact that it contains the whole message of God's love, that it is the personal message of that love *to me*, not doctrine but promise, not the display of God's metaphysical essence but of His redeeming purpose, in a word, of Himself as my God. Filled with this new light as to the meaning of Scripture, Luther displays profound contempt for the grubbing theologians who treated the Bible as a mere storehouse of proof texts, dealing with it, as he says of Tetzel, "like a sow with a bag of oats." The Bible is a living thing. The Middle Ages had no eye for anything but doctrinal mysteries, and where these were lacking saw only, as Luther complained, bare dead histories "which had simply taken place and concerned men no more." Nay, say the Reformers. This history is the story of God's dealings with His people of old. The heart of love which He opened to them, is still a heart of love to us. The great pre-eminence of the Bible history is that in it God speaks —speaks not in the language of doctrine but of personal grace, which we have a right to take home to us now, just as it was taken home by His ancient people.[2]

In a word, the Bible is a book of Experimental Religion, in which the converse of God with His people is depicted in all its stages up to the full and abiding manifestation of saving love in the person of Jesus Christ. God has no message to the believing soul which the Bible does not set forth, and set forth not in bare formulas but in living and experimental form, by giving the actual history of the need which the message supplies, and by showing how holy men of old received the message as a light to their own darkness, a comfort and a stay to their own souls. And so to appropriate the divine message for our wants, we need no help of ecclesiastical tradition, no authoritative Churchly exegesis. All that we need is to put ourselves by the side of the psalmist, the prophet, or the apostle, to enter by spiritual sympathy into his experience, to feel our sin and need as he felt them, and to take home to us, as he took them, the gracious words of divine love. This it is which makes the Bible perspicuous and precious to every one who is taught of the Spirit.

The history of the Reformation shows that these views fell upon the Church with all the force of a new discovery. It was nothing less than the resurrection of the living Word, buried for so many ages under the dust of a false interpretation. Now we all acknowledge the debt which we owe to the Reformers in this matter. We are agreed that to them we owe our open Bible; but we do not always understand what this gift means. We are apt to think and speak as if the Reformation had given us the Bible by removing artificial restrictions on its translation and circulation among the laity. There is a measure of truth in this view.

But, on the other hand, there were translations in the vulgar tongues long before Luther. The Bible was never wholly withdrawn from the laity, and the preaching of the Word was the characteristic office of the Friars, and the great source of that popular influence which they strained to the uttermost against the Reformation.

The real importance of Luther's work was not that he put the Bible into the hands of the laity, but that he vindicated for the Word a new use and a living interest which made it impossible that it should not be read by them. We are not disciples of the Reformation merely because we have the Bible in our hands and appeal to it as the supreme judge. Luther's opponents appealed to the Bible as confidently as he did. But they did not understand the Bible as he did. To them it was a book revealing abstract doctrines. To him it was the record of God's words and deeds of love to the saints of old, and of the answer of their inmost heart to God. This conception changes the whole perspective of Biblical study, and, unless our studies are conformed to it, we are not the children of the Reformation.

The Bible on the Reformation view is a history, the history of the work of redemption, from the fall of man to the ascension of the risen Saviour and the mission of the Spirit by which the Church still lives. But the history is not a mere chronicle of supernatural deeds and revelations. It is the inner history of the converse of God with man that gives the Bible its peculiar worth. The story of God's grace is expounded to us by the psalmists, prophets, and apostles, as they realised it in their own lives. For the progress of Revelation was not determined arbitrarily. No man can learn anything aright about God and His love, unless the new truth come home to his heart and grow into his life. What is still true of our appropriation of revealed truth was true also of its first communication. Inspired men were able to receive and set down new truths of Revelation as a sure rule for our guidance, because these truths took hold of them with a personal grasp, and supplied heartfelt needs. Thus the Record of Revelation becomes, so to speak, the autobiography of the Church—the story of a converse with God, in which the saints of old actually lived.

Accordingly, the first business of the Reformation theologian is not to crystallise Bible truths into doctrines, but to follow, in all its phases, the manifold inner history of the religious life which the Bible unfolds. It is his business to study every word of Scripture, not merely by grammar and logic, but in its relation to the life of the writer, and the actual circumstances in which God's Word came to him. Only in this way can we hope to realise the whole rich personal meaning of the Word of grace. For God never spoke a word to any soul that was not exactly fitted to the occasion and the man. Separate it from this context, and it is no longer the same perfect Word.

Now the great goodness of God to us, in His gift of the Bible, appears very specially in the copious material

He has supplied for our assistance in this task of historical exegesis. There are large passages in the Bible, especially in the Old Testament, which, taken apart from the rest of the book, would appear quite deficient in spiritual instruction. Crude rationalism often proposes to throw these aside as mere lumber, forming no integral part of the Record of Revelation. And, on the other hand, a narrowly timid faith sometimes insists that such passages, even in their isolation, must be prized as highly as the Psalms or the Sermon on the Mount. Both these views are wrong, and both err in the same way, by forgetting that a Bible which shall enable us to follow the inner life of the course of Revelation must contain, not only words of grace and answers of faith, but as much of the ordinary history, the everyday life, and the current thoughts of the people to whom Revelation came, as will enable us to enter into their circumstances, and receive the Word as they received it. From this point of view we can recognise the hand of a wise Providence in the circumstance that the Old Testament contains, in far larger proportion than the New, matter of historical and archæological interest, which does not serve a direct purpose of edification. For, in the study of the New Testament, we are assisted in the work of historical interpretation by a large contemporary literature of profane origin, whereas we have almost no contemporary helps for the study of Hebrew antiquity, beyond the books which were received into the Jewish Canon.[8]

The kind of Bible study which I have indicated is followed more or less instinctively by every intelligent reader. Every Christian takes home words of promise, of comfort, or of warning, by putting himself in the place of the first hearers of the Word, and uses the Bible devotionally by borrowing the answer spoken by the faith of apostles or psalmists. And the diligent reader soon learns that the profit of these exercises is proportioned to the accuracy with which he can compare his situations and needs with those underlying the text which he appropriates. But the systematic study of Scripture must rise above the merely instinctive use of sound principles. To get from the Bible all the instruction which it is capable of yielding, we must apprehend the true method of study in its full range and scope, obtain a clear grasp of the principles involved, and apply them systematically with the best help that scholarship supplies. Let us consider how this is to be done.

In the Bible, God and man meet together, and hold such converse as is the abiding pattern and rule of all religious experience. In this simple fact lies the key to all those puzzles about the divine and human side of the Bible with which people are so much exercised. We hear many speak of the human side of the Bible as if there were something dangerous about it, as if it ought to be kept out of sight lest it tempt us to forget that the Bible is the Word of God. And there is a widespread feeling that, though the Bible no doubt has a human side, a safe and edifying exegesis must confine itself to the divine side. This point of view is, however, thoroughly unprotestant and unevangelical—a survival of the mediæval exegesis which buried the true sense of Scripture. Of course, as long as you hold the mediæval view—that the whole worth of Revelation lies in abstract doctrines supernaturally communicated to the intellect and not to the heart—the idea that there is a human life in the Bible is purely disturbing. But if the Bible sets forth the personal converse of God with man, it is absolutely essential to look at the human side. The prophets and psalmists were not mere impassive channels through whose lips or pens God poured forth an abstract doctrine. He spoke not only through them, but to them and in them. They had an intelligent share in the Divine converse with them; and we can no more understand the Divine Word without taking them into account than we can understand a human conversation without taking account of both interlocutors. To try to suppress the human side of the Bible, in the interests of the purity of the Divine Word, is as great a folly as to think that a father's talk with his child can be best reported by leaving out everything which the child said, thought, and felt.

The first condition of a sound understanding of Scripture is to give full recognition to the human side, to master the whole situation and character and feelings of each human interlocutor who has a part in the drama of Revelation. *Nay, the whole business of scholarly exegesis lies with this human side.* All that earthly study and research can do for the reader of Scripture is to put him in the position of the man to whose heart God first spoke. What is more than this lies beyond our wisdom. It is only the Spirit of God which can make the Word a living word to our hearts, as it was a living word to him who first received it. This is the truth which the Westminster Confession expresses when it teaches, in harmony with all the Reformed Symbols, that our full persuasion and assurance of the infallible truth and divine authority of Scripture is from the inward work of the Holy Spirit, bearing witness by and with the Word in our hearts.

And here, as we at once perceive, the argument reaches a practical issue. We not only see that the principles of the Reformation demand a systematic study of Scripture upon lines of research which were foreign to the Church before the Reformation; but we are able to fix the method by which such study must be carried on. It is our duty as Protestants to interpret Scripture historically. The Bible itself has a history. It was not written at one time, or by a single pen. It comprises a number of books and pieces given to the Church by many instrumentalities and at various times. It is our business to separate these elements from one another, to examine them one by one, and to comprehend each piece in the sense which it had for the first writer, and in its relation to the needs of God's people at the time when it was written. In proportion as we succeed in this task, the mind of the Revealer in each of His many communications with mankind will become clear to us. We shall be able to follow His gracious converse with His people of old from point to point. Instead of appropriating at random so much of the Word as is at once perspicuous, or guessing darkly at the sense of things obscure, we shall learn to understand God's teaching in its natural connection. By this means we shall be saved from arbitrariness in our interpretations. For of this we may be assured, that there was nothing arbitrary in God's plan of revelation. He spoke to the prophets of old, as the Epistle to the Hebrews tells us, "in many parts and in many ways." There was variety in the method of His revelation; and each individual oracle, taken by itself, was partial and incomplete. But none of these things was without its reason. The method of revelation was a method of education. God spake to Israel as one speaks to tender weanlings (Isa. xxviii. 9), giving precept after precept, line upon line, here a little and there a little. He followed this course that each precept, as He gave it, might be understood, and lay a moral responsibility on those who received it (verse 13); and if our study follows close in the lines of the divine teaching, we too, receiving the Word like little children, shall be in the right way to understand it in all its progress, and in all the manifold richness of its meaning. But to do so, I again repeat, we must put ourselves alongside of the first hearers. What was clear and plain enough to the obedient heart then is not necessarily clear and plain to us now, if we receive it in a different attitude. God's Word was delivered in the language of men, and is not exempt from the necessary laws and limitations of human speech. Now it is a law of all speech, and especially of all speech upon personal matters, that the speaker expresses himself to the understanding of his hearer, presupposing in him a certain preparation, a certain mental attitude, a certain degree of familiarity with and interest in the subject. When a third person strikes into a conversation, he cannot follow it unless, as the familiar phrase has it, he knows where they are. So it is with the Bible. And here historical study comes in. The mind of God is unchangeable. His purpose of love is invariable from first to last. The manifold variety of Scripture, the changing aspects of Bible truth, depend on no change in Him, but wholly on the varying circumstances and needs of the men who received the Revelation. It is with their life and feelings that we must get into sympathy, in order to understand what God spoke to them. We must read the Bible as the record of the history of grace, and as itself a part of the history. And this we must do with all patience, not weary though our studies do not at each moment yield an immediate fruit of practical edification, if only they conduct us on the sure road to edification by carrying us along the actual path trodden by God's people of old; and, opening to us their needs, their hopes, their trials, even their errors and sins, enable our ears to receive the same voice which they heard behind them, saying, "This is the way; walk ye in it" (Isa. xxx. 21). It is the glory of the Bible that it invites and satisfies such study,—that its manifold contents, the vast variety of its topics, the extraordinary diversities of its structure and style, constitute an inexhaustible mine of the richest historical interest, in which generation after generation can labour, always bringing forth some new thing, and with each new discovery coming closer to a full understanding of the supreme wisdom and love of Him who speaks in all Scripture.

And now let us come to the point. In sketching the principles and aims of a truly Protestant study of Scripture I have not used the word criticism, but I have been describing the thing. Historical criticism may be defined without special reference to the Bible, for it is applicable, and is daily applied without dispute, to every ancient literature and every ancient history. The critical study of ancient documents means nothing else than the careful sifting of their origin and meaning in the light of history. The first principle of criticism is that every book bears the stamp of the time and circumstances in which it was produced. An ancient book is, so to speak, a fragment of ancient life; and to understand it aright we must treat it as a living thing, as a bit of the life of the author and his time, which we shall not fully understand without putting ourselves back into the age in which it was written. People talk of destructive criticism as if the critic's one delight were to prove that things which men have long believed are not true, and that books were not written by the authors whose names they bear. But the true critic has for his business, not to destroy, but to build up. The critic is an interpreter, but one who has a larger view of his task than the man of mere grammars and dictionaries,—one who is not content to reproduce the words of his author, but strives to enter into sympathy with his thoughts, and to understand the thoughts as part of the life of the thinker and of his time. In this process the occasional destruction of some traditional opinion is a mere incident.

Ancient books coming down to us from a period many centuries before the invention of printing have necessarily undergone many vicissitudes. Some of them are preserved only in imperfect copies made by some ignorant scribe of the dark ages. Others have been disfigured by editors, who mixed up foreign matter with the original text. Very often an important book fell altogether out of sight for a long time, and when it came to light again all knowledge of its origin was gone; for old books did not generally have title-pages and prefaces. They often lay in libraries with no note of the author's name save some words on a slip or tablet easily detached. And when such a roll was again brought into notice, with its title gone, some half-informed reader or copyist was very likely to give it a new title of his own devising, which was handed down thereafter as if it had been original. Or again, the true meaning and purpose of a book often became obscure in the lapse of centuries, and led to false interpretations. Once more, antiquity has handed down to us many writings which are sheer forgeries, like some of the Apocryphal books, or the Sibylline oracles, or the famous Epistles of Phalaris, which formed the subject of Bentley's great critical essay. In all such cases the historical critic must destroy the received view, in order to establish a true one. He must review doubtful titles, purge out interpolations, expose forgeries; but he does so only to manifest the truth, and put the genuine remains of antiquity on their true footing. A book that is really old and really valuable has nothing to fear from the critic, whose labours can only put its worth in a clearer light, and establish its authority on a surer basis.

In a word, it is the business of the critic to trace back the steps by which any ancient book has been transmitted to us, to find where it came from and who wrote it, to examine the occasion of its composition, and search out every link that connects it with the history of the ancient world and with the personal life of the author.

Now this is just what Protestant principles direct us to do with the several parts of the Bible. We have got to go back step by step, and retrace the history of the sacred volume up to the first origin of each separate writing which it contains. In doing this we must use every light that can be brought to bear on the subject.

Every fact is welcome, whether it come from Jewish tradition, or from a comparison of old MSS. and versions, or from an examination of the several books with one another and of each book in its own inner structure. It is not needful in starting to lay down any fixed rules of procedure. The ordinary laws of evidence and good sense must be our guides. And these we must apply to the Bible just as we should do to any other ancient book. That is the only principle we have to lay down. And it is plainly a just principle. For the transmission of the Bible is not due to a continued miracle, but to a watchful Providence ruling the ordinary means by which ancient books have all been handed down. And finally, when we have worked our way back through the long centuries which separate us from the age of Revelation, we must, as we have already seen, study each writing and make it speak for itself on the common principles of sound exegesis. We must not be afraid of the human side of Scripture. It is from that side alone that scholarship can get at any Biblical question. The common rules of interpretation tell us to read the book as nearly as we can from the standpoint of the author, and always to keep our eye fixed on his historical position, realising the fact that he wrote out of the experience of his own life and from the standpoint of his own time. And this, as has been shown, is the very rule which Protestant principles conduct us to. In this department of intellectual life science and faith have joined hands. There is no discordance between the religious and the scholarly methods of study. They lead to the same goal; and the more closely our study fulfils the demands of historical scholarship, the more fully will it correspond with our religious needs.

Now I know what is said in answer to all this. We have no objection, say the opponents of Biblical criticism, to any amount of historical study, but it is not legitimate historical study that has produced the current results of Biblical criticism. These results, say they, are based on the rationalistic assumption that the supernatural is impossible, and that everything in the Bible which asserts the existence of a real personal communication of God with man is necessarily untrue. My answer to this objection is very simple. We have not got to results yet; I am only laying down a method, and a method, as we have seen, which is in full accordance with, and imperatively prescribed by, the Reformation doctrine of the Word of God. We are agreed, it appears, that the method is a true one. Let us go on and apply it; and if in the application you find me calling in a rationalistic principle, if you can show at any step in my argument that I assume the impossibility of the supernatural, or reject plain facts in the interests of rationalistic theories, I will frankly confess that I am in the wrong. But, on the other hand, you must remember that all truth is one, that God who gave us the Bible has also given us faculties of reason and gifts of scholarship with which to study the Bible, and that the true meaning of Scripture is not to be measured by preconceived notions, but determined as the result of legitimate research. Only of this I am sure at the outset, that the Bible does speak to the heart of man in words that can only come from God—that no historical research can deprive me of this conviction, or make less precious the divine utterances that speak straight to the heart. For the language of these words is so clear that no readjustment of their historical setting can conceivably change the substance of them. Historical study may throw a new light on the circumstances in which they were first heard or written. In that there can only be gain. But the plain, central, heartfelt truths that speak for themselves and rest on their own indefeasible worth will assuredly remain to us. No amount of change in the background of a picture can make white black or black white, though by restoring the right background where it has been destroyed the harmony and balance of the whole composition may be immeasurably improved.

So it is with the Bible. The supreme truths which speak to every believing heart, the way of salvation which is the same in all ages, the clear voice of God's love so tender and personal and simple that a child can understand it—these are things which must abide with us, and prove themselves mighty from age to age apart from all scientific study. But those who love the truth will not shrink from any toil that can help us to a fuller insight into all its details and all its setting; and those whose faith is firmly fixed on the things that cannot be moved will not doubt that every new progress in Biblical study must in the end make God's great scheme of grace appear in fuller beauty and glory.

LECTURE II.

CHRISTIAN INTERPRETATION AND JEWISH TRADITION.

At our last meeting, I endeavoured to convey to you a general conception of the methods and objects of Biblical criticism, and to show that the very same rules for the prosecution of this branch of Biblical study may be derived independently from the general principles of historical science and from the theological principles of the Protestant Reformation. We ended by seeing that it was the duty of criticism to start with the Bible as it has been delivered to us, and as it now is in our hands, and to endeavour to trace back the history of its transmission, and of the vicissitudes through which it has passed, up to the time of the original authors, so that we may be able to take an historical view of the origin of each individual writing of the Old Testament, and of the meaning which it had to those who first received it and to him who first wrote it.

For this purpose, in speaking to a general audience, it is necessary for me to begin with the English Bible. The English Bible which we are accustomed to use gives us the Old Testament as it was understood by

Protestant scholars at the beginning of the seventeenth century. It is not necessary for our present purpose that I should dwell upon the minor differences which separate the Authorised Version from other English versions made about the same period or a little earlier. Some of these, particularly the Geneva Bible, are perhaps in certain respects preferable, while in others they are certainly inferior, to the translation of 1611. Speaking broadly, it is sufficient to say that the Authorised Version represents in a very admirable manner the understanding of the Old Testament which had been attained by Protestant scholarship at the beginning of the seventeenth century. We are now to look back and inquire what are the links connecting that English version of ours with the original autographs of the sacred writers.

The Protestant versions, of which our Bible is one, were products of the Reformation. To a certain extent they were products of the controversy with the Church of Rome. In other words, there were at that time two main views current in Europe, and among the scholars of Europe, as to the proper way of dealing with the Bible—as to the canon of Scripture, the authentic text, and the method of interpretation. We have to consider the differences that separated Protestant and Catholic exegesis. The Catholic exegesis, with which the Protestants had to contend, was the natural descendant of the exegesis of the Old Catholic Church, as it was formed in opposition to the heretics, as far back in part as the second century after Christ. At the time of Luther, as we have already seen, there was no dispute between Protestants and Catholics as to the authority of Scripture; both parties admitted the supreme authority, but they were divided on the question of the true meaning of Scripture. According to the Old Church, on which the Catholic party rested, the Bible was not clear and intelligible by its own light like an ordinary book. It was taken for granted that the use of the Bible lies in those doctrines higher than reason, those *noëtic truths*, as they were called, of a divine philosophy, which it contains. But the earliest fathers of the Catholic Church already saw quite clearly that those supposed abstract and noëtic truths did not lie on the surface of Scripture. To an ordinary reader the Bible appears something quite different from a body of supernatural mysteries and abstract philosophic doctrines. This observation was made by the earliest fathers, but it did not lead them, nor did it lead the Gnostic heretics, with whom they were engaged in controversy, to anticipate the great discovery of the Reformation, and to see that the real meaning of the Bible must just be its natural meaning. The fathers of the Church were not led to see in the Bible nothing more than it really contains— nothing more than a living, perspicuous message of divine truth. On the contrary, the orthodox and the Gnostics alike continued to look in the Bible for mysteries concealed under the plain text of Scripture— mysteries which could only be reached by some form of allegorical interpretation. Of course, the allegorical exegesis yielded to every party exactly those principles which that party desired. The orthodox found in the Bible the orthodox system of truth, the heretics found in it their own peculiar views; and so the controversy between the Gnostics and the Catholic Church could not be decided on the ground of the Bible alone, which both sides interpreted in an equally arbitrary manner. To tell the truth, it would have been very difficult indeed for Christian theologians in those days to reach a sound and satisfactory exegesis, conducted upon principles which we could now accept. Very few of the theologians in the churches of the Gentiles possessed the linguistic knowledge necessary to understand the original text. Hebrew scholars were few and far between, and the Doctors of the Church were habitually dependent upon the Alexandrian Greek translation, called the Septuagint or Version of the Seventy. To this translation we shall have to advert at greater length by-and-by. At present it is enough to say that it was a version composed in Egypt and current among the Jews of Alexandria a considerable time before the Christian era, and that it spread contemporaneously with the preaching of the Gospel through all parts of Christendom where Greek was understood. In many parts of the Old Testament, this translation was very obscure, and really did not yield to a natural method of exegesis any clear sense. But indeed, apart from the disadvantage of being thrown back upon the Septuagint, the

Christians could not have hoped to understand the Old Testament better than their Jewish contemporaries. Even if they had set themselves to study the original text, they would have required to take their whole knowledge of the Hebrew Bible from the Jews, who were the only masters that could then have instructed them in the language; and in fact, while the Western churches were mainly dependent on the Septuagint, and struck out an independent line of interpretation on the basis of that version, the exegesis of the Oriental churches continued to be largely guided by the teaching of the Synagogue. In Syria and beyond the river Euphrates, the Bible was interpreted by Christian scholars who spoke Syriac—a language akin to Hebrew—upon the methods of the Jewish schools; but by this time the Jews themselves had fallen into an abyss of artificial Rabbinical interpretation, from which no true light could be derived for the understanding of Scripture. The influence of the Jewish interpretation which ruled in the East can be traced, not only in the old Syriac translation called the Peshito, but in the writings of later Syriac divines. In the Homilies of Aphraates, for example, which belong to the fourth century, we find clear evidence that the Biblical training and exegetical methods of the author, who, living in the far East, was not a Greek scholar, were largely derived from the Jewish doctors; and the operation of the same influences can be followed far down into the Middle Ages.[1]

Accordingly, in the absence of a satisfactory and scientific interpretation, the conflict of opinions between the orthodox and the heretics was decided on another principle than that of exegesis. The apostles, it was said, had received the mysteries of divine truth from our Lord, and had committed them in plain and living words to the apostolic churches. That is a point to which the ancient fathers always recurred. The written word, they say, is necessarily ambiguous and difficult, but the spoken word of the apostles was clear and transparent. In the apostolic churches, then, the sum of true doctrine has been handed down in an accurate form; and the consent of the apostolic churches as to the mysteries of faith forms the rule of sound exegesis. Any interpretation of Scripture, say the fathers, is necessarily false if it differs from the *ecclesiastical canon*—that was the technical term which they used—if it differs, that is, from the received doctrinal testimony of the great apostolic churches, such as Corinth, Rome, and Alexandria, in which the word of the apostles was still held to live handed down by oral tradition.[2]

These were the principles of exegesis to which the Catholic Church adhered up to the time of the Reformation. New elements were added from time to time to the body of ecclesiastical tradition, and in particular a very great change took place with regard to the received edition of the Old Testament. When the theory of the ecclesiastical canon was first formed, the churches of Europe read either the Greek translation of the Septuagint or Latin versions formed from the Septuagint; but about the year 400 A.D., Jerome, a Hebrew scholar, and a very remarkable scholar indeed for that age, formed a new translation under the direct influence of Jewish tradition. His Hebrew learning he derived from the Jews, and resting on their teaching he made a new version direct from the Hebrew, which was greatly assailed at the time as a dangerous innovation, but which by-and-by came to be accepted in the Latin churches as the authentic and received edition of the Bible. When I say that Jerome's version was received by the Western churches, it is proper to observe that it was not received in all its purity, and that this *Vulgate* or received version (the word *vulgate* means "currently received"), as it actually existed in the Middle Ages and at the time of the Reformation, was not the pure text of Jerome, but was Jerome's version considerably modified by things which had been carried over from the older Latin translations taken from the Greek. Still, the Catholic Church supposed itself to receive the version of Jerome as the authoritative and vulgate version, and this new Vulgate replaced the old Vulgate, the Greek Septuagint translation made by the Jews in Egypt before the time of Christ.

Now the Reformers, who were well read in church history, sometimes met their opponents by pointing out that the ecclesiastical tradition on which the Catholics relied as the proper norm or rule of interpretation had itself undergone change in the course of centuries, and they often appealed with success to the earliest fathers against those views of truth which were current in their own times. But Luther's fundamental conception of revelation made it impossible for the Protestants to submit their understanding of the Bible even to the earliest and purest form of the ecclesiastical canon. The ecclesiastical canon—the rule of interpreting everything according to the consent of the apostolic churches—had, as we have seen, been first invented in order to get over the ambiguities of the allegorical method of interpretation. When Luther taught the people that the Bible can be understood like any other book, that the true meaning of its words is the natural sense which appeals to ordinary Christian intelligence, it was plain that for him this whole method of ecclesiastical tradition as the rule of exegesis no longer had any meaning or value.

The Church of Rome, after the Reformation arose, took up a definite and formal battle-ground against Protestantism in the Decrees of the Council of Trent. The positions laid down by the Doctors of Trent in opposition to the movement headed by Luther were these :—

I. The supreme rule of faith and life is contained in the written books and the unwritten traditions of Christ and his Apostles dictated by the Holy Spirit and handed down by continual succession in the Catholic Church. That was the way in which they expressed the authority of ecclesiastical tradition.

II. The canonical books are those books in all their

parts which are read in the Catholic Church and contained in the Latin Vulgate version, the authenticity of which is accepted as sufficiently proved by its long use in the Catholic Church.

III. The interpretation of Scripture must be conformed to the tenets of Holy Mother Church and the unanimous consent of the Fathers.

The Reformers traversed all these three positions; for, firstly, as we have seen, they denied the validity of unwritten tradition; secondly, they refused to admit the authority of the Vulgate, and appealed to the original text; thirdly, they denied the existence and still more the authority of the consent of the Fathers, and admitted no principle for the interpretation of the Bible that would not be sound if applied to another book. They affirmed that the reader has a right to form his own private judgment on the sense of Scripture; by which, of course, they did not mean that one man's judgment is as good as another's. They meant no more than that the sense of a controverted passage must be decided by argument and not by authority. The only rule of exposition which they laid down as possessing any authority for the Church was this,—that in a disputed point of doctrine the sense of an obscure passage must be ruled by passages which are more plain. And that, as you will easily observe, is, strictly speaking, not a rule of interpretation but a principle of theology. It rather tells us which passage we are to choose for the proof or disproof of any doctrine than helps us to get the exact sense of a disputed text. All that it really means is this—"Form your doctrines from plain texts, and do not be led astray from the teaching of plain passages by a meaning which some one may extort from an obscure one." So far as the principle is exegetical, it simply means that an all-wise Author cannot contradict Himself.

I do not require to say more upon the first and third positions of the Council of Trent; but the second position, as to the claims of the standard Vulgate edition, is a point which requires more attention. In making the Vulgate the standard edition, the Council of Trent implied two things :—(1) that the Vulgate contains all the canonical books, and none other, and that it presents these books in their true text; and (2) that the translation, if not perfect, is exempt from errors affecting doctrine. The Roman Catholics, of course, did not mean to assert that the Vulgate edition did in every particular represent the exact text and meaning of the original writers. In justice to them, we must say that for their contention that was not necessary, because all along what they wished to get at was not the meaning of the original writers, but the body of doctrine which had the seal of the authority of the Church; and therefore, from their point of view, the authenticity of the text of the Vulgate was sufficiently proved by the fact that the infallible Church had long used that text without finding any ground of complaint against it; and the authority of the translation, in like manner, was sufficiently supported by the fact that theologians had always been able to deduce from it the received doctrines of the Church. That, no doubt, was what they meant. Nevertheless, the two theses that they laid down were very curiously at variance with what Jerome, the author of the Vulgate version, had once and again said about the value of his own labours. They affirmed that the Vulgate contained all the canonical books and none else, and that it contained those books in the true text. Jerome, on the contrary, in that prologue to part of his translation which is generally called the *Prologus Galeatus*, regards all books as apocryphal which he did not translate directly from the Hebrew; and, following this rule, he excludes from the canon the Book of Wisdom, Ecclesiasticus, Judith, Tobit, Baruch, and also the two books of the Maccabees, although he had seen the first of these in Hebrew. The Council of Trent accepts all these books as canonical, and not only these books, but various additions to other books—to Ezra, Daniel, and Esther—which are not found in the Hebrew text.[3]

The second position of the doctors of Trent also reads curiously in the light of Jerome's own remarks. According to the Council of Trent, the whole translation of Jerome is accurate for all purposes of doctrine, but Jerome in his prefaces makes a very different claim for his version. What he says is this: "If you observe my version to vary from the Greek or Latin copies in your hands, ask the most trustworthy Jew you can find, and see if he does not agree with me."[4] Once and again Jerome claims this, and only this, for his version, that it agrees with the best Jewish tradition; in other words, Jerome sought in his version to correct the current Bibles of his day according to the Hebrew text, as the Jews of his time received it, and to give an interpretation on a level with the best Jewish scholarship. He did this partly by the aid of earlier translations from the Hebrew into the Greek (Aquila, Theodotion, but especially Symmachus) made after the time of Christ, and more in accordance than the Septuagint with the later Rabbinical scholarship;[5] and partly by the help of learned Jews. On one occasion, he tells us, he brought a famous Rabbi from Tiberias to instruct him. At another time he brought a Jewish scholar from Lydda; and in particular he speaks of one called Bar Anina, a teacher who came to him by night for fear of his co-religionists, while the translator resided in Jerusalem and Bethlehem.[6]

Now, in their argument with the Roman Catholics, the Protestants simply fell back upon these facts. They quoted Jerome against the Council of Trent, as is done, for example, in the sixth of the Articles of the Church of England.[7] They quoted Jerome, and therefore adopted his definition that all books which were not extant in Hebrew and admitted to the canon of the Jews in the day of Jerome are apocryphal and not to be cited in proof of a disputed doctrine. I ask you specially to note that that was all the Protestants in their earlier controversies did. They simply fell back upon Jerome. They said—" You find that great doctor, the most learned of his day, and other Fathers along with him, refusing to admit as canonical, and authoritative for the Church as proof of doctrine, any book which was not part of the Hebrew canon of the time." Beyond that they did not care to press the question of the canon. There were differences among themselves as to the value of the Apocrypha on the one hand, and as to the canonicity of Esther and some other books of the old canon upon the other. But it was enough for the Protestants in controversy with Rome to be able to refuse a proof text drawn from the Apocryphal books, upon the plain ground that the authority of these books was challenged even by many of the fathers. Calvin, in his *Antidote* to the Council of Trent is willing to leave the question of the canon open, contenting himself with the observation that the intrinsic qualities of the Apocryphal books display a manifest inferiority to the canonical writings.[8] That, I say, was all that the Protestants at first cared to lay down on this subject.

On the question of the true interpretation of Scripture they had much more to say. The revival of letters in the fifteenth century had raised a keen interest in ancient languages, and scholars who had mastered Greek as well as Latin were ambitious to add to their knowledge a third learned tongue, viz., the Hebrew. At first this ambition met with many difficulties. The original text of the Old Testament was preserved only among the scholars of the Synagogue. It was impossible to learn Hebrew except from Jewish teachers; and orthodox Jews refused to teach men who were not of their own faith. Gradually, however, these obstacles were surmounted. Towards the close of the fifteenth century, Hebrew Bibles began to be printed, and some knowledge of the Hebrew tongue became disseminated to a considerable extent; and at length, in the year 1506, John Reuchlin, the great supporter of Hebrew studies north of the Alps, put forth in Latin his *Rudiments* of the Hebrew language. This Latin work, which was something of the nature of both grammar and dictionary, was almost entirely taken from the Hebrew manuals of the famous Jewish scholar and lexicographer, Rabbi David Kimhi, who flourished about the year 1200 A.D. As soon as Christians were furnished in this way with text-books, the new learning spread rapidly. It ran over Europe just at the time when the Reformation was spreading, and the Reformers, always keenly alive to the best and most modern learning of their time, read the Old Testament in the original Hebrew, and often found occasion to differ from Jerome's version. Observe, they agreed with Jerome in principle. They, like him, aimed only at rendering the text as the best Hebrew scholars would do, and to them, as to him, the standard of scholarship was that of the most learned Jews. But when Jerome wrote, there was no such thing in existence as a Hebrew grammar and dictionary; there were no written commentaries to which a Christian scholar had access. The Reformers had the text-book of Reuchlin, the grammar and lexicon of Kimhi, the

commentaries of many Rabbis of the Middle Ages, with
other helps denied to Jerome, and therefore they knew
that their new learning put them in a position to
criticise his work. Often, indeed, they undervalued
Jerome's labours, and this ultimately led to controversies between Protestants and Catholics, which were
fruitful of instruction to both sides. But, on the whole,
the Reformers were right. They did know Hebrew
better than Jerome, and their versions, including our
English Bible, approached much more nearly than
his to the ideal common to both,—which was to give
the sense of the Old Testament as it was understood
by the best Jewish scholars. Of course, the Jewish
authorities themselves sometimes differed from one
another. In such cases, the Protestants leant sometimes on one authority, sometimes on another. Luther
takes a great deal from a commentator who has been
called the Rosenmüller of the Jews in the Middle Ages,
R. Solomon of Troyes, generally called Rashi, who died
A.D. 1105. Our Bible is mainly guided by the grammar
and lexicon of the later scholar, R. David Kimhi of
Narbonne, who has already been mentioned as the
author of the most current text-books of the Hebrew
language. But the point which I wish you to observe
is that the Reformers and their successors, up to the
time when all our Protestant versions were fixed, were,
for all purposes of learning, in the hands of the Rabbins.
Upon principle they stood with Jerome against the
Council of Trent, alike as to the question of the canon

and as to the question of interpretation. Their object in the sixteenth century, like his in the fourth, was simply to give to the vulgar the fruit of the best Jewish learning, applied to the translation of the Scriptures as they were received among the Jews from the time of Jerome downwards.

It may be asked why the Reformers stopped here. But the answer is clear enough. They stopped at that point because the learning of their time also stopped there. They went as far as the scholarship of the age would carry them. Luther, it will be remembered, first saw the practical value of philological study, when he was puzzling over the expression *pœnitentiam agite*, "do penance," which the Vulgate uses for the Greek word that in the English translation is rendered "repent." Was it possible, he said to himself, that Christ and the Apostles could really bid men do penance? Did the New Testament really stand on the side of his opponents, and of all the gross corruptions which the doctrine of penance had introduced? Melanchthon solved this difficulty by showing to Luther that the Greek word μετανοεῖτε, which Jerome had translated "do penance," really and etymologically meant "change your mind." From that moment the Reformation entered into a conscious alliance with the new learning, to which it was already akin in its independent love of truth, its rebellion against human authority, and its interest in the Bible as a real living book. Accordingly, all that early Protestantism did for the Old Testament, beyond the rejection of authoritative traditional interpretations and the allegorical sense, was to read it by the best light which scholarship then offered. All sound Hebrew scholarship then resided with the Jewish doctors, and so the Protestant scholars became their disciples.

But it would be absurd to suppose that the men who refused to accept the authority of *Christian* tradition as to the number of books in the canon, the best text of the Old Testament, or the principles upon which that text is to be translated, adopted it as a principle of faith that the *Jewish* tradition, the unchristian tradition, upon all these points is final. Luther again and again showed that he submitted to no such authority; and if the Reformers and their first successors did practically accept the results of Jewish scholarship upon all these questions, they did so merely because these results were in accordance with the best light then attainable. It was left for a later generation, which had lost the courage of the first Reformers because it had lost much of their clear insight into divine things, to substitute an authoritative Jewish tradition for the authoritative tradition of the Catholic Church—to swear by the Jewish canon and the Massoretic text as the Romanists swore by the Tridentine canon and the Vulgate text. The Reformers had too much reverence for God's Word to subject it to the bondage of any tradition. They would gladly have accepted any further light of learning, carrying them back behind the time of Rabbinical and unbelieving Judaism to the first ages of the Old Testament writings.

Scholarship moved onwards, and as research was carried farther it gradually became plain that it was possible for Biblical students, with the material still preserved to them, to get behind the Jewish Rabbins, upon whom our translators were still dependent, and to draw from the sacred stream at a point nearer its source. I have now to explain how this was seen to be possible.

From the time when the Old Testament was written, down to the sixteenth century, there was no continuous tradition of sound Hebrew learning except among the Jews. The little that Christians knew about the Old Testament at first hand had always come from the Rabbins. Among the Jews, on the contrary, there was a continuous scholarly tradition. The knowledge of Hebrew and the most received ways of explaining the Old Testament were handed down from generation to generation along with the original text. I ask you to understand precisely what this means. Long before the time of Christ, the Jews had ceased to speak Hebrew. In the New Testament, no doubt, we read once and again of the Hebrew tongue as spoken and understood by the people of Palestine; but the language which is called Hebrew in the New Testament was a dialect as unlike to the Hebrew of the Bible as German is to English—a different language, although a kindred one. This language is called Hebrew because it was spoken by the Hebrews, just as the Spanish Jews in Constantinople at the present day call their Spanish jargon Hebrew. It was a kind of Syriac or Aramaic, which the Jews had gradually learned in place of Hebrew, after their return from captivity, when they found themselves a small handful living in the midst of nations who spoke Aramaic, and with whom they had constant dealings. In those days Aramaic was the language of business and of government, just as English is in the Highlands of Scotland, and so the Jews forgot their own tongue, and learned Aramaic, as the Scottish Celts are now forgetting Gaelic for English. This process had already gone on to a great extent before the latest books of the Old Testament were completed. Such writers as the authors of Chronicles and Ecclesiastes write Hebrew in a way which shows that their thoughts often ran not in Hebrew but in Aramaic. They use Aramaic words and idioms which would have puzzled Moses and David, and in some of the later Old Testament books, in Ezra and in Daniel, although not in those parts of the former book which are autobiographical and written by Ezra himself, there actually are inserted in the Hebrew long Aramaic passages. Before the time of Christ, people who were not scholars had ceased to understand Hebrew altogether;[9] and in the synagogue, when the Bible was read, the *Meturgeman*, as he was called, that is a "dragoman," or qualified translator, had to rise and give the sense of the passage in the vulgar dialect. The Pentateuch was read verse by verse, or in lessons from the

Prophets three verses were read together, and then the Meturgeman rose, and did not read, but gave orally in Aramaic the sense of the original.[10] Hebrew then, by this time, was a learned language, acquired not in common life but in the school. In order to learn Hebrew, the young Jew had to go to school, but he had no grammar or lexicon, or other written help, to assist him. It was not possible for him therefore to study the language of the Old Testament as we study Latin or Greek. Everything was done by the oral instruction of the teacher, and by dint of sheer memory, without any scientific principle. In the first place, the pupil had to learn to read. In our Hebrew Bibles now, the pronunciation of each word is exactly represented. This is done by a double notation. The letters proper are the consonants, and the vowels are indicated by small marks placed above or below the line of the consonants. These small marks are a late invention. They did not exist in the time of Christ, or even four hundred years after his time, at the time of Jerome.[11] Before this invention the proper pronunciation of each difficult word had to be acquired from a master. When a pupil had learned to read a phrase correctly, he was taught the meaning of the words, and by such exercises, combined with the practice of constantly speaking Hebrew, which was kept up in the Jewish schools, as the practice of speaking Latin used to be kept up in our grammar schools, the pupil gradually got a practical command of the Hebrew tongue. It is easy to understand what kind of knowledge of

Hebrew this sort of study produced. The student acquired a certain practical fluency in speaking or writing "the language of the wise" as it was called. The language of the Bible itself was called "the holy tongue." The Hebrew as it was spoken in the schools, varying as we shall presently see to some considerable extent from the Hebrew of the Bible, was called "the language of the wise." We have many volumes of the composition of these scholars, chiefly legal works, with some old *midrashim*, as they are called, or sermonising commentaries on Scripture. These books no doubt are Hebrew in a certain sense, but they are as unlike to the Biblical Hebrew as a lawyer's deed is to a page of Cicero. The men who wrote such a jargon could not have any delicate perception for the niceties of the old classical language, especially as it is written in the most ancient books; and when they came to a difficult passage they could only guess at the sense, unless they possessed an interpretation of the hard text, and the hard words it contained, handed down to them from some older scholar.

Now let me ask you once more to realise precisely how these scribes, at and before the time of Christ, proceeded in dealing with the Bible. They had nothing before them but the bare text denuded of its vowels, so that the same words might often be read and interpreted in two different ways. A familiar example of this is given in Heb. xi. 21, where we read of Jacob leaning upon the top of his "staff;" but when we turn to our Hebrew

Bible, as it is now printed (Genesis xlvii. 31), we there find nothing about the "staff;" we find the "bed." Well, the Hebrew for "the bed" is "HaMMiTTaH," while the Hebrew for "the staff" is "HaMMaTTeH." The consonants in these two words are the same; the vowels are different; but the consonants only were written, and therefore, it was quite possible for one person to read the word as "bed," as is now the case in our English Bible, following the reading of the Hebrew scribes, and for the author of the Epistle to the Hebrews, on the other hand, to understand it as a "staff," following the interpretation of the Greek Septuagint.

Beyond the bare text, which in this way was often ambiguous, the scribes had no guide but oral teaching. They had no rules of grammar to go by; the kind of Hebrew which they themselves wrote often admitted grammatical constructions which the old language forbade, and when they came to an obsolete word or idiom, they had no guide to its meaning, unless their masters had told them that the pronunciation and the sense were so and so. Now, beyond doubt the Jewish scholars were most exact and retentive learners, and their masters spared no pains to teach them all that they knew. We in the West have little idea of the precision with which an Eastern pupil even now can take up and remember the minutest details of a lesson, reproducing them years afterwards in the exact words of his master. But memory, even when cultivated as it is cultivated in the schools of the East, is at best fallible; and even if we could suppose that the whole of the Bible had been taught word by word in the schools, in unbroken succession from the day on which each book was first written, it would still have required a continued miracle to preserve all these lessons perfectly and without writing through long generations. But in point of fact the traditional teaching of the Jews was neither complete, nor continuous, nor uniform.

It was not complete; that is, there never was an authoritative interpretation of the whole Bible. It was not continuous; that is, many interpretations, which at some time had general currency and authority, were figments of the Rabbins which they had not received by unbroken tradition from the time when Hebrew became a dead language, much less from the time when the passage was first written—interpretations not received by original tradition but devised by the Rabbins out of their own heads. And finally, the Rabbinical tradition was not uniform; that is, the interpretation and even the reading of individual texts was often a subject of controversy in the schools of the Scribes, and at different times we find different interpretations in the ascendant. The proof of these propositions lies partly in the records of Jewish learning still preserved in the Rabbinical literature; partly it lies in the translations and interpretations made at various times by Jewish scholars or under their guidance.

So long as the transmission and interpretation of the Bible were left to the unregulated labours of individual scholars or copyists, it is plain that individual theories and individual errors would have some influence on the work. The Bible had to be copied by the pen. Let us suppose then that the copyist, without any special instruction or guide, simply sat down to make a transcript, probably writing from dictation, of the MS. which he had bought or borrowed. In the first place, he was almost certain to make some slips, either of the pen or of the ear; but besides this, in all probability the volume before him would contain slips of the previous copyist. Was he to copy these mistakes exactly as they stood, and so perpetuate the error, or would he not in very many cases think himself able to detect and correct the slips of his predecessor? If he took the latter course, it was very possible for him to overrate his own capacity and make a new mistake. And so bit by bit, if there were no control, if each scribe acted independently, and without the assistance of a regular school, errors were sure to be multiplied, and the text would be certain to present many variations. Thus we know that even in recent times the Gaelic version of the Old Testament contains certain alterations upon the original text made in order to remove seeming contradictions. Much more were such changes to be anticipated in ancient times, when there was a far less developed sense of responsibility with regard to the verbal transcription of old texts. A uniform and scrupulous tradition, watching over the reading and the meaning of the text in all parts of the Jewish world, could only be transmitted by a regular school of scholars, or, as the Jewish records call them, a school of Scribes, that is, men of the book— men who were professionally occupied with the book of the law.

We are all familiar with these Scribes, or professed Biblical scholars, as they appear in the New Testament. Their principles at that epoch, as we know, were those of the Pharisees; in fact, the Pharisees were nothing else than the party of the Scribes, in opposition to the Sadducees or aristocratic party. To the Sadducees, or aristocratic party, the higher priestly nobility belonged. To the Pharisees, or party of the Scribes, belonged the great mass of Jewish scholars who were not closely associated with the higher ranks of the priesthood, together with many who, without being scholars, were eager to obey the law as the Scribes interpreted it. Those Scribes were the men who had in their hands the transmission and interpretation of the Old Testament; and our next task, in endeavouring to understand the steps by which the Old Testament has been handed down to us, must be to obtain a clear vision of their methods and objects, and of the work which they actually did upon the Old Testament as we now possess it. This subject will occupy our attention in next Lecture.

LECTURE III.

THE SCRIBES.[1]

THE subject with which we are to be occupied to-day is the part that was played by the Scribes in the preservation and transmission of the Old Testament. At the close of last Lecture we looked for a moment at the Scribes as they appear in the New Testament in association with the Pharisees. At that time, as one sees from the Gospels and the Acts, they constituted a party long established, and exercising a great and recognised influence in the Jewish state. In fact they go back as far as the later times of the Old Testament. Their father is Ezra, " the Scribe," as he is called *par excellence*, who came from Babylon to Judæa with the law of God in his hand (Ezra vii. 14), and with a heart "prepared to study the law of the Lord, to do it, and to teach in Israel statutes and judgments" (Ezra vii. 10). Ezra accomplished this task, not immediately, but with ultimate and complete success. He did so with the support of the Persian king, and with the immediate assistance of Nehemiah, who had been sent by Artaxerxes as governor of Jerusalem. At a great public meeting convened by Nehemiah, of which we read an account in chapters viii. to x. of the book which bears his name, the Law was openly read before the people at the Feast of Tabernacles, and, with confession and penitence, the Jews entered into a national covenant to make that law henceforth the rule of their lives. Now I do not ask at present what were the relations of the people to the Law before the time of Ezra. That question must come up afterwards; but any one who reads with attention the narrative in the book of Nehemiah must be satisfied that this work of Ezra, and the covenant which the people took upon them to obey the Law, were of epoch-making importance for the Jewish community. It was not merely a covenant to amend certain abuses in detailed points of legal observance; for the people in their confession very distinctly state that the Law had not been observed by their ancestors, their rulers, or their priests, up to that time (Neh. ix. 34); and in particular it is mentioned that the Feast of Tabernacles had never been observed according to the Law from the time that the Israelites occupied Canaan under Joshua, —that is, of course, never at all (Neh. viii. 17). Accordingly this covenant must be regarded as a critical epoch in the history of the community of Israel. From that time forward, with the assistance and under the approval of the Persian king, the Law—that is, the Pentateuch or Torah, as we now have it (for there can be no doubt that the Law which was in Ezra's hands was practically identical with our present Hebrew Pentateuch)—became the religious and municipal code of Israel. Now, as soon as the Torah was accepted as a practical code, the work of the Scribes became indispensable. For the Pentateuch, viewed as a code, is such a book as imperatively calls for a class of trained lawyers to be its interpreters. I do not ask at present whether, as most critics suppose, there are real contradictions between the laws given in different parts of the five books of Moses. At all events, it is a familiar fact that those who maintain that all the Pentateuchal laws can be reconciled, differ very much among themselves as to the precise method of reconciliation. No two commentators who attempt to digest all parts of the Pentateuch into a harmonious body of precepts agree in all their interpretations. In such an ambiguity of the Law it is manifest that the Scribes had an indispensable function as guides of the people to that interpretation which was in actual use in the practical administration of the code. Accordingly, by-and-by, in the time of the Chronicles (1 Chron. ii. 55), we find them organised in regular "families," or, as we should now say, "guilds," an institution quite in accordance with the whole spirit of the East, which forms a guild or trades-union of every class possessing special technical knowledge.[2]

We see, then, that before the close of the Old Testament Canon the Scribes not only existed, continuing the work of Ezra, but that they existed in the form of guilds or regular societies. What were their objects? There can be no doubt that from the first the objects of the Scribes were not philological, not scientific, but practical. Ezra's object was so. He came to make the Law the practical rule of Israel's life, and so it was still in later ages. The wisdom of the Scribes consisted of two parts, which in Jewish terminology were respectively called "Halacha" and "Haggada." "Halacha" was legal teaching, systematised legal precept; while "Haggada" was doctrinal and practical admonition, mingled with parable and legend. But of these two parts the "Halacha,"—that is, the system of rules applying the Pentateuchal law to every case of practice and every detail of life,—was always the chief thing. The difference between the learned theologian and the unlearned vulgar lay in knowledge of the Law. You remember what the Pharisees say in John vii. 49— "This people, which knoweth not the law, are cursed." The Law was the ideal of the Scribes. Their theory of the history of Israel was this.—In time past Israel had been chastised by God's wrath; the cause of this chastisement was that the people had neglected the Law. Forgetting the Law, Israel had passed and was still passing through many tribulations, and was subjected to the yoke of a foreign power. What was the duty of the Jews in this condition of things? According to the Scribes, it was not to engage in any political scheme whatever for throwing off the foreign yoke, but to establish the Law in their own midst,—to apply themselves, not only to obey the whole Torah, particularly in its ceremonial precepts, but so to develop these precepts that they might embrace every minute detail of life. Then, when by this means Israel had become a law-obeying nation in the fullest sense of the word, Jehovah Himself, in His righteousness, would intervene, miraculously remove the scourge, and establish the glory of His law-fulfilling people. These were the principles of the Scribes and the Pharisees, the principles spoken of by Paul in writing to the Romans, when he tells us that Israel, following after the law of righteousness, did not attain to the law of righteousness; that they, being ignorant of God's righteousness, and going about to establish their own righteousness, did not submit themselves unto the righteousness of God (Rom. ix. 31; x. 3).

Now, all that the Scribes did for the transmission, preservation, and interpretation of the Old Testament, was guided by these legal aims. In the first instance, they were not scholars, not preachers, but "lawyers" (νομικοί), as they are often called in the New Testament. In their juridical decisions they were guided partly by study of the Pentateuch, but partly also by observation of the actual legal usages of their time, by those views of the Law which were practically acknowledged, for example, in the ceremonial of the temple and the priesthood. There was thus, in the wisdom of the Scribes, an element of use and wont,—an element of common law, which of course existed in Jerusalem as in every other living community side by side with the codified written law; and this element of common law, or use and wont, was the source of the theory of legal tradition familiar to all

of us from allusions in the New Testament. According
to this theory, Moses himself had delivered to Israel an
oral law along with the written Torah. The oral law
was as old as the Pentateuch, and had come down in
authentic form through the prophets to Ezra. The
conception of an oral law, as old and venerable as the
written law, necessarily influenced the Scribes in all
their interpretations of Scripture. It introduced into
their handling of Scripture an element of uncertainty
and falsity, upon which Jesus Himself, as you will
remember, put His finger, with that unfailing insight
of His into the unsound parts of the religious state of
His time. Through their theory of the traditional law
the Scribes were led into many a departure from the
spirit, and even from the letter of the written Word
(Matt. xii. 1-8; xv. 1-20; xxiii.)

To the Scribes, then, the whole law, written and
oral, was of equal practical authority. What they
really sought to preserve intact, and hand down as
binding for Israel, was not so much the written text of
the Pentateuch as their own rules,—partly derived from
the Pentateuch, but partly, as we have seen, from other
sources,—which they honestly believed to be equally an
expression of the mind of the Revealer, even in cases
where they had no basis in Scripture, or only the
basis of some very strained interpretation. Now, you
can readily conceive that the traditional interpretation
of the law could not be stationary. In fact, we know
that it was not so. The subject has been gone into

with great care by Jewish scholars, who are more interested than we are in the traditional law; and they have been able to prove, from their own books and written records of the legal traditions, that that law underwent, from century to century, not a few changes. This was no more than natural. So long as a nation has a national life, lives and develops new practical necessities, there must also from time to time be changes in the law and its application. In part, then, the growth of the traditional law was owing to changes and new necessities of the national life. It would doubtless, from this source alone, have grown and changed very much more, but for the fact, that between Ezra and the time of Christ the Jews were almost continuously under foreign domination, so that they had not perfect freedom of civil or even religious development. At the same time, they always retained a certain amount of municipal independence; and so long as the municipal life remained active, the law necessarily underwent modifications from time to time.

But there was another reason for continual changes in the traditional law. The party headed by the Scribes, which finally developed into the Pharisees, were led by their exaggerated conceptions of the importance of legal and ceremonial righteousness as the one source of felicity in Israel—they were led, I say, by this exaggerated conception of legality to make, as they called it, a hedge round the Law—that is, constantly to expand the compass of legal precept; to extend the sphere of ceremonial observances outside of what lay in the Pentateuch and in the oldest form of tradition, so that it might be impossible for a man, if he observed all their traditional rules, to come even within sight of a possible breach of the Law. Now the Scribes and Pharisees who developed this tendency were not the governing class in Judæa. The governors of the nation in its internal matters were the priestly aristocracy, with the high priest at their head as a sort of hereditary prince over Israel. Nevertheless the great Rabbins of the party of Scribes were men whose legal ability gained for them a commanding position and influence; while the mass of the Pharisees, by their claim of special sanctity and special legality, also acquired great weight with the common people; and in consequence of this the authority of the party ultimately became so great that, as we learn from Josephus, the priestly aristocracy, who were the civil as well as the religious heads of the Jews, and who themselves were no more inclined than any other aristocracy to make changes that were not for their own personal profit, yet found themselves compelled by the pressure of public opinion to defer in almost every instance to the doctrines of the Scribes.[3] The municipal and legal administration took place by means of councils bearing the name of Synedria or Sanhedrin. There was a central council with judicial and administrative authority—the Great Sanhedrin in Jerusalem—and there were local councils in provincial towns. These councils were mainly occupied by Sadducees, or men of the aristocratic party; but ultimately the Scribes, as trained lawyers, gained a considerable proportion of seats in them; and during the latter time of the Maccabees under Queen Salome, and still more after the fall of the Hasmonean dynasty, when it was the policy of Herod the Great to crush the old nobility and play off the Pharisees against them, the influence of the Scribes in the national councils of justice came greatly to outweigh that of the aristocratic Sadducees. In this way, as you will observe, the interpreters of the law gained a very important place in the practical life of Israel; and they continued active, developing and applying their peculiar system, until the overthrow of the city by Titus in the year A.D. 70 deprived the law of much of its national importance. When the Temple was destroyed, and when the Jewish nationality was crushed, a great part of the public ordinances decreed by the Scribes fell into desuetude, though private and personal observances of ceremonial righteousness were still insisted upon. Further development became impossible, or was limited to a much narrower range; and after the last desperate struggle of the Jews for liberty under Hadrian, A.D. 132 to 135, the Scribes, no longer able to find a practical outlet for their influence in the guidance of the state, devoted themselves to systematising and writing down the traditional law in the stage which it had then reached. This systematisation took shape in the collection which is called the Mishna, which was completed by Rabbi Judah the Holy about A.D. 200.[4]

I have directed your attention to the history of the traditional law because its transmission was inseparably bound up with the transmission of the text of the Bible. As we have seen, the whole law, written and oral, was one in the estimation of the Scribes. The early versions and the early Jewish commentaries show us that the interpretation of the Pentateuch was guided by legal much rather than by philological principles. The Bible was understood by the help of the Halacha quite as much as the Halacha was based upon the Bible; and so, as the traditional law underwent many changes, these reacted upon the interpretation and even to a certain extent upon the reading of the text of the Pentateuch. Let me take an example of this from what we find in the Bible itself. In Neh. x. 32 we read that the people made a law for themselves, charging themselves with a yearly poll-tax of one-third of a shekel for the service of the Temple. In the time of Christ this tribute of one-third of a shekel had been increased to half a shekel (*didrachma;* Matt. xvii. 24, *margin*); and the impost which in the time of Nehemiah was a tax voluntarily taken upon themselves by the people without any written warrant, was in this later time supposed to be based upon Exodus xxx. 12-16. This view of the matter, indeed, is already taken by the Chronicler; for he speaks of a yearly Mosaic impost for the maintenance of the Temple (2 Chron. xxiv. 5, 6), and therefore even in his time the passage in the 30th chapter of Exodus must have been held to be the basis of the poll-tax. Yet that tax was a new tax; it was first assumed in the time of Nehemiah; and it is only an afterthought of the Scribes to base it upon the Pentateuch. This example illustrates one way in which the conception of the law changed in the hands of the Scribes. In other cases they actually took it upon themselves to alter Pentateuchal laws. For example, the tithes were transferred from the Levites to the priests, and the use of the liturgy prescribed in Deuteronomy xxvi. 12-15 on occasion of the tithing, which was not suitable after that change had been made, was abolished by John Hyrcanus, the Hasmonean prince and high priest.[5] These are but single examples out of many which might be adduced, but are enough to show that so long as the development of the oral law was running its course, the written law was treated by the Scribes with a certain measure of freedom.

Their real interest, I repeat, lay not in the sacred text itself, but in the practical system based upon it. That comes out very forcibly in repeated passages of the Rabbinical writings, in which the study of Scripture is spoken of almost contemptuously, as something far inferior to the study of the traditional legislative system.

Now, people often think of the Jews as entirely absorbed, from the very first, in the exact grammatical study and literal preservation of the written Word. Had this been so, they could never have devised so many expositions which are plainly against the idiom of the Hebrew language, but which flowed naturally and

easily from the legal positions then current. The early
Scribes had neither the inclination nor the philological
qualifications for exact scholarly study, and when they
did lay weight upon some verbal nicety of the sacred
Text, they did so in the interest of some legal theory of
their own, and upon principles to which we can assign
no value. No doubt the Scribes and their successors
in the Talmudic times (A.D. 200 to 600) must themselves have been quite aware that the meanings which
they forced upon texts, in order to carry out their legal
system, were not natural and idiomatic renderings. But
this did not greatly trouble them, for it was to them an
axiom that the oral and traditional laws were one
system, and, therefore, they were bound to harmonise
the two at any sacrifice of the rules of language. The
objections to such an arbitrary exegesis did not come to
be strongly felt till long after the Talmudic period,
when a new school of Jewish scholars arose, who had
grammatical and scientific knowledge, mainly derived
from the learning of the Arabs. When in the Middle
Ages these Rabbins introduced a stricter system of
grammatical interpretation, it soon came to be felt that
the Talmudic way of dealing with Scripture was often
quite forced and unnatural, and so it was found necessary to draw a sharp distinction between the traditional
Talmudic interpretation of any text, which continued to
have the value of an indisputable legal authority, and
the grammatical interpretation or *P'shat*, representing
that exact and natural sense of the passage which the

more modern study had enabled men to determine with sharpness and precision.

The mediæval Rabbins concentrated their attention on the plain grammatical sense of Scripture, and their best doctors, who were the masters of our Protestant translators, rose much above the Talmudical exegesis, although they never altogether shook off the false principle that a good sense must be got out of everything, and that if it cannot be got out of the text by the rules of grammar, these rules must just give way. Even our own Bible, which rests almost entirely upon the better or grammatical school of Jewish interpretation, does, in some passages, show traces of the Talmudical weakness of determining to harmonise things, and get over difficulties, even at the expense of strict grammar; but this false tendency was confined within narrow limits; and, on the whole, the influence of the Talmudists was almost completely conquered in the Protestant versions, though it is still felt in the harmonistic exegesis of the anti-critical school.[6]

A much more serious point is raised by the consideration that although we are able to correct the interpretations of the ancient Scribes, we have the text of the Hebrew Old Testament as they gave it to us; and we must therefore inquire whether they were in a position to hand down to us the best possible text. Let me illustrate the significance of this question, by referring to the history of the text of the New Testament. The books of the New Testament circulated in manuscript copies, and it is by a comparison of such old codices as still remain to us that scholars adjust the printed texts of their modern editions. The comparison shows that the old copies often differ in their readings. Some of the variations are mere slips of the transcriber, which any Greek scholar can correct as readily as one corrects a slip made in writing a letter; but others are more serious. Those of you who have not access to the Greek Testament, will find sufficient examples either in the small English New Testament, published by Tischendorf in 1869, which gives the readings of three ancient MSS., or in that very convenient book, Eyre and Spottiswoode's Sunday School Centenary Bible, which, on the whole, is the best edition of the English version for any one who wishes to look below the surface. Now if you consult such collections of various readings as are given in these works, you will find that, in various MSS., words, clauses, and whole sentences are inserted or omitted, and sometimes the insertions change the whole meaning of a passage. In one or two instances a complete paragraph appears in some copies, and is left out in others. The titles in particular offer great variations. The oldest MSS. do not prefix the name of Paul to the Epistle to the Hebrews, and they do not put the words "at Ephesus," into the first verse of the first chapter of Ephesians. Such changes as these show that the copyists of these times did not proceed exactly like law clerks copying a deed. They made additions from parallel passages, they wrote things upon the margin which afterwards got into the text; and, when copying from a blotted page, they sometimes had to make a guess at a word. In these and other ways mistakes came in and were perpetuated; and it takes the best scholarship, combined with an acuteness developed by long practice, to determine the true reading in each case, and to eliminate all corruptions.

Now, of course the ancients were quite aware that such variations existed among copies, and in later times they did their best to correct the text; but hardly any one will affirm that the shape which the New Testament ultimately took in the hands of the scholars of Constantinople, is as near to the first hand of the Apostles as the text which a good modern editor is able to make by comparing the oldest MSS. which are still preserved to us. Such is the state of the New Testament text, and such are the methods by which this text is corrected, through comparison of the most ancient MSS. But what is the state of things as regards the Old Testament? All MSS. of the Hebrew Bible (and we have none older than the ninth century after Christ) represent one and the same text. There are slight variations, but these are, almost without exception, such as might have been made even by a careful copyist acting under fixed rules, and do not affect the general state of the text. But we can go farther. We may say that the text of the Hebrew Old Testament which we now have is the same as lay before Jerome 400 years after Christ; the same as underlies certain translations into Chaldee called Targums, which were made in Babylon in the third century after Christ; indeed the same text as was received by the Jewish doctors of the second century, when the Mishna was being formed, and when the Jewish proselyte Aquila made his translation into Greek. I do not affirm that there were no various readings in the copies of the second or even of the fourth century, but the variations were slight and easily controlled, and such as would have occurred in MSS. carefully transcribed from one standard copy.[7]

The Jews, in fact, from the time when their national life was extinguished, and their whole soul concentrated upon the preservation of the monuments of the past, devoted the most strict and punctilious attention to the exact transmission of the received text, down to the smallest peculiarity of spelling, and even to certain irregularities of writing. Let me explain this last point. We find that when the standard manuscript had a letter too big, or a letter too small, the copies made from it imitated even this, so that letters of an unusual size appear in the same place in every Hebrew Bible. Nay, the scrupulousness of the transcribers went still further. In old MSS., when a copyist had omitted a letter—there was no running hand, it was a sort of printing with the pen, so that a letter might easily fall out,—and, when the error was detected, as the copy was revised, the reviser inserted the missing letter above the line as we should now do with a caret. If, on the other hand, the reviser found that any superfluous letter had been inserted, he cancelled it by pricking a dot above it. Now, when such corrections occurred in the standard MS. from which our Hebrew Bibles are all copied, the error and the correction were copied together, so that you will find, even in printed Bibles (for the system has been carried down into the printed text), letters suspended above the line to show that they had been inserted with a caret, and letters "pointed" with a dot over them to show that they form no proper part of the text.[8] This shows with what punctilious accuracy the one standard copy was followed. In a few cases, however, it was thought necessary to suggest a correction on the reading of the text. There were some words, for example, which it was not thought decorous to use in public reading in the synagogue, and for this and other reasons, a few modifications were prescribed in the reading of the text. But the rule was laid down that you must not on that account change the text itself. The reader simply learned to pronounce, in reading certain passages, a different word from that which he found written; and in many MSS. a note to this effect was placed on the margin. These notes are called *Keris*, the word *Keri* being the imperative "read!" while the expression actually written in the text, but not uttered, is called *Kethîb* (written). Now it is plain that such a system of mechanical transmission could not have been carried out with precision if copying had been left to uninstructed persons. The work of preserving and transmitting the received text became the specialty of a guild of technically trained scholars, called the Massorets, or "possessors of tradition," that is, of tradition as to the proper way of writing the Bible. The Massorets laboured for centuries; their work was not completed till at least 800 years after the time of Christ; and they collected many orthographical rules and great lists of peculiarities of writing to be observed in passages where any error was to be feared, which are still preserved either as marginal notes and appendices to MSS. of the Bible, or in separate works. Besides this, the scholars of the period after the close of the Talmud—that is, after the sixth Christian century, or thereby—devoted themselves to preserving not only the exact writing, but the exact reading and pronunciation of the Bible, according to the rules of the synagogal chanting. The final result of this labour was a system of vowel points and musical accents, which enable the trained reader to give exactly the correct pronunciation, and even the correct chanting tone of every word of the Hebrew Old Testament.

The development of all these precautions was the work of centuries, and had a history many parts of which are involved in obscurity. But the question that interests us, is to know where the text so carefully guarded came from. We have seen that all MSS. were scrupulously conformed to one standard copy; but where and when was that copy written, and how did it come to acquire such exceptional authority? All the evidence of variations and quotations later than the first Christian century points to the received text as already existing practically as we have it, but we cannot follow its history beyond that time. On the contrary, there is abundant evidence that in earlier ages Hebrew MSS. differed as much as, or more than, MSS. of the New Testament. We shall have to look at the proof of this in some detail by-and-by. For the present, it is enough to point out some of the chief sources of the evidence. The Samaritans, as well as the Jews, have preserved the Hebrew Pentateuch, writing it in a peculiar character. Well, the copies of the Samaritan Pentateuch, which they received from the Jews for the first time about 430 B.C., differ very considerably from our received Hebrew text. Some of the variations are corruptions wilfully introduced in favour of the schismatic temple on Mount Gerizim; but others have no polemical significance, affecting such points as the ages assigned to the patriarchs.[9] Then, again, the old Greek version, the Alexandrian version of the Septuagint, which, in part at least, was written before the middle of the third century B.C., contains many various readings, sometimes omitting large passages, or making considerable insertions; sometimes changing the order of chapters and verses; sometimes making only smaller changes, more similar to those with which we are familiar in Greek MSS. Nay, even among learned Jews who read Hebrew, the text was not fixed up to the first century of our era. For the *Book of Jubilees*, a

Hebrew work which was written apparently but a few years before the fall of the Temple, agrees with the Samaritan Pentateuch in some of the numbers in the patriarchal chronology, and in other readings.[10]

Now, observe the point to which we are thus brought. After the fall of the Jewish state, when the Scribes ceased to be an active party in a living commonwealth, and became more and more pure scholars, gathering up and codifying all the fragments of national literature and national life that remained to them, we find the text of the Old Testament carefully conformed to a single archetype. But we cannot trace this text back through the centuries when the nation had still a life of its own. Nay, we can be sure that in these earlier centuries copies of the Bible circulated, and were freely read even by learned men like the author of the *Book of Jubilees*, which had great and notable variations of text, not inferior in extent to those still existing in New Testament MSS. In later times every trace of these varying copies disappears. They must have been suppressed, or gradually superseded by a deliberate effort, which has been happily compared, by the German scholar Nöldeke, to the action of the Caliph Othman in destroying all copies of the Koran which diverged from the standard text that he had adopted. There can be no question who were the instruments in this work. The Scribes alone possessed the necessary influence to give one text or one standard MS. a position of such supreme authority. Moreover, we are able to explain how it came about that the fixing of a standard text took place about the Apostolic age, or rather a little later than that date, and not at any earlier time. We have already glanced at the political causes, which made the power of the Scribes greater in the time of Herod than it had ever been before. The doctors of the Law wielded a great authority, and were naturally eager to consolidate their legal system. In earlier times the oral and written law went independently side by side, and each stood on its own footing. Therefore, variations in the text did not seriously affect any practical question. But under Rabbi Hillel, a contemporary of Herod the Great, and the grandfather of the Gamaliel who is mentioned in the fifth chapter of Acts, a great change took place. It was the ambition of Hillel to devise a system of interpretation by which every traditional custom could be connected with some text from the Pentateuch, no matter in how arbitrary a way. This system was taken up and perfected by his successors, especially by Rabbi Akiba, who was a prominent figure in the revolt against Hadrian.[11] The new method of exegesis laid weight upon the smallest word, and sometimes even upon mere letters of Scripture; so that it became a matter of great importance to the new school of Rabbins to fix on an authoritative text. We have seen that when this text was fixed, the discordant copies must have been rigorously suppressed. The evidence for this is only circumstantial, but it is quite sufficient. There is no other explanation which will account for the facts, and the conclusion is confirmed by what took place among the Greek-speaking Jews with reference to their Greek Bible. The Bible of the Greek-speaking Jews, the Septuagint, had formerly enjoyed very great honour even in Palestine, and is most respectfully spoken of by the ancient Palestinian tradition; but it did not suit the newer school of interpretation, it did not correspond with the received text, and was not literal enough to fit the new methods of Rabbinic interpretation, while the Christians, on the contrary, found it a convenient instrument in their discussions with the Jews. Therefore it fell into disrepute, and early in the second century, just at the time when, as we have seen, the new text of the Old Testament had been fixed, we find its use superseded among the Greek-speaking Jews by a new translation, slavishly literal in character, made by a Jewish proselyte of the name of Aquila, who was a disciple of the Rabbi Akiba, and studiously followed his exegetical methods.[12]

This, then, was what the Scribes did.—They chose for us the Hebrew text which we have now got. Were they in a position to choose the very best text, to produce a critical edition which could justly be accepted as the standard, so that we lose nothing by the suppression of all divergent copies? Now, this at least we can say,—that if they fixed for us a satisfactory text, the Scribes did not do so in virtue of any great critical skill which they possessed in comparing MSS. and selecting the best readings. They worked from a false point of view. Their objects were legal, not philological. Their defective philology, their bad system of interpretation, made them bad critics; for it is the first rule of criticism that a good critic must be a good interpreter of the thoughts of his author. This judgment is quite confirmed by the accounts which are given in the Talmudical books of certain small and sporadic attempts made by the Scribes to exercise something like criticism upon the text. For example, in one passage of the Talmud, we read of three MSS. preserved in the Court of the Temple, each of which had one reading which the other MSS. did not share. The Scribes, we are told, rejected in each case the reading which had only one copy for it and two against it.[13] Now, every critic knows that to accept or reject a reading merely according to the number of MSS. for or against it is a method which, if applied on a large scale, would lead to a very bad text indeed. Then the early Scribes are related to have made certain changes in the text, apparently without manuscript authority, and merely in order to remove expressions which seemed irreverent or indecorous. We have seen that in later times, after the received text was fixed, the Jewish scholars did not venture to make such a change. They permitted themselves to make a change in the reading but not a change in the writing; but in earlier times, according to the statement of the Rabbinical books, a certain small number of alterations, chiefly on dogmatical grounds, was made even upon the writing of Scripture. These changes are called the

18 Tikkûnê Sopherîm (corrections or determinations of the Scribes). Thus in Job vii. 20, where the present text reads, "I am a burden to myself," the tradition explains that the original reading was, "I am a burden upon thee," that is, a burden upon Jehovah. That was corrected because it seemed to be a somewhat irreverent expression. Again, in Genesis xviii. 22, where our version says, "Abraham still stood before the Lord," tradition says that this was a change of the Scribes, the original reading being, "The Lord still stood before Abraham." Again, in Habakkuk i. 12, where our version and the present Hebrew text read, "Art thou not from everlasting, Jehovah my God, my Holy One? We shall not die," the tradition tells us that the original reading was, "Thou canst not die," which was changed because it seemed irreverent to mention the idea of God dying, even in order to negative it. Others of the eighteen cases recorded in the Jewish books as having been corrections of the Scribes are more doubtful, and a different explanation is more plausible, but on the whole it can hardly be questioned that the tradition expresses a fact, viz.—That the early guardians of the text did not hesitate to make small changes in order to remove expressions which they thought unedifying.[14] No doubt, such changes were made in a good many cases of which no record has been retained. For example, in our text of the Books of Samuel, Saul's son and successor is called Ishbosheth, but in 1 Chronicles viii. 33 he is called Eshbaal. Eshbaal means "Baal's man," a proper name of a well-known Semitic type, precisely similar to such Arabic names as Imrau-l-Cais, "the man of the god Cais." We must not, however, fancy that a son of Saul could be named after the Tyrian or Canaanite Baal. The word Baal is not the proper name of one deity, but an appellative noun meaning lord or owner, which the tribes of the Northern Semites applied each to their own chief divinity. In earlier times it appears that the Israelites did not scruple to apply the title of Baal to their national God Jehovah. Thus the golden calves at Bethel and Dan, which were certainly worshipped under the supposition that they represented Jehovah, were called Baalim by their devotees; and Hosea, when he prophesies the purification of Israel's religion, makes it a main point that the people shall no longer call Jehovah their Baal (Hosea ii. 16, 17; *comp.* xiii. 1, 2). This prophecy shows that in Hosea's time the use of the word was felt to be dangerous to true religion; and indeed there is no question that it led the mass of the people to confound the true God with the false Baalim of Canaan. And so in process of time scrupulous Israelites not only desisted from applying the title of Baal to Jehovah, and confined it to the Tyrian and Canaanite sun god, but taking literally the precept of Exod. xxiii. 13, "Make no mention of the name of other gods," they were wont, when they had occasion to refer to the false deity, to call him not Baal but Bosheth, "the shameful thing," as a euphemism for the hated name. This is how the name of "Eshbaal" was ultimately changed by scrupulous copyists or readers into "Ishbosheth," but we may be very certain that no king would ever have consented to bear such a name in his own lifetime as "The man of the shameful thing."

These, then, are specimens of the changes which we can still prove to have been made by early editors, and they are enough to show that these guardians of the text were not sound critics. Fortunately for us, they did not pretend to make criticism their main business. It would have been a very unfortunate thing for us indeed, if we had been left to depend upon a text of the Hebrew Bible which the Scribes had made to suit their own views. There can be no doubt, however, that the standard copy which they ultimately selected, to the exclusion of all others, owed this distinction not to any critical labour which had been spent upon it, but to some external circumstance that gave it a special reputation. Indeed, the fact, which we have already referred to, that the very errors and corrections and accidental peculiarities of the MS. were kept just as they stood, shows that it must have been invested with a peculiar sanctity; if indeed the meaning of the so-called extraordinary points—that is, of those suspended and dotted letters, and the like—had not already been forgotten when it was chosen to be the archetype of all future copies.

Now, if the Scribes were not the men to make a critical text, it is plain that they were also not in a position to choose, upon scientific principles, the very best extant MS.; but it is very probable that they selected an old and well-written copy, possibly one of those MSS. which were preserved in the Court of the Temple. Between this copy and the original autographs of the Sacred Writers there must have been many a link. It may have been an old manuscript, but it was not an exorbitantly old one. Of that there are two proofs. In the first place, it was certainly written with the "square" or "Chaldean" letters used in our modern Hebrew Bibles; but these letters are of Aramaic origin, and in old times the Hebrews used the quite different character called Phœnician. According to Jewish tradition, which ascribes everything to Ezra which it has not the assurance to refer to Moses, the change on the character in which the sacred books were written was introduced by Ezra; but we know that this is a mistake, for the Samaritans, who did not possess the Pentateuch until fifty years after Ezra, received it in the old Phœnician letter, which they retain in a corrupted form down to the present day. It is very doubtful whether there were any MSS. written in the Aramaic character before the third century B.C., and that therefore would be the earliest date to which we can refer the archetype of our present Hebrew copies. Another proof that the copy was not extraordinarily old lies in the spelling. In Hebrew, as in other languages, the rules of spelling varied in the course of centuries, and it is not impossible to say which of two orthographies is the older. Now, it can be proved that the copies which lay before the translators of the Septuagint in the third, and perhaps in the second, century B.C., often had an older style of spelling than existed in the archetype of our present Hebrew Bibles.[15] It does not follow of necessity that those older MSS. were also better and nearer to the original text; but certainly the facts which we have been developing give a new importance to the circumstance that the MSS. of the LXX. often contained readings very different from those of our Hebrew Bibles, even to the extent of omitting or inserting passages of considerable length.

In this connection there is yet another point worth notice. In these times Hebrew books were costly and cumbrous, written on huge rolls of leather, not even on the later and more convenient parchment. Copies therefore were not very numerous, and, being much handled, were apt to get worn and indistinct. For not only was leather an indifferent surface to write on, but the ink was of a kind that could be washed off, a prejudice existing against the use of a mordant.[16] No single copy therefore, however excellent, was likely to remain long in good readable condition throughout. And we have seen that collation of several copies, by which defects might have been supplied, was practised to but a small extent. Often indeed it must have been difficult to get copies to collate, and once at least the whole number of Bibles existing in Palestine was reduced to very narrow limits. For Antiochus Epiphanes (B.C. 168) caused all MSS. of the Law, and seemingly of the other sacred books, to be torn up and burnt, and made it a capital offence to possess a Pentateuch (1 Mac. i. 56, 57; Josephus, *Ant.* xii. 5). The text of books preserved only in manuscript might very readily suffer in passing through such a crisis, and it is most providential that the Septuagint version, translated at an earlier period and current in regions where Antiochus had no sway, still exists to carry our knowledge of the state of the text back beyond his time, confirming the substantial accuracy of our Hebrew Bibles, while at the same time it shows them to be not immaculate, and gives valuable help towards the correction of such errors as exist.

LECTURE IV.

THE SEPTUAGINT.[1]

WE have passed under review the vicissitudes of the Hebrew Text, as far back as the days of Antiochus Epiphanes. We have found that the absence of important various readings from the Hebrew MSS. now in existence does not prove that the text which they present is absolutely perfect and authoritative. The phenomena of the text prove, indeed, that all our MSS. go back to one archetype. But the archetype was not formed by a critical process which we can accept as conclusive. It was not so ancient but that a long interval lay between it and the first hand of the Biblical authors; and the comparative paucity of books in those early times, combined with the imperfect materials used in writing, and the deliberate attempt of Antiochus to annihilate the Hebrew Bible, exposed the text to so many dangers that it cannot but appear a most welcome and providential circumstance that the Greek translation, derived from MSS. of which some at least were presumably older than the archetype of our present Hebrew copies, and preserved in countries beyond the dominions of Antiochus, offers an independent witness as to the early state of the Biblical books, vindicating the substantial accuracy of the transmission of these records; while, at the same time, it displays a text not yet fixed in every point of detail, exhibits a series of important various readings, and sometimes indicates the existence of corruptions in the received Hebrew recension—corruptions which it not seldom enables us to remove, restoring the first hand of the sacred authors.

Nevertheless, there have been many scholars who altogether reject this use of the Septuagint. One of the few living representatives of this party is Keil, from whose *Introduction* (Eng. Trans., vol. ii. p. 306) I quote the following sentences:—

"The numerous and strongly marked deviations [of the Septuagint] from the Massoretic text have arisen partly at a later time, out of the carelessness and caprice of transcribers. But in so far as they existed originally, almost in a mass they are explained by the uncritical and wanton passion for emendation, which led the translators to alter the original text (by omissions, additions, and transpositions) where they misunderstood it in consequence of their own defective knowledge of the language, or where they supposed it to be unsuitable or incorrect for historical, chronological, dogmatic, or other reasons; or which, at least, led them to render it inexactly, according to their own notions and their uncertain conjectures."

If this judgment were sound, we should be deprived at one blow of the most ancient witness to the state of the text; and certainly, at one time, the opinion advocated by Keil was generally current among Protestant scholars. We have glanced, in a previous Lecture (*supra*, p. 43), at the reasons which led the early Protestants to place themselves, on points of Hebrew scholarship, almost without reserve in the hands of the Jews. They accepted the received Hebrew text as transmitted in the Jewish schools, and they naturally viewed with distrust the very different text of the Septuagint. However, the question of the real value of the Greek version was stirred early in the seventeenth century mainly by two French scholars, one of whom was a Catholic, John Morinus, priest of the Oratory, the other a Protestant, Ludovicus Cappellus.

The controversy raised by the publication of the *Exercitationes Biblicæ* of Morinus (Paris, 1633) was unduly prolonged by the introduction of dogmatic considerations which should have had no place in a scholarly argument as to the history of the Biblical text. These considerations lost much of their force when all parties were compelled to admit the value of the various readings of MSS. and versions for the study of the New Testament; and, since theological prejudice was overcome, it has gradually become clear to the vast majority of conscientious students that the Septuagint is really of the greatest value as a witness to the early state of the text.

It is very difficult to convey, in a popular manner, a sufficiently clear idea of the arguments by which this position is established. Even the few remarks which I shall make may, I fear, seem to you somewhat tedious; but I must ask your attention for them, because it is not a slight matter to inquire whether, in this version, older than the time of Antiochus Epiphanes, we have or have not a valuable testimony to the way in which the Old Testament has been transmitted, an independent basis for a rational and well-argued belief in the general soundness of the Hebrew text, and a measure of the degree of uncertainty which affects its readings in detail.

In judging of the Septuagint translation, we must not put ourselves on the standpoint of a translator in these days. We must begin by realising to ourselves the facts brought out in Lecture II., that Jewish scholars, before the time of Christ, had no grammar and no dictionary; that all their knowledge of the language was acquired by oral teaching; that their exegesis of difficult passages was necessarily traditional; and that, where tradition failed them, they had for their guidance only that kind of practical knowledge of the language which they got by the constant habit of reading the sacred text, and speaking some kind of Hebrew among themselves in the schools. We must also remember that, when the Septuagint was composed, the Hebrew language was either dead or dying, and that the mother-tongue of the translators was either Greek or Aramaic. It seems, indeed, that the work was done by persons who knew both Aramaic and Greek. In consequence of this, we must not be surprised to find that, when tradition was silent, the Septuagint translators made many mistakes. If they came to a difficult passage, say of a prophet, of which no traditional interpretation had been handed down in the schools, or which contained words the meanings of which had not been taught to them by their masters, they could do nothing better than make a guess,—sometimes guided by analogies and similar words in the Aramaic, sometimes perhaps by the Arabic, sometimes by other considerations. The value of the translation does not lie in the sense which they put upon such passages, but in the evidence that we can find as to what Hebrew words lay in the MSS. before them.

Now, apart from the natural limitation of scholarship derived entirely from tradition, we find that the Septuagint sometimes varies from the older text for reasons which are at once intelligible when we understand the general principles of the Scribes at the time. We have already seen, for example, that the Scribes in Palestine did not hesitate occasionally to make a dogmatic correction, removing from the writing, or at least from the reading, of Scripture some expression which they thought it indecorous to pronounce in public. We need not, therefore, be surprised to find, and indeed we do find, that the translators of the Septuagint did the same thing, and that they sometimes changed a phrase which they thought likely to be misunderstood, or to be used to establish some false doctrine. Thus, in Exodus xxiv. 10, the Hebrew text reads, "And they (that is, the leaders of Israel who went up towards Sinai with Moses) saw the God of Israel." This anthropomorphic expression, it was felt, could not be rendered literally without lending some countenance to the false idea that the spiritual God can be seen by the bodily eyes of men, and offering an apparent contradiction to Exodus xxxiii. 20. The Septuagint therefore changes it, and says, "They saw the place where the God of Israel had stood."

Again, we have already seen that the interpretation of the Scribes was largely guided by the Halacha, that is, by oral tradition ultimately based upon the common law and habitual usage of the sanctuary and of Jerusalem. The same influence of the Halacha is found in the Septuagint translation. Thus, in Lev. xxiv. 7, where the Hebrew text bids frankincense be placed on the shewbread, the Septuagint makes it "frankincense and salt," because salt, as well as frankincense, was used in the actual ritual of their period.

Such deviations of the Septuagint as these need not seriously embarrass the critic. He recognises the causes from which they came. He is able to estimate their extent approximately by what he knows of Palestinian tradition, and he is not likely, in a case of this sort, to be misled into the supposition that the Septuagint had a different text from the Hebrew. Once more, we find that the translators allowed themselves certain liberties which were also used by copyists of the time. Their object was to give the thing with perfect clearness where they understood it. Consequently they sometimes changed a "he" into "David" or "Solomon," or whoever the person might be who was alluded to; and they had no scruple in adding a word or two to complete the sense of an obscure sentence, or supply what appeared to be an ellipsis. Even our extant Hebrew MSS. indicate a tendency to make additions of this description. The original and nervous style of early Hebrew prose was no longer appreciated, and a diffuse smoothness, with constant repetition of standing phrases and elaborate expansion of the most trifling incidents, was the classical ideal of composition. The copyist or translator seldom omitted anything save by accident; but he was often tempted by his notions of style to venture on an expansion of the text. Let me take a single example. In passages in the Old Testament where we read of some one eating, a compassionate editor, as a recent critic humorously puts it, was pretty sure to intervene and give him something to drink. Sometimes we find the full reading in the Septuagint, sometimes in the Hebrew text. In 1 Samuel i. 9 the Hebrew tells us that Hannah rose up after she had eaten in Shiloh and after she had drunk, but the Septuagint has only the shorter reading, "After she had eaten." Conversely, in 2 Samuel xii. 21, where the Hebrew text says only, "Thou didst rise and eat bread," the Septuagint presents the fuller text, "Thou didst rise and eat bread, and drink." In cases of this sort, the shorter text is obviously the original. There was no motive for leaving out the drinking, but a copyist who loved completeness of statement naturally understood that a man would not eat without drinking likewise.

We must, then, put aside for our present purpose these three classes of variations. We have to put aside the cases where the translators misunderstood the text, and could not but misunderstand it because they had no tradition to guide them. We must not say that they were ignorant or capricious, because they were not able to make a good grammatical translation of a passage at a time when such a thing as grammar did not exist even in Palestine.

In the next place, we must put on one side the cases where their interpretation was influenced by exegetical considerations derived from the dogmatic theology of their time or from the traditional law. And, thirdly, we can attach no great importance to those variations in which, without changing the sense, the translator, or perhaps a copyist before him, gave a slight turn to an expression to remove ambiguity, or gain the diffuse fulness which he loved.

But after making every allowance for these cases a large class of passages remains, in which the Septuagint presents important variations from the Massoretic text. The test by which the value of these variations can be determined is the method of retranslation. A faithful translation from Hebrew into an idiom so different as the Greek cannot fail to retain the stamp of the original language. It will be comparatively easy to put it back into idiomatic Hebrew, and even the mistakes of the translator will often point clearly to the words of the original which he had before him. But where the translator capriciously departs from his original, the work of retranslation will at once become more difficult. For the capricious translator is one who substitutes his own thought for that of the author, and what he thinks in Greek will not so naturally lend itself to retroversion into the Hebrew idiom. The test of retranslation gives a very favourable impression of the fidelity of the Alexandrian version. With a little practice one can often put back whole chapters of the Septuagint into Hebrew, reproducing the original text almost word for word. The translation is not of equal merit throughout, and it is plain that different parts of the Bible were rendered into Greek by men of varying capacity; but in general, and under the limitations already indicated, it is safe to say that the translators were men of competent scholarship as scholarship then went, and that they did their work faithfully and in no arbitrary way. Now as we proceed with the work of retranslation, and when all has gone on smoothly for perhaps a whole chapter, in which we find no considerable deflection from the present Hebrew, we suddenly come to something which the practised hand has no difficulty in putting back into Hebrew, which indeed is full of such characteristic Hebrew idiom that it is impossible to ascribe it to the caprice of a translator thinking in Greek, but which, nevertheless, diverges from the Massoretic text. In such cases we can be morally certain that a various reading existed in the Hebrew MS. from which the Septuagint was derived. Nay, in some passages, the

moral certainty becomes demonstrative, for we find that
the translator stumbled on a word which he was unable
to render into Greek, and that he contented himself
with transcribing it in Greek letters. A Hebrew word
thus bodily transferred to the pages of the Septuagint,
and yet differing from what we now read in our Hebrew
Bibles, constitutes a various reading which cannot be
explained away. An example of this is found in 1 Sam.
xx., in the account of the arrangement made between
Jonathan and David to determine the real state of
Saul's disposition towards the latter. In the Hebrew
text (ver. 19) Jonathan directs David to be in hiding
"by the stone Ezel;" and at verse 41, when the plan
agreed on has been carried out, David at a given signal
emerges "from beside the Negeb." The Negeb is a
district in the south of Judea, remote from the city of
Saul, in the neighbourhood of which the events of our
chapter took place; and the attempt of the English
version to smooth away the difficulty is not satisfactory
either in point of grammar or of sense. But the Septuagint makes the whole thing clear. At verse 19 the
Greek reads "beside yonder Ergab," and at verse 41
"David arose from the Ergab." *Ergab* is the transcription in Greek of a rare Hebrew word signifying a *cairn*
or rude monument of stone, which does not occur elsewhere except as a proper name (Argob). The translators transcribed the word because they did not understand it, and the reading of the Massoretic text, which
involves no considerable change in the letters of the

Hebrew, probably arose from similar lack of knowledge on the part of Palestinian scholars.

The various readings of the Septuagint are not always so happy as in this case; but in selecting some further examples, it will be most instructive for us to confine ourselves to passages where the Greek gives a better reading than the Hebrew, and where its superiority can be made tolerably manifest even in an English rendering. It must, however, be remembered that complete proof that the corruption lies on the side of the Hebrew and not of the Greek can be offered only to those who understand these languages. Our first example shall be 1 Sam. xiv. 18.

Hebrew.	Septuagint.
And Saul said to Ahiah, Bring hither the ark of God. For the ark of God was on that day and [*not as E. V.* with] the children of Israel.	And Saul said to Ahiah, Bring hither the ephod, for he bare the ephod on that day before Israel.

The Authorised Version smooths away one difficulty of the Hebrew Text at the expense of grammar. But there are other difficulties behind. The ark was then at Gibeah of Kirjath-jearim (1 Sam. vii. 1; 2 Sam. vi. 3), quite a different place from Gibeah of Benjamin; and its priest was not Ahiah, but Eleazar ben Abinadab. Besides, Saul's object was to seek an oracle, and this was done, not by means of the ark, but by the sacred lot connected with the ephod of the priest (1 Sam. xxiii. 6, 9). This is what the Septuagint actually has got, and there can be no doubt that it is the right reading. The changes on the Hebrew letters required to get the one reading out of the other are far less considerable than one would imagine from the English.

Another example is the death of Ishbosheth (2 Sam. iv. 5, 6, 7) :—

Hebrew.	Septuagint.
[The assassins] came to the house of Ishbosheth in the hottest part of the day, while he was taking his midday siesta. (6) And hither they came into the midst of the house fetching wheat, and smote him in the flank, and Rechab and Baanah his brother escaped. (7) And they came into the house as he lay on his bed, . . . and smote him and slew him, *etc.*	They came to the house of Ishbosheth in the hottest part of the day, while he was taking his midday siesta. And lo, the woman who kept the door of the house was cleaning wheat, and she slumbered and slept, and the brothers Rechab and Baanah got through unobserved and came into the house as Ishbosheth lay on his bed, *etc.*

In the Hebrew there is a meaningless repetition in verse 7 of what has already been fully explained in the two preceding verses. The Septuagint text gives a clear and progressive narrative, and one which no "capricious translator" could have derived out of his own head. As in the previous case, the two readings are very like one another in the Hebrew letter.

Another reading, long ago appealed to by Dathe as one which no man familiar with the style of the translator could credit him with inventing, is found in Ahithophel's advice to Absalom (2 Sam. xvii. 3) :—

Hebrew.	Septuagint.
I will bring back all the people to thee. Like the return of the whole is the man whom thou seekest. All the people shall have peace.	I will make all the people turn to thee as a bride turneth to her husband. Thou seekest the life of but one man, and all the people shall have peace.

The cumbrousness of the Hebrew text is manifest. The Septuagint, on the contrary, introduces a graceful simile, thoroughly natural in the picturesque and poetically-coloured language of ancient Israel, but wholly unlike the style of the prosaic age when the translator worked.

You will observe that the examples which I have selected are all from the Books of Samuel, and this has a reason. In some parts of the Old Testament, and notably in Samuel and other early historical books, variations of the kind which I have illustrated are numerous; and there is often reason to conclude that the true reading is preserved in the Septuagint, or, at least, can be reached with its aid. In other books, and particularly in the greater part of the Pentateuch, the Septuagint deflects but little from the Hebrew text, and its variations seldom give a better reading. This is just what we should expect, for from a very early date the Pentateuch was read in the synagogues every Sabbath day (Acts xv. 21) in regular course, the whole being gone through in a cycle of three years. The Jews thus became so familiar with the words of the Pentateuch that copyists were in great measure secured from important errors of transcription; and it is also reasonable to suppose that the rolls written for the synagogue were transcribed with special care long before the full development of the elaborate precautions which were ultimately devised to exclude errors. Sections from the prophetic books were also read in the synagogue (Acts xiii. 15), but not in a complete and systematic manner. At the time of Christ, indeed, it would seem that the reader had a certain freedom of choice in the prophetic lessons (Luke iv. 17). Such books as Samuel had little place in the synagogue service, but the interest of the narrative caused them to be largely read in private. This use of the books gave no such guarantee against the introduction of various readings as was afforded by use in public worship. Private readers must no doubt have often been content to purchase or transcribe indifferent copies, and a student might not hesitate to make on his own copy notes or small additions to facilitate the sense, or even to add a paragraph which he had derived from another source, a procedure of which we shall find examples by and by. Under such circumstances, and in the absence of official supervision, the multiplication of copies opened an easy door to the multiplication of errors; which might, no doubt, have been again eliminated by a critical collation, but might very easily become permanent when, as we have seen, a single copy without critical revision acquired the position of the standard manuscript, to which all new transcripts were to be conformed.

In general, then, we must conclude, *first*, that many various readings once existed in MSS. of the Old Testament which have totally disappeared from the extant Hebrew copies; and, *further*, that the range and distribution of these variations were in part connected with the fact that all books of the Old Testament had not an equal place in the official service of the synagogue. But the force of these observations is sometimes met by an argument directed to depreciate the value of the Septuagint readings. It is not denied that the MSS. which lay before the Greek translators contained various readings; but it is urged that these MSS. were presumably of Egyptian origin, and that the Jews of Egypt had probably to content themselves with inferior copies, transmitted and multiplied in the hands of scholars who were neither so learned nor so scrupulous as the Scribes of Jerusalem. Upon this view we are invited to look upon the Septuagint as the witness to a corrupt Egyptian recension of the text, the various readings in which deserve little attention, and afford no evidence that Palestinian MSS. did not agree even at an early period with the present Massoretic text.

Now, we have already seen that this view is at any rate exaggerated, for we have had cases before us in which no sober critic will hesitate to prefer the so-called Egyptian reading. But it is to be observed further that the whole theory of a uniform Palestinian recension is a pure hypothesis. There is not a particle of evidence that there was a uniform Palestinian text in the sense in which our present Hebrew Bibles are uniform—or, in other words, to the exclusion even of such variations and corruptions as are found in MSS. of the New Testament—before the first century of our era. Nay, as we have seen, the author of the *Book of Jubilees*, a Palestinian scholar of the first century, used a Hebrew Bible which often agreed with the Septuagint or the Samaritan recension against the Massoretic text (*supra*, p. 73).

But let us look at the history of the Greek translation, and see what ground of fact there is for supposing that it was made from inferior copies, and could pass muster only in a land of inferior scholarship. The account of the origin of the Septuagint which was current in the time of Christ, and may be read in Josephus and Eusebius, is full of fabulous embellishments, designed to establish the authority of the version as miraculously composed under divine inspiration. The source of these fables is an epistle purporting to be written by one Aristeas, a courtier in Alexandria under Ptolemy Philadelphus.[2] This epistle is a forgery, but the author seems to have linked on his fabulous stories to some element of current tradition; and there is other evidence that in the second century B.C. the uniform tradition of the Jews in Egypt was to the effect that the Greek Pentateuch was written for the first or second Ptolemy, to be placed in the royal library collected by Demetrius Phalereus. This tradition is not wholly improbable, and at all events the date to which it leads us has generally commended itself to the judgment of scholars. That is, the Pentateuch was translated in Egypt before the middle of the third century B.C. The other books were translated later, but they probably followed pretty fast. The author of the prologue to the Apocryphal book of Ecclesiasticus, who wrote in Egypt about 130 B.C., speaks of the law, the prophets, and the other books of the fathers, as current in Greek in his time. The Septuagint version, then, was made in Egypt under the Ptolemies. Under these princes the Jewish colony in Egypt was not a poor or oppressed body; it was very numerous, very influential. Jews held important posts in the kingdom; and formed a large element in the population of Alexandria. Their wealth was so great that they were able to make frequent pilgrimages and send many rich gifts to the Temple at Jerusalem. They stood, therefore, on an excellent footing with the authorities of the nation in Palestine, and there is not the slightest evidence that they were regarded as heretics, using an inferior Bible, or in any way falling short of all the requisites of true Judaism. There was, indeed, a schismatic temple in Egypt, at Leontopolis; but that temple, so far as we can gather, by no means attracted to it the service and the worship of the greater part of the Greek-speaking Jews in Egypt. Their hearts still turned towards Jerusalem, and their intercourse with Palestine was too familiar and frequent to suffer them to fall into the position of an isolated and ignorant sect. In fact, we have the testimony of the author of the prologue to Ecclesiasticus that, when he came from Palestine to Egypt, he found there no small measure of learning and discipline in matters of religion.

All this makes it highly improbable that the Jews of Egypt would have contented themselves with a translation below the standard of Palestine, or that they would have found any difficulty in procuring manuscripts of the approved official recension, if such a recension had then existed. But the argument may be carried further. In the time of Christ there were many Hellenistic Jews resident in Jerusalem, with synagogues of their own, where the Greek version was necessarily in regular use. We find these Hellenists in Acts vi. living on the best terms with the religious authorities of the capital. Hellenists and Hebrews, the Septuagint and the original text, met in Jerusalem without schism or controversy. Yet many of the Palestinian scholars were familiar with Greek, and Paul cannot have been the only man born in the Hellenistic dispersion, and accustomed from infancy to the Greek version, who afterwards studied under Palestinian doctors, and became equally familiar with the Hebrew text. The divergences of the Septuagint must have been patent to all Jerusalem. Yet we find no attempt to condemn and suppress this version till the second century, when the rise of the new school of exegesis, and the consequent introduction of a fixed official text, were followed by the discrediting of the old Greek Bible in favour of the new translation by Aquila. On the contrary, early Rabbinical tradition expressly recognises the Greek version as legitimate. In some passages of the Jewish books mention is made of thirteen places in which those who "wrote for Ptolemy" departed from the Hebrew text. But these changes, which are similar in character to the "corrections of the Scribes" spoken of in last Lecture, are not reprehended; and in one form of the tradition they are even said to have been made by divine inspiration. The account of these thirteen passages contains mistakes which show that the tradition was written down after the Septuagint had ceased to be a familiar book in Palestine. It is remarkable that the graver variations of the Egyptian text are passed over in absolute silence, and had apparently fallen into oblivion. But the tradition recalls a time when Hebrew scholars knew the Greek version well, and noted its variations in a friendly spirit of tolerance. These facts are entirely inconsistent with the idea that the Egyptian text was viewed as corrupt. To the older Jewish tradition its variations appeared, not in the light of deviations from an acknowledged standard, but as features fairly within the limits of a faithful transmission or interpretation of the text. And so the comparison of the Septuagint with the Hebrew Bible not merely furnishes us with fresh critical material for the text of individual passages, but supplies a measure of the limits of variation which were tolerated two hundred years after Ezra, when the version was first written, and indeed from that time downwards until the apostolic age. For in the times of the New Testament the Greek and Hebrew Bibles were current side by side; and men like the apostles, who knew both languages, used either text indifferently, or even quoted the Old Testament from memory, as Paul often does, with a laxness surprising to the reader who judges by a modern rule, but very natural in the condition of the text which we have just characterised. It may be observed in passing that these considerations remove a great part of the difficulties which are commonly felt to attach to the citations of the Old Testament in the New. [3]

When we say that the readings of the Septuagint afford a fair measure of the limits of variation in the early history of the text, it is by no means implied that the Greek version, taken as a whole, is as valuable as the Hebrew text. A translation can never supply the place of a manuscript. There is always an allowance to be made for errors of translation and licences of interpretation; and even if we possessed the Septuagint in its original form it would be necessary to use it with great caution as an instrument of textual criticism. But in reality this use of the Septuagint is made greatly more difficult and uncertain by many corruptions which it underwent in the course of transmission. The text of the Septuagint was in a deplorable state even in the days of Origen at the close of the second Christian century. In his Hexaplar Bible, in which the Hebrew, the Septuagint, and the later Greek versions were arranged in parallel columns, Origen made a notable attempt to purify the text, and indicate its variations from the Hebrew. But the use made of Origen's labours by later generations rather increased the mischief, and in the present day it is an affair of the most delicate scholarship to make profitable use of the Alexandrian version for the confirmation or emendation of the

Hebrew. The work has often fallen into incompetent hands, and their rashness is a chief reason why cautious scholars are still apt to look with unjustifiable indifference on what, after all, is our oldest witness to the history of the text of the Old Testament, a valuable evidence for the general purity of the Hebrew Bible, and an important guide towards those corrections which can never be wholly unnecessary in a book transmitted from so early a date, on what is practically the authority of a single manuscript.

For our present purpose it is not necessary that I should conduct you over the delicate ground which cannot be safely trodden save by the most experienced scholarship. My object will be attained if I succeed in conveying to you by a few plain examples a just conception of the methods of the ancient copyists as they stand revealed to us in the broader differences between the Hebrew and the Septuagint. It will conduce to clearness if I indicate at the outset the conclusions to which these differences appear to point, and the proof of which will be specially contemplated in the details which I shall presently set before you. I shall endeavour to show that the comparison of the Hebrew and Greek texts carries us beyond the sphere of mere verbal variations with which textual criticism is generally busied, and introduces us to a series of questions affecting the composition, the editing, and the collection of the sacred books. This class of questions forms the special subject of the branch of critical science which is usually distinguished from the verbal criticism of the text by the name of Higher or Historical Criticism. The value of textual criticism is now admitted on all hands. The first collections of various readings for the New Testament excited great alarm, but it was soon seen to be absurd to quarrel with facts. Various readings were actually found in MSS., and it was necessary to make the best of them. But while textual criticism admittedly deals with facts, the higher criticism is often supposed to have no other basis than the subjective fancies and arbitrary hypotheses of scholars. When critics maintain that some Old Testament writings, traditionally ascribed to a single hand, are really of composite origin, and that many of the Hebrew books have gone through successive redactions,—or, in other words, have been edited and re-edited in different ages, receiving some addition or modification at the hand of each editor,—it is often supposed that these are mere theories devised to account for facts which may be susceptible of a very different explanation. It is thought incredible that inspired books should have been subjected to such treatment ; and, following the Newtonian rule that every hypothesis must have a basis in demonstrable fact, conservative theologians refuse to accept the critical theories till external evidence is produced that editors and compilers actually dealt with parts of the Bible in the way which critics assume. Here it is that the Septuagint comes in to justify the critics, and provide external evidence of the sort of thing which to the conservative school seems so incredible. The variations of the Greek and Hebrew text reveal to us a time when the functions of copyist and editor shaded into one another by imperceptible degrees. They not only prove that Old Testament books were subjected to such processes of successive editing as critics maintain, but that the work of redaction went on to so late a date that editorial changes are found in the present Hebrew text which did not exist in the MSS. of the Greek translators. The details of the evidence will make my meaning more clear, but in general what I desire to impress upon you is this. The evidence of the Septuagint proves that early copyists had a very different view of their responsibility from that which we might be apt to ascribe to them. They were not reckless or indifferent to the truth. They copied the Old Testament books knowing them to be sacred books, and they were zealous to preserve them as writings of Divine authority. But their sense of responsibility to the Divine word regarded the meaning rather than the form, and they had not that highly-developed sense of the importance of preserving every word and every letter of the original hand of the author which seems natural to us. When we look at the matter carefully, we observe that the difference between them and us lies, not in any religious principle, but in the literary ideas of those ancient times. From our point of view a book is the property of the author. You may buy a copy of it, but you do not thereby acquire a literary property in the work, or a right to tamper with the style and alter the words of the author even to make his sense more distinct. But this idea was too subtle for those ancient times. The man who had bought or copied a book held it to be his own for every purpose. He valued it for its contents, and therefore would not disfigure these by arbitrary changes. But, if he could make it more convenient for use by adding a note here, putting in a word there, or incorporating additional matter derived from another source, he had no hesitation in doing so. In short, every ancient scholar who copied or annotated a book for his own use was very much in the position of a modern editor, with the difference that at that time there was no system of footnotes, brackets, and explanatory prefaces, by which the insertions could be distinguished from the original text.

In setting before you some examples of the evidence which enables us to prove this thesis, I shall begin with the question of the titles which are prefixed to some parts of the Old Testament. A large proportion of the books of the Old Testament are anonymous. The Pentateuch, for example, bears no author's name on its front, although certain things in the course of the narrative are said to have been written down by Moses. All the historical books are anonymous, with the single exception of one of the latest of them, the memoirs of Nehemiah, in which the author's name is prefixed to the first chapter. This fact is characteristic. Why do the authors not give their names? Because the literary public was interested in the substance of the book, but was not concerned to know who had written it. That is the only conceivable reason. The idea of literary property, of the book belonging to the author instead of to the man who had bought the copy, did not exist then, or at least was very little developed.

This remark applies with full force only to works like the Historical Books, which were products of the study, and did not derive their value from their connection with the author's public life. It is not equally applicable to lyric poetry, where, as in the case of David's elegy on Saul and Jonathan, the interest of the poem frequently depends on the authorship. Least of all could the law of anonymity apply to the written collections of the sermons of the prophets, which were summaries of a course of public activity in which the personality of the prophet could not be separated from his words. Thus, while the historical books are habitually anonymous, and poetical pieces only sometimes bear an author's name, it is the rule that each group of prophecies, and often each individual oracle, has the name of the author attached. There are, indeed, a certain number of prophetic writings which have no title; but these, in all probability, are prophecies which were never spoken, which were composed in solitude, and circulated from the first in writing. They fall, therefore, under the general law of the anonymity of books which are not directly connected with a public interest attaching to the author's life.

The chief example of an anonymous prophecy is that which fills the last twenty-seven chapters of Isaiah. It is true that we have been accustomed by tradition to assume that this prophecy is the work of Isaiah,—or, in other words, that the title which stands at the beginning of the book of Isaiah covers the last twenty-seven chapters also. This seems a natural and plausible assumption from our point of view, and from our habits with regard to the use of title-pages stating everything that a volume contains; but no one who has been personally occupied with old Eastern MSS., and has observed the way in which copyists, on account of the scarcity and costliness of writing material, were accustomed to fill up blank pages at the end of a book by writing in some other work or passage which they wished to preserve, and that without any note or title whatever, will for a moment venture to affirm that the title at the beginning of the book must necessarily apply to the whole contents of the volume. And in old times, we must remember, the book of Isaiah was a volume. It was still a separate volume in the time of Christ, as we learn from Luke iv. 17. I do not at present press this point further, or attempt to decide whether these chapters are really the work of Isaiah, or whether, as modern criticism holds, they proceed from a later prophet. In either case, they form a distinct literary work; for those who uphold the traditional view of their authorship are agreed that they date from the latest times of Isaiah's life, and are not part of his public teaching directed to the immediate needs of his own age, but a sort of testament left for the consolation of the Babylonian exiles.[4] Even on this view, the fact that they have no separate title demands an explanation, which seems to flow naturally from the consideration that products of the study were in those days habitually anonymous.

It is easy to perceive, however, that as soon as a beginning was made with the custom of prefixing the author's name to a book—and we find this done at any rate by Nehemiah—the use of titles would grow, and readers would become curious to have the author's name in every case. It therefore becomes important to ask whether all the titles now found in the Old Testament go back to the original authors, or whether some of them are the conjectures of later copyists. This question is naturally suggested by what we find in manuscripts of the New Testament, many of which prefix the name of Paul to the Epistle to the Hebrews, although it is quite certain that the oldest copies left the Epistle anonymous. The Septuagint enables us to answer the question. The part of the Old Testament in which the system of titles has been carried out most fully is the Book of Psalms. The titles to the Psalms are to a large extent directions for their liturgical performance in the service of the Temple music; but they also contain the names of men—David, the Sons of Korah, and so forth. Are we to suppose that there is no title of a psalm in the Hebrew Bible which does not go back to the author of the psalm? Let us consult the Septuagint, and what do we find? We find, in the first place, that the Septuagint has the words "of" or "to David" in a number of psalms where the Hebrew has no author's name (Psalms x., xxxiii., xliii., lxvii., lxxi., xci., xciii. to xcix., civ., cxxxvii.); and, conversely, it omits the name of David from four, and the name of Solomon from one, of the Psalms of Degrees (Psalms cxxii., cxxiv., cxxxi., cxxxiii., cxxvii.). Now the large number of cases in which the Septuagint inserts the name of David is evidence of a tendency to ascribe to him an ever-increasing number of psalms. That tendency, we know, went on, till at length it became a common opinion that he was the author of the whole Psalter. We cannot therefore suppose that the Greek version, or the Hebrew MSS. on which it rested, would omit the name of David in any case where it had once stood; and the conclusion is inevitable that at least in four cases our Hebrew Bibles have the name of David where it has no right to be, and that the insertion was made by a copyist after the time when the text of the Septuagint branched off. But if this be so, it is impossible to maintain on principle that the titles of the Psalms are throughout authoritative; and if there is no principle involved, it is not only legitimate, but an absolute duty, to test every title by comparing it with the internal evidence supplied by the poem itself.

Similar variations, leading to similar conclusions,

are found in other parts of the Old Testament, and even in the prophetical books. In Jer. xxvii. 1 the Hebrew has a title which the Septuagint omits, and which every one can see to be a mere accidental repetition of the title of chap. xxvi. For the prophecy which the title ascribes to the beginning of the reign of Jehoiakim is addressed in the most explicit way to Zedekiah, king of Judah (verses 3, 12). So again the Septuagint omits the name of Jeremiah in the title to the prophecy against Babylon (chaps. l., li.), which, for other reasons, modern critics generally ascribe to a later prophet. Here, it is true, chap. li. 59-64 may seem to be a subscription establishing the traditional authorship. But a note at the end of the chapter in the Hebrew expressly says that the words of Jeremiah end with "they shall be weary,"—the close of ver. 58. This note is the real subscription to the prophecy, and it is also omitted by the Septuagint.[5]

I now pass to an example of editorial redaction, involving a series of changes running through the whole structure of a passage. For this purpose I select the twenty-seventh chapter of Jeremiah, the Hebrew title of which has already been shown to be an editorial insertion. We are now to see that the hand of an editor has been at work all through the chapter. Let me say at the outset that the example is a somewhat unusual one. There are not many parts of the Old Testament where the variations of the Greek and Hebrew are so extensive as in Jeremiah; but it is necessary to choose a well-marked case in order to convey a distinct conception of the limits of editorial interference. To facilitate comparison, I print a translation of the Hebrew text, putting everything in italics which is omitted by the Septuagint. The Greek has some other slight variations, which are not of consequence for our present purpose. The essential difference between the two texts is that the Hebrew, without omitting anything that is in the Greek, has a number of additional clauses and sentences.

In the reign of King Zedekiah a congress of ambassadors from the neighbouring nations was held at Jerusalem, to concert a rising against Nebuchadnezzar. The prophets and diviners encouraged this scheme; but Jeremiah was commanded by the Lord to protest against it, and declare that the empire of Nebuchadnezzar had been conferred on him by Jehovah's decree, and that it was vain to rebel. The prophetic message delivered in the name of the God of Israel ran thus:—

Jer. xxvii. 5.—I have made the earth, *the man and the beast which are upon the face of the earth*, by my great power and outstretched arm, and give it to whom I please. (6.) *And now I* have given all these lands [LXX. the earth] into the hand of Nebuchadnezzar. . . . (7.) *And all nations shall serve him and his son and his son's son, till the time of his land come also, and mighty nations and great kings make him their servant.* (8.) And the nation and kingdom which will not serve him, *Nebuchadnezzar, king of Babylon, and* put their neck under the yoke of the king of Babylon, will I punish, saith the Lord, with the sword, and with famine, *and with pestilence*, till I have consumed them by his hand. (9.) Therefore hearken ye not to your prophets,

I

... which say ye shall not serve the king of Babylon. (10.) For they prophesy lies to you to remove you from your land, *and that I should drive you out and ye should perish.* ...

(12.) And to Zedekiah, king of Judah, I spake with all these words, saying, Bring your neck *under the yoke of the king of Babylon,* and *serve him and his people, and live.* (13.) *Why will ye die, thou and thy people, by the sword, by famine, and by pestilence, as the Lord hath spoken against the nation that will not* serve the king of Babylon ? (14.) *Therefore hearken not unto the words of the prophets who speak unto you, saying, Serve not the king of Babylon;* for they [emphatic] prophesy lies unto you. (15.) For I have not sent them, saith the Lord, and they prophesy lies in my name. ...

(16.) And to the priests and to all this people [LXX. to all the people and the priests] I spake saying, Thus saith the Lord, Hearken not to the words of your prophets who prophesy to you, saying, Behold the vessels of the house of the Lord shall be brought back from Babylon *now quickly,* for they prophesy a lie unto you. (17.) *Hearken not unto them,* [LXX. I have not sent them], *serve the king of Babylon, and live; wherefore should this city be laid waste?* (18.) But if they are prophets, and if the word of the Lord is with them, let them intercede with the Lord of Hosts [LXX. with me], *that the vessels which are left in the house of the Lord, and the house of the king of Judah, and in Jerusalem, come not to Babylon.* (19.) For thus saith the Lord *of Hosts concerning the pillars and the sea and the bases,* and the rest of the vessels left in this city, (20.) Which Nebuchadnezzar king of Babylon took not when he carried Jeconiah *son of Jehoiakim king of Judah* captive from Jerusalem *to Babylon, and all the nobles of Judah and Jerusalem;* (21.) *For thus saith the Lord of Hosts, the God of Israel, concerning the vessels left in the house of God, and in the house of the king of Judah and Jerusalem;* (22.) They shall be taken to Babylon, *and there shall they be unto the day that I visit them,* saith the Lord; *then will I bring them up and restore them to this place.*

Throughout these verses the general effect of the omissions of the Septuagint is to make the style simpler, more natural, and more forcible. At verses

8, 10, 12, 13, 17, the additional matter of the Massoretic text is mere repetition of ideas fully expressed in the shorter recension; and at ver. 14 the omissions of the Septuagint give the proper oratorical value to the emphatic "they" of the original, which the prophet, in genuine Hebrew style, must have spoken with a gesture pointing to the false prophets who stood before the king. It is not to be thought that a later copyist added nerve and force to the prophecy by pruning the prolixities of the original text. Jeremiah is no mean orator and author, and the prolixities are much more in the wearisome style of the later Jewish literature.

But in some parts the two recensions differ in meaning as well as language. At verse 7 the Hebrew text inserts in the midst of Jeremiah's exhortation to submission a prophecy that the Babylonians shall be punished in the third generation. No doubt Jeremiah does elsewhere predict the fall of Babylon and the restoration of Israel. He had done so at an earlier date (xxv. 11-13). But is it natural that he should turn aside to introduce such a prediction here, in the very midst of a solemn admonition, on which it has no direct bearing? And is this a thing which a copyist would be tempted to omit? Much rather was it natural for a later scribe to introduce it. Again, at verse 16, the Hebrew text modifies the prediction of the restoration of the sacred vessels made by the false prophets, by the insertion of the words *now quickly*. There was no motive for the omission of these words, if they are original. But a later scribe, reflecting on the fact that the sacred vessels were restored by Cyrus, might well insert these words to deprive the false prophets of any claim to have spoken truly after all. In reality it does not need these words to prove them liars; for their prediction, taken in the context, plainly meant that the alliance should defeat Nebuchadnezzar and recover the spoil. But the words "now quickly" stand or fall with the prediction put into Jeremiah's mouth, in verse 22, that the vessels of the temple and the palace, including the brazen pillars, sea, and bases, should be taken indeed to Babylon, but be brought back again in the day of visitation. This is plainly the spurious insertion of a thoughtless copyist, who had his eye on chapter lii. 17. For it is true that the pillars, the sea, and the bases were carried to Babylon, but they were not and could not have been brought back. These huge masses could not have been transported entire across the mountains and deserts that separated Judea from Babylon. And so we are expressly told in chapter lii. that they were broken up and carried off as old brass, fit only for the melting-pot. Jeremiah and his hearers knew well that they could not reach Babylon in any other form, and in his mouth the prediction which we read in the Hebrew text would have been not only false, but palpably absurd. That such a prediction now stands in the text only proves what the thoughtlessness of copyists was capable of, and makes the reading of the Septuagint absolutely certain.

We conclude, then, from a plain argument of physical impossibility, that Jeremiah did not predict the restoration of the spoils of the Temple. And by this result we remove a serious inconsistency from his religious teaching. For the restoration to which Jeremiah constantly looks is not the re-establishment of the old ritual, but the bringing in of a spiritual covenant when God's law shall be written on the hearts of the people (chap. xxxi.). No prophet thinks more lightly of the service of the Temple (chap. vii.). He denies that God gave a law of sacrifice to the people when they left Egypt. They may eat their burnt-offerings as well as the other sacrifices, and God will not condemn them (vii. 21, 22). Even the ark of the covenant is in his eyes an obsolete symbol, which in the day of Israel's conversion shall not be missed and not be remade (iii. 16). To the false prophets and the people who followed them, the ark, the temple, the holy vessels, were all in all. To Jeremiah they were less than nothing, and their restoration was no part of his hope of salvation.[6]

LECTURE V.

THE SEPTUAGINT (*continued*)—THE CANON.

In last Lecture we began to examine those features of the Septuagint which bear witness to the kind of labour that was spent on the text by ancient editors. We have seen how editors or copyists sometimes added titles to anonymous pieces, and how by a series of small redactional changes, running from verse to verse through a chapter, the form and even the meaning of an important passage were sometimes considerably modified.

We now come to another branch of the subject, in which we have not to deal with mere arbitrary additions and corrections made by editors out of their own head, but with features of the text which illustrate the composite character of some of the Biblical books which we have been wont to look upon as continuous unities.

I begin with the *transpositions* of the Septuagint text, and choose as my first example the chapters comprising Jeremiah's prophecies against the heathen nations. In our Bibles, and in the Hebrew Bible, these prophecies occupy chapters xlvi. to li. In the Septuagint they follow the 13th verse of the twenty-fifth chapter, and appear in a different order. In the Hebrew the sequence is Egypt, Philistines, Moab, Ammon, Edom, Damascus, Kedar and Hazor, Elam, Babylon. The Septuagint sequence is Elam, Egypt, Babylon, Philistines, Edom, Ammon, Kedar and Hazor, Damascus, Moab. Can we then assume that in this case the translator of the Septuagint version, having before him a fixed and certain order of all Jeremiah's oracles, took the liberty to shift the prophecies against the nations through one another, and to put them in an entirely different part of the book? From what we have seen already as to the general way in which these translators acted, such an assumption is highly improbable. Rather we are to suppose that in their copy these prophecies already occupied a different place from what they hold in the Hebrew Bible.

What does that lead us to conclude? Variations in the order of the individual places may very well happen in collected editions of writings originally published separately, but not in a single book of one author. And that is just what the facts lead us otherwise to suppose, for we know that Jeremiah's prophecies were not all written down at one time, or in the order in which they now stand. We learn from chap. xxxvi. that a record of the first twenty-three years of his prophetic ministry was dictated by the prophet to Baruch in the fourth year of Jehoiakim. But this book does not correspond with the first part of the present book of Jeremiah, in which prophecies later than the reign of

Jehoiakim—such as chap. xxiv.—precede others which must have stood in the original collection (chap. xxvi.). Jeremiah's book, then, as we have it, is not a continuous record of his prophecies, which he himself kept constantly posted up to date, but a compilation made up from several prophetic writings originally published separately. In this compilation the natural order is not always observed, for it is plain that chap. xlv., containing a brief prophecy addressed to Baruch, "when he wrote these words in a book at the mouth of Jeremiah in the fourth year of Jehoiakim" (ver. 1), must originally have stood at the close of the collection spoken of in chap. xxxvi. It is easy then to understand that, when several distinct books of Jeremiah's words and deeds were brought together into one volume, there might be variations of order in different copies of the collection, just as modern editions of the collected works of one author frequently differ in arrangement.

It is very doubtful whether this group of prophecies appears just as they were first published, either in the Septuagint or in the Hebrew. The order of the individual prophecies seems to be more suitable in the Hebrew and English texts; for chap. xxv. 15 *seq.* contains a sort of brief summary or general conspectus of Jeremiah's prophecies against the nations, and here the order agrees very closely with that in our present Hebrew text as against the Septuagint; but then, on the other hand, the summary of Jeremiah's prophecies against the nations is found in the twenty-fifth chapter, whereas in our present edition the details under this general sketch begin at chap. xlvi. Much more natural in this respect is the arrangement of the Septuagint, placing all the details in immediate juxtaposition with the general summary; so that here we seem to have a case in which neither edition of Jeremiah's prophecies is thoroughly satisfactory and in good order. But the general conclusion is that the transpositions give us a key to the way in which the book came together, showing that it was not all written in continuous unity by Jeremiah himself as one book, but has the character of a compilation, or collected edition, of several writings. We observe, also, that the compilers did not execute their work with perfect skill; and so it would plainly be unreasonable to accuse every critic of rationalism who ventures to judge on internal or other evidence that the collection may possibly contain some chapters, such as l. li., which are not from the hand of Jeremiah at all.

Another example of the important inferences that may be drawn from the transpositions of the Septuagint occurs in the Book of Proverbs. I presume that many of us have been accustomed to think of the Proverbs as a single composition, written from first to last by Solomon. But here again we find such transpositions as indicate that the book is not so much one continuous writing as a collected edition of various proverbial books and tracts. For example, the first fourteen verses of Proverbs xxx., containing the words of Agur, are placed in the Septuagint collection after the 22d verse of chap. xxiv. Then immediately upon that follows chap. xxiv. 23-34, a little section which in the Hebrew has a separate title,—" These also are [words] of the wise." After that comes chap. xxx. 15. In our English Bible this verse does not appear to open a new section: we translate it—" The horseleach hath two daughters, *crying*, Give, give," an obscure and enigmatical expression, which has puzzled all commentators. Most probably the translation "horseleach" is incorrect. The verse begins — ["Words] of Alûkah. There are two daughters of 'Give, give,'"—that is, two insatiable things,—"yea, three that are never satisfied," etc. The words of Alûkah are followed in the Septuagint, as in the Hebrew, by the words of Lemuel (xxxi. 1-9). Then comes the collection of Salomonic proverbs formed by the scholars in the service of King Hezekiah (xxv.-xxix.); and the book closes with the description of the virtuous woman (xxxi. 10-31). You see how the fact that these several small collections of proverbs are grouped in such different order in the Septuagint and in the Hebrew respectively makes it probable that they originally existed as separate books; so that, when they came to be collected into one volume, differences of order might readily arise, which could hardly have happened if the whole had been the original composition of Solomon alone. And that is quite the conclusion to which critics have been drawn by evidence of another sort,—that the Proverbs are not all of one date, that the book no doubt contains proverbs of Solomon, but embraces in addition to them a variety of matter derived from other sources.[1]

Let us now pass to a similar example in the historical books. Many of you have probably observed the way in which the history of the reigns subsequent to Solomon in the Books of Kings is made up. There is what critics are accustomed to call the framework of the history, and there are details within the framework. The framework is precisely similar in form for each reign, consisting of notices of the accession and death of the king, with certain stated particulars under each head, including a reference to the royal chronicles of Judah or Israel, as the case may be, for full details of the reign. These notices form the chronological framework which binds the whole narrative together. But the details within the framework do not in themselves form a continuous story, and are plainly not all written by one hand, or constructed on a uniform plan. One reign is full of rich episodes and picturesque narrative, another is comparatively barren in detail, as well as in style; and sometimes we find sections which, in addition to variety of style and phrase, show marked peculiarities of grammatical form. From a closer examination of these phenomena, critics have been led to distinguish, on the one hand, a brief epitome of public affairs, with moral judgments on each sovereign, which runs through the whole work in close connection with the chronological framework, and appears to be based on the royal annals constantly cited as the original authority for the history; and, on the other hand, a variety of episodes which are but loosely connected with the general plan, and which in many cases cannot have been excerpted from any collection of official records. The official chronicles of the kings of Samaria, for example, could not have contained much of the history of Elijah and Elisha. We naturally ask whether this view, based on observation of the internal features of the book, finds any support of external evidence from the oldest version. The answer is that it does. In the Septuagint certain episodes of the history are removed to another place, or even exist in a somewhat different form, as if, at the time when this version was made, they still stood, so to speak, apart from the general structure of the narrative. For example, the first twenty verses of 1 Kings xiv., containing an account of the death of Abijah, and of his mother's journey to the prophet Ahijah, when he predicted the ruin of the house of Jeroboam, are not found in the Septuagint, but a somewhat different narrative of the same events is inserted in chapter xii. There are other transpositions of a similar kind elsewhere. For example, the history of the death of Naboth (1 Kings xxi.) stands in the Septuagint before chapter xx., so that the narrative of Ahab's Syrian wars is made continuous. It is easy to see that this gives a more natural order, and that the history of Naboth is really a distinct episode in Ahab's life. But, without pressing these transpositions beyond what they manifestly bear, it is at least safe to say that they are most readily explained in accordance with the view, otherwise probable, that the framework of the Books of Kings is filled up by narratives from several distinct sources, which were not worked up by the editor into a strictly continuous story, but retained so much of their original independent form that their precise order was to some extent a matter of indifference. This conclusion may not appear to have a very immediate practical importance. It does not change the substance of the record; but it teaches us to look on the historical books as to some extent composite in structure, a fact which has more important bearings on many questions of interest than one might at first sight be apt to suppose.

We come now to passages omitted or inserted in one or other form of the text. One of the most familiar and instructive of these is the story of David and Goliath (1 Sam. xvii.). The story, as it appears in our English Bible, presents inextricable difficulties. In the previous chapters we are told how David is introduced to the court of Saul, and becomes a favourite with the king. Then suddenly we have the account of a campaign, and we learn, without any explanation, that David, although he was Saul's armour-bearer, did not follow him to the field. He returns to his father Jesse, and is sent by Jesse to his elder brothers in the camp, who treat him with a degree of petulance not likely to be displayed even by elder brothers to a youth who already stood well at court. But, in fact, it appears from the close of the chapter that David is utterly unknown at court. Neither Saul nor Abner seems ever to have seen him before. Every one has been puzzled by these apparent contradictions. But in the Septuagint, verses 12 to 31, and then the verses from the 55th onwards to the 5th of the next chapter, are omitted, and when these are removed we get a perfectly consistent and natural account. We find David in the camp and in attendance on Saul, just as we should expect. He volunteers to fight Goliath, is victorious in the contest, and returns to his natural place in attendance on Saul's person. There is only one objection that can be raised to this shorter form of the text. It may be said that the story, as we have it in the Hebrew, is so puzzling that the Septuagint may have deliberately omitted the difficult verses in order to harmonise the narrative. But when we take the verses which are found in the Hebrew and not in the Septuagint and put them together, we find that they are fragments of an independent account of the affair, according to which David never had been at court, but was a mere shepherd boy, who, having been sent by his father to the camp with provisions for his brethren, volunteered to fight the Philistine. The unknown lad thus leaped into sudden fame. He was retained at court, and Jonathan, with impulsive generosity, at once received him as his dearest friend. It is not credible that, if the Septuagint translators had set themselves arbitrarily to cut down a narrative originally homogeneous, the verses which they omit would have palpably hung together as bits of a different and self-consistent account of the whole story. On the contrary, we are forced to conclude that the text of the Septuagint is complete in itself, and that the additions of the Hebrew are fragments of another account, a popular and less accurate version of the story, which must once have been current in a separate book. The story fell in this form into the hands of some ancient reader, who engrossed in his copy of the Books of Samuel as much of it as seemed to offer matter of fresh interest; and in this way the interpolation ultimately became fixed in the text of our Hebrew Bibles. At first sight this conclusion may appear startling. We do not like to think that the English or the Hebrew Bible can contain an interpolated narrative of inferior authenticity. But that is only one side of the case. The providence which permitted the interpolation has preserved to us the Greek version in evidence of the original state of the text, enabling us even at this day to restore the true form of an important narrative, and remove difficulties which have been a stumbling-block in the way of all thoughtful readers. To shut our eyes to the evidence of the Septuagint, or to refuse to weigh it by the ordinary methods of sound common sense, would be an act of timidity, not of reverence; and it is well to learn by so plain an example that He who gave us the Scriptures has suffered them to contain some difficulties which cannot be solved without the application of critical processes.

An equally striking example is found in the account given in the very next chapter of the gradual progress of Saul's hostility to David. When the women came out and praised David above Saul—

1 Sam. xviii. 8.—*Saul was very wroth and* the saying displeased him [LXX. Saul], and he said, They have ascribed unto David myriads, and to me they have ascribed thousands, *and what can he have more but the kingdom?* (9.) *And Saul eyed David from that day, and forward.* (10, 11.) *Next day Saul casts a javelin at David.* (12.) And Saul was afraid of David, *because the Lord was with him and was departed from Saul.* (13.) And Saul removed him from his person, and made him his captain over a thousand, and he went out and in before the people. (14.) And David was successful in all that he undertook, and the Lord was with him. (15.) And when Saul saw that he was so successful, he dreaded him. (16.) But all Israel loved David, because he went out and came in before them. (17-19.) *Saul promises Merab to David, but disappoints him.* (20-27.) Michal falls in love with David, and Saul avails himself of this opportunity to put him on a dangerous enterprise in the hope that he will fall. David, however, succeeds, and marries Michal.* (28.) And when Saul saw, *and knew* that the Lord was with David, and that *Michal the daughter of Saul* (LXX. all Israel) loved him, he came to fear David still more, *and hated David continually.* (29, 30.) *Thereafter David again distinguishes himself in war.* (xix. 1.) Saul proposes to his son and servants to kill David.

The words and verses printed in italics are omitted in the Septuagint. Read without them the progress of the narrative is perspicuous and consistent. Saul's jealousy is first roused by the praises bestowed on David, and he can no longer bear to have him constantly attached to his person. Without an open breach of relations, he removes him from court by giving him an important

* The words in 21 and 26, which refer to the incident of Merab, are not in LXX.

post. David's conduct, and the popularity he acquires in his new and more independent position, intensify Saul's former fears into a fixed dread. But there is still no overt act of hostility on the king's part; he hopes to lead David to destruction by stimulating his ambition to a desperate enterprise; and it is only when this policy fails, and David returns to court a universal favourite, with the new importance conferred by his alliance with the royal family, that Saul's fears wholly conquer his scruples, and he plans the assassination of his son-in-law. The three stages of this growing hostility are marked by the rising strength of the phrases in verses 12, 15, 28. The additions of the Hebrew text destroy the psychological truth of the narrative. Saul's fears reach the highest pitch as soon as his jealousy is first aroused, and on the very next day he attempts to slay David with his own hand. In the original narrative this attempt comes much later, and is accepted by David as a warning to flee at once (xix. 10). The other additions are equally inappropriate, and the episode of Merab is particularly unintelligible. It seems to hang together with xvii. 25, that is, with the interpolated part of the story of Goliath; and in 2 Sam. xxi. 8, Michal, not Merab, appears as the mother of Adriel's children. In that passage the English version has attempted to remove the difficulty by making Michal only the foster-mother, but the Hebrew will not bear such a sense.

Here, then, we have another case where all probability is in favour of the Greek text, and a fresh example of the principle alluded to in last Lecture, that, where there are two recensions of a passage, the shorter version is almost always to be recognised as that which is nearest to the hand of the original author. Sometimes, indeed, we meet with an insertion which is valuable because derived from an ancient source, such as the quotation from the Book of Jashar, preserved in the Septuagint of 1 Kings viii. 53. But seldom indeed did a copyist, unless by sheer oversight, omit anything from the copy that lay before him.[2]

These examples must suffice as indications of what can be learned from the Septuagint with regard to the way in which the Biblical books were compiled and edited. I pass to another point of difference between the Greek and Hebrew Bibles, which raises the question, what books were accepted by the Jews as sacred Scriptures; at what date the list of canonical books was closed; and what were the principles on which the list was formed.

The Hebrew Bible has twenty-four books, arranged in three great sections—the Law, the Prophets, and the Hagiographa. The first section is the Pentateuch, or, as the Hebrews call it, the "Five Fifths of the Law." The second section has two subdivisions, the prophetical histories, or "Earlier Prophets," and the prophetic books proper, which the Hebrews call the "Later Prophets." Each of these subdivisions contains four books; for the Hebrews count but one book of Samuel and one of Kings, and the Twelve Minor Prophets are reckoned as one book. The third section of the Hebrew Bible consists of what are called the Hagiographa, or "Ketûbîm," that is [sacred] writings. At the head of these stand three poetical books,—Psalms, Proverbs, and Job. Then come the five small books of Canticles, Ruth, Lamentations, Ecclesiastes, and Esther, which the Hebrews name the Megilloth, or "rolls." They have this name because they alone among the Hagiographa were used on certain annual occasions in the service of the synagogue, and for this purpose were written each in a separate volume. Last of all, at the end of the Hebrew Bible, stand Daniel, Ezra with Nehemiah (forming a single book), and the Chronicles. As the contents of these books are historical and prophetical, we should naturally have expected to find them in the section of Prophets. The reason why they hold a lower place will fall to be examined later. This number of twenty-four books, and the division into the Law, the Prophets, and the Hagiographa, were perfectly fixed during the Talmudic period, that is, from the third to the sixth century of our era. The order in each division was to some extent variable. The number of twenty-four books is first found in the Second (or Fourth) Book of Esdras, towards the close of the first Christian century.[3]

Another division into twenty-two books is adopted in the earliest extant list of the contents of the Hebrew Bible, that given by Josephus in his first book against Apion, chap. viii. The same scheme appears to have been adopted in the Book of Jubilees, and was still familiar in the time of Jerome, who prefers to reckon twenty-two books, joining Ruth to Judges, and Lamentations to Jeremiah; although he knows also the Talmudic enumeration of twenty-four books, and a third scheme which reckons twenty-seven, dividing Samuel, Kings, Chronicles, and Ezra-Nehemiah, as is done in our modern Bibles, and separating Jeremiah from Lamentations. It is proper to observe that the scheme of twenty-two books is conformed to the number of letters in the Hebrew alphabet. Jerome draws a parallel between this arrangement and the alphabetical acrostics in the Psalms, Lamentations, and Proverbs xxxi. 9-31, and there can be little doubt that it is artificial.[4]

It is often taken for granted that the list of Old Testament books was quite fixed in Palestine at the time of our Lord, and that the Bible acknowledged by Jesus was precisely identical with our own. But it must be remembered that this is only an inference back from the list of Josephus published at the very end of the first century. Before this date we have no catalogue of the sacred books. The nearest approach to one is the panegyric on the famous men of Israel in Ecclesiasticus xliv.-l., in which authors are expressly included. The writer takes up the Pentateuch, Joshua, Judges, Samuel, Kings, Isaiah, Jeremiah, Ezekiel, and the twelve Minor Prophets in order. He also mentions the psalms of David, and the songs, parables, and proverbs of Solomon. Daniel and Esther are passed over in silence, and Nehemiah is mentioned without Ezra. Neither Philo nor the New Testament enables us to make up a complete list of Old Testament books, for there are some of the Hagiographa (Esther, Canticles, Ecclesiastes) which are quoted neither by the apostles nor by their Alexandrian contemporary. On the other hand, there is no reason to believe that any books were received in the time of Christ which have now fallen out of the Canon.

When we turn to the Septuagint we find, in the first place, a very different arrangement of the books. There is no division into Law, Prophets, and Hagiographa; but the Law and the historical books come first, the poetical and didactic books follow, and the prophets stand at the end as in our English Bibles. But there is another difference. Interspersed through the books of the Hebrew Canon, MSS. and editions of the Septuagint contain certain additional writings which we call Apocrypha. The Apocrypha of the Septuagint are not precisely identical with those given in the English Authorised Version. The apocalyptic book called Second (or Fourth) Esdras is not extant in Greek. The Prayer of Manasseh is not in all editions of the Septuagint, but is found in the collection of hymns or canticles which some MSS. append to the Psalms. All our MSS. of the LXX. are of Christian origin, and these Canticles comprise the Magnificat and other New Testament hymns. On the other hand, the Septuagint reckons four books of Maccabees, while the English Apocrypha have only two.

The additional books contained in the Septuagint may be divided into three classes :—

I. Books translated from the Hebrew. Of these 1 Maccabees and Ecclesiasticus were still extant in Hebrew in the time of Jerome, and the books of Tobit and Judith were translated or corrected by him from Aramaic copies. Baruch, in his day, was no longer current among the Hebrews.

II. Books originally composed in Greek by Hellenistic Jews, such as the Second Book of Maccabees, the principal part of which is an epitome of a larger work by Jason of Cyrene, and the Wisdom of Solomon, which, though it professes to be the work of the Hebrew monarch, is plainly the production of an Alexandrian Jew trained in the philosophy of his time.

III. Books based on translations from the canonical books, but expanded and embellished with arbitrary and fabulous additions. In the Greek book of Esther the "Additions" given in the English Apocrypha are an integral part of the text. Similarly, the Septuagint Daniel embodies Susanna, the Song of the Three Children, and the Story of Bel and the Dragon. 1 Esdras is based on extracts from Chronicles, Ezra, and Nehemiah, but treats the text with great licence, and adds the fabulous history of Zerubbabel.

The style of literature to which this third class of Apocrypha belongs is perfectly familiar to students of the later Jewish literature. We possess many Jewish books of similar character containing popular reproductions of the canonical books interwoven with fabulous additions. This kind of literature is a branch of the Midrash, or treatment of the sacred books for purposes of popular edification. It seems to have had its origin in the Synagogue, where the early Meturgemans and preachers did not confine themselves to a faithful reproduction of Bible teaching, but added all manner of Haggada, ethical and fabulous, according to the taste of the time. But in Palestine the Haggadic Midrash was usually kept distinct from the text, and handed down either orally or in separate books. In Alexandria, on the contrary, the Jews seem to have been content, in certain instances, to receive books through a Midrash without possessing an exact version of the original text.

From the fact that the Apocrypha stand side by side with the canonical books in the MSS. and editions of the Septuagint, some have leaped to the conclusion that the Canon of the Alexandrian Jews contained all these books, or, in other words, that they were recognised in Alexandria as being divine and inspired in the same sense as the Law, the Prophets, and the Psalms. That conclusion, however, is a very hasty one. There are several reasons which prevent us from drawing such a rapid inference. In the first place, we observe that the number of Apocryphal books is not identical in all copies, and that some of the books are found in two recensions with very considerable variations of form.[5] This is a proof that there was no fixed canon upon the subject, and establishes a parallel between the place of the Apocrypha in MSS. of the Old Testament and the occurrence in New Testament MSS. of a varying number of such books as the Shepherd and the Epistles of Barnabas and Clement, which never enjoyed undisputed canonical authority in the Christian Church, though they had a certain ecclesiastical position in particular districts. In the second place, all our manuscripts of the Septuagint are of Christian origin. The presence of an Apocryphon in a Christian MS. shows that it had a certain measure of recognition in the Church, but does not prove that full canonical authority was ascribed to it in the Synagogue. Again, in the third place, the books must have been current one by one before they were collected into a single volume. We learn from the prologue to Ecclesiasticus and the subscription to the Apocryphal book of Esther that some of them at least were translated by private enterprise without having any official sanction. Whatever position, then, they ultimately attained, they were not translated as part of an official Canon. And finally, Philo, the greatest of Jewish Hellenists, who flourished in the time of our Lord, knew the Apocrypha indeed, for he seems sometimes to borrow the turn of a phrase from them, but he never quotes from them, much less uses them for the proof of doctrine as he habitually uses most of the books in our Old Testament. There are, then, sufficient reasons for hesitating to believe that the Alexandrian Jews received all these books as authoritative, in the same sense as the Law and the Prophets. But, on the other hand, we are bound to explain how such books ever came to stand so closely associated with the canonical books as they do in our Greek copies. If the line of demarcation between canonical and uncanonical books had been sharply fixed, it is hard to see how they could have got into the Septuagint at all. And how did it come to pass that certain of the Hagiographa were not used in Alexandria in their canonical form, but only in the shape of Haggadic reproductions, like the Greek Esther and Daniel? These phenomena point to a time when the idea of canonicity was not yet fixed, and when certain books, even of the Hebrew canon, were only pushing their way gradually towards universal recognition. The state of the case is best illustrated by the fact already referred to, that some of the oldest MSS. of the New Testament contain, in addition to the books now received, such writings as the Shepherd and the Epistles of Barnabas and Clement. Before the canon of the New Testament was fixed, several such books enjoyed considerable authority in different Churches. They were not accepted books, which, all over the Church, were undoubtedly received as authoritative, like the Gospels and the great Epistles of Paul; but they had a certain respect paid to them, and in some parts of the Christian Church were read at the public meetings for worship. Something of the same sort, surely, must have existed in the time when the Septuagint was formed; otherwise these books, not admitted over the whole Jewish world, would not have occurred in ancient copies alongside of books of undoubted authority. But, again, at the period when books like the Epistle of Barnabas had not been definitely relegated to a lower place, certain New Testament books now held as canonical were still more or less disputed. In Alexandria, in like manner, such a book as Esther cannot have been accepted as beyond dispute, for instead of a proper translation we find only a Midrash, circulating in two varying recensions, and not claiming by its subscription to be more than a private book brought to Alexandria in the fourth year of Ptolemy and Cleopatra by one Dositheos, who called himself a priest.

These facts force us to inquire upon what principles the Jews separated the sacred writings from ordinary books. But, before doing this, let me ask you rather to look at the Apocrypha as they appear to us in the light of modern historical research. All the books of the Apocrypha are comparatively modern. There is none of them, on the most favourable computation, which can be supposed to be older than the latest years of the Persian empire. They belong, therefore, to the age when the last great religious movement of the Old Testament under Ezra had passed away—when prophecy had died out, and the nation had settled down to live under the Law, looking for guidance in religion, not to a continuance of new revelation, but to the written Word, and to the interpretations of the Scribes. To place these books on the same footing with the Law and the Prophets, as is done by the Church of Rome, is quite impossible to the historical student. We receive the Bible as the record of revelation. Now, if we look at revelation, not from its Divine side, but from a human point of view, as a phenomenon in history, we may lay down the principle that revelation manifests itself among men in the production of new religious truths and original spiritual experiences. The record of revelation, then, is the record of the period in which the religion of Israel continued to grow, and develop new principles—to gain new insight into the ways of God with man. This growth continued during the long centuries in which spiritual truth, in the hands of the prophets, struggled for mastery against the heathenism of the great mass of the nation—against the constant inclination of the whole people to mingle with the Gentiles around them, and fall back into their false worship. After the time of Ezra, the battle was over, and the victory was won. The religious life of Israel became stereotyped, and no fresh religious start was made, unless, perhaps, in a very modified sense, at the rising under the Maccabees against the attempt of the Syrian Greeks to substitute heathenism for the religion of Israel. The spiritual religion could make no further progress so long as it was limited by national forms and a local attachment to the earthly temple. Further revelation, which should be an Old Testament revelation, was simply impossible. The spirit of prophecy could not reappear until Christianity broke through the national barrier of the old covenant, and transformed the religion of Israel into a religion for all mankind, freed from every limitation of place and of nationality.

Let me guard this argument against a possible misconception. When I say that the record of revelation is the record of the age of religious productivity that closed with the thorough establishment and general acceptance of the reform of Ezra which made relapse into heathenism impossible, and with the rise of the Scribes who taught as mere interpreters of the past, and not as men having authority, we are not necessarily to conclude that a book written after this date has no claim to be part of the historical record of revelation. For example, the book of Nehemiah, or, as we have now learned to call it, in accordance with the Hebrew usage, the joint book of Ezra and Nehemiah, which in all probability was also one book with Chronicles, carries down the list of high priests as far as Jaddua, who was in office at the time of Alexander (Neh. xii. 11). The book, therefore, was written, at the earliest, at the very end of the Persian period, though it incorporates earlier documents, such as the autobiography of Ezra and the memoir of Nehemiah. In its present form, then, the book may be as late as some of the earliest Apocrypha. But the account which it gives us of the reforms of Ezra and Nehemiah is a necessary part of the history of the last great step in the victory of spiritual religion in Israel, without which the record of revelation would not be complete. No such thing can be said in favour of the Apocrypha. They were not only written after the end of the living progress of the Old Testament revelation, but their contents add nothing to our knowledge of that progress, and therefore, on a purely historical argument, and without going into any knotty theological questions as to the precise nature of inspiration, we can say on broad grounds of common sense that these books must not be included in the Bible record, but that their value is simply that of documents for the history of the connection of the Old and the New Testament. They belong to a new literature which rose in Judæa after the cessation of prophetic originality, when the law and the tradition were all in all, when there was no man to speak with authority truths that he had received direct from God, but the whole intellect of Israel was either concentrated on the development of legal Halacha, or, in men of more poetical imagination, exercised itself in restating and illustrating the old principles of religion in ethical poetry, like that of Ecclesiasticus, or in romance and fable of a religious complexion, like the books of Judith and Tobit. Halacha, Midrash, and Haggada became the forms of all literary effort; or if any man tried a bolder flight, and sought for his work a place of higher authority, he did so by assuming the name of some ancient worthy. This last class of pseudepigraphic works, as they are called, consists largely of pseudoprophetic books in apocalyptic form, like 2 (4) Esdras.[6]

We have satisfied ourselves, then, by historical arguments, that there is a distinct line of demarcation between the Apocrypha and the books which present the record of that living progress of revelation which came to rest in the work of Ezra. But how far was this understood by those who separated out the books of our Hebrew Bible as canonical, and rejected all others? The Jews had a dim sort of consciousness after the time of Ezra that the age of revelation was past, and that the age of tradition had begun. The feeling that new revelation had almost ceased is found even in the latest prophecies of the Old Testament. In Zechariah xiii. the prophet predicts the near approach of a time when every one who calls himself a prophet, and puts on a prophet's garment, shall be at once recognised as a deceiver, and his own father and mother shall be the first to denounce the imposture. And in the last verse of Malachi—the last echo, as it were, of the prophetic literature of the Old Testament—Malachi does not look forward to a constant succession of prophets, such as is foretold in Deuteronomy. He sees no hope for the corrupt state of his times, except that the old prophet Elijah shall return to turn the hearts of the fathers to the children, and the hearts of the children to the fathers, lest God come and smite the earth with a curse. As time rolled on, the feeling that there was no new revelation among the people became still more strong. In 1 Maccabees ix. 27 we read that "there was great sorrow in Israel, such as there had not been since the days that no prophet had appeared among them;" and, according to Josephus, the strict succession of prophets ended in the reign of Artaxerxes Longimanus. The Scribes thoroughly sympathised with this view. Even when they made innovations, they always professed to do so as mere interpreters, claiming nothing more than to restore, to expound, or to fence in, the law given by Moses. Their position is aptly described in the phrase of the New Testament, where Jesus is said to teach "as one having authority, and not as the scribes." But, while the Jews had a general feeling that the age of revelation was past, they had no such clear perception of the reason of the change as we can have in the light of the New Testament; for they continued to look, not for a new revelation superseding the old covenant, but for the reappearance of prophets working in the service of the law and its ritual. In 1 Maccabees iv. 46 they put aside the stones of the polluted altar, not knowing what to do with them, but waiting till a prophet shall arise in Israel to tell it; and again (chap. xiv. 41), they agree to make Simon high priest until such time as a true prophet shall appear. The revival of prophecy was still looked for, but the idea of the function of prophecy was narrowed to things of no moment. Malachi had looked for a prophet to turn the hearts of the fathers to the children, and the hearts of the children to the fathers, lest God come and smite the earth with a curse. In the days of the Maccabees the true nature of prophecy had been so far forgotten that it was thought that the business of a prophet was to tell what should be done with the stones of a polluted altar, or which family was to hold the dignity of the high priesthood. Where the meaning of prophecy was so superficially conceived, it is not surprising that a sporadic reappearance of prophets was not thought impossible. Josephus, in a curious passage of his *Jewish War*, says that John Hyrcanus was the only man who united in his person the three highest distinctions, being at once ruler of his nation, and high priest, and gifted with prophecy; "for the Divinity so conversed with him that he was cognisant of all things that were to come" (*B. J.*, Bk. i. chap. ii. 8; compare the similar expressions of John xi. 51). Moreover, although the Scribes in general did not consider that they had the spirit of revelation, we find the author of Ecclesiasticus (chap. xxiv. 31, 32) claiming for his book an almost prophetic authority: "I will yet make instruction to shine as the morning, and will send forth her light afar off. I will pour forth doctrine as prophecy, and leave it unto eternal generations" (comp. i. 30, li. 13 *seq.*). The author is fully conscious that his whole wisdom is derived from the study of the law (xxiv. 30). He does not pretend that he or other scholars are the vehicles of new truths of revelation (chaps. xxxviii. xxxix.); but he is evidently not conscious that this circumstance constitutes an absolute difference between the teaching which, by his own admission, was nothing more than an enforcement of the principles of the law of Moses, and the old creative prophecy of Isaiah or

Jeremiah. This unclearness of view rests upon an error which not only was fatal to the Jews, but has continued to exercise a pernicious influence even on Christian theology down to our own day. The Jews, as we have already seen, identified religion with the Law, and the Law with the words of Moses.

All revelation was held to be comprised in the Torah. According to the Son of Sirach, the sacred Wisdom, created before the world and enduring to all eternity, which is established in Sion and bears sway in Jerusalem, the all-sufficient food of man's spiritual life, is identical with the book of the Covenant of God most High, the Law enjoined by Moses (Ecclesiasticus xxiv.). The secrets of this law are infinite, and all man's wisdom is a stream derived from this unfailing source. This doctrine of the pre-existent and eternal Law, comprising within itself the sum of all wisdom and all possible revelation, runs through the whole Jewish literature. It is brought out in a very interesting way in the old Jewish commentaries on Deut. xxx. 12:—
"The law is not in the heavens." "Say not," says the commentary, "another Moses shall arise and bring another law from heaven: there is no law left in heaven;" that is, according to the position of the Jews, the law of Moses contained the whole revelation of God's goodness and grace which had been given or which ever could be given.[7]

What place then was left for the Prophets, the Psalms, and the other books? They were inspired and authoritative interpretations and applications of the law of Moses, and nothing more. They were, therefore, simply the links in tradition between the time of Moses and the time of Ezra and the Scribes. And so clearly was this the Jewish notion, that the same word—*Kabbala*, doctrine traditionally received—is applied indifferently to all the books of the Old Testament except the Pentateuch, and to the oral tradition of the Scribes. The Pentateuch alone is *Mikra*, "reading," or, as we should call it, "Scripture." The Prophets, the Psalms, and the rest of the Old Testament, in common with the oral tradition of the Scribes, are mere Kabbala or traditional doctrine. From these premisses it necessarily follows that the other books are inferior to the Law. This consequence was drawn with full logical stringency. The Law and the Prophets were not written on the same roll, and, in accordance with a legal principle which forbade a less holy thing to be purchased with the price of one more holy, the Mishna directs that a copy of the other books may no more be bought with the price of a Pentateuch than part of a street may be bought with the price of a synagogue.[8]

I need not interrupt the argument to prove at length that this is a view which cannot be received by any Christian. It was refuted, once for all, by the apostle Paul when he pointed out, in answer to the Pharisees of his time, that the permanent value of all revelation lies, not in Law, but in Gospel. Now, it is certain that the prophetical books are far richer than the Law in evangelical elements. They contain a much fuller declaration of those spiritual truths which constitute the permanent value of the Old Testament Revelation, and a much clearer indication of the nature of the New and Spiritual Covenant under which we now live. There is more of Christ in the Prophets and the Psalms than in the Pentateuch, with its legal ordinances and temporary precepts adapted to the hardness of the people's hearts; and therefore no Christian can for a moment consent to accept that view of the pre-eminence of the Law which was to the Jews the foundation of their official doctrine of the canon. What then is the inference from these facts? We found, in Lecture II., that the early Protestants, for reasons very intelligible at their time, were content simply to accept the Canon as it came to them through the hands of the Jews. But it appears that, in defining the number and limits of the sacred books, the Jewish doctors started with a false idea of the test and measure of sacredness. Their tradition, therefore, does not conclusively determine the question of the Canon; and we cannot permanently acquiesce in it without subjecting their conclusions to a fresh examination by sounder tests.

And here let me say, in one word, anticipating the fuller discussion to follow in the next Lecture, that, as we find it a matter of thankfulness that the Scribes did not attempt to make a critical text of Scripture, so it is a matter of thankfulness for us that they did not, till a very late date, set themselves to establish an authoritative Canon of Scripture. A Canon, deliberately framed on the principles of the Scribes and Pharisees, could hardly have been satisfactory; but in reality the essential elements in the Canon were not determined by official authority. The great mass of the Old Testament books gained their canonical position because they commended themselves in practice to the experience of the Old Testament Church and the spiritual discernment of the godly in Israel. For the religious life of Israel was truer than the teaching of the Pharisees. The Old Testament religion was the religion of revelation; and the highest spiritual truths then known did not dwell in the Jewish people without producing, in practical life, a higher type of religious experience, and a truer insight into spiritual things, than was embodied in the doctrines of the Scribes.

The judgment which theological prejudice might pass on the several books of the record of revelation was controlled by the practical experience of those who found in the Scriptures food for their own daily life; and so, in God's providence, a result was attained which rested on sounder principles than those of the schools. Throughout the history of the Church, it has always been found that the silent experience of the pious people of God has been truer, and has led the Church in a safer path, than the public decrees of those who claim to be authoritative leaders of theological thought.

LECTURE VI.

THE HISTORY OF THE CANON.

In resuming the subject of the Old Testament Canon, I must again direct your attention to the testimonies cited in last Lecture which mark the epoch at which the Bible of the Jews in Palestine had attained the fixed dimensions in which we now possess it. The Fourth (or Second) Book of Esdras speaks of twenty-four publicly acknowledged books, and the *Book of Jubilees*, according to Syncellus and Cedrenus, reckoned twenty-two. These testimonies, however, are not certain. The extant text of the *Jubilees* does not contain a reference to the twenty-two books in the context where the Byzantines claim to have read it, and the number of the sacred books is lacking in some recensions of the text of Esdras.[1] The first unambiguous evidence as to the close of the canon is contained in the list of Josephus, composed towards the close of the first century. We can affirm with practical certainty that the twenty-two books of Josephus are those of our present Hebrew Canon; but the force of this evidence is disguised by the controversial purpose of the writer, which leads him to put his facts in a false light. The aim of Josephus in his work

against Apion is to vindicate the antiquity of the Hebrew
nation, and the credibility of its history as recorded in
his own *Archæology*. In this connection he maintains
that the Oriental nations kept official annals long before
the Greeks, and that the Jews in particular charged
their chief priests and prophets with the duty of preserving a regular record of contemporary affairs, not
permitting any private person to meddle in the matter.
This official record is contained in the twenty-two books
of the Old Testament. The older history, communicated by revelation, is found in the Pentateuch along
with the legal code. The other books, with the exception of four containing hymns and precepts of life, which
may be identified with the Psalms, Proverbs, Ecclesiastes,
and the Song of Solomon, are made to figure as a continuous history written by an unbroken succession of
prophets, each of whom recorded the events of his own
time, down to the reign of Artaxerxes Longimanus, when
the succession of prophets failed, and the sacred annals
stopped short. As Josephus places Ezra and Nehemiah
under Xerxes, and identifies his son Artaxerxes with the
Ahasuerus of Esther, he no doubt views Esther as the
latest canonical book. The number of thirteen pro-
phetico-historical books from Joshua to Esther is made
up by reckoning Job as a history. As the Song of
Solomon figures as a didactic book, it must have been
taken allegorically.[2]

According to Josephus, the close of the Canon is
distinctly marked by the cessation of the succession of

prophets in the time of Artaxerxes. On this view there never was or could be any discussion as to the number and limits of the canonical collection, which had from first to last an official character. Each new book was written by a man of acknowledged authority, and simply added to the collection as a new page would be added to the royal annals of an Eastern kingdom. It is plain that this view is not in accordance with facts. The older prophets were not official historiographers working in harmony with the priests for the regular continuance of a series of Temple annals; they were often in opposition to the sacred as well as the civil authorities of their nation. Jeremiah, for example, was persecuted and put in the stocks by Pashur the son of Immer, priest and chief governor of the Temple. Again, it is clear that there was no regular and unbroken series of sacred annals officially kept up from the time of Moses onwards. In the time of Josiah, the Law, unexpectedly found in the house of the Lord, appears as a thing that had been lost and long forgotten. Even a glance at the books of the Old Testament is enough to refute the idea of a regular succession of prophetic writers, each taking up the history just where the last had left it. In fact, Josephus in this statement simply gives a turn, for his own polemical purposes, to that theory of tradition which was current among the Pharisees of his time and is clearly expressed at the beginning of the treatise of the Mishna called *Pirkê Aboth*. In it we read that "Moses received the Torah from Sinai and delivered it to Joshua, Joshua delivered it to the elders, the elders to the prophets, and the prophets to the men of the Great Synagogue," from whom it passed in turn to the Zûgôth, as the Hebrews called them,—that is, the pairs of great doctors who, in successive generations, formed the heads of the Scribes. This whole doctrine of the succession of tradition is a dogmatical theory, not an historical fact; and in like manner Josephus's account of the Canon is a theory, and a theory inconsistent with the fact that we find no complete formal catalogue of Scriptures in earlier writers like the son of Sirach, who, enumerating the literary worthies of his nation, had every motive to give a complete list, if he had been in a position to do so; inconsistent also with the fact that questions as to the canonicity of certain books were still undecided within the lifetime of Josephus himself.

But the clearest evidence that the notion of canonicity was not fully established till long after the time of Artaxerxes lies in the Septuagint. The facts discussed in last Lecture are not to be explained by saying that there was one fixed Canon in Palestine and another in Alexandria. That would imply such a schism between the Hellenistic and Palestinian Jews, between the Jews who spoke Greek and those who read Hebrew, as certainly did not exist, and would assign to the Apocrypha an authority among the former which there is no reason to believe they ever possessed. The true inference from the facts is, that the Canon of the Old Testament was of gradual formation, that some books now accepted had long a doubtful position, while others were for a time admitted to a measure of reputation which made the line of demarcation between them and the canonical books uncertain and fluctuating. In short, we must suppose a time when the Old Testament Canon was passing through the same kind of history through which we know the New Testament Canon to have passed. In the early ages of the Christian Church we find the books of the New Testament divided into the so-called *Homologoumena*, or books universally acknowledged, and the *Antilegomena*, or books acknowledged in some parts of the Church but spoken against in others. The *Homologoumena* included those books which, either from their very nature or from their early and wide circulation, never could be questioned — books of admitted and undoubted apostolic authority, such as the Gospels and the great Epistles of Paul. The *Antilegomena* consisted of other books, some of which are now in our New Testament, but which for some reason were not from the first broadly circulated over the whole Church. Along with these, there were other books, not now held canonical, which in some parts of the Church were read in public worship, and received a certain amount of reverence. The history of the Canon unfolds the gradual process by which the number of *Antilegomena* was narrowed; either by the Church, through all its length and breadth, coming to be persuaded that some book not at first undisputed was yet worthy to be universally received as apostolic, or, conversely, by the spread of the conviction that other books, which for a time had been used in certain churches, were not fit to be put on a level with the Gospels and the great Epistles. We must suppose that a similar process took place with regard to the books of the Old Testament. About many of them there could be no dispute. Others were *Antilegomena*—books spoken against— and the number of such *Antilegomena*, which were neither fully acknowledged nor absolutely rejected, was naturally a fluctuating quantity up to a comparatively late date, when such a measure of practical agreement had been reached as to which books were really of sacred authority, that the theological heads of the nation could, without difficulty, cut short further discussion, and establish an authoritative list of Scriptures. The reason why a greater number of books of disputed position is preserved in Greek than in Hebrew is that the Rabbins of Palestine, from the close of the first century, when the Canon was definitely fixed, sedulously suppressed all Apocrypha, and made it a sin to read them.

This account of the origin of the Canon is natural in itself and agrees with all the facts, especially with the circumstance that the canonicity of certain books was a moot point among Jewish theologians till after the fall of the Temple. This fact gave no trouble to the Jews, who accepted the decision of R. Akiba and his compeers as of undisputed authority. But Christian theology could not give weight to Rabbinical tradition, and it is thus very natural that many attempts have been made to prove that an authoritative Canon was fixed in the days of Ezra and Nehemiah while the last prophets still lived.

Among the ancient fathers it was a current opinion that Ezra himself rewrote by inspiration the whole Old Testament, which had been destroyed or injured at the time of the Captivity. The source of this opinion is a fable in 2 (4) Esdras xiv. Esdras, according to this story, prayed for the Holy Spirit that he might rewrite the law that had been burned. His prayer was granted; and, retiring for forty days, with five scribes to write to his dictation, he produced ninety-four books. "And when the forty days were completed, the Most High spake, saying, Publish the first books which thou hast written, that the worthy and the unworthy may read them; but conserve the last seventy, and deliver them to wise men of thy people." To understand what this means, we must remember that this book of Esdras professes to be a genuine prophecy of Ezra the scribe. The author was aware that when he produced his book, which was not written till near the close of the first Christian century, it would be necessary to meet the objection that it had never been known before. Accordingly he and other forgers of the same period fell back on the assertion that certain of the sacred writings had always been esoteric books, confined to a privileged circle. The whole fable is directed to this end, and is plainly unworthy of the slightest attention. We have no right to rationalise it, as some have done, and read it as a testimony that Ezra may at least have collected and edited the Old Testament. But no doubt the currency which Fourth Esdras long enjoyed helped to fix the impression on men's minds that in some shape Ezra had a part in settling the Canon, and drove them to seek arguments for this view in other quarters.

Accordingly we find that a new form of the theory started up in the sixteenth century, and gained almost undisputed currency in the Protestant Churches. According to this view, the Canon was completed by a body of men known as the Great Synagogue. The Great Synagogue plays a considerable part in Jewish tradition; it is represented as a permanent council, under the presidency of Ezra, wielding supreme authority over the Jewish nation; and a variety of functions are ascribed to it. But the tradition never said that the Great Synagogue fixed the Canon. That opinion, current as it once was, is a mere conjecture of Elias Levita, a Jewish scholar contemporary with Luther. Not only so, but we now know that the whole idea that there ever was a body called the Great Synagogue holding rule in the Jewish nation is pure fiction. It has been proved in the clearest manner that the origin of the legend of the Great Synagogue lies in the account given in Neh. viii.-x. of the great convocation which met at Jerusalem and subscribed the covenant to observe the law. It was therefore a meeting, and not a permanent authority.

LECT. VI.   *SYNAGOGUE.*   157

It met once for all, and everything that is told about it, except what we read in Nehemiah, is pure fable of the later Jews.[8]

Two, then, of the traditions which seem to refer the whole Canon to Ezra and his time break down; but a third, found in 2 Maccabees, has received more attention in recent times, and has frequently been supposed, even by cautious scholars, to indicate at least the first steps towards the collection of the Prophets of the Hagiographa :—

> 2 Mac. ii. 13.—The same things were related in the records, and in the memoirs of Nehemiah, and how, founding a library, he collected the narratives about the kings and prophets [*according to another reading*, the books of the prophets], and the [writings] of David, and the letters of kings concerning sacred offerings. (14.) In like manner Judas collected the books scattered in consequence of the war that came on us, and we have them by us; of which if ye have need, send men to fetch them.

This passage stands in a spurious epistle, professedly addressed to the Jews in Alexandria by the Palestinian Jews. The epistle is full of fabulous details, which claim to be taken from written sources. If this claim is not pure fiction, the sources must have been apocryphal. The Memoirs of Nehemiah to which our passage appeals are one of these worthless sources, containing, as we are expressly told, the same fables, and therefore altogether unworthy of credence. But, in fact, the transparent object of the passage is to palm off upon the reader a whole collection of forgeries, by making out that the author and his friends in Palestine possess, and are willing to communicate, a number of valuable and sacred books not known in Egypt. Literary forgery had an incredible attraction for a certain class of writers in those ages. It was practised by the Hellenistic Jews as a regular trade, and it is in the interests of this fraudulent business that our author introduces the story about Nehemiah and his library. Even if Nehemiah did collect a library, which is likely enough, as he could not but desire to possess the books of the ancient prophets, that after all was a very different thing from forming an authoritative Canon.

Scholars have sometimes been so busy trying to gather a grain of truth out of these fabulous traditions, that they have forgotten to open their eyes and simply look at the Bible itself for a plain and categorical account of what Ezra and Nehemiah actually did for the Canon of Scripture. From Neh. viii.-x. we learn that Ezra did establish a Canon, that is, that he did lead his people to accept a written and sacred code as the absolute rule of faith and life; but this Canon of Ezra was the Pentateuch. The people entered into a covenant to keep the Law of Moses, which Ezra brought with him from Babylon (Ezra vii. 14). That was the establishment of the Pentateuch as the canonical and authoritative book of the Jews, and that is the position which it holds ever afterwards. So we have seen that to the author of Ecclesiasticus the Pentateuch, and no larger Canon, is the book of the Covenant of God most high, and the source of all sacred wisdom; while, to all Jewish theology, the Pentateuch stands higher than the other books in sanctity, and is viewed as containing within itself the whole compass of possible revelation. In the strictest sense of the word the Torah is not merely the Canon of Ezra, but remained the Canon of the Jews ever after, all other books being tested by their conformity with its contents.

That does not mean that the Divine authority of the Prophets was not recognised at the time of Ezra. Undoubtedly it was recognised, but it was not felt to be necessary to collect the prophetic books into one authoritative volume with the Law. Indeed, Ezra and Nehemiah could not have undertaken to make a fixed and closed collection of the Prophets, unless they had known that no other prophets were to rise after their time; and we have no reason to believe that they had such knowledge, which could only have come to them by special revelation. The other sacred books, after the time of Ezra, continued to be read and to stand each on its own authority, just as the books of the apostles did in the times of early Christianity. To us this may seem highly inconvenient. We are accustomed to regard the Bible as one book, and it seems to us an awkward thing that there should not have been a fixed volume comprising all sacred writings. The Jews, I apprehend, could not share these feelings. The use of a fixed Canon is either for the convenience of private reading, or for the limitation of public ecclesiastical lessons, or for the determination of appeals in matter of doctrine. And in none of these points did the Jews stand on the same ground with us. In these days the Bible was not a book, but a whole library. The Law was not written on the same skins as the Prophets, and each prophetical book, as we learn from Luke iv. 17, might form a volume by itself. In one passage of the Talmud, a volume containing all the Prophets is mentioned as a singularity. Very few persons, it may be presumed, could possess all the Biblical books, or even dream of having them in a collected form.[4]

Then, again, no part of the canonical books, except the Pentateuch, was systematically read through in the Synagogue. The Pentateuch was read through every three years. Lessons from the prophetical books were added at an early date, but up to the time of the Mishna this was not done on a fixed system, while the Hagiographa had no place in the Synagogue service until a comparatively late period, when the book of Esther, and still later the other four Megilloth, came to be used on certain annual occasions.[5] And, finally, in matters of doctrine, the appeal to the Prophets or Hagiographa was not sharply distinguished from appeal to the oral law. Both alike were parts of the *Kabbala*, the traditional and authoritative interpretation of the Pentateuch, which stood as the supreme standard above both.

It is true that the whole doctrine of oral tradition arose gradually and after the time of Ezra. But the one-sided legalism on which it rests could never have been developed if the books of the prophets, from the time of Ezra downwards, had been officially recognised as a part of public revelation, co-ordinate and equally fundamental with the law of Moses. The Prophets, in truth, with the other remains of the old sacred literature, were mainly regarded as books of private edification. While the Law was directly addressed to all Israel in all ages, the other sacred writings had a private origin, or were addressed to special necessities. Up to the time of the Exile, the godly of Israel looked for guidance to the living prophetic word in their midst, and the study of written prophecies or histories, which, according to many indications, was largely practised in the circles where the living prophets had most influence, was rather a supplement to the spoken word than a substitute for it. But in the time of the Exile, when the national existence with which the ancient religion of Israel was so closely intertwined was hopelessly shattered, when the voice of the prophets was stilled, and the public services of the sanctuary no longer called the devout together, the whole continuance of the spiritual faith rested upon the remembrance that the prophets of the Lord had foreseen the catastrophe, and had shown how to reconcile it with undiminished trust in Jehovah, the God of Israel. The written word acquired a fresh significance for the religious life, and

M

the books of the prophets, with those records of the ancient history which were either already framed in the mould of prophetic thought, or were cast in that mould by editors of the time of the Exile, became the main support of the faithful, who felt as they had never felt before, that the words of Jehovah were pure words, silver sevenfold tried, a sure treasure in every time of need.

The frequent allusions to the earlier prophets in the writings of Zechariah show how deep a hold their words had taken of the hearts of the godly in Israel; but the very profundity of this influence, belonging as it did to the sphere of personal religion rather than the public order of the theocracy, made it less necessary to stamp the prophetic series with the seal of public canonicity. These books had no need to be brought from Babylon with the approval of a royal rescript, or laid before the nation by the authority of a Tirshatha. The only form of public recognition which was wanting, and which followed in due course, was the practice of reading from the Prophets in the public worship of the synagogue. It required no more formal process than the natural use made of this ancient literature, to bring it little by little into the shape of a fixed collection, though, as we have seen in the example of Jeremiah, there was no standard edition up to a comparatively late date. In the time of Daniel we already find the prophetic literature referred to under the name of "the books" or Scriptures (Dan. ix. 2). The English version unfortunately omits the article, and loses the force of the phrase.

LECT. VI. *THE PROPHETS.* 163

The ultimate form of the prophetic collection is contained in the Earlier and Later Prophets of the Hebrew Bible, to which perhaps we must add Ruth and Lamentations, which, on the old scheme of twenty-two books, go with Judges and Jeremiah respectively, while the book of Joshua, on the other hand, appears to have stood originally in close connection with the Pentateuch. The authority of this collection, which was inextricably interlaced with the profoundest experiences of the spiritual life of Israel, was practically never disputed, and its influence on the personal religion of the nation was doubtless in inverse ratio to the preference assigned to the Pentateuch as the public and official code of Ezra's theocracy.[6]

Equally undisputed was the position of the Psalter, the hymn-book of the second Temple. The Psalter, as we shall see in a future Lecture, has a complicated history, and, along with elements of great antiquity, contains many pieces of a date subsequent to the Exile, or even to Ezra. In its finished form the collection is clearly later than the prophetical writings. But no part of the Old Testament appeals more directly to the believing heart, and none bears a clearer impress of inspiration in the individual poems, and of divine guidance in their collection. That the book containing the subjective utterance of Israel's faith, the answer of the believing heart to the word of revelation, continued to grow after the prophetic voice was still, and the written law had displaced the living word, was natural and necessary. In the Psalter we see how the ordinances of the new theocracy established themselves in the hearts of the people, as well as in the external order of the community at Jerusalem, and the spiritual aspects of the Law which escaped the legal subtilty of the Scribes are developed in such Psalms as the 119th, with an immediate force of personal conviction which has supplied a pattern of devotion to all following ages.

Thus three great masses of sacred literature, comprising those elements which were most immediately practical under the old dispensation, and make up the chief permanent value of the Old Testament for the Christian Church, took shape and attained to undisputed authority on broad grounds of history, and through processes of experimental verification, which made it unnecessary to seek complicated theological arguments to justify their place in the Canon. The Law, the Prophets, and the Psalms were inseparably linked with the very existence of the Old Testament Church. Their authority was not derived from the schools of the Scribes, and needed no sanction from them. And, though the spirit of legalism might mistake the true connection and relative importance of the Law and the other books, no Pharisaism was able to undermine the influence of those evangelical and eternal truths which kept true spirituality alive in Israel, while the official theology was absorbed in exclusive devotion to the temporary ordinances of the Law.

The Law, the Prophets, and the Psalms are the

substance and centre of the Old Testament, on which the new dispensation builds, and to which our Lord Himself appeals as the witness of the Old Covenant to the New. The rationalising exegesis which insists, against every rule of language, that the Psalms in Luke xxiv. 44 mean the Hagiographa as a whole misses the point of our Lord's appeal to the preceding history of revelation, and forgets that Ecclesiastes, Canticles, and Esther are not once referred to in the New Testament, and were still *antilegomena* in the apostolic age.

The Law, the Prophets, and the Psalms, form an intelligible classification, in which each element has a distinctive character. And this is still the case if we add to the Psalter the other two poetical books of Job and Proverbs, which stand beside the Psalms in our Hebrew Bibles. But the collection of the Hagiographa, as a whole, is not homogeneous. Why does not Daniel stand among the later prophets, Ezra and Chronicles among the historical books? Why is it that the Hagiographa were not read in the synagogue? With regard to the Psalms this is intelligible. They had their place, not in the synagogue, but in the Temple service. So, too, the books of Job and Proverbs, which belong to the philosophy of the Hebrews, and were specially adapted for private study, might seem less suitable for public reading — Job, in particular, requiring to be studied as a whole if one is to grasp its true sense. But this explanation does not cover the whole Hagiographa. Their position can only be explained by the lateness of their origin, or the lateness of their recognition as authoritative Scriptures. The miscellaneous collection of Hagiographa appended to the three great poetical books is the region of the Old Testament *antilegomena*, and in them we no longer stand on the ground of undisputed authority acknowledged by our Lord, and rooted in the very essence of the Old Testament dispensation.

The oldest explicit reference to a third section of sacred books is found in the prologue to Ecclesiasticus, written in Egypt about B.C. 130. The author speaks of "the many and great things given to us through the Law and the Prophets, and the others who followed after them;" and again, of "the Law and the Prophets, and the other books of the fathers," as the study of his grandfather and other Israelites, who aimed at a life conformed to the Law.

When the other books of the fathers are said to have been written by those who followed after the prophets, the sense may either be that their authors were later in time, or that they were subordinate companions of the prophets. In either case the author plainly regards these books as in some sense secondary to the prophetic writings; nor does it appear that in his time there was a distinct and definite name for this collection, or perhaps that there was a formal collection at all. The overplus of God-given literature, after the Law and the Prophets are deducted, is an inheritance from the fathers. We must not infer from this statement that all ancient books not comprised in the Law and the Prophets were accepted without criticism as a gift of God, and formed a third class of sacred literature. The author of Chronicles had still access to ancient books which are now lost; and the book of Ecclesiastes warns its readers against the futility of much of the literature of the time, and admonishes them to confine their attention to the words of the wise, the teachings of the masters of assemblies, *i.e.* the sages met in council, " the experienced circle of elders " praised in Ecclesiasticus xii. 11. There were many books in those days which claimed to be the work of ancient worthies, and such of them as we still possess display a very different spirit and merit from the acknowledged Hagiographa. There must have been a sifting process applied to this huge mass of literature, and the Hagiographa are the result. But it is not so easy to explain how this sifting took place and led to the collection which we now receive.

One thing is clear. The very separation of the Hagiographa from the books of cognate character which stand in the second section of the Hebrew Canon proves that the third collection was formed after the second had been closed. And since the prophetic collection was itself a gradual formation, fixed, not by external authority, but by silent consent, this brings the collection of the Hagiographa down long after the time of Ezra. With this it agrees that some of the books of the Hagiographa did not originate till the very end of the

Persian period at earliest. The genealogies in Chronicles and Nehemiah give direct proof of this fact, and the book of Ecclesiastes can hardly be dated before the Chronicles; while even so conservative a critic as Delitzsch now admits that Daniel probably did not exist in its present form till the time of the Maccabees. Neither Esther nor Daniel, nor indeed Ezra, is alluded to in the list of worthies in Ecclesiasticus. Again, the book of Psalms seems to have been long confined to use in the Temple. At least the Septuagint translation was made from a copy which shared many graphical errors of our present Hebrew. Both therefore must go back to one archetype, which seems to prove that copies were not multiplied till a pretty late date.

The determination of the collection of the Hagiographa must therefore have taken place at an epoch when the tradition of the Scribes was in full force, and we cannot confidently assert that their false theories had no influence on the work. If they had a share in determining the collection, we can tell with tolerable certainty what principles they acted on. For to them all sacred writings outside the Torah were placed on one footing with the oral law. In substance there was no difference between written books and oral tradition. Both alike were divine and authoritative expositions of the law. There was traditional Halacha expanding and applying legal precepts, but there was also traditional Haggada, recognised as a rule of faith and life, and embracing doctrinal topics, practical exhortation, embellishments and fabulous developments of Bible narratives.[7] The difference between these traditions and the sacred books lay only in the form. Tradition was viewed as essentially adapted for oral communication. Every attempt to reduce it to writing was long discouraged by the Scribes. It was a common possession of the learned, which no man had a right to appropriate and fix by putting it in a book of his own. The authority of tradition did not lie with the man who uttered it, but in the source from which it had come down; and any tradition not universally current and acknowledged as of old authority had to be authenticated by evidence that he who used it had heard it from an older scholar, whose reputation for fidelity was a guarantee that he in turn had received it from a sure source. The same test would doubtless be applied to a written book. Books admittedly new had no authority. Nothing could be accepted unless it had the stamp of general currency, or was authenticated by the name of an ancient author dating from the period antecedent to the Scribes. All this, as we see from the pseudepigraphic books, offered a great temptation to forgery, but it offered also a certain security that doubtful books would not be admitted till they had passed the test of such imperfect criticism as the Scribes could apply. And, besides all this, the ultimate criterion to which every book was subjected lay in the supreme standard of the Law. Nothing was holy which did not agree with the teaching of the Pentateuch.

For some of the Hagiographa the test of old currency was plainly conclusive. It does not appear that the book of Job was ever challenged, and the only trace of a discussion about the Proverbs is found in a late Jewish book, and in a form which commands little credence.[8] The same thing holds good of the Lamentations, which, indeed, in the time of Josephus, seem to have passed as an appendix to Jeremiah. Ruth, in like manner, is treated by Josephus as an appendix to Judges. The case of the other books is not so clear, and for all of them we have evidence that their position was long disputed, and only gradually secured.

The book of Ezra-Nehemiah has a special value for the history of the Old Covenant, and contains information absolutely indispensable, embodying contemporary records of the close of the productive period of Israel's history. Yet we find that the Alexandrian Jews were once content to receive it in the form of a Midrash, with many fabulous additions and a text arbitrarily mangled. The Chronicles, according to all appearances, were once one book with Ezra and Nehemiah, from which they have been so rudely torn that 2 Chron. now ends in the middle of a verse, which reappears complete at the beginning of Ezra. But the Chronicles now stand after Ezra-Nehemiah, as if it were an afterthought to admit them to equal authority. When the Greek book of Esdras was composed of extracts from Chronicles, as well as from Ezra and Nehemiah, the three books were probably still read as one work.[9]

With regard to Daniel, two facts point to late admission. Daniel is not mentioned among the worthies in Ecclesiasticus, and here again the ancient Greek Bible has a text encumbered with Haggadic additions.

The authority of the book of Esther, which is not used by Philo or the New Testament, is necessarily connected with the diffusion of the feast of Purim. Now, the book contains two ordinances on this head— the observance of the feast proper (Esther ix. 22), and the celebration of a memorial fast preceding it (Esther ix. 31). According to Jewish usage, the fast falls on the 13th of Adar. But this was the day when Judas Maccabæus defeated and slew Nicanor in the battle of Bethhoron, and was kept as a joyful anniversary in Palestine from that time onward (1 Mac. vii. 48). The day of Nicanor is still placed among the anniversaries on which fasting is forbidden in the *Megillath Ta'anith* after the death of Trajan. In Palestine, therefore, at the time of our Lord, the fast of Purim was not observed, and it may well be doubted whether even the subsequent feast was universally acknowledged. The Palestinian Talmud still contains traditions of opposition to its introduction. And here, again, it is a notable circumstance that the book is so freely handled in the two Greek recensions of the text, and that even the Aramaic Targums use an unwonted licence of purely romancing additions.

The book of Esther was not undisputed in the early Christian Church; and, according to Eusebius, Melito,

Bishop of Sardis in the middle of the second century, journeyed as far as Palestine to ascertain the Jewish Canon of his time, and brought back a list, from which Esther was excluded.[10]

The last stage in the history of the Jewish Canon is most clearly exhibited in the case of Ecclesiastes and the Song of Solomon, which were still controverted up to the very end of the first Christian century. In earlier times, as we have seen, no urgent necessity was felt to determine the precise compass of the sacred books. But in the apostolic age more than one circumstance called for a definite decision on the subject of the Canon. The school of Hillel, with its new and more powerful exegetical methods, directed to find a Scripture proof for every tradition, was naturally busied with the compass, as well as the text, of the ancient Scriptures. R. Akiba, a rigid spirit averse to all compromise, would admit no middle class between sacred books and books which it was a sin to read. "Those who read the outside books have no part in the life to come."[11] Such books were to be buried—thrust away in the rubbish room to which condemned synagogue rolls were relegated. But the immediately practical call for a precise definition of the compass of the sacred books arose from the circumstance that this question came to be necessarily associated with a point of ritual observance. The Rabbins, always jealous for the ceremonial sanctity of sacred things, were concerned to preserve MSS. of the Scriptures from being lightly handled or used for common purposes. They therefore devised, in accordance with their principle of hedging in the law, a Halacha to the effect that the sacred books communicate ceremonial uncleanness to hands that touch them, or to food with which they are brought in contact. This ordinance was well devised for the object in view, for it secured that such books should be kept in a place by themselves, and not lightly handled. But it now became absolutely necessary to know which books defile the hands. The Mishna contains a special treatise on "hands" (*Iadaim*), and here we find authentic information on the controversies to which the ordinance gave rise. Two books were involved. The schools of Shammai and Hillel were divided as to Ecclesiastes. But there was also discussion as to the Song of Solomon, and this point came up for special consideration at a great assembly held in Iamnia, about A.D. 90, where R. Akiba took a commanding place. Some of the doctors maintained that the canonicity of Canticles was a moot point. But Akiba struck in with his wonted energy, and silenced all dispute, "God forbid!" he cried. "No one in Israel has ever doubted that the Song of Solomon defiles the hands. For no day in the history of the world is worth the day when the Song of Solomon was given to Israel. For all the Hagiographa are holy, but the Song of Solomon is a holy of the holies. If there has been any dispute, it referred only to Ecclesiastes." [12]

In the characteristic manner of theological partisanship, Akiba speaks with most confident decision on the points where he knew his case to be weakest. So far was it from being true that no one had ever doubted the canonicity of Canticles that he himself had to hurl an anathema at those who sung the Song of Solomon with quavering voice in the banqueting house as if it were a common lay. The same tendency to cover the historical weakness of the position of disputed books by energetic protestations of their superlative worth appears in what the Palestinian Talmud relates of the opinions of the Doctors as to the roll of Esther. While some Rabbins, appealing to Deuteronomy v. 22, maintained that a day must come when the Hagiographa and the Prophets would become obsolete, and only the Law remain; nay, says Rabbi Simeon, Esther and the Halachoth can never become obsolete (Esther ix. 28).[13]

In speaking of these Old Testament *Antilegomena* I have confined myself to a simple statement of facts that are not open to dispute. It is matter of fact that the position of several books was still subject of controversy in the apostolic age, and was not finally determined till after the fall of the Temple and the Jewish state. Before that date the Hagiographa did not form a closed collection with an undisputed list of contents, and therefore the general testimony of Christ and the Apostles to the Old Testament Scriptures cannot be used as certainly including books like Esther, Canticles, and Ecclesiastes, which were still disputed among the orthodox Jews in the apostolic age, and to which the

New Testament never makes reference. These books have been delivered to us; they have their use and value, which are to be ascertained by a frank and reverent study of the texts themselves; but those who insist on placing them on the same footing of undisputed authority with the Law, the Prophets, and the Psalms, to which our Lord bears direct testimony, and so make the whole doctrine of the Canon depend on its weakest part, sacrifice the true strength of the evidence on which the Old Testament is received by Christians, and commit the same fault with Akiba and his fellow Rabbins, who bore down the voice of free inquiry with anathemas instead of argument.

LECTURE VII.

THE PSALTER.[1]

Up to this point we have been occupied with general discussions as to the transmission of the Old Testament among the Jews, and the collection of its books into a sacred canon. In the remaining part of our course we must deal with the origin of individual books; and as it is impossible in six lectures to go over the whole field of the Old Testament literature, I shall confine myself to the discussion of some cardinal problems referring to the three great central masses of the Old Testament, the Law, the Prophets, and the Psalms. The present Lecture will deal with the Book of Psalms.

The Psalter, as we have it, unquestionably contains Psalms of the Exile and the new Jerusalem. It is also generally admitted to contain Psalms of the period of David, thus embracing within its compass poems extending over a range of some five hundred years. How did such a collection come together? How was it formed, and how were the earlier Psalms preserved up to the date when they were embodied in our present Psalter?

In discussing this question, let us begin by looking at the nature and objects of the Psalter. The Book of

Psalms is a collection of religious and devotional poetry. It is made up mainly of prayers and songs of praise. But it is not a collection of all the religious poetry of Israel. That is manifest from the circumstance that, of the poems preserved in the historical books, only one is repeated in the Psalter. That one is the 18th Psalm, corresponding to 2 Samuel xxii., and even this exception is perhaps more apparent than real. We are already familiar with the fact that the historical books contain elements introduced at different times from different sources. Now 2 Sam. xxiv. 1 reads as if it had once followed on chap. xxi. 14, so that the Psalm belongs to a section of later insertion. With this it agrees that this Psalm and the last words of David are not placed in connection with the events of David's life to which they refer, and so it is very possible that these pieces were not found in the Book of Samuel when the first section of the Psalter was collected. But, be this as it may, the other specimens of religious poetry of the Hebrews preserved in the historical books are not repeated in the Psalter, so that the Book of Psalms cannot have been meant to include everything of sacred poetry that was known to exist. Again, the collection is not formed with an historical object. It is true that there are some titles which contain historical notes, but on the other hand there are many Psalms whose contents naturally suggest an inquiry as to the historical situation in which they were composed, but where we have no title or hint of any sort to answer that question. Again, although the Psalms represent a great range of individual religious experience, it is to be noticed that they avoid such situations and expressions as are of too unique a character to be used in the devotion of other believers. The feelings expressed in the Psalms are mainly such as can be shared by every devout soul, if not in every circumstance, yet at least in circumstances which frequently recur in human life. Some of the Psalms are manifestly written from the first with a general devotional purpose, as prayers or praises which can be used in any mouth. In others again the poet seems to speak, not in his private person, but in the name of the people of God as a whole; and even the Psalms more directly individual in occasion have so much catholicity of sentiment that they have served with the other hymns of the Psalter as a manual of devotion for the Church of all ages in both dispensations.

The Psalms, then, are a collection of religious poetry, chosen with a special view to the edification of the Old Testament Church. But further, the purpose immediately contemplated in the collection is not the private edification of the individual Israelite, but the public worship of the Old Testament Church in the Temple,— that is, necessarily (since some of the Psalms are later than the Exile), in the second Temple. This appears most clearly in the latter part of the book, where we meet with many Psalms obviously composed from the first for liturgical use. Some are doxologies; others are largely made up of extracts from earlier Psalms, in a way very natural in a liturgical manual of devotion, but not so natural in a poet merely composing a hymn for his personal use. The liturgical element is specially prominent in the Hallelujah Psalms, for these are hymns used in the part of the Temple service called the *hallel*, which, as we learn from the Chronicles (2 Chron. v. 12, 13), was associated with the trumpet-blowing of the priests. Again, throughout the Psalms, the Temple, Zion, the Holy City, are kept in the foreground. Once more, the same destination appears in the titles. The musical titles are full of technical terms which occur again in the Book of Chronicles in descriptions of the Levitical Psalmody of the Temple. The proper names in the titles have a similar reference. The sons of Korah were a guild of Temple musicians; Asaph was the father and patron of a similar guild; Heman and Ethan are named in the Chronicles as Temple singers of the time of David. Finally, the very name of the Psalter in the Hebrew Bible leads to the same conclusion. The Psalms are called *Tehillîm*, hymns, from the same root as Hallelujah, and with the same allusion to the Temple service of praise.[2]

The fact that the Psalter is a hymnal at once elucidates some important features in the book and suggests certain rules for its profitable use and study. The liturgical character of the Psalms explains their universality, and justifies the large use made of them in the Christian Church. As a liturgical collection, the Psalter expresses the feelings and hopes, the faith, the prayers and the praises of the Old Testament Church, their sense of sin, and their joyful apprehension of God's salvation. These are the subjective elements of religion, the answer of the believing heart to God. And precisely in these elements the religion of all ages is much alike. The New Testament revelation made a great change in the objective elements of religion. Old ideas and forms passed away, and new things took their place; but through all this growth of the objective side of revelation, the devotion of the faithful heart to God remains essentially one and the same. Our faith, our sense of sin, our trust upon God and His salvation, the language of our prayers and praises, are still one with those of the Old Testament Church. It is true that not a little of the colouring of the Psalms is derived from the ritual and order of the old dispensation, and has now become antiquated; but practical religion does not refuse those bonds of connection with the past. The believing soul is never anxious to separate its own spiritual life from the spiritual life of the fathers. Rather does it cling with special affection to the links that unite it to the Church of the Old Testament; and the forms which, in their literal sense, are now antiquated, become to us an additional group of figures in the rich poetic imagery of the Hebrew hymnal.

But the Psalter and the Old Testament in general are to us not merely books of devotion but sources of study for the better knowledge of the whole course of God's revelation. It is a law of all science that, to know a thing thoroughly, we must know it in its genesis and in its growth. To understand the ways of God with man, and the whole meaning of His plan of salvation, it is necessary to go back and see His work in its beginnings, examining the rudimentary stages of the process of revelation; and for this the Psalms are invaluable, for they give us the first answer of the believing heart to God under a dispensation where the objective elements of revelation were far less fully developed, and where spiritual processes were in many respects more naïve and childlike. While the simple Christian can always take up the Psalm-book and use it for devotion, appropriating those elements which remain the same in all ages, those who are called upon to study the Bible systematically, and who desire to learn all that can be learned from it, will also look at the Psalms from another point of view. Recognising the fact that many of them have an historical occasion, and that they express the life of a particular stage of the Old Testament Church, they will endeavour to study the history of the collection, and ascertain what can be learned of the epoch and situation in which each Psalm was written.

In entering upon this study, it is highly important to carry with us the fact that the Psalms are preserved to us, not in an historical collection, but in a hymn-book specially adapted for the use of the second Temple.

The plan of a hymn-book does not secure that every poem shall be given exactly as it was written by the first author. The practical object of the collection makes it legitimate and perhaps necessary that there should be such adaptations and alterations as may secure a larger scope of practical utility in ordinary services.

In a book which contains Psalms spreading over a period of 500 years, such a period as that which extends between Chaucer and Tennyson, or between Dante and Manzoni, changes of this kind could hardly be avoided; and so in fact we do find not a few variations in the text and indications of the hand of an editor retouching the original poems. Between Psalm xviii. and 2 Samuel xxii. there are some seventy variations not merely orthographical. The Psalter itself repeats certain poems with changes. Psalm liii. is a copy of Ps. xiv. with variations of text; Psalm lxx. repeats Ps. xl. 13-17; Ps. cviii. is verses 7-11 of Ps. lvii., followed by Ps. lx. 5-12. Another clear sign that we have not every Psalm in its original text lies in the alphabetical acrostics, Psalms ix.-x. xxv. xxxiv. xxxvii. cxi. cxii. cxix. cxlv., in which the initial letters of successive half verses, verses, or larger stanzas make up the alphabet. It is of the nature of an acrostic to be perfect. An acrostic poem which misses some letter or puts it in a false place is a failure; and therefore when we find that some of these acrostics are now imperfect, we must conclude that the text has suffered. In some cases it is still easy to suggest the slight change necessary to restore the original scheme. Elsewhere, as in the beautiful acrostic now reckoned as two Psalms (ix. and x.), the corruption in the text, or possibly the intentional change made to adapt the poem for public worship, is so considerable that the original text cannot be recovered.[3]

In general, then, we conclude that the oldest text of a sacred lyric is not always preserved in the Psalter. And so, again, we must not suppose that the notes of authors' names in a hymn-book have the same weight as the statements of an historical book. In a liturgical collection the author's name is of little consequence, and the editors who altered the text of a poem cannot be assumed *a priori* to have taken absolute care to preserve a correct record of its origin. But to this subject we shall recur presently.

Let us now look at the collection somewhat more closely; and, in the first place, note that in the Hebrew text the Book of Psalms is divided into five books, each of which has a separate heading not translated in our English Bible.[4] But another sign of the fivefold division of the Psalms can be followed in the English, for each of the books ends with a doxology. The scheme of the whole is as follows:—

Book I. Psalms 1-41.—Psalms ascribed to David, except 1, 2, 10 [which is part of 9], 33. *Doxology.*—Blessed be Jehovah, God of Israel, from everlasting and to everlasting. Amen and Amen.

Book II. Psalms 42-72.—42-49, Korahite [43 being part of 42];
50, Asaph ; 51-71, David, or anonymous ; 72, Solomon.
Doxology.—Blessed be Jehovah God, the God of Israel, who
alone doeth wondrous things. And blessed be His name
of glory for ever : and let the whole earth be filled with
His glory ; Amen and Amen.

Subscription.—The prayers of David the son of Jesse are ended.

Book III. Psalms 73-89.—73-83, Asaph ; 84, 85, 87, 88,
Korahite ; 86, David ; 88, Heman ; 89, Ethan. *Doxology.*
—Blessed be Jehovah for ever. Amen and Amen.

Book IV. Psalms 90-106.—90, Moses ; 101, 103, David.
Doxology.—Blessed be Jehovah, God of Israel, from ever-
lasting and to everlasting. *And let all the people say,* Amen :
Hallelujah.

Book V. Psalms 107-150.—108-110, 122,* 124,* 131,* 133,*
138-145, David ; 127,* Solomon ; 120-134, Pilgrimage
songs. Ends with a doxological Psalm.

The doxologies, with the exception of that in Book
IV., plainly form no part of the Psalms to which they
are attached, but mark the end of each book after the
pious fashion, not uncommon in Eastern literature, to
close the composition or transcription of a volume with
a brief prayer or words of praise. In Psalm cvi. the
case is different. The doxology includes a liturgical
direction that all the people shall say, "Amen, Hallelujah," which seems to imply that this doxology was
actually sung at the close of the Psalm. But the other
doxologies mark actual subdivisions in the Psalm-book,
and it naturally occurs to us to inquire whether these
subdivisions are not the boundaries of earlier collections, of which the first three books of our present
Psalter are made up.

* Not so in LXX.

A closer examination confirms this conjecture. The first book, Psalms i.-xli., is all Davidic, every Psalm bearing the title of David except Psalms i. ii. x. xxxiii. Now Psalm i. is clearly a preface to the collection. But in Talmudic times Psalm ii. was reckoned as forming one section with Psalm i., and so it is actually cited as the first Psalm in the correct text of Acts xiii. 33. Again, Psalm x. is the second part of the acrostic Psalm ix., and Psalm xxxiii. is certainly a late piece, and probably came into this part of the Psalter afterwards. The first book, therefore, is a formal collection of Psalms ascribed to David. So, again, in the second book, the Psalms ascribed to David form a connected group apart from the Korahitic and Asaphic Psalms, though including some anonymous pieces, and Psalm lxxii., which is entitled "of Solomon," but was perhaps viewed, as our version takes it, as a prayer of David for his son. In Book III. only Psalm lxxxvi. bears the name of David, and this title is unquestionably a mistake, for the Psalm is a mere cento of reminiscences from older parts of Scripture, and the prayer in verse 11, "Unite my heart to fear thy name," is based on the promise (Jer. xxxii. 39), "I will give them one heart . . . to fear me continually." It is the law of the religious life that prayer is based on promise, and not conversely.[5] It cannot be accident that has thus disposed the Davidic Psalms of Books I.-III. in two groups. But if the final collector had gathered these poems together for the first time, he would surely have made one group, not two. Nor can he have added the subscription to Psalm lxxii., "The prayers of David are ended," unless, indeed, we suppose that the titles ascribing Psalms of the fourth and fifth books to David are all additions of later copyists after the collection was closed. We conclude, then, that the first book once existed as a separate collection, and that the subscription to Psalm lxxii., with the doxology, marks the close of another once separate collection of Davidic Psalms.

Another evidence that the first three books of the Psalter contain collections formed by more than one editor lies in the names of God. Books I. IV. and V. of the Psalter use the names of God in the same way as most other parts of the Old Testament, where Jehovah is the prevailing term, and other names, such as Elohim (God), occur less frequently. But in the greater part of Books II. and III. (Psalms xlii.-lxxxiii.) the name of Jehovah is rare, and Elohim takes its place even where the substitution reads very awkwardly. For example, a common Old Testament phrase is "Jehovah my God," "Jehovah thy God," based upon Exodus xx. 2, where, in the preface to the ten commandments, we have, "I am Jehovah thy God." Some later writers seem to have avoided the name Jehovah, in accordance with a tendency which ultimately became so prevalent among the Jews that they now never pronounce the word Jehovah (Jahwe), but read Adonai (Lord) in its place. Such writers avoid the phrase "Jehovah my God," and simply say, "my God." But in the Elohim Psalms, and nowhere else in the Old Testament, we find the peculiar phrase " God my God," with Elohim in place of Jehovah. And so, even in Psalm l. 7, where the words of Exodus xx. 2 are actually quoted, we read "I am God thy God." Clearly this is no accident. The Psalms in which the name Elohim, and not Jehovah, is habitually used hang together. And, when we look more closely at the matter, we see that they not only hang together, but that the phenomenon of the names of God is due, not to the original authors of the Psalms, but to the collector himself; for some of these Elohim Psalms occur also in the earlier Jehovistic part of the Psalter. Psalm liii. is identical with Psalm xiv.; Psalm lxx. with part of Psalm xl.; and here, among other variations of text, we find Jehovah six times changed to Elohim, and only one converse change. That is a clear proof that the Elohim Psalms have been formed by an editor who, for some reason, preferred to suppress, as far as possible, the name Jehovah.

Now let us look a little more closely at this Elohistic collection. It forms the main part of the second and third Psalm Books. The Psalms that remain look like an appendix, containing some supplementary Korahite Psalms, and one Psalm ascribed to David, which we have seen to be late, and which may fairly be judged to be no part of the original Davidic collections. If we set the appendix on one side, we find in Books II. and

III. a single Elohistic collection with a well-marked editorial peculiarity running through it. This Elohistic Psalm Book consists of two kinds of elements. It contains, in the first place, Levitical Psalms,—that is, Psalms ascribed to Levitical choirs, the sons of Korah and Asaph, and, further, a collection of Davidic Psalms marked off as a distinct section by the subscription at the end of Psalm lxxii. and the accompanying doxology. As now arranged, the Davidic collection is wedged in between two masses of Levitical Psalms, and even separates the Asaphic Psalm l. from the body of the Asaphic collection, Psalms lxxiii.-lxxxiii. It is not probable that this was the original order, for if we simply take Psalms xli.-l., and lift them into the place between Psalms lxxii. and lxxiii., we get a complete and natural arrangement. We thus have a book containing, first, a collection of Davidic Psalms with a subscription, and then two collections of Levitical Psalms, the first Korahitic and the last Asaphic. We may fairly accept this as the original order, which possibly was changed by the final collector in order that he might show by a distinct mark that the two Davidic collections in his work were originally separate. Perhaps, also, he may have been influenced by the fact that Psalms l. and li. are both suitable for the service of sacrifices of praise. Such is the account it seems reasonable to give of Books II. and III.

We come next to Books IV. and V. They also are really one book, for the doxology of Psalm cvi. belongs to the Psalm, and there is no clear mark of difference in subject, character, or editorial treatment in the Psalms which precede and follow it. But, taken as a unity, Books IV. and V. are marked by a liturgical character more predominant than in the other books. They are also of later collection than the Elohistic Psalm-book, for Psalm cviii. is made up of two Elohim Psalms, retaining the predominant use of Elohim, although the other Psalms of the last two books are Jehovistic. As the Elohim Psalms got their peculiar use of the names of God from the collector, and not from their authors, we may safely affirm that Books II. and III. existed in their collected form before Psalm cviii. was composed.

Thus the five books of the Psalms reduce themselves for us to three books, the second one having a subdivision. The first book, which from every point of view proclaims itself the oldest, consists of Davidic Psalms; the second book, now our second and third, consists (except in the appendix) of Elohistic Psalms, and these again are subdivided into a collection of Davidic Psalms and a twofold series of Levitical Hymns; and finally, the fourth and fifth books contain the latest Psalms, mainly written from the first with a liturgical purpose, and not merely adapted for liturgical use like many of the poems in the earlier part of the collection.

We come next to inquire into the age of these three collections. Most of the Psalms in Books IV. and V. are certainly late, not only in collection, but in authorship. Observe, in the first place, the discontinuance of the musical titles. Such titles as "To the chief musician (?) upon Neginoth," "upon Sheminith," and so forth, are frequent in the first three Psalm Books, but are not found in the last two. Now these titles were the technical terms of the Temple music, still recognised as such by the Chronicler, but which had become unknown and unintelligible in the time of the Septuagint. It seems as if they had already gone out of use when Books IV. and V. were collected, and this again would imply that by that time the national music of Israel had undergone a revolution, which can hardly have been due to anything else than the influence of foreign art. One naturally thinks of the great change on the whole civilisation and art of the East which was caused by the introduction of Greek influence. Can we suppose that the Psalter was completed so late? Many scholars answer in the negative, but there are good names and strong reasons on the other side, and at any rate the matter is not so certain as to forbid us to suggest such an explanation.[6] A curious and interesting feature in the musical titles in the earlier half of the Psalter is that many of them indicate the tune to which the Psalm was set, by quoting phrases like Aijeleth hash-shahar, or Jonath elem rechokim, which are evidently the names of familiar songs. Of the song which gave the title Al-taschith, "Destroy not," a trace is still preserved in Isa. lxv. 8. "When the new wine is found in the cluster," says the prophet, men say, "Destroy it not, for a blessing is in it." These words in the

Hebrew have a distinct lyric rhythm. They are the first line of one of the vintage songs so often alluded to in Scripture. And so we learn that the early religious melody of Israel had a popular origin, and was closely connected with the old joyous life of the nation. In the time when the last books of the Psalter were composed, the Temple music had passed into another phase, and had differentiated itself from the melodies of the people, just as we should no longer think of using as church music the popular airs to which Psalms and hymns were set in Scotland at the time of the Reformation.

In the fifth Psalm Book a special group consists of the Songs of Degrees, or more literally, "Songs of Ascent." [7] To ascend is the Hebrew technical term for going up to Jerusalem on pilgrimage. The songs of ascent, therefore, can hardly be anything else than a collection of hymns to be sung by pilgrims to the sanctuary; and with this interpretation the contents of the collection harmonise, some of the Psalms either directly alluding to the pilgrimage (cxxii.), or expressing such sentiments as would rise to the lips of the pilgrims when the mountains of Zion and the Temple first presented themselves to their gaze (cxxi. cxxviii.). The custom of going up to the feasts at Jerusalem with music and song is ancient (Isa. xxx. 29), but the pilgrimage Psalms of our Psalter are plainly, in part, later than the Exile, for they speak of captivity and deliverance. They are, therefore, Psalms of the second Temple.

Nay, Psalm cxxii. is later than the work of Ezra and Nehemiah, for it speaks of "Jerusalem the rebuilt, like a city well knit together." This language could not be used before the time of Nehemiah, when the walls were fallen and great part of the area of the city waste (Neh. ii. 17, vii. 4). From the English version it seems as if the Psalm were written under the dynasty of David, but in vv. 4, 5 the correct translation is "went up," "were set."

On all these grounds we are led to refer the collection Psalms xc.-cl., and even the origin of many of the pieces it contains, to a date subsequent to the reorganisation of the theocracy by Ezra and Nehemiah, when we know that the Temple service of song was specially provided for. It does not follow that the collection contains no ancient songs which had been passed over in the earlier collections of Books I.-III. Yet on more than one ground it is difficult to attach much weight to the titles referring seventeen of its Psalms to David. In the earlier half of the Psalter the Davidic Psalms form two well-marked groups which contain internal evidence that they were once separate collections. It is indeed hard to see how ancient poems could be preserved for long centuries without being so collected. But in Books IV., V. there is no trace of a third collection of Davidic Psalms. Nay, they occur sporadically up and down the books, which could hardly have occurred had the collector found these Psalms with their titles. Again, we have seen in Lecture III. that the pilgrimage Psalms ascribed to David did not bear his name in the Septuagint, though the tendency at that time was all in the direction of ascribing to David as many poems as possible. In Psalm cxxii. the title appears to have been suggested by the name of David occurring in ver. 5, though that verse, which speaks of the thrones of the house of David as a recollection of the past, really bears clear evidence that the title is false. So again in Psalm cxliv. 10 the singer says, "Thou that givest deliverance to kings, who didst save David from the hurtful sword, save me." Here David is distinguished from the Psalmist, yet the mere name of David was enough to suggest the title to some copyist. Such facts not only break down the authority of the titles, but show how very hasty were the inferences on which they were adopted. Similar arguments apply to other Psalms, and in particular the argument of language, of which Psalm cxxxix. is a peculiarly strong case. This Psalm belongs to the period when Hebrew was being largely superseded as a vernacular by Aramaic. It contains at least four Aramaic forms which are not such loan-words as one nation may borrow from another to enrich its vocabulary, but Aramaic pronunciations of roots also found in the Hebrew. The differences and affinities between Aramaic and Hebrew are similar to those between English and German. By the rule known as Grimm's law, old English words beginning with T correspond to German words with Z, so that English *ten* is German *zehn*, and

English *to* German *zu*. Now, if we find a man speaking or writing English who puts *zu* for *to* or *zehn* for *ten*, we know at once that German, not English, is his vernacular. His English is imperfect; he is not merely using a loan-word like *Zeitgeist* or any other German term which English writers borrow for a definite purpose. So it is in Psalm cxxxix. The Psalmist pronounces words with a guttural ('Ayin) when the Hebrew form has a sharp *S* (Çade); and thus he declares himself a man whose vernacular was Aramaic, as clearly as the Ephraimites revealed their tribe by saying *Sibbóleth*.

Let us now turn back to the middle section, consisting of the second and third Psalm Books, and let us take up first the Levitical part of that section. It consists partly of songs entitled, "Of the sons of Korah." That does not necessarily mean songs composed by the sons of Korah. The sons of Korah were a guild of Temple singers, and the Psalms belonging to this guild are simply a collection of Psalms which they were accustomed to sing.

The second collection of Levitical Psalms bears the title of "Asaph." The sons of Asaph were also a guild of singers. According to the Chronicles they had their name from an Asaph who lived in the time of David. He is not mentioned in the earlier books, and the only interest attaching to him lies in the guild that bore his name. In Semitic idiom "sons of Asaph" means no more than the guild of Asaph, and the guild taken collectively might also be simply called Asaph, just as

Judah means the sons of Judah. That the title "of Asaph" does not imply that David's Asaph wrote all the Psalms so named is universally admitted, for some of these are certainly late poems. The Asaphic Psalms are on the same footing with those of the sons of Korah, forming a second Levitical collection in the hands of a different guild.

These two collections have a curious general feature in common. They contain no confession of sin. In some of them Israel appears as divided into a righteous class to whom the singer belongs and a wicked class against whom he prays. Elsewhere, the whole nation seems to speak with one voice, and claims to be righteous, and suffering not for its own sin. Whenever sin is acknowledged in those Psalms, it is the sin of a former generation. Now it is manifest that this refers us to a very peculiar historical position. Before the time of Ezra and Nehemiah, it is impossible that the really godly could have held such language. Previous to the Exile, the prophets and all the deeper religious hearts of Israel knew well that all national suffering was chastisement for national sin. No Israelite before the Exile could say what is said in Psalm xliv., and practically repeated elsewhere, that the people, in spite of their afflictions, have not forgotten God or been false to His covenant, that they have not stretched out their hands to a strange god, that they are persecuted not for sin, but for God's sake, and because of their adherence to Him. Individuals like Jeremiah and other righteous men complained of persecution in the old time, but then that persecution proceeded from the godless mass of the nation; whereas here the complaint is that the whole nation has been chastised—that its armies have been defeated, that Jerusalem has been taken, and that the blood of God's saints has been shed like water round its walls, where their corpses lie unburied, not for sin, but for their adherence to God's covenant. And with these go other marks of a late date. The synagogues are mentioned in Psalm lxxiv. as burned, but there were no synagogues before the Exile; and prophecy is spoken of as having failed. Now the first trace of the feeling that Israel suffers, not for sin, but in spite of its obedience to God, appears in the prophet Malachi; and there the prophet rebukes it and points out in the clearest way that in reality the Israelites were punished for their sin. But here, you observe, we have a persecution for religion. That must be later than Ezra and Nehemiah—later than the time when Israel became a law-abiding people. At what time then? The defilement of the Temple and the destruction of its beauty referred to in Psalms lxxiv. and lxxix. cannot, so far as our knowledge of the history goes—it must be admitted that we know but little of the history after the time of Nehemiah—refer to any earlier date than the reign of Artaxerxes II., when the Persian general Bogoses defiled the Temple; but some of the features, and particularly the fact that the calamities befalling Israel are ascribed to religious persecution, point rather to the time when the Greek kings sought to put down the spiritual religion of Israel by force, and to restore the worship of false gods. This conclusion, indeed, is refused by many scholars, and I do not put it forth categorically. What appears to be certain is that the Levitical Psalms, as we now have them, cannot refer to any calamity that fell on the nation before the work of Ezra and Nehemiah.

On the other hand, the Korahite collection certainly embodies older Psalms. Psalm xlv. in particular, which is the epithalamium of a king of Israel, must be older than the Exile, and perhaps was omitted from the earlier collections because its religious use depends on a typical application to the Messiah.

We have still to consider the two Davidic collections. The second of these, as we now have it, is incorporated in the Elohistic collection which, as we have just seen, was formed after the time of Ezra. The first Davidic collection stands by itself as a separate Psalm Book, in which, with the exceptions already explained, every Psalm is referred to David. It is plain that, under these circumstances, the titles in the first Psalm Book have quite a different value from the scattered titles in the latter part of the Psalter. They form a system, and cannot be referred to the arbitrary insertions of successive copyists. Only two views seem to be possible. One of these is that the collector of Psalms i.-xli. may have deliberately confined himself to Psalms which he knew to be David's. In that case two possibilities arise. The Psalms may have been known as David's because they already existed in writing with titles to that effect. Or, on the other hand, the collector having satisfied himself that they were Davidic may have added the titles himself.

But a different view is also possible. The collection may not have been framed from the first exclusively with an eye to Davidic poems. But in process of time it may have come to be called "Psalms of David" because it contained some of his poems, just as all the proverbs are now called "Proverbs of Solomon." And thus, when the first Psalm Book was taken up into a larger collection, each Psalm may have received a title derived from the current name of the book in which it was found.

The question between these several possibilities would be decided, if we could show reason to suppose that David wrote down all his own Psalms, and prefixed his name to them one by one. This, however, not only cannot be proved, but is highly improbable for many reasons. We have seen that the Psalms of Books IV. and V., and also the Korahite and Asaphic collections, are mainly anonymous, and that many of the titles which do name an author are certainly erroneous additions of copyists. Can we suppose that later psalmists habitually omitted their names, but that David as habitually used his? But again, it is not in accordance with Eastern usage to suppose that the early poets of Israel wrote down their compositions at all. Poems were published, not in writing, but by being sung or recited. In the books of Samuel, David is said to have spoken, not written, the pieces there given as his. That is the regular practice of the East. The songs of the Arabian poets circulated exclusively by word of mouth, and the oldest pieces of Arabic poetry now extant were not written down for a century and a half, when the scholars of Islam collected them for philological purposes.[8] It is often assumed, in connection with the account given in Chronicles of the institution of the Levitical service of song, that David wrote down his poems for the Levites. But this is mere assumption. All Eastern analogy, and the unquestionably late date of the extant Psalm Books of Asaph and the sons of Korah, lead us to suppose that the Temple singers, like the Arabian *Râwîs*, long preserved their songs by word of mouth, and sang without book. Beyond question, the earliest written collections of poetry, like the Book of Jashar and the Book of the Wars of the Lord, were historical, not liturgical.

These are general presumptions against the supposition that the Psalms were first published with their titles. But the conclusive argument is that the first Psalm Book contains pieces which David certainly did not write. Psalms xx. and xxi. are not spoken by a king, but addressed to the king by his people. So viewed, they are a natural and beautiful expression of Israel's faith. But to suppose that David wrote for the people the words in which they should express their feelings towards his throne is to sacrifice the fresh spontaneity of the Psalms to mere theory. Again, in Psalm xxxiv. the title speaks of Abimelech as king of Gath in the time of David. In reality Abimelech was a contemporary of Abraham, and the king in David's time was named Achish. Again, several of the Psalms of the first book not only speak of Zion as God's holy mountain, which David might do after he had brought the ark to Jerusalem, but allude to the Temple, in which the singer of Psalm xxvii. desires to live continually. But the House of God at Zion, in David's time, was not a temple but a tent. There had been a temple at Shiloh, but it was destroyed. And in Psalm xxvii. 10, the words, "My father and my mother have forsaken me, but Jehovah taketh me up," are quite inappropriate to David. These are individual difficulties, but arguments equally strong and of wider scope can be drawn from the general situation of many of the Psalms. The singer in Psalms ix.-x. writes after Zion had become God's dwelling-place. But he lives in an evil time, when Israel is oppressed by the heathen established in the land. Under this oppression, God's people are represented as poor and needy. The weak and the orphan suffer from their tyranny and pride, and God's help has been so long withdrawn that they openly scoff at His majesty. There are many other Psalms in the collection which presuppose a similar situation, where the psalmist identifies himself with the poor and needy, with the oppressed righteous people of

God suffering in silence at the hands of the wicked, who are strong and prosperous in the land, so that their victims have no hope but to wait in patient endurance for the interposition of Jehovah (xii., xxxv., xxxvii., xxxviii., etc.). Most of these Psalms are referred by the defenders of the titles to the time when David was pursued by Saul. But it is quite unhistorical to represent Saul as a man who persecuted and spoiled all the quiet and godly souls in Israel; even David and his friends were never helpless sufferers—the quiet or timid in the land (xxxv. 20), dumb amidst all oppression (xxxviii. 13, 14). And such a Psalm as xxxvii., where the Psalmist calls himself an old man, must, on the traditional view, be spoken by David late in his prosperous reign; yet here we have the same situation—the wicked rampant, the righteous suffering in silence, as if David were not a king who sat on his throne doing justice and judgment to all his people (2 Sam. viii. 15). If Psalms ix., x., xxxvii. represent the state of things in the time of David, the Books of Samuel are the most partial of histories, and the reign of the son of Jesse was not the golden age which it appeared to all subsequent generations.

These considerations forbid us to accept the titles as an authoritative part of the text. They represent a tradition which may be as old as the first collection of Psalms i.-xli., but may equally well and more probably have grown up round that collection during the time when it circulated as a separate book. The tradition separates the first Psalm Book from the properly Levitical collections, and doubtless expresses the fact that these are the oldest Psalms, belonging to the early ages of Hebrew psalmody from David downwards; but in assigning any individual psalm to David we must be guided by other arguments than those of the titles. The date at which the collection was formed can hardly be assigned with precision. The later books were collected after the time of Ezra, but this contains no poem which demands so recent a date. Psalm xxxi. presents great affinities to the thought and language of Jeremiah, and may be the work of that prophet. Psalm xiv. is most naturally referred to the Babylonian Exile. The collection can hardly be thought to fall much later. We have seen with what affection the godly of Israel clung to the words of the prophets and their associates when the captivity deprived them of the outward means of grace. In such a time the old Psalms of Zion would acquire a new value, and there was every motive to bring them together in as full a collection as possible. The prayer for the redemption of Israel, which stands as a supplementary verse at the close of the acrostic Psalm xxv., may be read with great probability as a prayer of the Captivity.[9]

We have still to look at the second Davidic collection contained in the Elohistic Psalm Book. This collection is later than Book I., Psalm liii. being a repetition of Psalm xiv., and Psalm lxx. an extract from Psalm xl. The titles, therefore, have still less authority for us than those in the earlier book. In many cases they are unquestionably incorrect, as appears most clearly where they refer to special events in David's life. Psalm lii. is said to refer to Doeg. It actually speaks of a rich and powerful man, an enemy of the righteous in Israel, whom God will lay low, while the psalmist is like a green olive tree in the house of God, whose mercy is his constant support. Now David had nothing to fear from Doeg. The danger was all for the priests of Nob. How could the psalmist in such a case confine himself to thanking God for his own deliverance, and not express in a single word his sympathy with the unhappy priests who perished for the aid they gave him? Psalm liv. is said to be spoken against the Ziphites. In reality it speaks of strangers and tyrants, standing Old Testament names for foreign oppressors. In Psalm lv. the singer lives among foes in a city whose walls they occupy with their patrols, exercising constant violence within the town, from which the psalmist would gladly escape to the desert. The enemy is in alliance with one who had once been an associate of the psalmist, and joined with him in the service of the sacred feasts. Hence the Psalm is often applied to Ahithophel; but the whole situation is as different as possible. In Psalm lix. we are asked to find a psalm composed by David when he was watched in his house by Saul. In reality the singer speaks of heathen foes besieging the city— *i.e.*, Jerusalem—whom God is prayed to cast down, that His power may be manifest over all the earth. It is impossible to attach authority to a group of titles so full of palpable incongruities; and, apart from the titles, it is difficult to find sufficient ground for ascribing a single psalm of the second collection to David. Even Delitzsch, the able defender of the general correctness of the headings, admits that David was not the author of Psalms lxv. and lxix., and hesitates as to some of the others.[10]

The general result of this discussion is not purely negative. We are unable to accept the titles as our guide to the historical study of the Psalms, because they are often inconsistent with the far more valuable evidence of the sacred poems themselves. The titles would be authoritative if they were as old as the Psalms; but in fact some of them are the mere conjectures of individual copyists, and even in the two great collections of poems ascribed to David there is no proof that they express a tradition earlier than the formation of these collections. But it is noteworthy that the earliest Psalm Book was received in the Jewish Church as a Davidic hymnal. This opinion was not based on authentic knowledge that every Psalm in the collection is really David's; for some of the Psalms are certainly of later date. But the tradition expresses a conviction that David was closely connected with the early psalmody of Israel. There is little direct evidence in the old Hebrew literature to support this conviction. In the Books of Samuel the king is never lost in the psalmist, as is the case in the current conception of

David's life; and when we observe that the two hymns in 2 Sam. xxii., xxiii. appear to be foreign to the original context of the narrative, it may appear doubtful whether the oldest story of his life set forth David as a psalmist at all. It is very curious that the book of Amos (vi. 5) represents David as the chosen model of the dilettanti nobles of Ephraim, who lay stretched on beds of ivory, anointed with the choicest perfumes, and mingling music with their cups in the familiar manner of oriental luxury. Yet we know that David took a personal part in the procession which brought the ark up to Jerusalem with music and dance (2 Sam. vi.). Dancing, music, and song are in early times the united expression of lyrical inspiration. Sacred melody was accompanied by dances in the days of Miriam, and even in the time of the latest Psalms (cxlix. 3, cl. 4). We have every right to conclude that the lyrical talents of Israel's most gifted singer were devoted to the service of Jehovah, which King David placed high above all considerations of royal dignity (2 Sam. vi. 21). But the passage makes it clear that in those days religion was not separated from ordinary life, and that the gladness of the believing heart found natural utterance in sportful forms of unconstrained mirth. At a much later date, as we have seen, melodies of the Temple service were borrowed from the joyous songs of the vintage, and so it was possible that David should give the pattern alike for the songs of the sanctuary and for the worldly airs of the nobles of Samaria. The sacred music of Israel was of popular origin, and long retained its popular type (Amos v. 23; Isa. xxx. 29; Jerem. xxxiii. 11). On the solemn feast days the Temple resounded with clamours like those of a conquering army (Lam. ii. 7). A sacred poetry of such popular origin must necessarily reflect the religious life, not of one or two great poets, but of Israel as a nation in all the vicissitudes of a long history; and a judicious criticism learns to seek in the Psalter, not merely the autobiography of David, but a long and weighty chapter in the life of the Old Testament Church.

That this standpoint enables us to expound many Psalms with far more force and truth than the traditional exegesis can only be proved in a detailed commentary. I allude, in closing, only to two points.

Christian theology has always been largely occupied with the typical references of the Psalms, following the authority of our Lord Himself, who read in the Psalter the pattern of His own experience as the founder of the New Dispensation. So long as the primary reference of so large a part of the Psalms was confined to the experiences of David's life, the typical interpretation often seemed arbitrary. It was not possible to establish a principle of real connection between the events of David's life and the experiences of our Lord which they foreshadowed. But the newer exegesis observes that in many of these typical Psalms the primary reference is not to events of an individual life, but to the experience of God's people as a whole, who speak by personification with a single voice. And thus the typical reference becomes easy and natural. For our Lord as the Head of the Church, the Captain of the faithful, who takes on Him the whole burden of His people, and stands as their representative before the Father, can appropriate to Himself the whole experience of the Old Testament Church, in so far as the life of that Church is a part of the life of the Church Universal of which He is the Head.

Another point in which criticism removes a serious difficulty is the interpretation of the imprecatory Psalms, which can never be explained as having a private reference to David without introducing an element of personal vindictiveness of a kind greatly calculated to give offence. The injuries done to David by Ahithophel and others, to whom these Psalms are currently supposed to refer, were largely personal. David could not say that he was persecuted as the representative of God's cause in Israel, and without sin on his part. On any interpretation, these Psalms bear, more than most others, the impress of the limitations of the Old Covenant; but at least the element of personal vindictiveness disappears when we assign them, as we have every right to do, to later times of persecution, when the fortunes at stake were not those of an individual, but of the cause of God's truth against treachery within and persecuting heathenism without.

LECTURE VIII.

THE TRADITIONAL THEORY OF THE OLD TESTAMENT HISTORY.[1]

THE book of Psalms has furnished us with an example of what can be learned by critical study in a subject of limited compass, which can be profitably discussed without any wide digression into general questions of Old Testament history. The criticism of the Prophets and the Law opens a much larger field, and brings us face to face with fundamental problems.

We know, as a matter of historical fact, that the Pentateuch, as a whole, was put into operation as the rule of Israel's life at the reformation of Ezra, with a completeness which had never been aimed at from the days of the conquest of Canaan (*supra*, p. 56). From this time onwards the Pentateuch, in its ceremonial as well as its moral precepts, was the acknowledged standard of Israel's righteousness (Neh. xiii.; Mal. i. 7 *seq.*, iii. 8 *seq.*, iv. 4; Acts xv. 5). According to the theory of the later Jews, which has passed into current Christian theology, it had always been so. The whole law of the Pentateuch was given in the wilderness, or on the plains of Moab, and Moses conveyed to the

Israelites before they entered Canaan, everything that it was necessary for them to know as a revelation from God. The law was a rule of absolute validity, and the keeping of it was the whole of Israel's religion. No religion could be acceptable to God which was not conformed to the legal ordinances. On this theory the ceremonial part of the law must always have been the prominent and most characteristic feature of the Old Covenant. In the Levitical legislation, the feasts, the sacrificial ritual, the ordinances of ceremonial purity, are always in the foreground as the necessary forms in which alone the inner side of religion, love to God and man, can find acceptable expression. Not that religion is made up of mere forms, but everything in religion is reduced to rule and has some fixed ceremonial expression. There is no room for religious spontaneity.

According to this theory, it is not possible to distinguish between ceremonial and moral precepts of the law, as if the observance of the latter might excuse irregularity in the former. The object of God's covenant with Israel was to maintain a close and constant bond between Jehovah and His people, different in kind from the relations of mankind in general to their Creator. Israel was chosen to be a holy people. Now, according to the Pentateuch, holiness is not exclusively a moral thing. It has special relation to the observances of ritual worship and ceremonial purity. "Ye shall distinguish between clean beasts and unclean, and not make yourselves abominable by any beast, fowl, etc., which I have separated from you as unclean. And ye shall be holy unto me: for I Jehovah am holy, and have severed you from the nations to be mine" (Lev. xx. 25, 26). If a sacrifice is eaten on the third day, "it is abominable; it shall not be accepted. He that eateth it shall bear his guilt, for he hath profaned Jehovah's holy thing: that soul shall be cut off from his people" (Lev. xix. 8). "That which dieth of itself, or is torn of beasts, no priest may eat to defile himself therewith. I am Jehovah; and they shall keep my ordinance and not take sin on themselves by profaning it and die therein. I Jehovah do sanctify them" (Lev. xxii. 8, 9). No stronger words than these could be found to denounce the gravest moral turpitude.

The whole system is directed to the maintenance of holiness in Israel, as the condition of the benefits which Jehovah promises to bestow on His people in the land of Canaan. And therefore every infringement of law, be it merely in some point of ceremony which we might be disposed to think indifferent, demands an atonement, that the relation of God to His people may not be disturbed. To provide such atonement is the great object of the priestly ritual which culminates in the annual ceremony of the day of expiation. Atonement implies sacrifice, the blood or life of an offering presented on the altar before God. "It is the blood that atones by the life that is in it" (Lev. xvii. 11; Hebrews ix. 22). But the principle of holiness demands that the sacrificial act itself, and the altar on which the blood is offered, be hedged round by strict ritual precautions. At the altar, Jehovah, in His awful and inaccessible holiness, meets with the people, which is imperfectly holy and stands in need of constant forgiveness. There is danger in such a meeting. Only the priests, who live under rules of intensified ceremonial purity, and have received a peculiar consecration from Jehovah Himself, are permitted to touch the holy things, and it is they who bear the sins of Israel before God to make atonement for them (Lev. x. 17). Between them and Israel at large is a second cordon of holy ministers, the Levites. It is death for any but a priest to touch the altar, and an undue approach of ordinary persons to the sanctuary brings wrath on Israel (Num. i. 53). Accordingly, sacrifice, atonement, and forgiveness of sin are absolutely dependent on the hierarchy and its service. The mass of the people have no direct access to their God in the sanctuary. The maintenance of the Old Testament covenant depends on the priestly mediation, and above all on that one annual day of expiation when the high priest enters the Holy of Holies and "cleanses the people that they may be clean from all their sins before Jehovah" (Lev. xvi. 30). The whole system, you perceive, is strictly knit together. The details are necessary to the object aimed at. The intermission of any part of the ceremonial scheme involves an accumulation of unforgiven sin, with the consequence of divine wrath on the nation and the withdrawal of God's favour.

To complete this sketch of the theory of the Pentateuch it is only necessary to add that the hierarchy had no dispensing power. If a man sins, he has recourse to the sacramental sacrifice appointed for his case. The priest makes atonement for him, and he is forgiven. But knowingly and obstinately to depart from any ordinance is to sin against God with a high hand, and for this there is no forgiveness. "He hath despised the word of the Lord and broken his commandment: that soul shall be cut off in its guilt" (Num. xv. 30, 31).

Such is the system of the law as contained particularly in the middle books of the Pentateuch, and practically accepted from the days of Ezra. It is not strange that the later Jews should have received it as the sum of all revelation, for manifestly it is a complete theory of the religious life. Its aim is to provide everything that man requires to live acceptably with God, the necessary measure of access to Jehovah, the necessary atonement for all sin, and the necessary channel for the conveyance of God's blessing to man. It is, I repeat, a complete theory of the religious life, to which nothing can be added without an entire change of dispensation. Accordingly, the Jewish view of the law as complete, and the summary of all revelation, has passed into Christian theology, with only this modification that, whereas the Jews think of the dispensation of the law as final, and the atonement which it offers as sufficient, we have learned to regard the dispensation as temporary and its atonement as typical, prefiguring the atonement of Christ. But this modification of the Jewish view of the Torah does not diminish the essential importance of the law for the life of the old dispensation. The ceremonies were not less necessary because they were typical; for they are still to be regarded as divinely appointed means of grace, to which alone God had attached the promise of blessing.

Now, as soon as we lay down the position that the system of the ceremonial law, embracing, as it does, the whole life of every Jew, was completed and prescribed as an authoritative code for Israel before the conquest of Canaan, we have an absolute rule for measuring the whole future history of the nation and the whole significance of subsequent revelation under the Old Testament.

On the one hand, the religious history of Israel can be nothing else than the history of the nation's obedience or disobedience to the law. Nothing could be added to the law and nothing taken from it till the time of fulfilment, when the type should pass away and be replaced by the living reality of the manifestation of Christ Jesus. So long as the old dispensation lasted, the law remained an absolute standard. The Israelite had no right to draw a distinction between the spirit and the letter of the law. The sacrifices and other typical ordinances might not be of the essence of religion. But obedience to God's word undoubtedly was so, and that word had in the most emphatic manner enjoined the sacrifices and other ceremonies, and made the forgiveness of Israel's sins to depend on them. The priestly atonement was a necessary part of God's covenant. "The priest shall make atonement for him, and he shall be forgiven." To neglect these means of grace is, according to the Pentateuch, nothing less than the sin committed with a high hand, for which there is no forgiveness.

Again, on the other hand, the position that the whole legal system was revealed to Israel at the very beginning of its national existence strictly limits our conception of the function and significance of subsequent revelation. The prophets had no power to abrogate any part of the law, to dispense with Mosaic ordinances, or institute new means of grace, other methods of approach to God in lieu of the hierarchical sacraments. For the Old Testament way of atonement is set forth in the Pentateuch as adequate and efficient. According to Christian theology, its efficiency as a typical system was conditional on the future bringing in of a perfect atonement in Christ. But for that very reason it was not to be tampered with until Christ came. The prophets, like the law itself, could only point to a future atonement; they were not themselves saviours, and could do nothing to diminish the need for the temporary provisions of the hierarchical system; and, as a matter of fact, the prophets did not abolish the Pentateuch or any part of the Levitical system. Nay, it is just as their work closes that we find the Pentateuchal code solemnly advance to a position of public authority under Ezra which it had never held before.

Hence the traditional view of the Pentateuch necessarily regards the prophets as ministers and exponents of the law. Their business was to enforce the observance of the law on Israel and to recall the people from backsliding to a strict conformity with its precepts. According to the Jewish view, this makes their work less necessary and eternal than the law. Christian theologians avoid this inference, but they do so by laying stress on the fact that the reference to a future and perfect atonement, which lay implicitly in the typical ordinances of the ceremonial law, was unfolded by the prophets in the clear language of evangelical prediction. We view the prophets, therefore, as exponents of the spiritual elements of the law, who showed the people that its precepts were not mere forms but veiled declarations of the spiritual truths of a future dispensation which was the true substance of the shadows of the old ritual. This theory of the work of the prophets is much more profound than that of the Rabbins. But it implies, as necessarily as the Jewish view, that the prophets were constantly intent on enforcing the observance of the ceremonial as well as the moral precepts of the Pentateuch. Neglect of the ritual law was all the more culpable when the spiritual meaning of its precepts was made plain.

I think that it will be admitted that in this sketch I have correctly indicated the theory of the Old Testament dispensation which orthodox theologians derive from the traditional view as to the date of the Pentateuch. I ask you to observe that it is essentially the

Rabbinical view supplemented by a theory of typology; but I also ask you to observe that it is perfectly logical and consistent in all its parts. It is, so far as one can see, the only theory which can be built on the premisses. It has only one fault. The standard which it applies to the history of Israel is not that of the contemporary historical records, and the account which it gives of the work of the prophets is not consistent with the writings of the prophets themselves.

This may seem a strong statement, but it is not lightly made, and it expresses no mere personal opinion, but the growing conviction of an overwhelming weight of the most earnest and sober scholarship. The discrepancy between the traditional view of the Pentateuch and the plain statements of the historical books and the Prophets is so marked and so fundamental that it can be made clear to every reader of Scripture. It is this fact which compels us, in the interests of practical theology—nay even in the interests of Christian apologetic—to go into questions of Pentateuch criticism. For if the received view which assigns the whole Pentateuch to Moses is inconsistent with the concordant testimony of the Earlier and Later Prophets, we are brought into this dilemma:—Either the Old Testament is not the record of a self-consistent scheme of revelation, of one great and continuous work of a revealing and redeeming God, or else the current view of the origin of the Pentateuch must be given up. Here it is that criticism comes in to solve a problem which in its origin is not merely critical, but springs of necessity from the very attempt to understand the Old Testament dispensation as a whole. For the contradiction which cannot be resolved on traditional assumptions is at once removed when the critic points out within the Pentateuch itself clear marks that the whole law was not written at one time, and that the several documents of which it is composed represent successive developments of the fundamental principles laid down by Moses, successive redactions of the sacred law of Israel corresponding to the very same stages in the progress of revelation which are clearly marked in the history and the prophetic literature. Thus the apparent discordance between the several parts of the Old Testament record is removed, and we are able to see a consistent divine purpose ruling the whole dispensation of the Old Covenant, and harmoniously displayed in every part of the sacred record. To develop this argument in its essential features, fitting the several parts of the record into their proper setting in the history of revelation, is the object which I propose for our discussion of the Law and the Prophets. Of the critical or constructive part of the argument I can give only the main outlines, for many details in the analysis of the Pentateuch turn on nice questions of Hebrew scholarship. But the results are broad and intelligible, and possess that evidence of historical consistency on which the results of special scholarship are habitually accepted by the mass of intelligent men in other branches of historical inquiry.

Such, then, is the plan of our investigation; and, first of all, let us compare the evidence of the Bible history with the traditional theory already sketched. In working out this part of the subject I shall confine your attention in the first instance to the books earlier than the time of Ezra, and in particular to the histories in the Earlier Prophets, from Judges to Second Kings. I exclude the book of Joshua because it in all its parts hangs closely together with the Pentateuch. The difficulties which it presents are identical with those of the Books of Moses, and can only be explained in connection with the critical analysis of the law. And, on the other hand, I exclude for the present the narrative of Chronicles, which was written long after the reformation of Ezra, and has not the character of a primary source for the earlier history. The earlier historical books from Judges to Kings bring down the history in continuous form to the Captivity, and attained their final shape soon after that event. But the great mass of the records which they embody is much earlier. We have already seen (*supra*, p. 123 *seq.*) that they are in part based on official annals, while in great part they are made up in accordance with the system already explained, on which Hebrew historians were wont verbally to incorporate older documents in their narratives. Thus in substance they are vastly older than the Chronicles, and possess many essential characteristics of contemporary histories. It is the rule of all historical study to begin with the records that stand nearest to the events recorded, and are written under the living impress of the life of the time described. Many features of the old Hebrew life, which are reflected in lively form in the Earlier Prophets, were obsolete long before the time of the Chronicler, and could not be revived except by archæological research. The whole life of the old kingdom was buried and forgotten; Israel was no longer a nation, but a municipality and a church. No theory of inspiration, save the theory of the Koran, which boasts that its fabulous legends were supernaturally conveyed to Mohammed without the use of documents or tradition, can deny that a history written under these conditions is but a secondary source for the study of the life of the ancient kingdom.[2] It is manifest that the Chronicler, writing at a time when the institutions of Ezra had universal currency, had no complete knowledge of the greatly different praxis of Israel before the Exile. And therefore, when his statements seem to present the history in a somewhat different light from those of the earlier books, we must no more take him as our commentator than we take S. Paul as our guide to the Old Testament chronology. We must let the earlier books speak for themselves, and the right understanding of the statement of the Chronicles must then be considered as a separate question. I do not now speak of individual details, in which the later history may often preserve some useful notice derived from sources no longer extant. Our present concern is with the general picture of the life and worship of ancient Israel presented in the historical books; and here the only rule of sound study is to begin with the sources which draw from the life.

Every reader of the Old Testament history is familiar with the fact that from the days of the Judges down to the Exile the law was never strictly enforced in Israel. The history is a record of constant rebellion and shortcomings, and the attempts at reformation made from time to time were comparatively few and never thoroughly carried out. The deflections of the nation from the standard of the Pentateuch come out most clearly in the sphere of worship. In the time of the Judges the religious condition of the nation was admittedly one of anarchy. The leaders of the nation, divinely appointed deliverers like Gideon and Jephthah, who were zealous in Jehovah's cause, were as far from the Pentateuchal standard of righteousness as the mass of the people. Gideon erects a sanctuary at Ophrah, with a golden ephod—apparently a kind of image— which became a great centre of illegal worship (Jud. viii. 24 *seq.*); Jephthah offers his own daughter to Jehovah; the Lord departs from Samson, not when he marries a daughter of the uncircumcised, but when his Nazarite locks are shorn.

The revival under Samuel, Saul, and David was marked by great zeal for Jehovah, but brought no reform in matters of glaring departure from the law. Samuel sacrifices on many high places, Saul builds altars, David and his son Solomon permit the worship at the high places to continue, and the historian recognises this as legitimate because the Temple was not yet built (1 Kings iii. 2-4). In Northern Israel this state of things was never changed. The high places were an established feature in the kingdom of Ephraim, and Elijah himself declares that the destruction of the altars of Jehovah—all illegitimate according to the Pentateuch—is a breach of Jehovah's covenant (1 Kings xix. 10). In the Southern Kingdom it was not otherwise. It is recorded of the best kings before Hezekiah that the high places were not removed by them; and in the eighth century B.C. the prophets describe the worship of Ephraim and Judah in terms practically identical. Even the reforms of Hezekiah and Josiah were imperfectly carried through; and important points of ritual, such as the due observance of the Feast of Tabernacles, were still neglected (Neh. viii. 17). These facts are not disputed. The question is how we are to interpret them.

The prophets and the historical books agree in representing the history of Israel as a long record of disobedience to Jehovah, of which captivity was the just punishment. But the precise nature of Israel's sin is often misunderstood. We are accustomed to speak of it as idolatry, as the worship of false gods in place of Jehovah; and in a certain sense this corresponds with the language of the sacred books. In the judgment of the prophets of the eighth century the mass of the Israelites, not merely in the Northern Kingdom but equally in Judah, had rebelled against Jehovah, and did not pay Him worship in any true sense. But that was far from being the opinion of the false worshippers themselves. They were not in conscious rebellion against Jehovah and His covenant. On the contrary, their religion was based on two principles, one of which is the fundamental principle of all Old Testament revelation, while the second is the principle that underlies the whole system of ritual ordinance in the Pentateuch. The first principle in the popular religion of Israel, acknowledged by the false worshippers as well as by the prophets, was that Jehovah is Israel's God and Redeemer, and that Israel is the people of Jehovah in a distinctive sense. And with this went a second principle, that Israel is bound to do homage to its God in sacrifice, and to serve Him diligently and assiduously according to a fixed ritual.

Let me explain this point more fully. There is no doubt that the worship of Baal, Ashtoreth, Moloch, and other gods of the heathen peoples of Canaan was not uncommon in Israel; and once at least, in the time of Ahab, there was an attempt to give such worship a national character; but as a rule such worship took a secondary place, and those who fell into it did not do so to the exclusion of the worship of Jehovah as the great God of Israel. And the attempt of Ahab was purely transitory. It was put down by a great revolution under Jehu; and even Ahab himself, as we learn from 1 Kings xxii., never entirely broke with the prophets of Jehovah. The national sin was not denial that Jehovah is Israel's God, with a paramount claim to the service and worship of the nation. On the contrary, the prophets represent their contemporaries as full of zeal for Jehovah, and confident that they have secured His help by their great assiduity in His service (Amos iv. 4 *seq.*, v. 18 *seq.*; Hosea vi.; Isa. i. 11 *seq.*; Micah iii. 11; Jer. vii.).

To obtain a precise conception of what this means, we must look more closely at the notion of worship under the Old Testament dispensation. To us worship is a spiritual thing. We lift up our hearts and voices to God in the closet, the family, or the church, persuaded that God, who is spirit, will receive in every place the worship of spirit and truth. But this is strictly a New Testament conception, announced as a new thing by Jesus to the Samaritan woman, who raised a question as to the disputed prerogative of Zion or Gerizim as the place of acceptable worship. Under the New Covenant neither Zion nor Gerizim is the mount of God. Under the Old Testament it was otherwise. Access to God—even to the spiritual God—was limited by local conditions. There is no worship without access to the deity before whom the worshipper draws nigh to express his homage. We can draw near to God in every act of prayer in the heavenly sanctuary, through the new and living way which Jesus has consecrated in His blood. But the Old Testament worshipper sought access to God in an earthly sanctuary which was for him, as it were, the meeting place of heaven and earth. Such holy points of contact with the divine presence were locally fixed, and their mark was the altar, where the worshipper presented his homage, not in purely spiritual utterance, but in the material form of an altar-gift. The promise of blessing, or, as we should now call it, of answer to prayer, is in the Old Testament strictly attached to the local sanctuary. "In every place where I set the memorial of my name, I will come unto thee and bless thee" (Exod. xx. 24). Every visible act of worship is subjected to this condition. In the mouth of Saul, "to make supplication to Jehovah" is a synonym for doing sacrifice (1 Sam. xiii. 12). To David, banishment from the land of Israel and its sanctuaries is a command to serve other gods (1 Sam. xxvi. 19; compare Deut. xxviii. 36, 64). And the worship of the sanctuary imperatively demands the tokens of material homage, the gift without which no Oriental would approach even an earthly court. "None shall appear before me empty" (Exod. xxiii. 15). Prayer without approach to the sanctuary is not recognised as part of the "service of Jehovah;" and for him who is at a distance from the holy place, a vow, such as Absalom made at Geshur in Syria (2 Sam. xv. 8), is the natural surrogate for the interrupted service of the altar. The essence of a vow is a promise to do sacrifice or other offering at the sanctuary (Deut. xii. 6; Lev. xxvii.; 1 Sam. i. 21. Compare Gen. xxviii. 20 *seq.*).

This conception of the nature of divine worship is

the basis alike of the Pentateuchal law and of the popular religion of Israel described in the historical books and condemned by the prophets. The sanctuary of Jehovah, the altar and the altar-gifts, the sacrifices and the solemn feasts, the tithes and the free-will offerings, were never treated with indifference (Amos iv. 4, viii. 5; Hosea viii. 13; Isa. i. 11 *seq.*; Jer. vii.). On the contrary, the charge which the prophets constantly hurl against the people is that they are wholly absorbed in affairs of worship and ritual service, and think themselves to have secured Jehovah's favour by the zeal of their external devotion without the practice of justice, mercy, and moral obedience.

The condition of religious affairs in Northern Israel is clearly described by the prophets Amos and Hosea. These prophets arose under the dynasty of Jehu, the ally of Elisha and the destroyer of Baal-worship, a dynasty in which the very names of the kings denote devotion to the service of Jehovah. Jehovah was worshipped in many sanctuaries and in forms full of irregularity from the standpoint of the Pentateuch. There were images of Jehovah under the form of a calf or steer in Bethel and Dan, and probably elsewhere. The order of the local sanctuaries, and the religious feasts celebrated at them, had much in common with the idolatry of the Canaanites. Indeed many of the high places were old Canaanite sanctuaries. Nevertheless these sanctuaries and their worship were viewed as the fixed and normal provision for the maintenance of living relations between Israel and Jehovah. Hosea predicts a time of judgment when this service shall be suppressed. "The children of Israel shall sit many days without sacrifice and without *maççēba*, without ephod and teraphim." This language expresses the entire destruction of the religious order of the nation, a period of isolation from all access to Jehovah, like the isolation of a faithless spouse whom her husband keeps shut up, not admitting her to the privileges of marriage (Hos. iii.).[8] It appears, then, that sacrifice and *maççēba*, ephod and teraphim, were recognised as the necessary forms and instruments of the worship of Jehovah. They were all old traditional forms, not the invention of modern will-worship. The *maççēba*, or consecrated stone, so often named in the Old Testament where our version unfortunately renders "image," is as old as the time of Jacob, who set up and consecrated the memorial stone that marked Bethel as a sanctuary. It was the necessary mark of every high place, Canaanite as well as Hebrew, and is condemned in the Pentateuchal laws against the high places along with the associated symbol of the sacred tree or pole (*Ashēra*, E. V. *grove*), which was also a feature in the patriarchal sanctuaries. (The oak of Moreh, Gen. xii. 6, 7; the tamarisk of Beersheba, Gen. xxi. 33; Gen. xxxi. 45, 54; Gen. xxxiii. 20, with xxxv. 4; Jos. xxiv. 26; Hos. iv. 13.) The ephod is also ancient. It must have been something very different from the ephod of the high priest, but is to be compared with the ephods of Gideon and Micah (Jud.

viii. 27, xvii. 5), and with that in the sanctuary of Nob (1 Sam. xxi. 9). Finally, teraphim are a means of divination (Ezek. xxi. 21; Zech. x. 2) as old as the time of Jacob, and were found in Micah's sanctuary and David's house (1 Sam. xix. 13; E. V. *image*).[4]

It appears, then, that the national worship of Jehovah, under the dynasty of Jehu, was conducted under traditional forms which had a fixed character and general recognition. These forms were ancient. There is no reason to think that the worship of the northern sanctuaries had undergone serious modifications since the days of the Judges. The sanctuaries themselves were of ancient and, in great part, of patriarchal consecration. Beersheba, Gilgal, Bethel, Shechem, Mizpah, were places of the most venerable sanctity, acknowledged by Samuel and earlier worthies. Of the sanctuary at Dan we know the whole origin and history. It was founded by the Danites who carried off Micah's Levite and holy things; and the family of the Levite, who was himself a grandson of Moses, continued in office through the age of David and Samuel down to the Captivity (Jud. xviii. 30). It was a sanctuary of purely Israelite origin, originally instituted by Micah for the service of Jehovah, and equipped with every regard to the provision of an acceptable service. "Now I know," said Micah, "that Jehovah will do me good, since I have got the Levite as my priest." This trait indicates an interest in correct ritual which never died out. In truth ritual is never deemed unimportant in a religion so little spiritual as that of the mass of Israel. All worships that contain heathenish elements are traditional, and nothing is more foreign to them than the arbitrary introduction of forms for which there is no precedent of usage.

That this traditional service and ritual was not Levitically correct needs no proof. Let us rather consider the features which marked it as unspiritual and led the prophets to condemn it as displeasing to God.

In the first place, we observe that though Jehovah was worshipped with assiduity, and worshipped as the national God of Israel, there was no clear conception of the fundamental difference between Him and the gods of the nations. This appears particularly in the current use of images, like the golden calves, which were supposed to be representations or symbols of Jehovah. It is not easy to say how far image-worship was essential to the popular religion. Amos, in his preaching at Bethel, makes no mention of the golden calves, though he speaks of images of the star gods, Moloch and Chiun (Keiwan or Saturn). But the whole service is represented by the prophets as gross, sensual, and unworthy of a spiritual deity (Amos ii. 7, 8; Hosea iv. 13, 14). We know that many features in the worship of the high places were practically identical with the abominations of the Canaanites, and gave no expression to the difference between Jehovah and the false gods. Thus it came about that the Israelites fell into what is called *syncretism* in religion. They were unable sharply to distinguish between the local worship of Jehovah and the worship of the Canaanite Baalim. The god of the local sanctuary was adored as Jehovah, but a local Jehovah was practically a local Baal. This confusion of thought may be best illustrated from the local Madonnas of Roman Catholic shrines. Every Madonna is a representation of the one Virgin; but practically each Virgin has its own merits and its own devotees, so that the service of these shrines is almost indistinguishable from polytheism, of which, indeed, it is often an historical continuation. In Phœnicia one still sees grottoes of the Virgin Mary which are old shrines of Ashtoreth, bearing the symbols of the ancient worship of Canaan. So it was in those days. The worship of the one Jehovah, who was Himself addressed in old times by the title of Baal or Lord (*supra*, p. 79), practically fell into a worship of a multitude of local Baalim, so that a prophet like Hosea can say that the Israelites, though still imagining themselves to be serving the national God, and acknowledging His benefits, have really turned from Him to deities that are no gods.

In this way another fault came in. The people, whose worship of Jehovah was hardly to be distinguished from a gross polytheism, could not be averse to worship other gods side by side with the national deity. Thus we find that the services of Ashtoreth, Tammuz, or other deities which could not even in popular conception be identified with Jehovah, obtained a certain currency, at least in sections of the nation. This worship was always secondary, and was put down from time to time in movements of reformation which left the high places of Jehovah untouched (1 Sam. vii. 3; 1 Kings xv. 12 *seq.*; 2 Kings x. 28, 29, xi. 18).

This sketch of the popular religion of Israel is mainly drawn from the Northern Kingdom. But it is clear from the facts enumerated that it was not a mere innovation due to the schism of Jeroboam. Jeroboam, no doubt, lent a certain *éclat* to the service of the royal sanctuaries, and the golden calves gave a very different conception of Jehovah from that which was symbolised by the ark on Zion. But the elements of the whole worship were traditional, and were already current in the age of the Judges. Gideon's golden ephod and the graven image at Dan prove that even image-worship was no innovation of Jeroboam. And it is certain that the worship of the Judæan sanctuaries was not essentially different from that of the northern shrines. The high places flourished undisturbed from generation to generation. The land was full of idols (Isa. ii.). Jerusalem appears to Micah as the centre of a corrupt Judæan worship, which he parallels with the corrupt worship of Samaria (Micah i. 5, iii. 12, v. 11 *seq.*, vi. 16).

Where then did this traditional worship, so largely diffused through the mass of Israel, have its origin, and what is its historical relation to the laws of the Pentateuch ? No doubt many of its corrupt features may be explained by the influence of the Canaanites; and from the absolute standard of spiritual religion applied by the prophets it might even be said that Israel had forsaken Jehovah for the Baalim. But from the standpoint of the worshippers it was not so. They still believed themselves loyal to Jehovah. Their great sanctuaries were patriarchal holy places like Bethel and Beersheba, or purely Hebrew foundations like Dan. With all its corruptions, their worship had a specifically national character. Jehovah never was a Canaanite God, and the roots of the popular religion, as we have already seen, were that acknowledgment of Jehovah as Israel's God, and of the duty of national service to Him, which is equally the basis of Mosaic orthodoxy.[5] These are principles which lie behind the first beginnings of Canaanite influence. But in the Pentateuch these principles are embodied in a ritual altogether diverse in system and theory, as well as in detail, from the traditional ritual of the high places. The latter service is not merely a corrupt copy of the Mosaic system, with elements borrowed from the Canaanites. In the Levitical ritual the essentials of Jehovah-worship are put in a form which made no accommodation to heathenism possible, which left no middle ground between the pure worship of Jehovah, as maintained by the Aaronic priesthood in the one sanctuary, and a deliberate rejection of Israel's God for the idols of the heathen.

To understand this point we must observe that according to the Levitical system God is absolutely inaccessible to man, except in the priestly ritual of the central sanctuary. Controversial writers on the law of the one sanctuary have often been led to overlook this point by confining their attention to the law of the sanctuary in Deuteronomy, which speaks of the choice of one place in Canaan where Jehovah will set His name as a practical safeguard against participation in the worship of Canaanite high places. But if the whole Pentateuch is one Mosaic system, the law of Deuteronomy must be viewed in the light of the legislation of the Middle Books. Here the theory of the one sanctuary is worked out on a basis independent of the question of heathen shrines. According to the Old Testament, worship is a tryst between man and God in the sanctuary, and the question of the legitimate sanctuary is the question of the place where Jehovah has promised to hold tryst with His people, and the conditions which He lays down for this meeting. The fundamental promise of the Levitical legislation is Exod. xxix. 42 *seq*. The place of tryst is the Tent of Tryst or Meeting, incorrectly rendered in the Authorised Version, "The tabernacle of the congregation." "There will I hold tryst with the children of Israel, and it shall be sanctified by my glory. And I will sanctify the tent of meeting and the altar, and I will sanctify Aaron and his sons to do priestly service to me. And I will dwell in the midst of the children of Israel, and will be their God." The tent of meeting is God's *mishkan*, His dwelling-place, which He sets in the midst of Israel (Lev. xxvi. 11). The first condition of divine blessing in Lev. xxvi. is reverence for the sabbath and the sanctuary, and the total rejection of idols and of the *maççēba* which was the mark of the high places. There is no local point of contact between heaven and earth, no place where man can find a present God to receive his worship, save this one tent of meeting, where the ark with the Cherubim is the abiding symbol that God is in the midst of Israel, and the altar stands at the door of the tabernacle as the legitimate place of Israel's gifts. This sanctuary with its altar is the centre of Israel's holiness. It is so holy that it is hedged round by a double cordon of sacred ministers. For the presence of Jehovah is a terrible thing, destructive to sinful man. The Old Testament symbol of Jehovah's manifestation to His people is the lightning flash from behind the thunder cloud, fire involved in smoke, an awful and devouring brightness consuming all that is not holy. Therefore the dreadful spot where His holiness dwells may never be approached without atoning ritual and strict precautions of ceremonial sanctity provided for the priests, and for none other. Even the Levites may not touch either ark or altar, lest both they and the priests die (Num. xviii. 3). Still less dare the laity draw near to the tabernacle (Num. xvii. 13 [28]). It is only the sons of Aaron who, by their special consecration, can bear with impunity "the guilt of the sanctuary" (xviii. 1); and so every sacred offering of the Israelite, every gift which expresses the people's homage, must pass through their hand and do toll to them (Num. xviii.

8 *seq*.). Thus the access of the ordinary Israelite to God is very restricted. He can only stand afar off while the priest approaches Jehovah as his mediator, and brings back a word of blessing. And even this mediate access to God is confined to his visits to the central sanctuary. The stated intercourse of God with His people is not the concern of the whole people, but of the priests, who are constantly before God, offering up on behalf of the nation the unbroken service of the continual daily oblations. This is a great limitation of the freedom of worship. But it is no arbitrary restriction. On the Levitical theory, the imperfection of the ordinary holiness of Israel leaves no alternative open. For the holiness of God is fatal to him who dares to come near His dwelling-place.

On this theory the ritual of the sanctuary is no artificial scheme devised to glorify one holy place above others, but the necessary scheme of precaution for every local approach to God. Other sanctuaries are not simply less holy, places of less solemn tryst with Jehovah; they are places where His holiness is not revealed, and therefore are not, and cannot be, sanctuaries of Jehovah at all. If Jehovah were to meet with man in a second sanctuary, the same consequences of inviolable holiness would assert themselves, and the new holy place would again require to be fenced in with equal ritual precautions. In the very nature of the covenant, there is but one altar and one priesthood through which the God of Israel can be approached.

The popular religion of Israel, with its many sanctuaries, proceeds on a theory diametrically opposite. Opportunity of access to Jehovah is near to every Israelite, and every occasion of life that calls on the individual, the clan, or the village, to look Godwards is a summons to the altar. In the family every feast was an eucharistic sacrifice. In affairs of public life it was not otherwise. The very phrases in Hebrew for " making a covenant " or " inaugurating war " point to the sacrificial observances that accompanied such acts. The earlier history relates scarcely one event of importance that was not transacted at a holy place. The local sanctuaries were the centres of all Hebrew life. How little of the history would remain if Shechem and Bethel, the two Mizpahs and Ophra, Gilgal, Ramah, and Gibeon, Hebron, Bethlehem, and Beersheba, Kadesh and Mahanaim, Tabor and Carmel, were blotted out of the pages of the Old Testament![6]

This different and freer conception of the means of access to God, the desire which it embodies to realise Jehovah's presence in acts of worship, not at rare intervals only but in every concern of life, cannot be viewed as a mere heathenish corruption of the Levitical system. This fact comes out most clearly in the point which brings out the contrast of the two systems in its completest form.

In the traditional popular Jehovah-worship, to slay an ox or a sheep for food was a sacrificial act, and the flesh of the victim was not lawful food unless the blood or life had been poured out before Jehovah. The currency of this view is presupposed in the Pentateuchal legislation. Thus in Lev. xvii. it appears as a perpetual statute that no animal can be lawfully slain for food, unless it be presented as a peace-offering before the central sanctuary, and its blood sprinkled on the altar. One has no right to slay an animal on other conditions. The life, which lies in the blood, comes from God and belongs to Him. The man who does not recognise this fact, but eats the flesh with the blood, "hath shed blood, and shall be cut off from his people" (verse 4; comp. Gen. ix. 4). In Deuteronomy this principle is presupposed, but relaxed by a formal statute. Those who do not live beside the sanctuary may eat flesh without a sacrificial act, if they simply pour out the blood upon the ground (Deut. xii. 20 *seq.*). The old rule, it would seem, might still hold good for every animal slain within reach of the holy place. Now, under the conditions of Eastern life, beef and mutton are not everyday food. In Canaan, as among the Arabs at this day, milk is the usual diet (Prov. xxvii. 26, 27; Jud. iv. 19). The slaughter of a victim for food marks a festal occasion, and the old Hebrew principle modified in Deuteronomy means that all feasts are religious, that sacred occasions and occasions of natural joy and festivity are identical.[7] Under the full Levitical system this principle was obsolete, or at least could assert itself only in the vicinity of the sanctuary, and in connection with the three great festive gatherings at Passover, Pentecost, and the Feast of Tabernacles. But in the actual history of the nation the principle was not yet obsolete. Thus in 1 Sam. xiv., when the people, in their fierce hunger after the battle of Michmash, fly on the spoil and, slaying beasts on the ground, eat them with the blood—*i.e.*, as we see from Lev. xvii., without offering the blood to Jehovah—Saul rebukes their transgression, erects a rude altar in the form of a great stone, and orders the people to kill their victims there. A feast and a sacrifice are still identical in the book of Proverbs, which speaks the ordinary language of the people. Compare Prov. xv. 17 with xvii. 1, and note the inducement offered to the foolish young man in chap. vii. 14. In Hosea ii. 11 all mirth is represented as connected with religious ceremonies. But the most conclusive passage is Hosea ix. 3 *seq.*, where the prophet predicts that in the Exile all the food of the people shall be unclean, because sacrifice cannot be performed beyond the land of Israel. They shall eat, as it were, the unclean bread of mourners, "because their necessary food shall not be presented in the house of Jehovah." In other words, all animal food not presented at the altar is unclean; the whole life of the people becomes unclean when they leave the land of Jehovah to dwell in an "unclean land" (Amos vii. 17). We see from this usage how closely the practice of sacrifice in every corner of the land was interwoven with the whole life of the nation, and how absolute was the contrast between the traditional conception of sacrificial intercourse between Jehovah and His people and that which is expressed in the Levitical law. But we see also that the popular conception is not a new thing superadded to the Levitical system from a foreign source, but an old traditional principle of Jehovah-worship prior to the law of Deuteronomy. When did this principle take root in the nation? Not surely in the forty years of wandering, when, according to the express testimony of Amos v. 25, sacrifices and offerings were not presented to Jehovah.

But let this pass in the meantime. We are not now concerned to trace the history of the ordinances of worship in Israel, but only to establish a clear conception of the essential difference between the old popular worship and the finished Levitical system. The very foundation of revealed religion is the truth that man does not first seek and find God, but that God in His gracious condescension seeks out man, and gives him such an approach to Himself as man could not enjoy without the antecedent act of divine self-communication. The characteristic mark of each dispensation of revealed religion lies in the provision which it makes for the acceptable approach of the worshipper to his God. Under the Levitical dispensation all approach to God is limited to the central sanctuary, and passes of necessity through the channel of the priestly mediation of the sons of Aaron. The worshipping subject is, strictly speaking, the nation of Israel as a unity, and the function of worship is discharged on behalf of the nation by the priests of God's choice. The religion of the individual rests on this basis. It is only the maintenance of the representative national service of the sanctuary which gives to every Israelite the assurance that he stands under the protection of the national covenant with Jehovah, and enables him to enjoy a measure of such personal spiritual fellowship with God as can never be lacking in true religion. But the faith with which the Israelite rested on God's redeeming love had little direct opportunity to express itself in visible acts of homage. The sanctuary was seldom accessible, and in daily life the Hebrew believer could only follow with an inward longing and spiritual sympathy the national homage which continually ascended on behalf of himself and all the people of God in the stated ritual of the Temple. Hence that eager thirst for participation in the services of the sanctuary which is expressed in Psalms like the forty-second: "My soul thirsteth for God the living God; when shall I come and appear before the face of God?" "Send forth thy light and thy truth; let them guide me; let them bring me to thy holy mountain, even unto thy dwelling-place." This thirst, seldom satiated, which fills the Psalter with expressions of passionate fervour in describing the joys of access to God's house, was an inseparable feature of the Levitical system. After the Exile, the necessity for more frequent acts of overt religion was partly supplied by the synagogues; but these, in so far as they provided a sort of worship without sacrifice, were already an indication that the dispensation was inadequate and must pass away. All these experiences are in the strongest contrast to the popular religious life before the Captivity. Then the people found Jehovah, and rejoiced before Him, in every corner of the land, and on every occasion of life.

This contrast within the Old Testament dispensation presents no difficulty if we can affirm that the popular religion was altogether false, that it gave no true access to Jehovah, and must be set on one side in describing the genuine religious life of Israel. But it is a very different thing if we find that the true believers of ancient Israel—prophets like Samuel, righteous men like David—placed themselves on the standpoint of the local sanctuaries, and framed their own lives on the assumption that God is indeed to be found in service non-Levitical. If the whole Pentateuchal system is really as old as Moses, the popular worship has none of the marks of a religion of revelation; it sought access to God in services to which He had attached no promise. And yet we shall find, in next Lecture, that for long centuries after Moses, all the true religion of Israel moved in forms which departed from the first axioms of Levitical service, and rested on the belief that Jehovah may be acceptably worshipped under the popular system, if only the corruptions of that system are guarded against. It was not on the basis of the Pentateuchal theory of worship that God's grace ruled in Israel during the age of the Judges and the Kings, and it was not on that basis that the prophets taught.

LECTURE IX.

THE LAW AND THE HISTORY OF ISRAEL BEFORE THE EXILE.

IN last Lecture I tried to exhibit to you the outlines of the popular worship of the mass of Israel in the period before the Captivity, as sketched in the books of Kings and in the contemporary prophets. In drawing this sketch I directed your attention particularly to two points. On the one hand, the popular religion has a basis in common with the Pentateuchal system: both alike acknowledge Jehovah as the God of Israel, who brought His people out of the land of Egypt; both recognise that Israel's homage and worship are due to Jehovah, and that the felicity of the people in the land of Canaan is dependent on His favour. But along with this we found that between the popular worship and the system of the Pentateuch there is a remarkable contrast. In the Levitical system access to God is only to be attained through the mediation of the Aaronic priests at the central sanctuary. The whole worship of Israel is narrowed to the sanctuary of the ark, and there the priests of God's consecration conduct that representative service which is in some sense the worship of the whole people. The ordinary Israelite meets with God in the sanctuary only on special occasions, and during the great part of his life must be content to stand afar off, following with distant sympathy that continual service which is going on for him at Jerusalem in the hands of the Temple priests. In the popular religion, on the contrary, the need of constant access to God is present to every Israelite. Opportunities of worship exist in every corner of the land, and every occasion of importance, whether for the life of the individual or for the family, village, or clan, is celebrated by some sacrificial rite at the local sanctuary. We saw, further, that, as these two types of religion are separated by a fundamental difference, so also it is impossible to suppose that the popular worship is merely a corruption of the Levitical theory under the influence of Canaanite idolatry. It is indeed very natural to suppose that the system of the Law, the distance that it constitutes between Jehovah and the ordinary worshipper, was too abstract for the mass of Israel. It can well be thought that the mass of the people in those days could not be satisfied with the kind of representative worship conducted on their behalf in the one sanctuary, and that they felt a desire to come themselves into immediate contact with the Deity in personal acts of service embodied in sacrifice. But if the Levitical theory was the starting-point it is pretty clear that this would rather lead the unspiritual part of Israel to worship other gods side by side with Jehovah, local and inferior deities, just as in the Roman Catholic Church the distance between God and the ordinary layman leads the mass of the people, who have no boldness of access to God the Father or God the Son, separated from them in the sacred mystery of the mass, to approach the saints and address themselves to them as more accessible deities. But that is not what we find in Israel. We do not find that a sense of the inaccessibility of Jehovah, as represented in the system of the Pentateuch, led Israel for the most part to serve other gods, although that also happened in special circumstances. They held that Jehovah Himself could be approached and acceptably worshipped at a multitude of sanctuaries not acknowledged in the system of the Law, and at which, according to that system, God had given no promise whatever to meet with His people. It can hardly be questioned that the idea of meeting with Jehovah at the local sanctuaries and of doing acceptable service to Him there had survived from a time previous to the enactment of the law of the middle books of the Pentateuch. This is confirmed by the fact that the lineaments of the popular religion as displayed in the historical books have much that is akin to the worship of the patriarchs, and in particular that many of the sanctuaries of Israel were venerated as patriarchal shrines.

Nevertheless, if Moses left the whole Levitical system as a public code, specially intrusted to the priests and leaders of the nation, that code must have influenced at least the *élite* of Israel. Its provisions must have been kept alive at the central sanctuary, and, in particular, the revealing God, who does not contradict Himself, must have based upon the law His further communications to the people, and His judgment upon their sins spoken through His prophets. He cannot have stamped with His approval a popular system entirely ignoring the fundamental conditions of His intercourse with Israel. And the history must bear traces of this. God's word does not return unto Him void without accomplishing that which He pleaseth, and succeeding in the thing whereto He sends it (Isa. lv. 11).

Now it is certain that the first sustained and thorough attempt to put down the popular worship, and establish an order of religion conformed to the written law, was under King Josiah. An essay in the same direction had been made by Hezekiah at the close of the eighth century B.C. (2 Kings xviii. 4, 22). Of the details of Hezekiah's reformation we know little. It was followed by a violent and bloody reaction under his successor Manasseh, and in Josiah's time the whole work had to be done again from the beginning. Hezekiah evidently acted in harmony with Isaiah and his fellow-prophets; but neither in the history nor in their writings is anything said of the written law as the rule and standard of reformation. In the case of Josiah it was otherwise. The reformation in his eighteenth year (B.C. 521) was based on the Book of the Law found in the Temple, and was carried out in pursuance of a solemn covenant to obey the law, made by the king and the people in the house of Jehovah. This is an act strictly parallel to the later covenant and reformation under Ezra. But it did not amount, like Ezra's reformation, to a complete establishment of the whole ritual system of the Pentateuch. The book of Nehemiah expressly says as much with respect to the Feast of Tabernacles. And the same fact comes out in regard to the order of the priestly ministrations at the Temple. For, while Josiah put to death the priests of the high places of Ephraim, he brought the priests of the Judæan high places to Jerusalem, where they were not allowed to minister at the altar, but "ate unleavened bread in the midst of their brethren" (2 Kings xxiii. 8, 9). The reference here is to the unleavened bread of the Temple oblations, which, on the Levitical law, was given to the sons of Aaron, to be eaten in the court of the sanctuary (Lev. vi. 14-18; Num. xviii. 9). It appears, then, that the priests of the local high places were recognised as brethren of the temple priests, and admitted to a share in the sacred dues, though not to full altar privileges. This was unquestionably a grave Levitical irregularity, for, though it appears from Ezek. xliv. 10 *seq.* that the priests of the high places were Levites, it is not for a moment to be supposed that they were all sons of Aaron (compare Neh. vii. 63 *seq.*). This point will come up again along with other indications that the worship in the Temple at Jerusalem was not established by Josiah in full conformity with the Levitical system. All that I ask you to carry with you at present is that Josiah's reformation, although based upon the law, and explicitly taking it as the standard, did not go the whole length of that Pentateuchal system which we now possess. In truth, when we compare the reformation of Josiah, as set forth in Second Kings, with what is written in the Pentateuch, we observe that everything that Josiah acted upon is found written in one or other part of Deuteronomy. So far as the history goes, there is no proof that his "Book of the Covenant" was anything more than the book of Deuteronomy, which, in its very form, appears to have once been a separate volume.[1]

No one can read 2 Kings xxii., xxiii. without observing how entirely novel was the order of things which Josiah introduced. Before the Book of the Law was read to him, Josiah was interested in holy things, and engaged in the work of restoring the Temple. But the necessity for a thorough overturn of the popular sanctuaries came on him as a thing entirely new. It is plain, too, that he had to consider established privileges and a certain legitimate status on the part of the priests of the high places. There was in Judæa a class of irregular priests called *Kemarîm*, instituted by royal authority (E. V. *idolatrous priests*, 2 Kings xxiii. 5), whom he simply put down. But the priests of the popular high places were recognised priests of Jehovah, and, instead of being punished as apostates, they received support and a certain status in the Temple. We now see the full significance of the toleration of the high places by the earlier kings of Judah. They were tolerated because they were not known to be any breach of the religious constitution of Israel. Even the Temple priests knew of no such constitution. The high places were not interfered with by King Jehoash when his conduct was entirely directed by the high priest Jehoiada (2 Kings xii. 2, 3). Yet Jehoiada had every motive for suppressing the local sanctuaries, which diminished the dues of the central altar, and he could hardly have failed to move in this direction if he had had the law at his back. It seems, however, that the written covenant of Jehovah with Israel, preserved in the Temple, was not yet identical with Josiah's Book of the Covenant (2 Kings xxiii. 2). In the account of the dedication of the Temple (2 Kings viii. 9, 21), the covenant is identified with the two tables of stone preserved in the ark.

These facts do not mean, merely, that the law was disobeyed. They imply that the complete system of the Pentateuch was not known in the period of the kings of Judah, even as the theoretical constitution of Israel. No one, even among those most interested, shows the least consciousness that the Temple and its priesthood have an exclusive claim on all the worship of Israel. And the local worship, which proceeds on a diametrically opposite theory, is acknowledged as a part of the established ordinances of the land.

Here, then, the question rises, Was the founding of

the Temple on Zion undertaken as part of an attempt to give practical force to the Levitical system? Was this, at least, an effort to displace the traditional religion and establish the ordinances of the Pentateuch? The whole life of Solomon answers this question in the negative. His royal state, of which the Temple and its service were a part, was never conformed to the law. He not only did not abolish the local sanctuaries, but built new shrines, which stood till the time of Josiah, for the gods of the foreign wives whom, like his father David (2 Sam. iii. 3), he married against the Pentateuchal law (1 Kings xi.; 2 Kings xxiii. 13). And when the book of Deuteronomy describes what a king of Israel must not be, it reproduces line for line the features of the court of Solomon (Deut. xvii. 16 *seq.*). Even the ordinances of Solomon's Temple were not Levitically correct. The two brazen pillars which stood at the porch (1 Kings vii. 21) were not different from the forbidden *maççēba*, or from the twin pillars of Hercules, from which their Tyrian artist probably copied them;[2] and 1 Kings ix. 25 can hardly bear any other sense than that the king officiated at the altar in person three times a year. That implies an entire neglect, on his part, of the strict law of separation between the legitimate priesthood and laymen; but the same disregard of the exclusive sanctity of the Temple priesthood, and of that twofold cordon of Aaronites and Levites which the law demands to protect the Temple from profanation, reappears in later times, and indeed was a standing feature in the whole history of Solomon's Temple. The prophet Ezekiel, writing after the reforms of King Josiah, and alluding to the way in which the Temple service was carried on in his own time, complains that uncircumcised foreigners were appointed as keepers of Jehovah's charge in His sanctuary (Ezek. xliv. 6 *seq.*).[3] Who were these foreigners, uncircumcised in flesh and uncircumcised in heart, by whom the sanctity of the Temple was habitually profaned? The history still provides details to make this quite clear to us.

There was one important body of foreigners in the service of the kings of Judah from the time of David downwards. David instituted a bodyguard of Kerethim and Pelethim, or rather of Cretans and Philistines (2 Sam. xv. 18), to whom the Hebrew of 2 Sam. xx. 23 adds a name which has been obliterated in our English version, the Carians. These foreign soldiers were a sort of janissaries attached to the person of the sovereign, after the common fashion of Eastern monarchs, who deem themselves most secure when surrounded by a band of followers uninfluenced by family connections with the people of the land. The constitution of the bodyguard appears to have remained unchanged to the fall of the Judæan state. The Carians are again mentioned in the Hebrew text of 2 Kings xi. 4, and the prophet Zephaniah, writing under King Josiah, still speaks of men connected with the court, who were clad in foreign garb and leaped over the threshold. To leap over the threshold of the sanctuary is a Philistine custom (1 Sam. v. 5); and when the prophet adds that these

Philistines of the court fill their master's house with violence and fraud, we recognise the familiar characters of Oriental janissaries (Zeph. i. 8, 9).

The foreign guards, whom we thus see to have continued to the days of Zephaniah, are unquestionably identical with the uncircumcised foreigners whom Ezekiel found in the Temple. For the guard accompanied the king when he visited the sanctuary (1 Kings xiv. 28), and the Temple gate leading to the palace was called "the gate of the foot-guards" (2 Kings xi. 19). Nay, so intimate was the connection between the Temple and the palace that the royal bodyguard were also the Temple guards, going in and out in courses every week (2 Kings xi. 9). It was the centurions of the Carians and the footguards who aided Jehoiada in setting King Jehoash on the throne; and 2 Kings xi. 11, 14, pictures the coronation of the young king while he stood by a pillar, "according to custom," surrounded by the foreign bodyguard, who formed a circle about the altar and the front of the shrine, in the holiest part of the Temple court (compare Joel ii. 17).[4] Thus it appears that as long as Solomon's Temple stood, and even after the reforms of Josiah, the function of keeping the ward of the sanctuary, which by Levitical law is strictly confined to the house of Levi, on pain of death to the stranger who comes near (Num. iii. 38), devolved upon uncircumcised foreigners, who, according to the law, ought never to have been permitted to set foot within the courts of the Temple. From this fact the inference is inevitable, that under the first Temple the principles of Levitical sanctity were never recognised or enforced. Even the high priests had no conception of the fundamental importance which the middle books of the Pentateuch attach to the concentric circles of ritual holiness around and within the sanctuary, an importance to be measured by the consideration that the atoning ritual on which Jehovah's forgiving grace depends presupposes the accurate observance of every legal precaution against profanation of the holy things. This being so, we cannot be surprised to find that the priests of the Temple were equally neglectful, or rather equally ignorant, of the correct system of atoning ordinances which form the very centre of the Levitical Law to which all other ordinances of sanctity are subservient. The sin offering and the trespass offering are not once mentioned before the Captivity. On the contrary, we read of an established custom in the time of the high priest Jehoiada that sin money and trespass money were given to the priests (2 Kings xii. 16; comp. Hos. iv. 8; Am. ii. 8). This usage, from a Levitical point of view, can be regarded as nothing but a gross case of simony, the secularising for the advantage of the priests of one of the most holy and sacred ordinances of the Levitical system. Yet this we find fixed and established, not in a time of national declension, but in the days of the reforming high priest who extirpated the worship of Baal.

In truth the first Temple had not that ideal position which the law assigns to the central sanctuary. It did not profess to be the one lawful centre of all worship, and its pre-eminence was not wholly due to the ark, but lay very much in the circumstance that it was the sanctuary of the kings of Judah, as Bethel, according to Amos vii. 13, was a royal chapel of the monarchs of Ephraim. The Temple was the king's shrine; therefore his bodyguard were its natural servants, and the sovereign exercised a control over all its ordinances, such as the Levitical legislation does not contemplate and could not approve. We find that King Jehoash introduced changes into the destination of the Temple revenues. In his earlier years the rule was that the priests received pecuniary dues and gifts of various kinds so different from those detailed in the Pentateuch that it is impossible for us to explain each one; but, such as they were, the priests appropriated them subject to an obligation to maintain the fabric of the Temple. King Jehoash, however, found that while the priests pocketed their dues nothing was done for the repair of the Temple, and he therefore ordained that all moneys brought into the Temple should be paid over for the repairs of the house, with the exception of the trespass and sin money, which remained the perquisite of the priests. Such interference with the sacred dues is inconceivable under the Levitical system, which strictly regulates the destination of every offering.

But, indeed, the kings of Judah regarded the treasury of the Temple as a sort of reserve fund available for political purposes, and Asa and Hezekiah drew upon this source when their own treasury was exhausted (1 Kings xv. 18; 2 Kings xviii. 15).

With this picture before us, we are no longer surprised to find that Urijah, or Uriah, the priest and friend of Isaiah, whom the prophet took with him as a faithful witness to record (Isa. viii. 2), co-operated with King Ahaz in substituting a new altar, on a pattern sent from Damascus, for the old brazen altar of Solomon, and in general allowed the king to regulate the altar service as he pleased (2 Kings xvi. 10 *seq*.). The brazen altar, which, according to the book of Numbers, even the Levites could not touch without danger of death, was reserved for the king to inquire by.

The force of these facts lies in the circumstance that they cannot be explained as mere occasional deviations from Levitical orthodoxy. The admission of uncircumcised strangers as ministers in the sanctuary is no breach of a spiritual precept which the hard heart of Israel was unable to follow, but of a ceremonial ordinance adapted to the imperfect and unspiritual state of the nation. An interest in correct ritual is found in the least spiritual religions, and there is ample proof that it was not lacking in Israel, even in the barbarous times of the Judges. The system of ceremonial sanctity was calculated to give such *éclat* to the Temple and its priesthood that there was every motive for maintaining it in force if it was known at all. But in reality it was violated in every point. All the divergences from Levitical ritual lie in this direction. The sharp line of distinction between laymen's privileges and priestly functions laid down in the Law has its *rationale* in the theory and practice of atonement. In the Temple we find irregular atonements, a lack of precise grades of holiness, incomplete recognition of the priestly prerogative, subordination of the priesthood to the palace carried so far that Abiathar is deposed from the priesthood, and Zadok, who was not of the old priestly family of Shiloh, set in his place by a mere fiat of King Solomon.[5] And, along with this want of clear definition in the inner circles of ceremonial holiness, we naturally find that the exclusive sanctity of the nation was not understood in a Levitical sense; for not only Solomon but David himself intermarried with heathen nations, and Absalom, the son of a Syrian princess, was the recognised heir to the throne on account of his mother's dignity, and became, through his daughter, the progenitor of the later kings of Judah. All these facts hang together; they show that the priests of the Temple, and righteous kings like David, were as ignorant of the Levitical theory of sanctity as the mass of the vulgar and the unrighteous kings.

The Temple of Solomon never stood contrasted with the popular high places as the seat of the Levitical system, holding forth in their purity the typical ordinances of atonement which the popular worship ignored. The very features which separate the religion of the ritual law from the traditional worship of the high places are those which the guardians of the Temple systematically ignored.

Let us now go back beyond the age of Solomon to the period of the Judges, and the age of national revival which followed under Samuel, Saul, and David. We need not again dwell on the fact that the whole religion of the time of the Judges was Levitically false. Even the divinely chosen leaders of the nation knew not the law (*supra*, p. 220). What is important for our argument is to observe that breaches of the law were not confined to times of rebellion against Jehovah. From the standpoint of the Pentateuchal ritual, Israel's repentance was itself illegal in form. Acts of true worship, which Jehovah accepted as the tokens of a penitent heart and answered by deeds of deliverance, were habitually associated with illegal sanctuaries. At Bochim the people wept at God's rebuke and sacrificed to the Lord (Jud. ii. 5). Deborah and Barak opened their campaign at the sanctuary of Kedesh. Jehovah Himself commanded Gideon to build an altar and do sacrifice at Ophrah, and this sanctuary still existed in the days of the historian (Judges vi. 24). Jephthah spake all his words "before the Lord" at Mizpah or Ramoth Gilead, the ancient sanctuary of Jacob, when he went forth in the spirit of the Lord to overthrow the Ammonites (Jud. xi. 11, 29; Gen. xxxi. 45, 54), and his vow before the campaign was a vow to do sacrifice in Mizpah.

We are accustomed to speak of the sacrifices of Gideon and Manoah as exceptional, and, no doubt, they were so if our standard is the law of the Pentateuch. But in that case all true religion in that period was exceptional; for all God's acts of grace mentioned in the book of Judges, all His calls to repentance, and all the ways in which He appears from time to time to support His people, and to show Himself their living God, ready to forgive in spite of their disobedience, are connected with this same local worship. The call to repentance is never a call to put aside the local sanctuaries and worship only before the ark at Shiloh. On the contrary, the narrator assumes, without question, the standpoint of the popular religion, and never breathes a doubt that Jehovah was acceptably worshipped in the local shrines. In truth, no other judgment on the case was possible; for through all this period Jehovah's gracious dealings with His people expressed His acceptance of the local worship in unambiguous language. If the Pentateuchal programme of worship and the rules which it lays down for the administration of the dispensation of grace existed in these days, they were at least absolutely suspended. It was not according to the law that Jehovah administered His grace to Israel during the period of the Judges.

Nevertheless the fundamental requisites for a practical observance of the Pentateuchal worship existed in these days. The ark was settled at Shiloh; a legitimate priesthood ministered before it. There is no question that the house of Eli were the ancient priesthood of the ark. It was to the clan, or *father's house*, of Eli, according to 1 Sam. ii. 27 *seq.*, that Jehovah appeared in Egypt, choosing him as His priest from all the tribes of

Israel. The priesthood was legitimate, and so was the sanctuary of Shiloh, which Jeremiah calls Jehovah's place, where He set His name at the first (Jer. vii. 12). Here therefore, if anywhere in Israel, the law must have had its seat; and the worship of Shiloh must have preserved a memorial of the Mosaic ritual.

We have an amount of detailed information as to the ritual of Shiloh, which shows the importance attached to points of ceremonial religion. Shiloh was visited by pilgrims from the surrounding country of Ephraim, not three times a year according to the Pentateuchal law, but at an annual feast. This appears to have been a vintage feast, like the Pentateuchal Feast of Tabernacles, for it was accompanied by dances in the vineyards (Jud. xxi. 21), and according to the correct rendering of 1 Sam. i. 20, 21, it took place when the new year came in, that is, at the close of the agricultural year, which ended with the ingathering of the vintage (Exod. xxxiv. 22). It had not a strictly national character, for in Judges xxi. 19 it appears to be only locally known, and to have the character of a village festival. Indeed a quite similar feast was observed at Shechem (Jud. ix. 27).[6]

There was, however, a regular sacrifice performed by each worshipper in addition to any vow he might have made (1 Sam. i. 21), and the proper due to be paid to the priests on these offerings was an important question. The great offence of Eli's sons was that they "knew not Jehovah and the priests' dues from the people." They made irregular exactions, and, in parti-

S

cular, would not burn the fat of the sacrifice till they had secured a portion of uncooked meat (1 Sam. ii. 12 *seq.*). Under the Levitical ordinance this claim was perfectly regular; the worshipper handed over the priest's portion of the flesh along with the fat, and part of the altar ceremony was to wave it before Jehovah (Lev. vii. 30 *seq.*, x. 15). But at Shiloh the claim was viewed as illegal and highly wicked. It caused men to abhor Jehovah's offering, and the greed which Eli's sons displayed in this matter is given as the ground of the prophetic rejection of the whole clan of priests of Shiloh (1 Sam. ii. 17, 29).

The importance attached to these details shows how essential to the religion of those days was the observance of all points of established ritual. But the ritual was not that of the Levitical law. Nay, when we look at the worship of Shiloh more closely, we find glaring departures from the very principles of the Pentateuchal sanctuary. The ark stood, not in the tabernacle, but in a temple with doorposts and folding-doors, which were thrown open during the day (1 Sam. i. 9, iii. 15). Access to the temple was not guarded on rules of Levitical sanctity. According to 1 Sam. iii. 3, Samuel, as a servant of the sanctuary who had special charge of the doors (ver. 15), actually slept " in the temple of Jehovah where the ark of God was." To our English translators this statement seemed so incredible, that they have ventured to change the sense against the rules of the language. One can hardly wonder at them, for, according to the Law, the place of the ark could be entered only by the high priest once a year, and with special atoning services. And, to make the thing more surprising, Samuel was not of priestly family. His father was an Ephrathite, and he himself came to the Temple by a vow of his mother to dedicate him to Jehovah. By the Pentateuchal law such a vow could not make Samuel a priest. But here it is taken for granted that he becomes a priest at once. As a child he ministers before Jehovah, wearing the ephod which the law confines to the high priest, and not only this, but the high priestly mantle (*me'îl*, E. V. coat, 1 Sam. ii. 18, 19). And priest as well as prophet Samuel continued all his life, sacrificing habitually at a variety of sanctuaries. These irregularities are sufficiently startling. They profane the holy ordinances, which, under the Law, are essential to the legitimate sanctuary. And, above all, it is noteworthy that the service of the great day of expiation could not have been legitimately performed in the temple of Shiloh, where there is no awful seclusion of the ark in an inner *adyton*, veiled from every eye, and inaccessible on ordinary occasions to every foot. These things strike at the root of the Levitical system of access to God. But of them the prophet who came to Eli has nothing to say. He confines himself to the extortions of the younger priests.

The Law was as little known in Shiloh as among the mass of the people, and the legitimate priesthood, the successors of Moses and Aaron, are not judged by

God according to the standard of the Law. Where, then, during this time was the written priestly Torah preserved ? If it lay neglected in some corner of the sanctuary, who rescued it when the Philistines destroyed the Temple after the battle of Ebenezer ? Was it carried to Nob by the priests, who knew it not, or was it rescued by Samuel, who, in all his work of reformation, never attempted to make its precepts the rule of religious life ?

The capture of the ark, the fall of Shiloh, and the extension of the Philistine power into the heart of Mount Ephraim were followed by the great national revival successively headed by Samuel, Saul, and David. The revival of patriotism went hand in hand with zeal for the service of Jehovah. In this fresh zeal for religion, affairs of ritual and worship were not neglected. Saul, who aimed at the destruction of necromancy, was also keenly alive to the sin of eating flesh with the blood (1 Sam. xiv. 33) ; the ceremonially unclean might not sit at his table (1 Sam. xx. 26) ; and there are other proofs that ritual observances were viewed as highly important (1 Sam. xxi. 4 *seq.* ; 2 Sam. xi. 4), though the details agree but ill with the Levitical ordinances. The religious patriotism of the period finds its main expression in frequent acts of sacrifice. On every occasion of national importance the people assemble and do service at some local sanctuary, as at Mizpah (1 Sam. vii. 6, 9), or at Gilgal (x. 8, xi. 15, xiii. 4, 9, etc.). The seats of authority are sanctuaries, Ramah, Bethel, Gilgal

(vii. 16, 17, comp. x. 3), Beersheba (viii. 2, comp. Amos v. 5, viii. 14), Hebron (2 Sam. ii. 1, xv. 12). Saul builds altars (1 Sam. xiv. 35). Samuel can make a dangerous visit most colourably by visiting a local sanctuary like Bethlehem, with an offering in his hand (1 Sam. xvi.); and in some of these places there are annual sacrificial feasts (1 Sam. xx. 6). At the same time the ark is settled on the hill (Gibeah) at Kirjath-jearim, where Eleazar ben Abinadab was consecrated its priest (1 Sam. vii. 1). The priests of the house of Eli were at Nob, where there was a regular sanctuary with shewbread, and no less than eighty-five priests wearing a linen ephod (1 Sam. xxii. 18).

It is quite certain that Samuel, with all his zeal for Jehovah, made no attempt to bring back this scattered worship to forms of legal orthodoxy. He continued to sacrifice at a variety of shrines; and his yearly circuit to Bethel, Gilgal, and Mizpah, returning to Ramah, involved the recognition of all these altars (1 Sam. x. 3, xi. 15, vii. 6, 9, ix. 12).

In explanation of this it is generally argued that the age was one of religious interregnum, and that Jehovah had not designated a new seat of worship to succeed the ruined sanctuary of Shiloh. This argument might have some weight if the law of the one sanctuary and the one priesthood rested only on the book of Deuteronomy, which puts the case as if the introduction of a strictly unified cultus was to be deferred till the peaceful occupation of Palestine was

completed (Deut. xii. 8 *seq.*). But in the Levitical
legislation the unification of cultus is not attached to a
fixed place in the land of Israel, but to the movable
sanctuary of the ark and to the priesthood of the house
of Aaron. All the law of sacrificial observances is
given in connection with this sanctuary, and on the
usual view of the Pentateuch was already put into force
before the Israelites had gained a fixed habitation. In
the days of Samuel the ark and the legitimate priesthood still existed. They were separated, indeed,—the
one at Kirjath-jearim, the other at Nob. But they might
easily have been reunited; for the distance between
these towns is only a forenoon's walk. Both lay in that
part of the land which was most secure from Philistine
invasion, and formed the centre of Saul's authority.
For the Philistines generally attacked the central mountain district of Canaan from the north by the easy roads
leading into the heart of the land from the plain of
Jezreel, and the country south of the gorge of Michmash
was the rallying ground of Hebrew independence. Yet
it is just in this narrow district, which a man might
walk across in a day, that we find a scattered worship,
and no attempt to concentrate it on the part of Samuel
and Saul. There was no plea of necessity to excuse
this if Samuel knew the Levitical law. Why should he
go from town to town making sacrifice in local high
places from which the sanctuary of Nob was actually
visible? The Law does not require such tribute at the
hands of individuals. Except at the great pilgrimage

feasts the private Israelite is not called upon to bring any other sacrifice than the trespass or sin offering when he has committed some offence. But Samuel's sacrifices were not sin offerings; they were mere peace offerings, the material of sacrificial feasts which under the law had no urgency (1 Sam. ix., xvi.). What was urgent on the Levitical theory was to re-establish the stated burnt-offering and the due atoning ritual before the ark in the hands of the legitimate priesthood and on the pattern of the service in the wilderness. But in place of doing this Samuel falls in with the local worship as it had been practised by the mass of the people while Shiloh still stood. He deserts the legal ritual for a service which, on the usual theory, was mere willworship. The truth plainly is that Samuel did not know of a systematic and exclusive system of sacrificial ritual confined to the sanctuary of the ark. He did not know a model of sacred service earlier than the choice of Shiloh, which could serve the people when Shiloh was destroyed. His whole conduct is inexplicable unless, with the prophet Jeremiah, he does not recognise the Levitical law of stated sacrifice as part of the divine ordinances given in the time of Moses (Jer. vii. 22). Grant with Jeremiah that sacrifice is a free expression of Israel's homage which Jehovah has not yet regulated by law, and at once the conduct of Samuel is clear, and Jehovah's acceptance of his service intelligible.

At length, in the reign of David, the old elements of

the central worship were reunited. The ark was brought up from Kirjath-jearim to Jerusalem, and Abiathar, the representative of the house of Eli, was there as priest. Israel was again a united people, and there was no obstacle to the complete restitution of the Levitical cultus, had it been recognised as the only true expression of Israel's service. But still we find no attempt to restore the one sanctuary and the exclusive privilege of the one priesthood. According to the Law, the consecration of the priesthood is not of man but of God, and Jehovah alone can designate the priest who shall acceptably approach Him. The popular religion has another view. To offer sacrifice is the privilege of every Israelite. Saul though a layman had done so, and if his sacrifice at Gilgal was a sin, the offence lay not in the presumption of one who was not of the house of Aaron, but in the impatience which had moved without waiting for the promised presence of the prophet (1 Sam. xiii. 8 *seq.*; compare xiv. 35). The priest therefore was the people's delegate; his consecration was from them not from Jehovah (Jud. xvii. 5, 12; 1 Sam. vii. 1). In this respect David was not more orthodox than Saul. When he brought up the ark to Jerusalem he wore the priestly ephod, offered sacrifices in person, and, to make it quite clear that in all this he assumed a priestly function, he blessed the people as a priest in the name of Jehovah (2 Sam. vi. 14, 18). Nor were these irregularities exceptional; in 2 Sam. viii. 18 we read that David's sons were priests. This statement, so incredible on the traditional theory, has led our English version, following the Jewish tradition of the Targum, to change the sense, and substitute "chief rulers" for priests. But the Hebrew word means priests, and can mean nothing else. Equally irregular was David's relation to the high places. His kingdom was first fixed at the sanctuary of Hebron, and long after the ark was brought up to Jerusalem he allowed Absalom to visit Hebron in payment of a sacrificial vow (2 Sam. xv. 8, 12). But in fact the book of Kings expressly recognises the worship of the high places as legitimate up to the time when the Temple was built (1 Kings iii. 2 *seq.*). The author or final editor of the history, who carries the narrative down to the Captivity, occupied the standpoint of Josiah's reformation. He knew how experience had shown the many high places to be a constant temptation to practical heathenism; and though he is aware that *de facto* the best kings tolerated the local shrines for centuries after the temple was built, he holds that the sanctuary of Zion ought to have superseded all other altars. But before the temple the high places were in his judgment legitimate. This again is intelligible enough if he was guided by the law of Deuteronomy, and understood the one sanctuary of Deuteronomy to be none other than the temple of Jerusalem. But it is not consistent with the traditional view of the Levitical legislation as a system completed and enforced from the days of the wilderness in a form dependent only on the existence of the Aaronic priesthood and the ark. And so we actually find that the author of Chronicles, who stands on the basis of the Levitical legislation and the system of Ezra's reformation, refuses to accept the simple explanation that the high places were necessary before the temple, and assumes that in David's time the only sanctuary strictly legitimate was the great high place of Gibeon, at which he supposes the brazen altar to have stood (1 Chron. xvi. 39 *seq.*, xxi. 29 *seq.*; 2 Chron. i. 3 *seq.*) Of all this the author of Kings knows nothing. From his point of view the worship of the high places had a place and provisional legitimacy of its own without reference to the ark or the brazen altar.[7]

The result of this survey is that, through the whole period from the Judges to Ezekiel, the Law in its finished system and fundamental theories was never the rule of Israel's worship, and its observance was never the condition of the experience of Jehovah's grace. Although many individual points of ritual resembled the ordinances of the Law, the Levitical tradition as a whole had as little force in the central sanctuary as with the mass of the people. The contrast between true and false worship is not the contrast between the Levitical and the popular systems. The freedom of sacrifice which is the basis of the popular worship is equally the basis of the faith of Samuel, David, and Elijah. The reformers of Israel strove against the constant lapses of the nation into syncretism, or the worship of foreign gods, but they did not do so on the ground of the Levitical theory of Israel's absolute separation from the nations or of a unique holiness radiating from the one sanctuary and descending in widening circles through priests and Levites to the ordinary Israelite. The history itself does not accept the Levitical standard. It accords legitimacy to the popular sanctuaries before the foundation of the temple, and represents Jehovah as accepting the offerings made at them. With the foundation of the temple the historian regards the local worship as superseded, but he does so from the practical point of view that the worship there was in later times of heathenish character (2 Kings xvii.). Nowhere does the condemnation of the popular religion rest on the original consecration of the tabernacle, the brazen altar, and the Aaronic priesthood as the exclusive channels of veritable intercourse between Jehovah and Israel.

A dim consciousness of this witness of history is preserved in the fantastic tradition that the Law was lost and restored by Ezra. In truth the people of Jehovah never lived under the law, and the dispensation of Divine grace never followed its pattern till Israel had ceased to be a nation. The history of Israel refuses to be measured by the traditional theory as to the origin and function of the Pentateuch. In next Lecture we must inquire whether the prophets confirm or modify this result.

LECTURE X.

THE PROPHETS.[1]

A SPECIAL object of the finished Pentateuchal system, as enforced among the Jews from the days of Ezra, was to make the people of Jehovah visibly different from the surrounding nations. The principle of holiness was a principle of separation, and the ceremonial ordinances of holiness, whether in daily life or in the inner circles of the temple worship, were so many visible and tangible fences set up to divide Israel, and Israel's religion, from the surrounding Gentiles and their religion. Artificial as this system may appear, the history proves that it was necessary. The small community of the new Jerusalem was under constant temptations to mingle with the "people of the land." Intermarriages, such as Ezra and Nehemiah suppressed by a supreme effort, opened a constant door to heathen ideas and heathen morality. The religion of Jehovah could not be preserved intact without isolating the people of Jehovah from their neighbours, and this again could only be done through a highly developed system of national customs and usages, enlisting in the service of religious purity the force of habit, and the natural conservatism of

Eastern peoples in all matters of daily routine. Long before the time of Christ the ceremonial observances had so grown into the life of the Jews that national pride, inborn prejudice, a disgust at foreign habits sucked in with his mother's milk, made the Israelite a peculiar person, naturally averse to contact with the surrounding Gentiles, and quite insensible to the temptations which had drawn his ancestors into continual apostasy. The hatred of the human race, which, to foreign observers, seemed the national characteristic of the Jews under the Roman Empire, was a fault precisely opposite to the facility with which the Israelites, before the Captivity, had mingled with the heathen and served their gods. This change was undoubtedly due to the discipline of the Law, the strict pedagogue, as St. Paul represents it, charged to watch the steps of the child not yet fit for liberty. Without the Law the Jews would have been absorbed in the nations, just as the Ten Tribes were absorbed and disappeared in their captivity.

But we have seen in the last two Lectures that this legal discipline of ceremonial holiness was not enforced in Israel before Josiah, nor, indeed, in all its fulness, at any time before Ezra. The ordinary life of Israel was not guarded against admixture with the nations. David married the Princess Maacah of Geshur; Solomon took many strange wives; Jehoram, in his good father's lifetime, wedded the half-heathen Athaliah. The 45th Psalm celebrates the marriage of a king, the anointed of

Jehovah, with a daughter of Tyre, and people of lower estate were not more concerned to keep themselves apart from the Gentiles. Great sections of the nation were indeed of mixed blood. The population of Southern Judah was of half-Arab origin, and several of the clans in this district bear names which indicate their original affinity with Midian or Edom; while we know that in the time of the Judges and later many cities like Shechem were half Israelite and half Canaanite. This mixture of blood asserted itself in social customs inconsistent with the Pentateuchal law, and precisely identical with the usages of the heathen Semites. Marriage with a half-sister, a known practice of the Phœnicians and other Semites, had the precedent of Abraham in its favour, was not thought inadmissible in the time of David (2 Sam. xiii. 13), and was still a current practice in the days of Ezekiel (xxii. 11). I choose this instance as peculiarly striking, but it is not an isolated case. There is ample proof in other ways that relics of the system of female kinship, and peculiar laws of marriage and succession proper to the heathen Semites, lingered in Israel down to a late date.[2] The social system of the nation was not yet consolidated on distinctive principles. Even in the practices of worship the sanctuaries of Jehovah had much in common with heathen shrines, and this holds good, not merely of the local high places, but, as we saw in last Lecture, of the Temple of Solomon itself, where the ceremonial of Levitical exclusiveness was never enforced according to the Pentateuch. I am now speaking of practice, not of theory, and I apprehend that even those who maintain that the whole Pentateuch was then extant as a theoretical system must admit that before the Exile the pedagogic ordinances of that system were not the practical instrument by which the distinctive relation of Israel to Jehovah was preserved, and the people hindered from sinking altogether into Canaanite heathenism.

It was through an instrumentality of a very different kind that Israel, with all its backslidings, was prevented from wholly forgetting its vocation as the people of Jehovah, that a spark of higher faith was kept alive in all times of national declension, and the basis laid for that final work of reformation which at length made Israel the people of the Law not only in name but in reality. That instrumentality was the word of the prophets.

The conception that in Jehovah Israel has a national God and Father, with a special claim on its worship, is not in itself a thing peculiar to revealed religion. Other Semitic tribes had their tribal gods. Moab is the people of Chemosh, and the members of the nation are called sons and daughters of the national deity even in the Israelite lay, Numbers xxi. 29 (compare Malachi ii. 11). All religion was tribal or national. "Thy people," says Ruth, "shall be my people, and thy God my God" (Ruth i. 16). "Hath any nation changed its god?" asks Jeremiah (ii. 11). Jehovah Himself, according to Deut. iv. 19, has appointed the heavenly host and other false deities to the heathen nations, while He conversely is Himself the "portion of Jacob" (Jer. x. 16; comp. Deut. xxix. 26). In the early times, to be an Israelite and to be a worshipper of Jehovah is the same thing. To be banished from the land of Israel, the inheritance of Jehovah, is to be driven to serve other gods (1 Sam. xxvi. 19).

These are ideas common to all Semitic religions. But in Semitic heathenism the relation between a nation and its god is natural. It does not rest on choice either on the nation's part or on the part of the deity. The god, so far as we can judge, appears to have been conceived as father of his people in a physical sense. At any rate, the god and the worshippers formed a natural unity, which was also bound up with the land they occupied. It was deemed necessary for settlers in a country to "know the manner of the god of the land" (2 Kings xvii. 26). The dissolution of the nation destroys the national religion, and dethrones the national deity. The god can no more exist without his people than the nation without its god.

The mass of the Israelites hardly seem to have risen above this conception. The Pentateuch knows the nation well enough to take it for granted that in their banishment from "the land of Jehovah," where He can no longer be approached in the sanctuaries of the popular worship, they will serve other gods, wood and stone (Deut. xxviii. 36; comp. Hosea ix.). Nay, it is plain that a great part of Israel imagined, like their heathen neighbours, that Jehovah had need of them as much as they had need of Him, that their worship and service could not be indifferent to Him, that He must, by a natural necessity, exert His power against their enemies and save His sanctuaries from profanation. This indeed was the constant contention of the prophets who opposed Micah and Jeremiah (Micah iii. 11; Jer. vii. 4 *seq.*, xxvii. 1 *seq.*); and from their point of view, the captivity of Judah was the final and hopeless collapse of the religion of Jehovah. The religion of the true prophets was very different. They saw Jehovah's hand even in the fall of the state. The Assyrian and the Babylonian were His servants (Isa. x. 5 *seq.*; Jer. xxvii. 6), and the catastrophe which overwhelmed the land of Israel, and proved that the popular religion was a lie, was to the spiritual faith the clearest proof that Jehovah is not only Israel's God, but the Lord of the whole earth. As the death and resurrection of our Lord are the supreme proof of the spiritual truths of Christianity, so the death of the old Hebrew state and the resurrection of the religion of Jehovah in a form independent of the old national life is the supreme proof that the religion of the Old Testament is no mere natural variety of Semitic monolatry, but a dispensation of the true and eternal religion of the spiritual God. The prophets who foresaw the catastrophe without alarm and without loss of faith stood on a foundation diverse from that of natural religion. They were the organs of a spiritual revelation, who had stood, as they

T

themselves say, in the secret counsel of Jehovah (Amos iii. 7; Jer. xxiii. 18, 22), and knew the law of His working, and the goal to which He was guiding His people. It was not the law of ordinances, but the living prophetic word in the midst of Israel, that separated the religion of Jehovah from the religion of Baal or Chemosh, and gave it that vitality which survived the overthrow of the ancient state, and the banishment of Jehovah's people from His land.

The characteristic mark of a true prophet is that he has stood in the secret counsel of Jehovah, and speaks the words which he has heard from His mouth. "The Lord Jehovah," says Amos, "will not do anything without revealing his secret to his servants the prophets. The lion hath roared, who will not fear? The Lord Jehovah hath spoken, who can but prophesy?" But the prophets do not claim universal foreknowledge. The secret of Jehovah is the secret of His relations to Israel. "The secret of Jehovah belongs to them that fear him, and he will make them know his covenant" (Psalm xxv. 14). "If they have stood in my secret counsel, let them proclaim my words to my people, that they may return from their evil way" (Jer. xxiii. 22). The word secret or privy counsel (*sôd*) is that used of a man's intimate personal circle. The prophets stand in this circle. They are in sympathy with Jehovah's heart and will, their knowledge of His counsel is no mere intellectual gift but a moral thing. They are not diviners but intimates of Jehovah. Balaam, in spite of his predictions, is not in the Old Testament called a prophet. He is only a soothsayer (Josh. xiii. 22).

Why has Jehovah a circle of intimates within Israel, confidants of His moral purpose and acquainted with what He is about to do? The prophets themselves supply a clear answer to this question. There are personal relations between Jehovah and His people, analogous to those of human friendship and love. "When Israel was a child I loved him, and called my son out of Egypt. . . . I taught Ephraim to go, holding them by their arms. . . . I drew them with human bands, with cords of love" (Hosea xi. 1). "You alone have I known," says Jehovah through Amos, "of all the families of the earth" (Amos iii. 2). This relation between Jehovah and Israel is not a mere natural, unintelligent and physically indissoluble bond such as unites Moab to Chemosh. It rests on free love and gracious choice. As Ezekiel xvi. 6 puts it, Jehovah saw and pitied Jerusalem, when she lay as an infant cast forth to die, and said unto her, Live. The relation is moral and personal, and receives moral and personal expression. Jehovah guides His people by His word, and admits them to the knowledge of His ways. But He does not speak directly to every Israelite (Deut. xviii. 15 *seq.*). The organs of His loving and personal intercourse with the people of His choice are the prophets. "By a prophet Jehovah brought Israel out of Egypt, and by a prophet he was preserved" (Hosea xii. 13). "I brought you up from the land of Egypt, and led you in the wilderness forty years to possess the land of the Amorites. And I raised up of your sons for prophets, and of your young men for Nazarites. Is it not even thus, O ye children of Israel?" (Amos ii. 10, 11). The prophets, you perceive, regard their function as an essential element in the national religion. It is they who keep alive the constant intercourse of love between Jehovah and His people which distinguishes the house of Jacob from all other nations; it is their work which makes Israel's religion a moral and spiritual religion.

To understand this point we must remember that in the Old Testament the distinctive features of the religion of Jehovah are habitually represented in contrast to the religion of the heathen nations. It is taken for granted that the religion of the nations does in a certain sense address itself to man's legitimate needs. The religion of Israel would not be the all-sufficient thing it is, if the nation did not find in Jehovah the true supply of those wants for which other nations turn to the delusive help of the gods who are no gods. Now, in all ancient religions, and not least in Semitic heathenism, it is a main object of the worshipper to obtain oracles from his god. The uncertainties of human life are largely due to man's ignorance. His life is environed by forces which he cannot understand or control, and which seem to sport at will with his existence and his happiness. All these forces are viewed as supernatural, or rather—for in these questions it is important to eschew metaphysical notions not known to early thinkers—they are divine beings, with which man can enter into league only by means of his religion. They are to be propitiated by offerings, and consulted by enchantments and soothsayers. In Semitic heathenism the deity whom a tribe worships as its king (Moloch) or lord (Baal) is often identified with some supreme power of nature, with the mighty sun, the lord of the seasons, or with the heavens that send down rain, or with some great planet whose stately march through the skies appears to regulate the cycles of time. These are the higher forms of religion. In lower types the deity is a sort of fetich or totem more immediately identified with earthly objects, —animals, trees, or the like. But in any case the god is a member of the chain of hidden natural agencies on which man is continually dependent, and with which it is essential to establish friendly relations. Such relations are attainable, for man himself is physically connected with the natural powers. They produced him; he is the son of his god as well as his servant; and so the divinity, if rightly questioned and carefully propitiated, will speak to the worshipper and aid him by his counsel as well as his strength. In all this there is, properly speaking, no moral element. The divine forces of nature seem to be personified, for they hear and speak. But, strictly speaking, the theory of such religion is the negation of personality. It is on the physical side of his being that man has relations to the godhead. Readers of Plato will remember how clearly this comes out in the *Timæus*, where the faculty of divination is connected with the appetitive and irrational part of man's nature.[3] That, of course, is a philosophical explanation of popular notions. But it indicates a characteristic feature in the religion of heathenism. It is not as an intellectual and moral being that man has fellowship with deities that are themselves identified with physical powers. The divine element in man through which he has access to his god lies in the mysterious instincts of his lower nature; and paroxysms of artificially produced frenzy, dreams, and diseased visions are the accepted means of intercourse with the godhead.

Accordingly an essential element in the religion of the heathen Semites was divination in its various forms, of which so many are enumerated in Deut. xviii. 10, 11. The diviner procured an oracle, predicting future events, detecting secrets, and directing the worshipper what choice to make in difficult points of conduct. Such oracles were often sought in private life, but they were deemed altogether indispensable in the conduct of the state, and the soothsayers were a necessary part of the political establishment of every nation. The Old Testament takes it for granted that Jehovah acknowledges and supplies in Israel the want which in other nations is met by the practice of divination. The place of the soothsayer is supplied by the prophets of Jehovah. "These nations, which thou shalt dispossess, hearken unto soothsayers and diviners; but as for thee,

Jehovah thy God suffereth thee not to do so. A prophet from the midst of thee, of thy brethren, like unto me, will Jehovah thy God raise up unto thee; unto him shall ye hearken" (Deut. xviii. 14 *seq.*).

In the popular religion, where the attributes of Jehovah were not clearly marked off from those of the heathen Baalim, little distinction was made between prophet and soothsayer. The word prophet, *nabî'*, is not exclusively Hebrew. It appears to be identical with the Assyrian Nebo, the spokesman of the gods, answering to the Greek Hermes. And we know that there were prophets of Baal, whose orgies are described in 1 Kings xviii., where we learn that they sought access to their god in exercises of artificial frenzy carried so far that, like modern fanatics of the East, they became insensible to pain, and passed into a sort of temporary madness, to which a supernatural character was no doubt ascribed, as is still the case in similar religions. This Canaanite prophetism then was a kind of divination, based, like all divination, on the notion that the irrational part of man's nature is that which connects him with the deity. It appears that there were men calling themselves prophets of Jehovah, who occupied no higher standpoint. Saul and his servant went to Samuel with the fourth part of a shekel as fee to ask him a question about lost asses, and the story is told as if this were part of the business of a common seer. In the time of Isaiah, the stay and staff of Jerusalem, the necessary props of the state, included not only judges and warriors but prophets, diviners, men skilled in presages, and such as understood enchantments (Isa. iii. 2, 3, Heb.). Similarly Micah iii. 5 *seq.* identifies the prophets and the diviners, and places them alongside of the judges and the priests as leaders of the nation. "The heads thereof give judgment for bribes, and the priests give legal decisions for hire, and the prophets divine for money; yet they lean upon Jehovah and say, Is not Jehovah among us? none evil can come upon us." You observe that this false prophecy, which is nothing else than divination, is practised in the name of Jehovah, and has a recognised place in the state. And so, when Amos appeared at Bethel to speak in Jehovah's name, the priest Amaziah identified him with the professional prophets who were fed by their trade (Amos vii. 12), and formed a sort of guild, as the name "sons of the prophets" indicates.

With these prophets by trade Amos indignantly refuses to be identified. "I am no prophet," he cries, "nor the member of a prophetic guild, but an herdsman, and a plucker of sycomore fruit. And Jehovah took me as I followed the flock, and said unto me, Go, prophesy unto my people Israel." These words of the earliest prophetic book clearly express the standpoint of spiritual prophecy. With the established guilds, the official prophets, if I may so call them, the men skilled in enchantment and divination, whose business was a trade involving magical processes that could be taught and learned, Amos, Isaiah, and Micah have nothing in common; they declaim against the accepted prophecy of their time, as they do against all other parts of the national religion which were no longer discriminated from heathenism. They accept the principle that prophecy is essential to religion. They admit that Jehovah's guidance of His people must take the form of continual revelation, supplying those needs which drive heathen nations and the unspiritual masses of Israel to practise divination. But the method of true revelation has nothing in common with the art of the diviner. "When they say unto you, Consult the familiar spirits and wizards that peep and mutter: should not a people consult its God? shall they go to the dead on behalf of the living?" (Isa. viii. 19). Jehovah is a living God, a moral and personal being. He speaks to His prophets, not in magical processes or through the visions of poor phrenetics, but by a clear intelligible word addressed to the intellect and the heart. The characteristic of the true prophet is that he retains his consciousness and self-control under revelation. He is filled with might by the spirit of Jehovah (Micah iii. 8). Jehovah speaks to him as if He grasped him with a strong hand (Isa. viii. 11). The word is within his heart like a burning fire shut up in his bones (Jer. xx. 9), so that he cannot remain silent. But it is an intelligible word, which speaks to the prophet's own heart and conscience, forbidding Isaiah to walk in the way of the corrupt nation, filling Micah with power to declare unto Jacob his transgression, supporting the heart of Jeremiah with an inward joy amidst all his trials (Jer. xv. 16). The first condition of such prophecy are pure lips and a heart right with God. Isaiah's lips are purged and his sin forgiven before he can go as Jehovah's messenger (Isa. vi.); and to Jeremiah the Lord says, "If thou return, then will I bring thee back, and thou shalt stand before me: and if thou take forth the precious from the vile, thou shalt be as my mouth: let them—the sinful people—turn to thee, but turn not thou to them" (Jer. xv. 19). Thus the essence of true prophecy lies in moral converse with Jehovah. It is in this moral converse that the prophet learns the divine will, enters into the secrets of Jehovah's purpose, and so by declaring God's word to Israel keeps alive a constant spiritual intercourse between Jehovah and His people.

According to the prophets this spiritual intercourse is the essence of religion, and the "word of Jehovah," in the sense now explained, is the characteristic and distinguishing mark of His grace to Israel. When the word of Jehovah is withdrawn, the nation is hopelessly undone. Amos describes as the climax of judgment on the Northern Kingdom a famine not of bread but of hearing Jehovah's word. Men shall run from end to end of the land to seek the word of Jehovah, and shall not find it. In that day the fair virgins and the young men shall faint for thirst, and the guilty people shall fall to rise no more (Amos viii. 11 *seq.*). Conversely the hope of Judah in its adversity is that "thine eyes shall see thy teacher, and thine ears shall hear a word behind thee saying, This is the way, walk ye in it, when ye turn to the right hand or the left" (Isa. xxx. 20). And so the function of the prophet cannot cease till the days of the new covenant, when Jehovah shall write His revelation in the hearts of all His people, when one man "shall no more teach another saying, Know Jehovah: for they shall all know me from the least of them unto the greatest of them, saith Jehovah: for I will forgive their iniquity, and remember their sin no more" (Jer. xxxi. 33 *seq.*). When we compare this passage with Isaiah vi., we see that under this new covenant the prophetic consecration is extended to all Israel, and the function of the teacher ceases, because all Israel shall then stand in the circle of Jehovah's intimates, and see the king in His beauty as Isaiah saw Him in prophetic vision (Isa. xxxiii. 17). The same thought appears in another form in Joel ii. 28, where it is represented as a feature in the deliverance of Israel that God's spirit shall be poured on all flesh, and young and old, freemen and slaves, shall prophesy. But nowhere is the idea more clear than in the last part of the book of Isaiah, where the true people of Jehovah and the prophet of Jehovah appear as identical. "Hearken unto me, ye that know the right, *the people in whose hearts my revelation dwells;* fear ye not the reproach of man, neither be ye afraid of their revilings. . . . *I have put my words in thy mouth*, and I have covered thee in the shadow of my hand, planting the heavens and laying the foundation of the earth, and saying to Zion, Thou art my people" (Isa. li. 7, 16).

We see then that the ideal of the Old Testament is a dispensation in which all are prophets. "Would that all the people of Jehovah were prophets," says Moses in Num. xi. 29, "and that Jehovah would put his spirit upon them." If prophecy were merely an institution for the prediction of future events, this wish would be futile. But the essential grace of the prophet is a heart purged of sin, and entering with boldness into the inner circle of fellowship with Jehovah. The spirit of Jehovah, which rests on the prophet, is not merely a spirit of wisdom and understanding, a spirit of counsel and might, but a spirit to know and fear the Lord (Isa. xi. 2). The knowledge and fear of Jehovah is the sum of all prophetic wisdom, but also of all religion; and the Old Testament spirit of prophecy is the forerunner of the New Testament spirit of sanctification. That this spirit, in the Old Covenant, rests not upon all the faithful but only upon chosen organs of revelation corresponds to the limitations of the dispensation, in which the primary subject of religion is not the individual but the nation, so that Israel's personal converse with Jehovah can be adequately maintained, like other national functions, through the medium of certain chosen and representative persons. The prophet is thus a mediator, who not only brings God's word to the people but conversely makes intercession for the people with God (Isa. xxxvii. 4; Jer. xiv. 11, xv. 1, etc.).

The account of prophecy given by the prophets themselves involves, you perceive, a whole theory of religion, pointing in the most necessary way to a New Testament fulfilment. But the theory moves in an altogether different plane from the Levitical ordinances, and in no sense can it be viewed as a spiritual commentary on them. For under the Levitical system Jehovah's grace is conveyed to Israel through the priest; according to the prophets it comes in the prophetic word. The systems are not identical; but may they at least be regarded as mutually supplementary?

In their origin priest and prophet are doubtless closely connected ideas. Moses is not only a prophet but a priest (Deut. xviii. 15; Hos. xii. 13; Deut. xxxiii. 8; Psalm xcix. 6). Samuel also unites both functions; and there is a priestly as well as a prophetic oracle. In early times the sacred lot of the priest appears to have been more looked to than the prophetic word. David ceases to consult Gad when Abiathar joins him with the ephod. (Compare 1 Sam. xiv. 18, xxii. 10, xxiii. 9, xxviii. 6 with xxii. 5.) Indeed, so long as sacrificial acts were freely performed by laymen, the chief distinction of a priest doubtless lay in his qualification to give an oracle. The word which in Hebrew means priest is in old Arabic the term for a soothsayer (*kôhen, kâhin*), and in this, as in other points, the popular religion of Israel was closely modelled on the forms of Semitic heathenism, as we see from the oracle in the shrine of Micah (Jud. xviii. 5. Comp. 1 Sam. vi. 2; 2 Kings x. 19).[4] The official prophets of Judah appear to have been connected with the priesthood and the sanctuary until the close of the kingdom (Isa. xxviii. 7; Jer. xxiii. 11, xxvi. 11; comp. Hosea iv. 5). They were in fact part of the establishment of the temple subject to priestly discipline (Jer. xxix. 26, xx. 1 *seq.*). They played into the priests' hands (Jer. v. 31), had a special interest in the affairs of worship (Jer. xxvii. 16; *supra*, p. 114 *seq.*), and appear in all their conflicts with Jeremiah as the partisans of the theory that Jehovah's help is absolutely secured by the temple and its services.

But the prophecy which thus co-operates with the priests is not spiritual prophecy. It is a kind of prophecy which the Old Testament calls divination, which traffics in dreams in place of Jehovah's word (Jer. xxiii. 28), and which, like heathen divination, presents features akin to insanity that require to be repressed by physical constraint (Jer. xxix. 26). Spiritual prophecy, in the hands of Amos, Isaiah, and their successors, has no such alliance with the sanctuary and its ritual. It develops and enforces its own doctrine of the intercourse of Jehovah with Israel, and the conditions of His grace, without assigning the slightest value to priests and sacrifices. The sum of religion, according to the prophets, is to know Jehovah, and obey His precepts. Under the system of the law enforced from the days of Ezra onwards an important part of these precepts are ritual. Malachi, prophesying in or after the days of Ezra, accepts this position as the basis of his prophetic exhortations. The first proof of Israel's sin is to him neglect of the sacrificial ritual. The language of the older prophets up to Jeremiah is quite different. "What are your many sacrifices to me? saith Jehovah: I delight not in the blood of bullocks, and lambs, and he-goats. When ye come to see my face, who hath asked this at your hands, to tread my courts? Bring no more vain oblations . . . my soul hateth your new moons and your feasts; they are a burden upon me; I am weary to bear them" (Isa. i. 11 *seq.*). "I hate, I despise your feast days, and I will not take pleasure in your solemn assemblies. Take away from me the noise of thy songs, and let me not hear the melody of thy viols. But let justice flow as waters, and righteousness like a perennial stream" (Amos v. 21 *seq.*). It is sometimes argued that such passages mean only that Jehovah will not accept the sacrifice of the wicked, and that they are quite consistent with a belief that sacrifice and ritual are a necessary accompaniment of true religion. But there are other texts which absolutely exclude such a view. Sacrifice is not necessary to acceptable religion. Amos proves God's indifference to ritual by reminding the people that they offered no sacrifice and offerings to Him in the wilderness during those forty years of wandering which he elsewhere cites as a special proof of Jehovah's covenant grace (Amos ii. 10, v. 25).[5] Micah declares that Jehovah does not require sacrifice; He asks nothing of His people, but "to do justly, and love mercy, and walk humbly with their God" (Micah vi. 8). And Jeremiah vii. 21 *seq.* says in express words, "Put your burnt offerings to your sacrifices and eat flesh. For

I spake not to your fathers and gave them no command
in the day that I brought them out of Egypt concerning
burnt offerings or sacrifices. But this thing commanded
I them, saying, Obey my voice, and I will be your God,
and ye shall be my people," etc. (Compare Isa. xliii. 23
seq.) The position here laid down is perfectly clear.
When the prophets positively condemn the worship of
their contemporaries, they do so because it is associated
with immorality, because by it Israel hopes to gain God's
favour without moral obedience. This does not prove
that they have any objection to sacrifice and ritual in
the abstract. But they deny that these things are
of positive divine institution, or have any part in
the scheme on which Jehovah's grace is administered in
Israel. Jehovah, they say, has not enjoined sacrifice.
This does not imply that He has never accepted sacrifice, or that ritual service is absolutely wrong. But it is
at best mere form, which does not purchase any favour
from Jehovah, and might be given up without offence.
It is impossible to give a flatter contradiction to the
traditional theory that the Levitical system was enacted
in the wilderness. The theology of the prophets before
Ezekiel has no place for the system of priestly sacrifice
and ritual.

All this is so clear that it seems impossible to misunderstand it. Yet the position of the prophets is not
only habitually explained away by those who are
determined at any cost to maintain the traditional view
of the Pentateuch, but is still more seriously misunder-

stood by a current rationalism not altogether confined to those who, on principle, deny the reality of positive revelation. It is a widespread opinion that the prophets are the advocates of natural religion, and that this is the reason of their indifference to a religion of ordinances and ritual. On the naturalistic theory of religion, *ethical monotheism* is the natural belief of mankind, not, indeed, attained at once in all races, but worked out for themselves by the great thinkers of humanity, continually reflecting on the ordinary phenomena of life and history. It is held that natural religion is the only true religion, that the proof of its truth lay open to all men in all countries, and that Christianity itself, so far as it is true, is merely the historical development, in one part of the world, of those ideas of ethical monotheism which other nations than Israel might have worked out equally well on the basis of their own experience and reflection. From this point of view the prophets are regarded as advanced thinkers, who had not yet thrown aside all superstition, who were hampered by a belief in miracle and special revelation, but whose teaching has abiding value only in proportion as it reduced these elements to a subordinate place and struck out new ideas essentially independent of them. The prophets, we are told, believed themselves to be inspired. But their true inspiration was only profound thinking. They were inspired as all great poetic and religious minds are inspired; and when they say that God has told them certain things as to His nature and attributes, this only means that they have reached a profound conviction of spiritual truths concealed from their less intelligent contemporaries. The permanent truths of religion are those which spring up in the breast without external revelation or traditional teaching. The prophets had grasped these truths with great force, and so they were indifferent to the positive forms which made up the religion of the mass of their nation. This theory has had an influence extending far beyond the circle of those who deliberately accept it in its whole compass. Even popular theology is not indisposed to solve the apparent contradiction between the Prophets and the Pentateuch, by saying that the former could afford to overlook the positive elements of Israel's religion, because their hearts were filled with spiritual truths belonging to another sphere.

But the prophets themselves put the case in a very different light. According to them it is their religion which is positive, and the popular worship which is largely traditional and of human growth. That Jehovah is the Judge, the Lawgiver, the King of Israel, is a proposition which they accept in the most literal sense. Jehovah's word and thoughts are as distinct from their own words and thoughts as those of another human person. The mark of a false prophet is that he speaks "the vision of his own heart, not from Jehovah's mouth" (Jer. xxiii. 16). The word of Jehovah, the commandments and revelations of Jehovah, are given to them internally, but are not therefore identical with their own reflections. They have an external authority, the authority of Him who is the King and Master of Israel. This is not the place for a theory of revelation. But it is well to observe, as a matter of plain fact, that the inspiration of the prophets presents phenomena quite distinct from those of any other religion. In the crasser forms of religion the supernatural character of an oracle is held to be proved by the absence of self-conscious thought. The dream, the ecstatic vision, the frenzy of the Pythoness, seem divine because they are not intelligent. But these things are divination, not prophecy. Jeremiah draws an express contrast between dreams and the word of Jehovah (Jer. xxiii. 25-28). And the visions of the prophets, which were certainly rare, and by no means the standard form of revelation, are distinguished by the fact that the seer retains his consciousness, his moral judgment, his power of thinking (Isa. vi.). On the other hand, the assertion so often made that the prophets identify the word of Jehovah with their own highest thoughts, just as the Vedic poets do, ignores an essential difference between the two cases. The prophets drew a sharp distinction between their own word and God's word, which these poets never do. Nor is spiritual prophecy, as other scholars hold, a natural product of Semitic religion. Semitic religion, like other religions, naturally produces diviners; but even Mohammed had no criterion apart from his hysterical fits to distinguish his own thoughts from the revelations of Allah.[6]

According to the prophets, all true knowledge of God is reached, not by human reflection, but by the instruction of Jehovah Himself. Religion is to know Jehovah, to fear Him and obey His commandments, as one knows, fears, and obeys a father and a king. The relations of Jehovah to Israel are of a perfectly matter-of-fact kind. They rest on the historical fact that He chose the people of Israel, brought them up from Egypt, settled them in Canaan, and has ever since been present in the nation, issuing commands for its behaviour in every concern of national life. In every point of conduct Israel is referred, not to its own moral reflections and political wisdom, but to the Word of Jehovah.

According to the traditional view, the Word of Jehovah is embodied in a book-revelation. The Torah, instruction, or, as we should say, revelation of God, is a written volume deposited with the priests, which gives rules for all national and personal conduct, and also provides the proper means for regaining God's favour when it has been lost through sin. But to the prophets the Torah has a very different meaning.

The prophets did not invent the word Torah. It is a technical term of the current traditional religion. A Torah is any decision or instruction on matters of law and conduct given by a sacred authority. Thus *môreh*, or giver of Torah, may mean a soothsayer. The oak of the Torah-giver (Gen. xii. 6) is identical with the soothsayers' oak (Jud. ix. 37). You remember, in illustration of this name, that Deborah gave her prophetic judgments under "the palm-tree of Deborah" between Ramah and Bethel. More frequent are allusions to the Torah of the priests, which in like manner denotes, not a book which they had in their hands, but the sacred decisions given, by the priestly oracle or otherwise, in the sanctuary, which in early Israel was the seat of divine judgment (Exod. xviii. 19, xxi. 6, where for *the judges* read *God;* 1 Sam. ii. 25). Thus in Deut. xxxiii. 10 the business of the Levites is to give Torah to Israel and to offer sacrifice to God. In Jer. xviii. 18 the people give as a ground of their security against the evils predicted by Jeremiah that Torah shall not perish from the priest, counsel from the wise, and the word from the prophet. The priests are "they that handle the Torah" (Jer. ii. 8). Micah complains that the priests give Torahs or legal decisions for hire (Micah iii. 11). In these passages the Torah is not a book but an oral decision, and this the grammatical form of the word, as an infinitive of the verb "to give a decision or instruction," shows to be the primitive sense.

We have seen how spiritual prophecy branched off and separated itself from the popular prophecy which remained connected with the sanctuary and the priests. In doing so it carried its own spiritual Torah with it. When God bids Isaiah "bind up the testimony, seal the Torah among my disciples," the reference is to the revelation just given to the prophet himself (Isa. viii. 16). To this Torah and testimony, and not to wizards and consulters of the dead, Israel's appeal for Divine guidance lies (verse 20). The Torah is the living prophetic word. "Hear the word of Jehovah," and "Give ear to the Torah of our God," are parallel injunctions by which the prophet demands attention to his divine message (Isa. i. 10). The Torah is not yet a finished and complete system, booked and reduced to a code, but a living word in the mouth of the prophets. In the latter days the proof that Jehovah is King in Zion, exalting His chosen hill above all the mountains of the earth, will still be that Torah proceeds from Zion and the word of Jehovah from Jerusalem, so that all nations come thither for judgment, and Jehovah's word establishes peace among hostile peoples (Isa. ii. 2 *seq.*; Micah v. 1 *seq.*). It is this continual living instruction of Jehovah present with His people which the prophets, as we have already seen, regard as essential to the welfare of Israel. No written book would satisfy the thirst for God's Word of which Amos speaks. The only thing that can supersede the Torah of the prophets is the Torah written in every heart and spoken by every lip. "This is my covenant with them, saith Jehovah: my spirit that is upon thee, and my words which I have put in thy mouth shall not depart out of thy mouth, nor out of the mouth of thy seed, nor out of the mouth of thy seed's seed, saith Jehovah, from henceforth and for ever" (Isa. lix. 21). God's Word, not in a book but in the heart and mouth of His servants, is the ultimate ideal as well as the first postulate of prophetic theology.

How then did this revelation, which is essentially living speech, pass into the form of a written word such as we still possess in the books of the Old Testament? To answer this question as the prophets themselves would do, we must remember that among primitive nations, and indeed among Eastern nations to this day, books are not the foundation of sound knowledge. The ideal of instruction is oral teaching, and the worthiest shrine of truths that must not die is the memory and heart of a faithful disciple. The ideal state of things is that in which the Torah is written in Israel's heart, and all his children are disciples of Jehovah (Isa. liv. 13). But this ideal was far from the actual reality, and so in religion, as in other branches of knowledge, the written roll to which truth is committed supplies the lack of faithful disciples. This comes out quite clearly in the case of the prophetic books. The prophets write the words which their contemporaries refuse to hear. So Isaiah seals his revelation among the disciples of Jehovah; that is, he takes them as witnesses to a document which is, as it were, a formal testimony against Israel (Isa. viii. 1 *seq.*, 16). So Jeremiah, after three-and-twenty years spent in speaking to a rebellious people, writes down his prophecies that they may have another opportunity to hear and repent (Jer. xxxvi.). Jehovah's Word has a scope that reaches beyond the immediate occasion, and a living force which prevents it from returning to Him without effect; and if it is not at once taken up into the hearts of the people, it must be set in writing for future use and for a testimony in time to come. Thus the prophets become authors, and they and their disciples are students of written revelation. One passage of an older seer is cited as the text of further prophetic discourse both in Isaiah ii. and in Micah v.; and the prophecy against Moab (Isa. xv., xvi.) is followed by the note of a later prophet. "This is the word which Jehovah spake against Moab long ago. But now Jehovah speaks, saying, Within three short years the glory of Moab shall be abased" (Isa. xvi. 13, 14). Thus we see how the beginnings of prophetic literature in the eighth century coincide with the great breach between spiritual prophecy and the popular religion. Elisha had no need to write, for his word bore immediate fruit in the overthrow of the house of Omri and the destruction of the worshippers of Baal. The old prophecy left its record in social and political successes. The new prophecy that begins with Amos spoke to a people that would not hear, and looked to no immediate success, but only to a renovation of the remnant of Israel to follow on a completed work of judgment. When the people forbid the prophets to preach, they begin perforce to write (Amos ii. 12, vii. 12, 13; Micah ii. 6; Jer. xxxvi. 5 *seq.*).

But, though the properly prophetic literature begins in the eighth century B.C., do not the prophets, it may be asked, base their teaching on an earlier written revelation of another kind? They certainly hold that the religion of Israel is as old as the Exodus. They speak of Moses. "By a prophet," says Hosea, "Jehovah brought Israel out of Egypt." "I brought thee up out of the land of Egypt, and redeemed thee out of the house of bondage," says Micah; "and I sent before thee Moses, Aaron, and Miriam." Do not these references presuppose the written law of Moses? This question requires careful consideration.

There is no doubt that the prophets regard themselves as successors of Moses. He is, as we see from Hosea, the first prophet of Israel. But the prophets of the eighth century never speak of a written law of Moses. The only passage which has been taken to do so is Hosea viii. 12. And here the grammatical translation is, "Though I wrote to him my Torah in ten thousand precepts, they would be esteemed as a strange thing." It is simple matter of fact that the prophets do not refer to a written Torah as the basis of their teaching; and we have seen that they absolutely deny the existence of a binding ritual law. But, on the other hand, it is clear that the Torah is not a new thing in the eighth century. The false religion of the mass of the nation is always described as a corruption of truths which Israel ought to know. "Thou hast forgotten the Torah of thy God," says Hosea to the priests (Hos. iv. 6). It cannot fairly be doubted that the Torah which the priests have forgotten is Mosaic Torah. For the prophets do not acknowledge the priests as organs of revelation. Their knowledge was essentially traditional. Such traditions are based on old-established law, and they themselves undoubtedly referred their wisdom to Moses, who, either directly or through Aaron,—for our argument it matters not which,—is the father of the priests as well as the father of the prophets (Deut. xxxiii. 4, 8 *seq.*; 1 Sam. ii. 27 *seq.*). That this should be so lies in the nature of the case. Jehovah as King of Israel must from the first have given permanent laws as well as precepts for immediate use. What is quite certain is that, according to the prophets, the Torah of Moses did not embrace a law of ritual. Worship by sacrifice, and all that belongs to it, is no part of the divine Torah to Israel. It forms, if you will, part of natural religion, which other nations share with Israel, and which is no feature in the distinctive precepts given at the Exodus. There is no doubt that this view is in accordance with the Bible history, and with what we know from other sources. Jacob is represented as paying tithes; all the patriarchs build altars and do sacrifice; the law of blood is as old as Noah; the consecration of firstlings is known to the Arabs; the autumn feast of the vintage is Canaanite as well as Hebrew; and these are but examples which might be largely multiplied.

The true distinction of Israel's religion lies in the character of the Deity who has made Himself personally known to His people, and demands of them a life conformed to His spiritual character as a righteous and forgiving God. The difference between Jehovah and the gods of the nations is that He does not require sacrifice, but only to do justly, and love mercy, and walk humbly with God. This standpoint is not confined to the prophetic books; it is the standpoint of the ten commandments, which contain no precept of positive worship. But according to many testimonies of the preexilic books, it is the ten commandments, the laws written on the two tables of stone, that are Jehovah's covenant with Israel. In 1 Kings viii. 9, 21 these tables are identified with the covenant deposited in the sanctuary. And with this the book of Deuteronomy agrees (Deut. v. 2, 22). Whatever is more than the words spoken at Horeb is not strictly covenant, but prophetic teaching, continual divine guidance addressed to those needs which in heathen nations are met by divination, but which in Israel are supplied by the personal word of the revealing God ministered through a succession of prophets (Deut. xviii. 9 *seq.*). Even Ezra (ix. 11) still speaks of the law which forbids intermarriage with the people of Canaan as an ordinance of the prophets (plural). Yet this is now read as a Pentateuchal law (Deut. vii.).

To understand this view, we must remember that among the pure Semites even at the present day the sphere of legislation is far narrower than in our more complicated society. Ordinary affairs of life are always regulated by consuetudinary law, preserved without writing or the need for trained judges, in the memory and practice of the family and the tribe. It is only in cases of difficulty that an appeal is taken to the judge—

the Kadhi of the Arabs. It was not otherwise in the days of Moses. It was only hard matters that were brought to him, and referred by him, not to a fixed code of law, but to Divine decision (Exod. xviii. 19-26), which formed a precedent for future use. Of this state of things the condition of affairs under the Judges is the natural sequel. But Moses did more than any Kadhi. He was a prophet as well as a judge. As such he founded in Israel the great principles of the moral religion of the righteous Jehovah. All else was but a development of the fundamental revelation of Horeb, and from the standpoint of prophetic religion it is not of importance whether these developments were given directly by Moses, or only by the prophets his successors. But all true Torah must move in the lines of the original covenant. The standard of the prophets is the moral law, and because the priests had forgotten this they declare them to have forgotten the law, however copious their Torah, and however great their interest in details of ritual. Forgotten or perverted by the priests (Hos. iv. 6 ; Zeph. iii. 4), the true Torah of Jehovah is preserved by the prophets. But the prophets before Ezekiel have no concern in the law of ritual. They make no effort to recall the priests to their duty in this respect, except in the negative sense of condemning such elements in the popular worship as are inconsistent with the spiritual attributes of Jehovah.

From the ordinary presuppositions with which we are accustomed to approach the Old Testament, there is one point in this position of the prophets which still creates a difficulty. If it is true that they exclude the sacrificial worship from the positive elements of Israel's religion, what becomes of the doctrine of the forgiveness of sins, which we are accustomed to regard as mainly expressed in the typical ordinances of atonement? It is necessary, in conclusion, to say a word on this head. The point, I think, may be put thus. When Micah, for example, says that Jehovah requires nothing of man but to do justly, to love mercy, and to walk humbly with God, we are apt to take this utterance as an expression of Old Testament legalism. According to the law of works, these things are of course sufficient. But sinful man, sinful Israel, cannot perform them perfectly. Is it not therefore necessary for the law to come in with its atonement to supply the imperfection of Israel's obedience? I ask you to observe that such a view of the prophetic teaching is the purest rationalism, necessarily allied with the false idea that the prophets are advocates of natural morality. The prophetic theory of religion has nothing to do with the law of works. Religion, they teach, is the personal fellowship of Jehovah with Israel, in which He shapes His people to His own ends, impresses His own likeness upon them by a continual moral guidance. Such a religion cannot exist under a bare law of works. Jehovah did not find Israel a holy and righteous people; He has to make it so by wise discipline and loving guidance, which refuses to be frustrated by the people's shortcomings and sins. The continuance of Jehovah's love in spite of Israel's transgressions, which is set forth with so much force in the opening chapters of Hosea, is the forgiveness of sin.

Under the Old Testament the forgiveness of sins is not an abstract doctrine but a thing of actual experience. The proof, nay the substance, of forgiveness is the continued enjoyment of those practical marks of Jehovah's favour which are experienced in peaceful occupation of Canaan and deliverance from all trouble. This practical way of estimating forgiveness is common to the prophets with their contemporaries. Jehovah's anger is felt in national calamity, forgiveness is realised in the removal of chastisement. The proof that Jehovah is a forgiving God is that He does not retain His anger for ever, but turns and has compassion on His people (Micah vii. 18 *seq.*; Isa. xii. 1). There is no metaphysic in this conception, it simply accepts the analogy of anger and forgiveness in human life.

In the popular religion the people hoped to influence Jehovah's disposition towards them by gifts and sacrifices (Micah vi. 4 *seq.*), by outward tokens of penitence. It is against this view that the prophets set forth the true doctrine of forgiveness. Jehovah's anger is not caprice but a just indignation, a necessary side of His moral kingship in Israel. He chastises to work penitence, and it is only to the penitent that He can extend forgiveness. By returning to obedience the people regain the marks of Jehovah's love, and again experience His goodness in deliverance from calamity and happy possession of a fruitful land. According to the prophets, this law of chastisement and forgiveness works directly, without the intervention of any ritual sacrament. Jehovah's love is never withdrawn from His people, even in their deepest sin and in His sternest chastisements. "How can I give thee up, Ephraim? How can I cast thee away, Israel? My heart burns within me, my compassion is all kindled. I will not execute the fierceness of my wrath; I will not turn to destroy thee: for I am God and not man, the Holy One in the midst of thee" (Hos. xi. 8). This inalienable Divine love, the sovereignty of God's own redeeming purpose, is the ground of forgiveness. "I, even I, am he that blotteth out thine iniquity for mine own sake" (Isa. xliii. 25). And so the prophets know, with a certainty that rests in the unchangeable heart of God, that through all chastisement, nay through the ruin of the state, the true remnant of Israel shall return to Jehovah, not with sacrifices, but with lips instead of bullocks, as Hosea puts it, saying, Take away all iniquity and receive us graciously (Hos. xiv. 2). All prophetic prediction is but the development in many forms, and in answer to the needs of Israel in various times, of this supreme certainty, that God's love works triumphantly in all His judgments; that Israel once redeemed from Egypt shall again be redeemed not only from bondage but from sin; that Jehovah will perform the truth to Jacob, the mercy to Abraham, which He sware to Israel's fathers from the days of old (Micah vii. 20). Accordingly, the texts which call for obedience and not sacrifice (Micah vi.; Jer. vii. etc.), for humanity instead of outward tokens of contrition (Isa. lviii.), come in at the very same point with the atoning ordinances of the ritual law. They do not set forth the legal conditions of acceptance without forgiveness, but the requisites of forgiveness itself. According to the prophets, Jehovah asks only a penitent heart and desires no sacrifice; according to the ritual law, He desires a penitent heart approaching Him in certain sacrificial sacraments. The law adds something to the prophetic teaching, something which the prophets do not know, and which, if both are parts of one system of true revelation, was either superseded before the prophets rose, or began only after they had spoken. But the ritual law was not superseded by prophecy. It comes into full force only at the close of the prophetic period in the reformation of Ezra. And so the conclusion is inevitable that the ritual element which the law adds to the prophetic doctrine of forgiveness became part of the system of God's grace only after the prophets had spoken.[7]

LECTURE XI.

THE PENTATEUCH : THE FIRST LEGISLATION.

THE results of our investigation up to this point are not critical but historical, and, if you will, theological. The Hebrews before the Exile knew a twofold Torah, the Torah of the priests and that of the prophets. Neither Torah corresponds with the present Pentateuch. The prophets altogether deny to the law of sacrifice the character of positive revelation; their attitude to questions of ritual is the negative attitude of the ten commandments, content to forbid what is inconsistent with the true nature of Jehovah, and for the rest to leave matters to their own course. The priests, on the contrary, have a ritual and legal Torah which has a recognised place in the state, but neither in the old priestly family of Eli nor in the Jerusalem priesthood of the sons of Zadok did the rules and practice of the priests correspond with the finished system of the Pentateuch.

These results have a much larger interest than the question of the date of the Pentateuch. It is more important to understand the method of God's grace in Israel than to settle when a particular book was written; and we now see that, whatever the age of the Pentateuch as a written code, the Levitical system of communion with God, the Levitical sacraments of atonement, were not the forms under which God's grace worked, and to which His revelation accommodated itself, in Israel before the Exile.

The Levitical ordinances, whether they existed before the Exile or no, were not yet God's word to Israel at that time. For God's word is the expression of His practical will. And the history and the prophets alike make it clear that God's will for Israel's salvation took quite another course.

The current view of the Pentateuch is mainly concerned to do literal justice to the phrase "The Lord spake unto Moses, saying" thus and thus. But to save the literal "unto Moses" is to sacrifice the far more important words "The Lord spake." The time when these ritual ordinances became God's word—that is, became a divinely sanctioned means for checking the rebellion of the Israelites and keeping them as close to spiritual religion as their imperfect understanding and hard hearts permitted—was subsequent to the work of the prophets. As a matter of historical fact, the Law continues the work of the prophets, and great part of the Law was not yet known to the prophets as God's word.

The ritual law is, strictly speaking, a fusion of prophetic and priestly Torah. Its object is to provide a scheme of worship, in the pre-Christian sense of that word, consistent with the unique holiness of Jehovah, and yet not beyond the possibility of practical realisation in a nation not yet ripe to enter into present fruition of the evangelical predictions of the prophets. From the time of Ezra downwards this object was practically realised. But before the Captivity it not only was not realised, but was not even contemplated. Ezekiel, himself an exile, is the first prophet who proposes a reconstruction of ritual in conformity with the spiritual truths of prophecy. And he does so, not like Ezra by recalling the nation to the law of Moses, but by sketching an independent scheme of ritual, which unquestionably had a great influence on the subsequent development. Jeremiah, like Ezekiel, was a priest as well as a prophet, but there is nothing in Jeremiah which recognises the necessity for such a scheme of ritual as Ezekiel maps out.

When the Levitical law first comes on the stage of actual history at the time of Ezra, it presents itself as the Law of Moses. People who have not understood the Old Testament are accustomed to say, with the usual presumption of unhistorical rationalism, that this is either literally true or a lie. The Pentateuch is either the literary work of Moses, or it is a barefaced imposture. The reverent and thoughtful student, who knows the complicated difficulties of the problem, will not willingly accept this statement of the question. If we are tied up to make a choice between these two alternatives, it is impossible to deny that all the historical evidence that has come before us points in the direction of the second. If our present Pentateuch was written by Moses, it was lost as completely as any book could be. The prophets know the history of Moses and the patriarchs, they know that Moses is the founder of the Torah, but they do not know that complete system which we have been accustomed to suppose his work. And the priests of Shiloh and the Temple do not know the very parts of the Torah which would have done most to raise their authority and influence. At the time of Josiah a book of the Law is found, but it is still not the whole Pentateuch, for it does not contain the full Levitical system. From the death of Joshua to Ezra is, on the usual chronology, just one thousand years. Where was the Pentateuch all this time, if it was unknown to every one of those who ought to have had most interest in it?

It is plain that no thinking man can be asked to accept the Pentateuch as the literal work of Moses without some evidence to that effect. But evidence a thousand years after date is no evidence at all, when the intervening period bears unanimous witness in a different sense. By insisting that the whole Pentateuch is one work of Moses and all of equal date, the traditional view cuts off all possibility of proof that its kernel is Mosaic. For it is certain that Israel, before the Exile, did not know all the Pentateuch. Therefore, if the Pentateuch is all one, they did not know any part of it. If we are shut up to choose between a Mosaic authorship of the whole five books and the sceptical opinion that the Pentateuch is a mere forgery, the sceptics must gain their case.

It is useless to appeal to the doctrine of inspiration for help in such a strait; for all sound apologetic admits that the proof that a book is credible must precede belief that it is inspired.

The true way of escape from the sceptical conclusions must be sought in another direction. We must ask whether the facts of the case do shut us up to the dangerous alternative, so eagerly pressed by the enemies of revelation and so naïvely accepted by light-hearted advocates of the traditional view.

The Pentateuch is known as the Law of Moses in the age that begins with Ezra. What is the sense which the Jews themselves, from the age of Ezra downwards, attach to this expression? In one way they certainly take a false and unhistorical sense out of the words. They assume that the law of ordinances, or rather the law of works, moral and ceremonial, was the principle of all Israel's religion. They identify Mosaism with Pharisaism. That is certainly an error, as the History and the Prophets prove. But, on the other hand, the Jews are accustomed to use the word Mosaic quite indifferently of the direct teaching of Moses and of precepts drawn from Mosaic principles and adapted to later needs. According to a well-known passage in the Talmud, even the Prophets and the Hagiographa were implicitly given to Moses at Sinai. So far is this idea carried that the Torah is often identified with the Decalogue, in which all other parts of the Law are involved. Thus the words of Deut. v. 22, which refer to the Decalogue, are used as a proof that the five books of Moses can never pass away.[1] The beginnings of this way of thought are clearly seen in Ezra ix. 11, where a law of the Pentateuch is cited as an ordinance of the prophets. Mosaic law is not held to exclude post-Mosaic developments. That the whole law is the Law of Moses does not necessarily imply that every precept was developed in detail in his days, but only that the distinctive law of Israel owes to him the origin and principles in which all detailed precepts are implicitly contained. The development into explicitness of what Moses gave in principle is the work of continuous divine teaching in connection with new historical situations.

This way of looking at the Law of Moses is not an invention of modern critics; it actually existed among the Jews. I do not say that they made good use of it; on the contrary, in the period of the Scribes, it led to a great overgrowth of traditions, which almost buried the written word. But the principle is older than its abuse, and it seems to offer a key for the solution of the serious difficulties in which we are involved by the apparent contradictions between the Pentateuch on the one hand and the historical books and the Prophets on the other.

If the word Mosaic was sometimes understood as meaning no more than Mosaic in principle, it is easy to see how the fusion of priestly and prophetic Torah in our present Pentateuch may be called Mosaic, though many things in its system were unknown to the history and the prophets before the Exile. For Moses was priest as well as prophet, and both priests and prophets referred the origin of their Torah to him. In the age of the prophetic writings the two Torahs had fallen apart. The prophets do not acknowledge the priestly ordinances of their day as a part of Jehovah's commandments to Israel. The priests, they say, have forgotten or perverted the Torah. To reconcile the prophets and the priesthood, to re-establish conformity between the practice of Israel's worship and the spiritual teachings of the prophets, was to return to the standpoint of Moses, and bring back the Torah to its original oneness. Whether this was done by bringing to light a forgotten Mosaic book or by recasting the traditional and consuetudinary law in accordance with Mosaic principles is a question purely historical, which does not at all affect the legitimacy of the work.

It is always for the interest of truth to discuss historical questions by purely historical methods, without allowing theological questions to come in till the historical analysis is complete. This indeed is the chief reason why scholars indifferent to the religious value of the Bible have often done good service by their philological and historical studies. For though no one can thoroughly understand the Bible without spiritual sympathy, our spiritual sympathies are often bound up with theological prejudices which have no real basis in Scripture; and it is a wholesome exercise to see how the Bible history presents itself to men who approach the Bible from an altogether different point of view. It is easier to correct the errors of a rationalism with which we have no sympathy, than to lay aside prejudices deeply interwoven with our most cherished and truest convictions.

In strict method, then, we ought now to prosecute the question of the origin of the Pentateuch by the ordinary rules of historical inquiry; and only when a result has been reached should we pause to consider the theological bearings of what we have learned. But we have all been so much accustomed to look at the subject from a dogmatical point of view that a few remarks at this stage on the theological aspect of the problem may be useful in clearing the path of critical investigation.

Christian theology is interested in the Law as a stage in the dispensation of God's purpose of grace. As such it is acknowledged by our Lord, who, though He came to supersede the Law, did so only by fulfilling it, or, more accurately, by filling it up, and supplying in actual substance the good things of which the Law presented only a shadow and unsubstantial form. The Law, according to the Epistle to the Hebrews, was weak and unprofitable; it carried nothing to its goal, and must give way to a better hope, by which we draw near to God (Heb. vii. 18, 19). The Law on this view never actually supplied the religious needs of Israel; it served only to direct the religious attitude of the people, to prevent them from turning aside into devious paths and looking for God's help in ways that might tempt them to forget His spiritual nature and fall back into heathenism. For this purpose the Law presents an artificial system of sanctity, radiating from the sanctuary and extending to all parts of Israel's life. The type of religion maintained by such a system is certainly inferior to the religion of the prophets, which is a thing not of form but of spirit. But the religion of the prophets could not become the type of national religion until Jehovah's spirit rested on all his people, and the knowledge of Him dwelt in every heart. This was not the case under the old dispensation. The time to which Jeremiah and Isaiah xl.-lxvi., look forward, when the prophetic word shall be as it were incarnate in a regenerate nation, did not succeed the restoration from Babylon. On the contrary, the old prophetic converse of Jehovah with His people flagged and soon died out, and the word of Jehovah, which in old days had been a present reality, became a memory of the past and a hope for the future. It was under these circumstances that the dispensation of the Law became a practical power in Israel. It did not bring Israel into such direct converse with Jehovah as prophecy had done. But for the mass of the people it nevertheless formed a distinct step in advance, for it put an end to the anomalous state of things in which practical heathenism had filled the state, and the prophets preached to deaf ears. The legal ritual did not satisfy the highest spiritual needs, but it practically extinguished idolatry. It gave palpable expression to the spiritual nature of Jehovah, and, around and within the ritual, prophetic truths gained a hold of Israel such as they had never had before. The book of Psalms is the proof how much of the highest religious truth, derived not from the Law but from the Prophets, dwelt in the heart of the nation, and gave spiritual substance to the barren forms of the ritual.

These facts, quite apart from any theory as to the age and authorship of the Pentateuch, vindicate for the Law the position which it holds in the teaching of Jesus and in Christian theology. That the Law was a divine institution, that it formed an actual part in the gracious scheme of guidance which preserved the religion of Jehovah as a living power in Israel till shadow became substance in the manifestation of Christ, is no theory but an historical fact, which no criticism as to the origin of the books of Moses can in the least degree invalidate. On the other hand, the work of the Law, as we have now viewed it, was essentially subsidiary. As S. Paul puts it in Rom. v. 20, the Law came in from the side ($\nu\acute{o}\mu o\varsigma$ $\delta\grave{e}$ $\pi a\rho\epsilon\iota\sigma\hat{\eta}\lambda\theta\epsilon\nu$). It did not lie in the right line of direct development, which, as the Epistle to the Hebrews points out, leads straight from Jeremiah's conception of the New Covenant to the fulfilment in Christ. Once more we are thrown back on S. Paul's explanation. The Law was but a pedagogue, an usher to accompany the schoolboy in the streets, and lead him to the appointed meeting with his true teacher.

This explanation of the function of the Law is that of

the New Testament, and it fits in with all the historical facts that we have had before us. But current theology, instead of recognising the historical proof of the divine purpose of the Law, is inclined to stake everything on the Mosaic authorship of the whole system. If the Law is not written by Moses, it cannot be part of the record of revelation. But if it could be proved that Moses wrote the Law, what would that add to the proof that its origin is from God? It is not true as a matter of history that Pentateuch criticism is the source of doubts as to the right of the Law to be regarded as a divine dispensation. The older sceptics, who believed that Moses wrote the Pentateuch, attacked the divine legation of Moses with many arguments which criticism has deprived of all force. You cannot prove a book to be God's word by showing that it is of a certain age. The proof of God's word is that it does His work in the world, and carries on His truth towards the final revelation in Christ Jesus. This proof the Pentateuch can adduce, but only for the time subsequent to Ezra. In reality, to insist that the whole Law is the work of Moses is to interpose a most serious difficulty in the way of its recognition as a divine dispensation. Before the Exile the law of ceremonies was not an effectual means to prevent defection in Israel, and Jehovah Himself never dispensed His grace according to its provisions. Is it possible that He laid down in the wilderness, with sanctions the most solemn, and with a precision which admitted no exception, an order of worship and ritual which has no further part in Israel's history for well-nigh a thousand years?

But I do not urge this point. I do not desire to raise difficulties against the common view, but to show that the valid and sufficient proof that the Law has a legitimate place in the record of Old Testament revelation, and that history assigns to it the same place as it claims in Christian theology, is derived from a quarter altogether independent of the critical question as to the authorship and composition of the Pentateuch. This being premised, we can turn with more composure to inquire what the Pentateuch itself teaches as to its composition and date.

The Pentateuch, as we have it, is not a formal lawbook, but a history beginning with the Creation and running on continuously into the book of Joshua. The Law, or rather several distinct legal collections, are inserted in the historical context. Confining our attention to the main elements, we can readily distinguish three principal groups of laws or ritual ordinances in addition to the ten commandments.

I. The collection Exod. xxi.-xxiii. This is an independent body of laws, with a title, "These are the judgments which thou shalt set before them." It is inserted in immediate connection with the fundamental revelation of the ten commandments on Horeb, and contains a very simple system of civil and religious polity, adequate to the wants of a primitive agricultural people. I shall call this the First Legislation.

II. The Law of Deuteronomy. The book of Deuteronomy contains a good deal of matter rather hortatory than legislative. The Deuteronomic code proper begins at chap. xii., with the title, "These are the statutes and judgments which ye shall observe to do," etc.; and closes with the subscription (Deut. xxvi. 16 *seq.*), " This day Jehovah thy God hath commanded thee to do these statutes and judgments," etc. The Deuteronomic Code, as we may call Deut. xii.-xxvi., is not a mere supplement to the First Legislation. It is an independent reproduction of its substance, sometimes merely repeating the older laws, but at other times extending or modifying them. It covers the whole ground of the old law, except the law of treason (Exod. xxii. 28) and the details as to compensations to be paid for various injuries. The Deuteronomic Code presupposes a regular establishment of civil judges (Deut. xvi. 18), and the details of compensation in civil suits might naturally be left in their hands.[2]

III. Quite distinct from both these codes is the Levitical Legislation. The Levitical ordinances, including directions for the equipment of the sanctuary and priesthood, sacrificial laws, and the whole system of threefold sanctity in priests, Levites, and people, are scattered through several parts of Exodus and the books of Leviticus and Numbers. They do not form a compact code; but, as a whole, they are clearly marked off from both the other legislations, and might be removed from the Pentateuch without making the rest unintelligible. The

First Legislation and the Code of Deuteronomy take the land of Canaan as their basis. They give directions for the life of Jehovah's people in the land He gives them. The Levitical Legislation starts from the sanctuary and the priesthood. Its object is to develop the theory of a religious life which has its centre in the sanctuary, and is ruled by principles of holiness radiating forth from Jehovah's dwelling-place. The first two Legislations deal with Israel as a nation; in the third Israel is a church, and as such is habitually addressed as a "congregation" (*ēdah*), a word characteristic of the Levitical Law.

These three bodies of law are, in a certain sense, independent of the historical narrative of the Pentateuch in which they now occur. For the first two Legislations this is quite plain. They are formal codes which may very well have existed as separate law books before they were taken up into the extant history. The Levitical Legislation seems at first sight to stand on a different footing. Individual portions of it, such as the chapters at the beginning and end of Leviticus, have a purely legal form; but a great part of the ordinances of law or ritual takes the shape of narrative. Thus, the law for the consecration of priests is given in a narrative of the consecration of Aaron and his sons. The form is historical, but the essential object is legal. The law takes the form of recorded precedent. There is nothing surprising in this. Among the Arabs, to this day, traditional precedents are the essence of law, and the

Kadhi of the Arabs is he who has inherited a knowledge of them. Among early nations precedent is particularly regarded in matters of ritual; and the oral Torah of the priests doubtless consisted, in great measure, of case law. But law of this kind is still essentially law, not history. It is preserved, not as a record of the past, but as a guide for the present and the future. The Pentateuch itself shows clearly that this law, in historical form, is not an integral part of the continuous history of Israel's movements in the wilderness, but a separate thing. For in Exodus xxxiii. 7, which is non-Levitical, we read that Moses took the tabernacle and pitched it outside the camp, and called it the tent of meeting. But the Levitical account of the setting up of the tabernacle, with the similar circumstance of the descent of the cloud upon it, does not occur till chap. xl. (comp. Num. ix. 15). Again, in Numbers x. we have first the Levitical account of the fixed order of march of the Israelites from Sinai with the ark in the midst of the host (vv. 11-28), and immediately afterwards the historical statement that when the Israelites left Sinai the ark was not in their midst but went before them a distance of three days' journey (vv. 33-36).[8] It is plain that though the formal order of march with the ark in the centre, which the author sets forth as a standing pattern, is here described in the historical guise of a record of the departure of Israel from Sinai, the actual order of march on that occasion was different. The same author cannot have

written both accounts. One is a law in narrative form ;
the other is actual history. These examples are forcible
enough, but they form only a fragment of a great chain
of evidence which critics have collected. By many
marks, and particularly by extremely well-defined peculiarities of language, a Levitical document can be separated out from the Pentateuch, containing the whole
mass of priestly legislation and precedents, and leaving
untouched the essentially historical part of the Pentateuch, all that has for its direct aim to tell us what befell
the Israelites in the wilderness, and not what precedents
the wilderness offered for subsequent ritual observances.
As the Pentateuch now stands, the two elements of law
and history are interspersed, not only in the same book,
but often in the same chapter. But originally they
were quite distinct.[4]

The Pentateuch, then, is a history incorporating at
least three bodies of law. The history does not profess
to be written by Moses, but only notes from time
to time that he wrote down certain special things
(Exod. xvii. 14, xxiv. 4, xxxiv. 27 ; Num. xxxiii. 2 ;
Deut. xxxi. 9, 22, 24). These notices of what Moses
himself wrote are so far from proving him the author
of the whole Pentateuch that they rather point in the
opposite direction. What he wrote is distinguished
from the mass of the text, and he himself is habitually
spoken of in the third person. It is common to explain
this as a literary artifice analogous to that adopted by
Cæsar in his *Commentaries*. But it is a strong thing to

suppose that so artificial a way of writing is as old as Moses, and belongs to the earliest age of Hebrew authorship. One asks for proof that any Hebrew ever wrote of himself in the third person, and particularly that Moses would write such a verse as Numbers xii. 3, "The man Moses was very meek above all men living."

The idea that Moses is author of the whole Pentateuch, except the last chapter of Deuteronomy, is derived from the old Jewish theory in Josephus that every leader of Israel wrote down by Divine authority the events of his own time, so that the sacred history is like a day-book constantly written up to date. No part of the Bible corresponds to this description, and the Pentateuch as little as any. For example, the last chapter of Deuteronomy, which on the common theory is a note added by Joshua to the work in which Moses had carried down the history till just before his death, cannot really have been written till after Joshua was dead and gone. For it speaks of the city Dan. Now Dan is the new name of Laish, which that town received after the conquest of the Danites in the age of the Judges, when Moses's grandson became priest of their idolatrous sanctuary. But if the last chapter of Deuteronomy is not contemporary history, what is the proof that the rest of that book is so? There is not an atom of proof that the hand which wrote the last chapter had no share in the rest of the book.

As a matter of fact, the Pentateuchal history was

written in the land of Canaan, and if it is all by one hand it was not composed before the period of the kings. Genesis xxxvi. 31 *seq.* gives a list of kings who reigned in Edom "before there reigned a king of the children of Israel." This carries us down at least to the time of Saul; but the probable meaning of the passage is that these kings ruled before Edom was subject to an Israelite monarch, which brings us to David at any rate. Of course this conclusion may be evaded by saying that certain verses or chapters are late additions, that the list of Edomite kings, and such references to the conquest of Canaan as are found in Deut. ii. 12, iv. 38, are insertions of Ezra or another editor. This might be a fair enough thing to say if any positive proof were forthcoming that Moses wrote the mass of the Pentateuch; but in the absence of such proof no one has a right to call a passage the insertion of an editor without internal evidence that it is in a different style or breaks the context. And as soon as we come to this point we must apply the method consistently, and let internal evidence tell its whole story. That, as we shall soon see, is a good deal more than those who raise this potent spirit are willing to hear.

The proof that the Pentateuch was written in Canaan does not turn on mere isolated texts which can be separated from the context. It lies equally in usages of language that cannot be due to an editor. There has been a great controversy about Deut. i. 1 and other similar passages, where the land east of the Jordan is said to be across Jordan, proving that the writer lived in Western Palestine. That this is the natural sense of the Hebrew word no one can doubt, but we have elaborate arguments that Hebrew was such an elastic language that the phrase can equally mean "on this side Jordan," as the English Version has it. The point is really of no consequence, for there are other phrases which prove quite unambiguously that the Pentateuch was written in Canaan. In Hebrew the common phrase for "westward" is "seaward," and for southward "towards the Négeb." The word Négeb, which primarily means "parched land," is in Hebrew the proper name of the dry steppe district in the south of Judah. These expressions for west and south could only be formed within Palestine. Yet they are used in the Pentateuch, not only in the narrative but in the Levitical description of the tabernacle in the wilderness (Exod. xxvii.). But at Mount Sinai the sea did not lie to the west, and the Négeb was to the north. Moses could no more call the south side the Négeb side of the tabernacle than a Glasgow man could say that the sun set over Edinburgh. The answer attempted to this is that the Hebrews might have adopted these phrases in patriarchal times, and never given them up in the ensuing four hundred and thirty years; but that is nonsense. When a man says "towards the sea" he means it. The Egyptian Arabs say seaward for northward, and so the Israelites must have done when they were in Egypt. To an Arab in Western Arabia, on the contrary, seaward means towards the Red Sea.

Again, the Pentateuch displays an exact topographical knowledge of Palestine, but by no means so exact a knowledge of the wilderness of the wandering. The narrator knew the names of the places famous in the forty years' wandering; but for Canaan he knew local details, and describes them with exactitude as they were in his own time (*e.g.*, Gen. xii. 8, xxxiii. 18, xxxv. 19, 20). Accordingly, the patriarchal sites can still be set down on the map with definiteness; but geographers are unable to assign with certainty the site of Mount Sinai, because the narrative has none of that topographical colour which the story of an eyewitness is sure to possess. Once more, the Pentateuch cites as authorities poetical records which are not earlier than the time of Moses. One of these records is a book, the Book of the Wars of Jehovah (Num. xxi. 14); did Moses, writing contemporary history, find and cite a book already current containing poetry on the wars of Jehovah and His people, which began in his own times? Another poetical authority cited is a poem circulating among the *Môshelîm* or reciters of sarcastic verses (Num. xxi. 27 *seq.*). It refers to the victory over Sihon, which took place at the very end of the forty years' wandering. If Moses wrote the Pentateuch, what occasion could he have to authenticate his narrative by reference to these traditional depositaries of ancient poetry?

The Pentateuch, then, was not written in the wilderness; but moreover it is not, even in its narrative parts a single continuous work, but a combination of several narratives originally independent. The first key to the complex structure of the history was found in the use of the names of God in Genesis. Some parts of Genesis habitually speak of Jehovah, others as regularly use the word Elohim; and as early as 1753 the French physician Astruc showed that if the text of Genesis be divided into two columns, all the Elohim passages standing on one side, and the Jehovah passages on the other, we get two parallel narratives which are still practically independent. This of course was no more than a hint for further investigation. In reality there are two independent documents in Genesis which use Elohim. A third uses Jehovah, and the process by which the three were finally interwoven into one book is somewhat difficult to follow. Astruc supposed that these documents were all older than Moses, and that he was the final editor. But later critics have shown that the same documents can be traced through the whole Pentateuch, and even to the end of the book of Joshua. To prove this in detail would occupy several lectures. I can only give one or two illustrations to prove that these results are not imaginary.

A modern writer, making a history with the aid of older records, masters their contents and then writes a wholly new book. That is not the way of Eastern historians. If we take up the great Arabic historians—say Tabary, Ibn el Athîr, Ibn Khaldûn, and Abulfeda—we often find passages occurring almost word for word in each. All use directly or indirectly the same sources, and copy these sources verbally as far as is consistent with the scope and scale of their several works. Thus a comparatively modern book has often the freshness and full colour of a contemporary narrative, and we can still separate out the old sources from their modern setting. So it is in the Bible, as we have already seen in the case of the books of Kings. It is this way of writing that makes the Bible history so vivid and interesting, in spite of its extraordinary brevity in comparison with the vast periods of time that it covers. Think only what a mass of veracious detail we were able to gather in Lecture IX. for the state of ritual in ancient Israel. No compend on the same scale written on modern principles could have preserved so much of the genuine life of antique times. It stands to reason that the Pentateuch should exhibit the same features, and the superciliousness with which traditionalists declare the labours of the critics to be visionary is merely the contempt of ignorance, which has never handled old Eastern histories, and judges everything from a Western and modern standpoint.

Every one can see that, when we have this general key to the method of ancient Eastern historians, it is quite a practical undertaking to try to separate the sources from which a Hebrew author worked. It will not always be possible to carry the analysis out fully; but it is no hopeless task to distribute the main masses of the story between the several authors whose books he used. Marked peculiarities of language, of which the use of the names of God is the most celebrated but not the most conclusive, are a great help; and along with these a multitude of other indications come in, in the process of analysis.

A very clear case is the account of the flood. As it now stands the narrative has the most singular repetitions, and things come in in the strangest order. But as soon as we separate the Jehovah and Elohim documents all is clear. The first narrative tells that Jehovah saw the wickedness of men and determined to destroy them. But Noah found grace in His eyes, and was called to enter the ark with a pair of all unclean beasts, and clean beasts and fowls by sevens; for, he is told, after seven days a forty days' rain will ensue and destroy all life. Noah obeys the command, the seven days elapse, and the rain follows as predicted, floating the ark but destroying all outside of it. Then the rain ceases and the waters sink. As soon as the rain is over Noah opens the window of the ark, and sends out the dove and the raven. After fourteen days the dove, sent out for the third time, does not return, and Noah removing the covering of the ark finds the ground dry, builds an altar and does sacrifice, receiving the promise that the flood shall not again recur and disturb the course of the seasons. The parallel Elohistic narrative is equally complete. It also relates God's anger with mankind. Noah receives orders to build the ark and take in the animals in pairs (there is no mention of the sevens of clean beasts). The flood begins when Noah is six hundred years old, and he enters the ark. The fountains of the great deep are broken up, and the windows of heaven opened; but on the same day, Noah, his family, and the pairs of animals enter the ark. The waters rise till they cover the hills, and swell for a hundred and fifty days, when they are assuaged by a great wind, and the fountains of the deep and the windows of heaven are closed, and so just five months after the flood commenced the ark rests on a point in the mountains of Ararat. After the one hundred and fifty days the waters fail, and continue to decrease for two months and a half, till the tops of the mountains are seen. In other three months the face of the earth was freed of water, but it was not till the lapse of a full solar year that Noah was permitted to leave the ark, when he received God's blessing, the so-called Noachic ordinances, and the sign of the bow. These two accounts are plainly independent, and each is complete in itself. It is impossible that the work of one author could so divide itself into two narratives, and have for each narrative a different name of God.[5]

The proof that the same variety of hands runs through to the end of the book of Joshua would carry us too far, and is the less necessary because the fact will hardly be denied by those who admit the existence of separate sources in the Pentateuch at all. For those who cannot follow the details of the original text it is more profitable to concentrate attention on the legal parts of the Pentateuch. What has been said is enough to show that the Pentateuch is a much more complex book than appears at first sight, and that in its present form it was written after the time of Moses, nay after that of Joshua. It is now no longer permissible to insist that the reference to the kingship of Israel over Edom and similar things are necessarily isolated phenomena. We cannot venture to assert that the composition of the Pentateuch out of older sources of various date took place before the time of the kings. How much of it is early, how much comparatively late, must be determined by a wider inquiry, and for this the laws give the best starting-point.

The post-Mosaic date of the narrative does not in itself prove that the laws were not all written by Moses. Two of our three legislative *Corpora* are independent of the history. The third is at least independent of the main thread of the narrative, and deals with history only for legal and ritual purposes. But does the Pentateuch represent Moses as having written the legal codes which it embodies? So far as the ritual of Levitical legislation is concerned, we can answer this question at once with a decisive negative. It is nowhere said that Moses wrote down the description of the tabernacle and its ordinances, or the law of sacrifice. And in many places the laws of this legislation are expressly set forth as oral. Moses is commanded to speak to Aaron or to the Israelites, as the case may be, and communicate to them God's will. This fact is significant when we remember that the

Torah of the priests referred to by the prophets is plainly oral instruction. There is nothing in the Pentateuch that does not confirm the prior probability that ritual law was long an affair of practice and tradition, resting on knowledge that belonged to the priestly guild. But the priests, according to Hosea, forgot the Torah, and we have seen that neither at Shiloh nor in Jerusalem did the ritual law exist in its present form, or even its present theory. Thus we are reduced to this alternative:—either the ritual law was written down by the priests immediately after Moses gave it to them, or at least in the first years of residence in Canaan, and then completely forgotten by them; or else it was not written till long after, when the priests who forgot the law were chastised by exile, and a new race arose who accepted the rebukes of the prophets. The former hypothesis implies that a book specially meant for the priests, and kept in their custody, survived many centuries of total neglect and frequent removals of the sanctuary, and that too at a time when books were written in such a way that damp soon made them illegible. Yet the text of this book, which the priests had forgotten, is much more perfect than that of the Psalms or the books of Samuel. These are grave difficulties; and they must become decisive when we show that an earlier code, contradicting the Levitical legislation in important points, was actually current in early times as the divine law of Israel.

While the Pentateuch does not make Moses the author of the Levitical code, it tells that he wrote down certain laws. He wrote down the words of Jehovah's covenant with Israel (Exod. xxxiv. 27, 28; Exod. xxiv. 4, 7). In the former passage the words of the covenant are expressly identified with the Ten Words on the tables of stone. In the latter passage the same thing seems to be meant; for, though at first sight the "words of Jehovah" in Exod. xxiv. 4 may be thought to include the "judgments," or code of civil and other laws, we observe at ver. 3 that the "words of Jehovah"—the commandments spoken from Sinai—are distinguished from the "judgments." Indeed, details of damages for civil injuries and the like, with the law of blood-revenge, common to the Hebrews with their Arab cousins, could hardly be reckoned as part of the covenant on which Jehovah's relation to Israel was permanently based.

Till we come to the book of Deuteronomy, then, we find no statement that Moses wrote down more than the ten commandments. In Deut. xxxi. 9, 24, on the other hand, the account of Moses's last address to the people is followed by the statement that he wrote "the words of this law" in a book, which he deposited with the Levites to be preserved beside the ark. Now Deut. xxxi., which speaks of Moses in the third person, is distinct from the code in which he speaks of himself in the first person. Do the words of this chapter imply that the person—not Moses—who wrote it had before him the

Deuteronomic code as a book which he knew to have existed separately, and accepted as the actual writing of Moses? It may be so, but the inference is not certain. The narrative certainly implies that the present Deuteronomic code answers to what Moses wrote, that it is the divine Torah as the narrator was guided to present it to his readers. But then we must remember that there is, as we have seen, an elasticity about the phrase Torah. Among the later Jews it may mean something as narrow as the ten commandments, or it may mean something much wider, and yet the summary and the expansion are not viewed as two Torahs, but as the same Torah in two forms. It was already so in the days of Deuteronomy. For, according to Deut. xxvii. 8, "all the words of this law" are to be written on the plaistered stones of Mount Ebal; and here, as Calvin points out, we can only understand the sum and substance of the law. In view of this elasticity of the word Torah, it cannot be thought certain that the author of Deut. xxxi. means to convey, as an historical fact, that the very code of Deut. xii.-xxvi., in all its fulness, was written down word for word by Moses. It must be remembered that even the speeches introducing and closing the code are not an exact transcript of Moses's words as taken down by a shorthand reporter. They are plainly a free reproduction of the spirit of what he had to say to Israel—the only thing that ancient historians, who had no Hansard to refer to, could possibly give in the case of speeches which they had not heard, or even, in general, of such as they had heard.

There is nothing in these statements of the Pentateuch, when looked at fairly, which does not leave it quite an open question when and by what stages the divine Torah, of which Moses was the originator, assumed the form it has in the extant written codes.

Now it is a very remarkable fact, to begin with, that all the sacred law of Israel is comprised in the Pentateuch, and that, apart from the Levitical legislation, it is presented in codified form. On the traditional view, three successive bodies of law were given to Israel within forty years. Within that short time many ordinances were modified, and the whole law of Sinai recast on the plains of Moab. But from the days of Moses there was no change. With his death the Israelites entered on a new career, which transformed the nomads of Goshen into the civilised inhabitants of vineyard land and cities in Canaan. But the Divine laws given them beyond Jordan were to remain unmodified through all the long centuries of development in Canaan, an absolute and immutable code. I say, with all reverence, that this is impossible. God no doubt could have given, by Moses's mouth, a law fit for the age of Solomon or Hezekiah, but such a law could not be fit for immediate application in the days of Moses and Joshua. Every historical lawyer knows that in the nature of things the law of the wilderness is different from the law of a land of high agriculture and populous cities. God can do all things, but He cannot contradict Himself, and He who shaped the eventful development of Israel's history must have framed His law to correspond with it.

It is no conjecture, but plain historical fact stated in Exod. xviii., that Moses judged his contemporaries by bringing individual hard cases before Jehovah for decision. This was the actual method of his Torah, a method strictly practical, and in precise conformity with the genius and requirements of primitive nations. The events of Sinai, and the establishment of the covenant on the basis of the Ten Words, did not cut short this kind of Torah. On the contrary, there is clear proof that direct appeal to a Divine judgment continued to be practised in Israel. The First Legislation (Exod. xxi. 6, xxii. 8) speaks of bringing a case to God, and receiving the sentence of God, where our version has "the judges." The sanctuary was the seat of judgment, and the decisions were Jehovah's Torah. So still, in the time of Eli, we read that, if man offend against man, God gives judgment as daysman between them (1 Sam. ii. 25). Jehovah is in Israel a living judge, a living and present lawgiver. He has all the functions of an actual king present among his people (Isa. xxxiii. 22). So the prophets still view Jehovah's law as a living and growing thing, communicated to Israel as to weanlings, "precept upon precept, line upon line, here a little and there a little" (Isa. xxviii. 9 *seq.*); and their religion, drawn direct from Jehovah, is contrasted with the traditional religion, which is "a command of men learned and taught" (Isa. xxix. 13). A code is of necessity the final result and crystallised form of such a living divine Torah, just as in all nations consuetudinary and judge-made law precedes codification and statute law. The difference between Israel and other nations lay essentially in this, that Jehovah was Israel's Judge, and therefore Israel's Lawgiver. This divine Torah begins with Moses. As all goes back to his initiative, the Israelites were not concerned to remember the precise history of each new precept; and, when the whole system developed under continuous divine guidance is summed up in a code, that code is simply set down as Mosaic Torah. We still call the steam-engine by the name of Watt, though the steam-engine of to-day has many parts that his had not.

The Bible has not so narrow a conception of revelation as we sometimes cling to. According to Isaiah xxviii. 23 *seq.* the rules of good husbandry are a "judgment" taught to the ploughman by Jehovah, part of Jehovah's Torah (verse 26). The piety of Israel recognised every sound and wholesome ordinance of daily and social life as a direct gift of Jehovah's wisdom. "This also cometh forth from Jehovah of hosts, whose counsel is miraculous, and His wisdom great." Accordingly Jehovah's law contains, not only institutes of direct revelation in our limited sense of that word, but old consuetudinary usages, laws identical with those of other early peoples, which had become sacred by being taken up into the God-given polity of Israel, and worked into harmony with the very present reality of His redeeming sovereignty. We shall best picture to ourselves what the ancient Hebrews understood by divine statutes, by a brief survey of the manner of life prescribed in the First Legislation.

The society contemplated in this legislation is of very simple structure. The basis of life is agricultural. Cattle and agricultural produce are the elements of wealth, and the laws of property deal almost exclusively with them. The principles of civil and criminal justice are those still current among the Arabs of the desert. They are two in number, retaliation and pecuniary compensation. Murder is dealt with by the law of blood-revenge, but the innocent manslayer may seek asylum at God's altar. With murder are ranked manstealing, offences against parents, and witchcraft. Other injuries are occasions of self-help or of private suits to be adjusted at the sanctuary. Personal injuries fall under the law of retaliation, just as murder does. Blow for blow is still the law of the Arabs, and in Canaan no doubt, as in the desert, the retaliation was usually sought in the way of self-help. The principle of retaliation is conceived as legitimate vengeance, xxi. 20, 21, *margin*. Except in this form there is no punishment, but only compensation, which in some cases is at the will of the injured party (who has the alternative of direct revenge), but in general is defined by law.

Degrading punishments, as imprisonment or the bastinado, are unknown, and loss of liberty is inflicted only on the thief who cannot pay a fine. The slave retains definite rights. He recovers his freedom after seven years, unless he prefer to remain a bondman, and to seal this determination by a symbolical act at the door of the sanctuary. His right of blood-revenge against his master is limited, and, instead of the *lex talionis*, for minor injuries he can claim his liberty. Women do not enjoy full social equality with men. Women slaves were slaves for life, but were usually married to members of the family or servants of the household. The daughter was her father's property, who received a price for surrendering her to a husband; and so a daughter's dishonour is compensated by law as a pecuniary loss to her father. The Israelites directly contemplated in these laws are evidently men of independent bearing and personal dignity, such as are still found in secluded parts of the Semitic world under a half-patriarchal constitution of society where every freeman is a small landholder. But there is no strong central authority. The tribunal of the sanctuary is arbiter, not executive. No man is secure without his own aid, and the widow or orphan looks for help, not to man, but to Jehovah Himself. But if the executive is weak, a strict regard for justice is inculcated. Jehovah is behind the law, and He will vindicate the right. He requires of Israel humanity as well as justice. The Gêr, or stranger living under the protection of a family or community, has no legal status, but he must not be oppressed.[6] The Sabbath is enforced as an ordinance of humanity, and to the same end the produce of every field or vineyard must be left to the poor one year in seven. The precepts of positive *cultus* are simple. He who sacrifices to any God but Jehovah falls under the ban. The only ordinance of ceremonial sanctity is to abstain from the flesh of animals torn by wild beasts. The sacred dues are the firstlings and first fruits: the former must be presented at the sanctuary on the eighth day. This, of course, presupposes a plurality of sanctuaries, and in fact Exodus xx. 24, 25, explains that an altar of stone may be built, and Jehovah acceptably approached, in every place where He sets a memorial of His name. The stated occasions of sacrifice are the feast of unleavened bread, in commemoration of the exodus, the feast of harvest, and that of ingathering. These feasts mark the cycle of the agricultural year, and at them every male must present his homage before Jehovah. The essential points of sacrificial ritual are abstinence from leaven in connection with the blood of the sacrifice, and the rule that the fat must be burnt the same night.

You see at once that this is no abstract divine legislation. It is a social system adapted for a very definite national life. On the common view, many of its precepts were immediately superseded by the Levitical or Deuteronomic code, before they ever had a chance of being put in operation in Canaan. But this hypothesis, so dishonouring to the Divine Legislator, who can do nothing in vain, is refuted by the whole tenor of the code, which undoubtedly is as living and real a system of law as was ever written. The details of the system are almost all such as are found among other nations. The law of Israel does not yet aim at singularity; it is enough that it is pervaded by a constant sense that the righteous and gracious Jehovah is behind the law, and wields it in conformity with His own holy nature. The law, therefore, makes no pretence at ideality. It contains precepts adapted, as our Lord puts it, to the hardness of the people's heart. The ordinances are not ideally perfect, and fit to be a rule of life in every state of society, but they are fit to make Israel a righteous, humane, and God-fearing people, and to facilitate a healthy growth towards better things.

The important point that reference to Jehovah and His character determines the spirit rather than the details of the legislation cannot be too strongly accentuated. The civil laws are exactly such as the comparative lawyer is familiar with in other nations. Even the religious ordinances are far from unique in their formal elements. The feast of unleavened bread has a special reference to the deliverance from Egypt, which is the historical basis of Israel's distinctive religion. But even this feast has also an agricultural reference; and the two others, which are purely agricultural, are quite analogous to what is found in other nations. The Canaanite vintage feast at Shechem is a close parallel to the feast of ingathering (*suprá*, p. 257). The sacred dues have also their analogies outside Israel. It is enough to refer to the offering of a firstling sheep or camel observed by the heathen Arabs under the name of *fara'*. The distinctive character of the religion appears in the laws directed against polytheism and witchcraft, in the prominence given to righteousness and humanity as the things which are most pleasing to Jehovah and constitute the true significance of such an ordinance as the Sabbath, and, above all, in the clearness with which the law holds forth the truth that Jehovah's goodness to Israel is no mere natural relation such as binds Moab to Chemosh, that His favour to His people is directed by moral principles and is forfeited by moral iniquity. In this code we read already the foundation of the thesis of Amos that just because Jehovah knows Israel He observes and punishes the nation's sins (Amos iii. 2 ; Exod. xxii. 23, 27, xxiii. 7).

Now, we have seen that before the Exile the most characteristic features of the Levitical legislation, and so the most prominent things in our present Pentateuch, had no influence on Israel, either on the righteous or the wicked. This result involved us in great perplexity. For, if the traditional view of the age of the Pentateuch is correct, there was through all these centuries an absolute divorce between God's written law and the practical workings of His grace. And the perplexity was only increased when we found that, nevertheless, there was a Torah in Israel before the prophetic books, to which the prophets appeal as the indisputable standard of Jehovah's will. But the puzzle is solved when we compare the history with this First Legislation. It did

LECT. XI. *LEGISLATION.* 341

not remain without fruit in Israel, and it, as we have just seen in the case of Amos, affords a firm footing for the prophetic word. There is abundant proof that the principles of this legislation were acknowledged in Israel. The appeal to God as judge appears in 1 Sam. ii. 25 ; the law of blood-revenge administered, not by a central authority, but by the family of the deceased, occurs in 2 Sam. iii. 30, xiv. 7, etc.; the altar is the asylum in 1 Kings i. 50, and elsewhere ; the thief taken in the breach (Exod. xxii. 2) is alluded to by Jer. ii. 34 ; and so forth. The sacred ordinances agree with those in the history, or, if exceptions are noted, they are stigmatised as irregular. The plurality of altars accords with this law. The annual feasts—at least that of the autumn, which seems to have been best observed—are often alluded to ; and the night service of commemoration for the exodus appears in Isa. xxx. 29. The rule that the pilgrim must bring an offering was recognised at Shiloh (1 Sam. i. 21). So, too, the complaint against Eli's sons for their delay in burning the fat is based on the same principle as Exod. xxiii. 18. The use of leavened bread with the sacrifice is rebuked by Amos iv. 5, and seems to have had some symbolical significance of a purely Canaanite character.[7] The prohibition to eat blood, which is essentially one with the prohibition of torn flesh, is sedulously observed by Saul, and Saul also distinguishes himself by suppressing witchcraft. The proof that this law was known and acknowledged in all its leading provisions is as complete as the proof that the Levitical law was still unheard of. This result confirms, and at the same time supplements, our previous argument. We have now brought the history into positive relation to one part of the Pentateuch, and the critical analysis of the Books of Moses has already filled up one of those breaches between law and history which the traditional view can do nothing to heal.

LECTURE XII.

THE DEUTERONOMIC CODE AND THE LEVITICAL LAW.

IN the First Legislation the question of correct ritual has little prominence. The simple rules laid down are little more than the necessary and natural expression of that principle which we saw in Lecture VIII. to be the presupposition of the popular worship of Israel, even when it diverged most widely from the Levitical forms. Jehovah alone is Israel's God. It is a crime, analogous to treason, to depart from Him and sacrifice to other gods. As the Lord of Israel and Israel's land, the giver of all good gifts to His people, He has a manifest claim on Israel's homage, and receives at their hands such dues as their neighbours paid to their gods, such dues as a king receives from his people (comp. 1 Sam. viii. 15, 17). The occasions of homage are those seasons of natural gladness which an agricultural life suggests. The joy of harvest and vintage is a rejoicing before Jehovah, when the worshipper brings a gift in his hand, as he would do in approaching an earthly sovereign, and presents the choicest first-fruits at the altar, just as his Canaanite neighbour does in the house of Baal (Jud. ix. 27). The whole worship is spontaneous and natural. It has hardly the character of a positive legislation, and its distinction from heathen rites lies less in the outward form than in the different conception of Jehovah which the true worshipper should bear in his heart. To a people which "knows Jehovah," this unambitious service, in which the expression of grateful homage to Him runs through all the simple joys of a placid agricultural life, was sufficient to form the visible basis of a pure and earnest piety. But its forms gave no protection against deflection into heathenism and immorality when Jehovah's spiritual nature and moral precepts were forgotten. The feasts and sacrifices might still run their accustomed round when Jehovah was practically confounded with the Baalim, and there was no more truth or mercy or knowledge of God in the land (Hosea iv. 1).

Such, in fact, was the state of things in the eighth century, the age of the earliest prophetic books. The declensions of Israel had not checked the outward zeal with which Jehovah was worshipped. Never had the national sanctuaries been more sedulously frequented, never had the feasts been more splendid or the offerings more copious. But the foundations of the old life were breaking up. The external prosperity of the state covered an abyss of social disorder. Profusion and luxury among the higher classes stood in startling contrast to the misery of the poor. Lawlessness and open crime were on the increase. The rulers of the nation grew fat upon oppression, but there was none who was grieved for the wound of Joseph. These evils were earliest and most acutely felt in the kingdom of Ephraim, where Amos declares them to be already incurable under the outwardly prosperous reign of Jeroboam II. With the downfall of Jehu's dynasty the last bonds of social order were dissolved, and the Assyrian found an easy prey in a land already reduced to practical anarchy. The smaller realm of Judah seemed at first to show more hopeful symptoms (Hosea iv. 15). But the separation of the kingdoms had not broken the subtle links that connected Judah with the greater Israel of the North. At all periods the fortunes and internal movements of Ephraim had powerfully reacted on the Southern Kingdom. Isaiah and Micah describe a corruption within the house of David altogether similar to the sin of Samaria. "The statutes of Omri were kept, and all the works of the house of Ahab" (Micah vi. 16).

The prominence which the prophets assign to social grievances and civil disorders has often led to their being described as politicians, a democratic Opposition in the aristocratic state. This is a total misconception. The prophets of the eighth century have no political views, they propose no practical scheme of political readjustment, and they give only the indirectest hints of the causes which were so rapidly dissolving the body politic of Israel. The work of the prophets is purely religious; they censure what is inconsistent with the knowledge and fear of Jehovah, but see no way of remedy save in the repentance and return to Him of all classes of society, after a sifting work of judgment has destroyed the sinners of Jehovah's people without suffering one grain of true wheat to fall to the ground (Amos ix. 9 *seq.*; Isa. vi., etc.). But to the prophets the observance of justice and mercy in the state are the first elements of religion. The religious subject, the worshipping individual, Jehovah's son, was not the individual Israelite, but the nation *qua* nation, and the Old Testament analogue to the peace of conscience which marks a healthy condition of spiritual life in the Christian was that inner peace and harmony of the estates of the realm which can only be secured where justice is done and mercy loved. The ideal of the prophets in the eighth century is not different from that of the First Legislation. In the old law the worship of feasts and sacrifices is the natural consecration, in act, of a simple, happy society, nourished by Jehovah's good gifts in answer to the labour of the husbandman, and cemented by a regard for justice and habits of social kindliness. When the old healthy harmony of classes was dissolved, when the rich and the poor were no longer knit together by a kindly sympathy and patriarchal bond of dependence, but confronted one another as oppressor and oppressed, when the strain thus put on all social relations burst the weak bonds of outer order and filled the land with unexpiated bloodshed, the pretence of homage to Jehovah at His sanctuary was but the crowning proof that Israel knew not his God.

"When ye spread forth your hands, I will hide mine eyes from you; yea, when ye make many prayers I will not hear: your hands are full of blood" (Isa. i. 15).

The causes of the inner disintegration of Israel were manifold, and we cannot pause to examine them fully. But in this, as in all similar cases which history exhibits, the strain which snapped the old bands of social unity proceeded mainly from the effects of warlike invasion reacting on a one-sided progress in material prosperity, to which the order of the state had not been able to readjust itself. The luxury of the higher classes, described by Amos and Isaiah, shows that the nobles of Israel were no longer great farmers, as Saul and Nabal had been, living among the peasantry and sharing their toil. The connection with Tyre, which commenced in the days of David, opened a profitable foreign market for the agricultural produce of Palestine (Ezek. xxvii. 17), and introduced foreign luxuries in return. The landowners became merchants and forestallers of grain (Amos viii. 5; Hos. xii. 7). The introduction of such a commerce, throwing the Hebrews into immediate relations with the great emporium of international traffic, necessarily led to accumulation of wealth in a few hands, and to the corresponding impoverishment of the class without capital, as exportation raised the price of the necessaries of life. In times of famine, or under the distress wrought by prolonged and ferocious warfare with Syria, the once independent peasantry fell into the condition now so universal in the East. They were loaded with debt, cheated on all hands, and often had to relinquish their personal liberty (Amos ii. 6, 7; Micah iii. 2 *seq.*, vi. 10 *seq.*, etc.). The order of the state, entirely based on the old precommercial state of things when trade was the affair of the Canaanites—Canaanite, in old Hebrew, is the word for a trader—was not able to adjust itself to the new circumstances. How entirely commercial avocations were unknown to the old law appears from the circumstance that the idea of capital is unknown. It is assumed in Exod. xxii. 25 that no one borrows money except for personal distress, and all interest is conceived as usury (comp. Psalm xv. 5). In proportion, therefore, as the nation began to share the wealth and luxury of the Canaanite trading cities of the coast, it divorced itself from the old social forms of the religion of Jehovah. The Canaanite influence affected religion in affecting the national life, and it was inevitable that the worship of the sanctuary, which had always been in the closest *rapport* with the daily habits of the people, should itself assume the colour of Canaanite luxury and Canaanite immorality. This tendency was not checked by the extirpation of professed worship of the Tyrian Baal. Jehovah Himself in His many shrines assumed the features of the local Baalim of the Canaanite sanctuaries, and those horrible orgies of unrestrained sensuality, of which we no longer dare to speak in unveiled words, polluted the temples where Jehovah still reigned in name, and where His help was confidently expected to save Israel from Damascus and Assyria.

The prophets, as I have already said, never profess to devise a scheme of political and social reformation to meet these evils. Their business is not to govern, but to teach the nation to know Jehovah, and to lay bare the guilt of every departure from Him. It is for the righteous ruler to determine how the principles of justice, mercy, and God-fearing can be made practically operative in society. Thus the criticism of the prophets on established usages is mainly negative. The healing of Israel must come from Jehovah. It is useless to seek help from political combinations, and it is a mistake to fancy that international commerce and foreign culture are additions to true happiness. This judgment proceeds from no theories of political economy. It would be a fallacy to cite the prophets as witness that commerce and material civilisation are bad in themselves. All that they say is that these things, as they found them in their own time, have undone Israel, and that the first step towards deliverance must be a judgment which sweeps away all the spurious show of prosperity that has come between Jehovah's people and the true knowledge of their God (Isa. ii.; Micah v.). Israel must again pass through the wilderness. All the good gifts of fertile Canaan must be taken away by a desolating calamity. Then the valley of trouble shall again become a gate of hope, and Jehovah's covenant shall renew its course on its old principles, but with far more perfect realisation (Hos. ii.). The prophetic pictures of Israel's final felicity are at this time all framed on the pattern of the past. The days of David shall return under a righteous king (Micah v. 2 *seq.*; Hos. iii. 5 ; Isa. xi. 1 *seq.*), and Israel shall realise, as it had never done in the past, the old ideal of simple agricultural life, in which every good gift is received directly from Jehovah's hand, and is supplied by Him in a plenty that testifies to His perfect reconciliation with His people (Hos. ii. 21 *seq.* ; Amos ix. 11 *seq.*; Micah iv. 4, vii. 14 ; Isa. iv. 2).

This picture is ideal. It was never literally fulfilled to Israel in Canaan, and now that the people of God has become a spiritual society dissociated from national limitations and relation to the land of Canaan, it never can be fulfilled save in a spiritual sense. The restoration of Israel to Palestine would be no fulfilment of prophecy now, for the good things of the land never had any other value to the prophets than that of an expression of Jehovah's love to the people of His choice, which is now much more clearly declared in Christ Jesus, and brought nigh to the heart by His spirit. But the ideal supplied a practical impulse. It did not provide the sketch of a new legislation which could cure the deeper ills of the state without the divine judgment which the prophets foretold, but it indicated evils that must be cleared away, and with which the old divine laws were unable to grapple.

One point, in particular, became thoroughly plain

The sacrificial worship was corrupt to the core, and could never again be purified by the mere removal of foreign elements from the local high places. The first step towards reformation must lie in the abolition of these polluted shrines, and to this task the adherents of the prophets addressed themselves.

At this point in the history the centre of interest is transferred from Ephraim to Judah. In Ephraim the sanctuaries perished with the fall of the old kingdom, or sank, if possible, to a lower depth in the worship of the mixed populations introduced by the conqueror. In Judah there was still some hope of better things. The party of reform was for a space in the ascendant under King Hezekiah, when the miraculous overthrow of the Assyrian vindicated the authority of the prophet Isaiah and justified his confident prediction that Jehovah would protect His sacred hearth on Mount Zion. But the victory was not gained in a moment. Under Manasseh a terrible reaction set in, and the corrupt popular religion crushed the prophetic party, not without bloodshed. The truth was cast down, but not overthrown. In Josiah's reign the tide of battle turned, and then it was that "the book of the Torah" was found in the Temple. Its words smote the hearts of the king and the people, for though the book had no external credentials it bore its evidence within itself, and it was stamped with the approval of the prophetess Huldah. The Torah was adopted in formal covenant, and on its lines,—the lines of the Deuteronomic Code, as we have already seen (*supra*, p. 246),—the reformation of Josiah was carried out.

The details of the process of reformation which culminated in the eighteenth year of Josiah are far from clear, but a few leading points can be established with precision. The central difference between the Deuteronomic Code, on which Josiah acted, and the old code of the First Legislation, lies in the principle that the Temple at Jerusalem is the only legitimate sanctuary. The legislator in Deuteronomy expressly puts forth this ordinance as an innovation, "Ye shall not do, as we do here this day, every man whatsoever is right in his own eyes" (Deut. xii. 8). Moreover, it is explained that the law which confines sacrifice to one altar involves modifications of ancient usage. If the land of Israel becomes so large that the sanctuary is not easily accessible, bullocks and sheep may be eaten at home, as game is eaten, without being sacrificed, the blood only being poured on the ground. We have already seen that the earlier custom here presupposed, on which every feast of beef or mutton was sacrificial, obtained long after the settlement of Israel in Canaan, on the basis of the principle of many altars laid down in Exod. xx. 24, and presupposed in the First Legislation. But further, the book of Deuteronomy, which reproduces almost every precept of the older code, with or without modification, remodels the ordinances which presuppose a plurality of sanctuaries. According to Exod. xxii. 30, the firstlings are to be offered on the eighth day. This is impracticable under the law of one altar; and so in Deut. xv. 19 *seq.* it is appointed that they shall be eaten year by year at the sanctuary, and that meantime no work shall be done with the firstling bullock, and that a firstling sheep shall not be shorn. Again, the asylum for the manslayer in Exod. xxi. 12-14 is Jehovah's altar, and so, in fact, the altar was used in the time of David and Solomon. But under the law of Deuteronomy there are to be three fixed cities of refuge (Deut. xix. 1 *seq.*).

The law, then, is quite distinctly a law for the abolition of the local sanctuaries, as they are recognised by the First Legislation, and had been frequented under it without offence during many centuries in the land of Canaan. The reason for the change of law comes out in Deut. xii. 2 *seq.* The one sanctuary is ordained to prevent assimilation between Jehovah-worship and the Canaanite service. The Israelites in the eighth century did service on the hill-tops and under the green trees (Hos. iv. 13; Isa. i. 29), and in these local sanctuaries practically merged their Jehovah-worship in the abominations of the heathen. The Deuteronomic law designs to make such "syncretism" henceforth impossible by separating the sanctuary of Jehovah from all heathen shrines. And so, in particular, the old marks of a sanctuary, the *maççēba* and *ashēra* (*supra*, p. 226), which had been used by the patriarchs, and continued to exist in sanctuaries of Jehovah down to the eighth century, are declared illegitimate (Deut. xvi. 21; Josh.

xxiv. 26; 1 Sam. vi. 14, vii. 12; 2 Sam. xx. 8; 1 Kings i. 9; Hosea iii. 4; 1 Kings vii. 21). This detail is one of the clearest proofs that Deuteronomy was unknown till long after the days of Moses. How could Joshua, if he had known such a law, have erected a *maççēba* or sacred pillar of unhewn stone under the sacred tree by the sanctuary at Shechem? Nay, this law was still unknown to Isaiah, who attacks idolatry, but recognises *maççēba* and altar as the marks of the sanctuary of Jehovah. "In that day," he says, prophesying the conversion of Egypt, "there shall be an altar to Jehovah within the land of Egypt, and a *maççēba* at the border thereof to Jehovah" (Isa. xix. 19). Isaiah could not refer to a forbidden symbol as a *maççēba* to Jehovah. He takes it for granted that Egypt, when converted, will serve Jehovah by sacrifice (ver. 21), and do so under the familiar forms which Jehovah has not yet abrogated.

This passage gives us a superior limit for the date of the Deuteronomic Code. It was not known to Isaiah, and therefore the reforms of Hezekiah cannot have been based upon it. Indeed the prophets of the eighth century, approaching the problem of true worship, not from the legal and practical side, but from the religious principles involved, never get so far as to indicate a detailed plan for the reorganisation of the sanctuaries. Micah proclaims God's wrath against the *maççēbas* and *ashēras;* but they perish in the general fall of the cities of Judah with all their corrupt civilisation

(Micah v. 10 *seq.*). Even Jerusalem and the Temple of Zion must share the general fate (chap. iii. 12). Such a prediction offers no occasion for a plan of reformed worship. In the prophecies of Isaiah again, where the *maççēba* is still recognised as legitimate, the idols of the Judæan sanctuaries are viewed as the chief element in the nation's rebellion, and the mark of repentance is to cast them away (Isa. xxx. 22, xxxi. 6 *seq.*, ii. 7, 20). It does not seem impossible that Isaiah would have been content with this reform, for he never proclaims war against the local sanctuaries as he does against their idols. He perceives indeed that not only the idols but the altars come between Israel and Jehovah, and lead the people to look to the work of their own hands instead of to their Maker (Isa. xvii. 7 *seq.*). Yet even here the contrast is not between one altar and many, but between the material and man-made sanctuary and the Holy One of Israel. The prophetic thought seems to hesitate on the verge of transition to the spiritual worship of the New Covenant. But the time was not yet ripe for so decisive a change.

To Isaiah, Jehovah's presence with His people is still a local thing. It could not, indeed, be otherwise, for the people of Jehovah was itself a conception geographically defined, bound up with the land of Canaan, and having its centre in Jerusalem. In the crisis of the Assyrian wars, the fundamental religious thought that Jehovah's gracious purpose, and therefore Jehovah's people, are indestructible, took in Isaiah's mind the

definite form of an assurance that Jerusalem could not
fall before the enemy. "Jehovah hath founded Zion,
and the poor of his people shall trust in it" (Isa.
xiv. 32). Jehovah, who hath his fire in Zion, and his
furnace in Jerusalem, will protect his holy mountain,
hovering over it as birds over their nest (Isa. xxxi. 5, 9).
Zion is the inviolable seat of Jehovah's sovereignty,
where He dwells as a devouring fire, purging the sin of
His people by consuming judgment, but also asserting
His majesty against all invaders (Isa. xxxiii. 13 *seq.*,
iv. 4 *seq.*). This conception is nowhere specially connected with the Temple. Rather is it the whole plateau
of Zion (chap. iv. 5) which is the seat of Jehovah's presence with His people. But, according to the whole
manner of thought in the Old Testament, the seat of
Jehovah's presence to Israel, the centre from which His
Torah goes forth (Isa. ii. 3), the mountain of Jehovah
and Jehovah's house (Isa. xxx. 29, ii. 2), the hearth of
God (*Ariel*, Isa. xxix. 1), the place of solemn and festal
assembly (Isa. iv. 5, xxxiii. 20), must be the place of
acceptable sacrifice, if sacrifice is to continue at all.
Isaiah, perhaps, was not concerned to draw this inference. His thoughts were rather full of the spiritual
side of Jehovah's presence to His people, the word of
revelation guiding their path (xxx. 20, 21), the privilege
of dwelling unharmed in the fire of Jehovah's presence,
and seeing the King in His glory, which belongs to the
man that walketh in righteousness, and speaketh up-
right words; who despiseth the gain of oppression,

shaking his hands from the holding of bribes, stopping his ears from the hearing of blood, and shutting his eyes from looking on evil (xxxiii. 14 *seq.*). But a practical scheme of reformation, resting on these premisses, and deriving courage from the fulfilment of Isaiah's promise of deliverance, could hardly fail to aim at the unification of worship in Jerusalem. Hezekiah may at first have sought only to purge the sanctuaries of idols. But the whole worship of these shrines was bound up with their idolatrous practices, while the Temple on Zion, the sanctuary of the ark, might well be purged of heathenish corruptions, and still retain in this ancient Mosaic symbol a mark of Jehovah's presence palpable enough to draw the homage even of the masses who had no ears for the lofty teaching of Isaiah. The history informs us that Hezekiah actually worked in this direction. We cannot tell the measure of his success, for what he effected was presently undone by Manasseh; but, at least, it was under him that the problem first took practical shape.

It is very noteworthy, and, on the traditional view, quite inexplicable, that the Mosaic sanctuary of the ark is never mentioned in the Deuteronomic Code. The author of this law occupies the standpoint of Isaiah, to whom the whole plateau of Zion is holy; or of Jeremiah; who forbids men to search for the ark or remake it, because Jerusalem is the throne of Jehovah (Jer. iii. 16, 17). But he formulates Isaiah's doctrine in the line of Hezekiah's practical essay to suppress the high places, and he develops a scheme for fuller and effective execution of this object with a precision of detail that shows a clear sense of the practical difficulties of the undertaking. It was no light thing to overturn the whole popular worship of Judah. It is highly probable that Hezekiah failed to produce a permanent result because he had not duly provided for the practical difficulties to which his scheme would give rise. The Deuteronomic Code has realised these difficulties, and meets the most serious of them by the modifications of the old law already discussed, and by making special provision for the priests of the suppressed shrines.

The First Legislation has no law of priesthood, no provision as to priestly dues. The permission of many altars, which it presupposes, is given in Exodus xx. 24-26 in a form that assumes the right of laymen to offer sacrifice,[1] as we actually find them doing in so many parts of the history (*supra*, p. 264). Yet a closer observation shows that the old law presupposes a priesthood, whose business lies less with sacrifice than with the divine Torah which they administer in the sanctuary as successors of Moses. For the sanctuary is the seat of judgment (*supra*, p. 334), and this implies a qualified *personnel* through whom judgment is given. According to the unanimous testimony of all the older records of the Old Testament, this priesthood, charged with the Torah administered at the sanctuary, is none other than the house of Levi, the kinsmen or descendants of Moses, who already in his time were the bodyguard of the ark, and so the guardians of the sanctuary at which he dispensed Divine judgments. (See especially Deuteronomy xxxiii. 8; 1 Samuel ii. 27 *seq.*). The history of the Levites after the Conquest is veiled in much obscurity. The principal branch of the family, which remained with the ark, is known to us as the house of Eli, which lost its supremacy in fulfilment of the prophecy in 1 Samuel ii., when Solomon deposed Abiathar and set Zadok in his place (1 Kings ii. 26, 27). According to the prophecy just alluded to, Zadok did not belong to the priestly family originally chosen by Jehovah, but he was the head of a body of Levites (2 Samuel xv. 24). Another Levitical family which claimed direct descent from Moses held the priesthood of the sanctuary of Dan, and in the later times of the kingdom all the priests of local sanctuaries were viewed as Levites. Whether this implies that they were all lineal descendants of the old house of Levi may well be doubted. But in early times guilds are hereditary bodies, modified by a right of adoption, and it was understood that the priesthood ran in the family to which Moses belonged. In the time of Ezekiel the Jerusalem priesthood consisted of the Levites of the guild of Zadok. The subordinate ministers of the Temple were not Levites, but, as we have already seen, the foreign janissaries, and presumably other foreign slaves, the progenitors of the *Nethînîm*, who appear in the list of returning exiles in Ezra ii. with names for the most part not Israelite. The Levites who are not Zadokites are by Ezekiel expressly identified with the priests of the high places (Ezek. xliv. 9 *seq.*; *supra*, p. 249 and *note*). These historical facts—for they are no conjecture, but the express testimony of the sacred record—are presupposed in the Code of Deuteronomy. The priests, according to Deuteronomy xxi. 5, are the sons of Levi; "for them hath Jehovah thy God chosen to minister to him and to bless in his name, and according to their decision is every controversy and every stroke." Deuteronomy knows no Levites who cannot be priests, and no priests who are not Levites. The two ideas are absolutely identical. But these Levites, who are priests of Jehovah's own appointment, were, in the period when the code was composed, scattered through the land as priests of the local sanctuaries. They had no territorial possessions (Deut. xviii. 1), and were viewed as Gêrîm, or strangers under the protection of the community in the places where they sojourned (verse 6). Apart from the revenues of the sanctuary, their position was altogether dependent (xiv. 27, 29, etc.).[2]

In the abolition of the local sanctuaries it was necessary to make provision for these Levites. And this the new code does in two ways: it provides, in the first place, that any Levite from the provinces who chooses to come up to Jerusalem shall be admitted to equal privileges with his brethren the Levites who stand there before Jehovah—not to the privilege of a servant in the sanctuary, but to the full priesthood, as is expressly conveyed by the terms used. Thus ministering, he receives for his support an equal share of the priestly dues paid in kind (Deut. xviii. 6 *seq.*). Those Levites, on the other hand, who remain dispersed through the provinces receive no emolument from the sanctuary, and, having no property in land (xviii. 1), have a far from enviable lot, which the legislator seeks to mitigate by recommending them in a special manner, along with the widow and the orphan, to the charity of the landed classes under whose protection they dwell (xii. 12, 18; xiv. 27, 29; xvi. 11, 14; xxvi. 11 *seq.*). The method of such charity is to some extent defined. Once in three years every farmer is called upon to store up a tithe of the produce of his land, which he retains in his own hands, but must dispense to the dependents or Levites who come and ask a meal. The legislator, it is plain, aims at something like a voluntary poor-rate. The condition of the landless class, with whose sufferings the prophets are so often exercised, had become a social problem, owing to the increase of large estates and other causes (Isa. v. 8; Micah ii.), and demands a remedy; but it is not proposed to enforce the assessment through the executive. The matter is left to every man's conscience as a religious duty, of which he is called to give account before Jehovah in the sanctuary (xxvi. 12 *seq.*). And the bond between charity and religion is drawn still closer by the provision that the well-to-do landholder, when he comes up to the sanctuary to make merry before God, feasting on the firstlings, tithes, etc., must bring with him his dependents and the Levite who is within his gates, that they too may have their part in the occasions of religious joy. This law of charity appears to supersede the old rule of leaving the produce of every field to the poor one year in seven, which is obviously a more primitive and less practical arrangement. In place of this, the Deuteronomic Code requires that, at the close of every seven years, there shall be a release of Hebrew debtors by their creditors (xv. 1 *seq.*).

I return to the Levites, in order to point out that the comparison of Deut. xviii. with 2 Kings xxiii. 8 *seq.* effectually disproves the idea of some critics that the Deuteronomic Code was a forgery of the temple priests, or of their head, the high priest Hilkiah. The proposal to give the Levites of the provinces—that is, the priests of the local sanctuaries—equal priestly rights at Jerusalem could not commend itself to the temple hierarchy. And in this point Josiah was not able to carry out the ordinances of the book. The priests who were brought up to Jerusalem received support from the temple dues, but were not permitted to minister at the altar. This proves that the code did not emanate from Hilkiah and the Zadokite priests, whose class interests were strong enough to frustrate the law which, on the theory of a forgery, was their own work.

Whence, then, did the book derive the authority which made its discovery the signal for so great a reformation? How did it approve itself as an expression of the Divine will, first to Hilkiah and Josiah, and then to the whole nation? To this question there can be but one answer. The authority that lay behind Deuteronomy was the power of the prophetic teaching which half a century of persecution had not been able to suppress. After the work of Isaiah and his fellows, it was impossible for any earnest movement of reformation to adopt other principles than those of the prophetic word on which Jehovah Himself had set His seal by the deliverance from Assyria. What the Deuteronomic code supplied was a clear and practical scheme of reformation on the prophetic lines. It showed that it was possible to adjust the old religious constitution in conformity with present needs, and this was enough to kindle into new flame the slumbering fire of the word of the prophets. The book became the programme of Josiah's reformation, because it gathered up in practical form the results of the great movement under Hezekiah and Isaiah, and the new divine teaching then given to Israel. It was of no consequence to Josiah—it is of equally little consequence to us—to know the exact date and authorship of the book. Its prophetic doctrine, and the practical character of the scheme which it set forth—in which the new teaching and the old Torah were fused into an intelligible unity —were enough to commend it.

The law of the one sanctuary, which is aimed against assimilation of Jehovah-worship to the religion of

Canaan, and seeks entirely to separate the people from the worship of Canaanite shrines, is only one expression of a thought common to the prophets, that the unique religion of Jehovah was in constant danger from intercourse between Israel and the nations. Isaiah complains that the people were always ready to "strike hands with the children of strangers," and recognises a chief danger to faith in the policy of the nobles, who were dazzled with the splendour and courted the alliance of the great empires on the Nile and the Tigris (Isa. ii. 6, xxx. 1 *seq.*; compare Hosea vii. 8, viii. 9, xiv. 3). The vocation of Israel as Jehovah's people has no points of contact with the aims and political combinations of the surrounding nations, and Micah looks forward to a time when Israel shall be like a flock feeding in solitude in the woods of Bashan or Carmel. Isaiah expresses this unique destiny of Israel in the word *holiness*. Jehovah is the Holy One of Israel, and conversely His true people are a holy seed. The notion of holiness is primarily connected with the sanctuary and acts of worship. The old Israelite *consecrated himself* before a sacrifice. In the First Legislation the notion of Israel's holiness appears only in the law against eating flesh torn in the field, of which the blood had not been duly offered to God on His altar. But Isaiah raises the notion beyond the sphere of ritual, and places Israel's holiness in direct relation to the personal presence of Jehovah on Zion in the centre of His people as their living Sanctuary, whose glory fills all the earth (Isa.

vi. 3, iv. 3 *seq.*). The Code of Deuteronomy appropriates this principle; but in its character of a law, seeking definite practical expression for religious principles, it develops the idea of unique holiness and separation from the profane nations in prohibitive ordinances. The essential object of the short law of the kingdom (xvii. 14 *seq.*) is to guard against admixture with foreigners and participation in foreign policy. Other precepts regulate contact with the adjoining nations (xxiii. 3 *seq.*), and a vast number of statutes are directed against the immoralities of Canaanite nature-worship, which, as we know from the prophets and the books of Kings, had deeply tainted the service of Jehovah. Not a few details, which to the modern eye seem trivial or irrational, disclose to the student of Semitic antiquity an energetic protest against the moral grossness of Canaanite heathenism. These precepts give the law a certain air of ritual formalism, but the formalism lies only on the surface, and there is a moral idea below. The ceremonial observances of Deuteronomy are inversions of heathen usages. A good example lies in the list of forbidden foods. We know as a fact that some of the unclean animals were sacramentally eaten in certain heathen rituals (Isa. lxvi. 17, lxv. 4, lxvi. 3), and in general the rules as to eating and not eating certain animals among the heathen Semites, as in other primitive nations, were directly connected with the worship of animal deities, the totems of certain races or families. The worship of unclean animals is mentioned in Ezekiel

viii. 10, 11, in a form that indicates the existence of family totems within Israel; and it is impossible to doubt that the laws of clean and unclean beasts are aimed at heathen usages connected with this worship. Just so our own prejudice against the use of horse flesh is a relic of an old ecclesiastical prohibition framed at the time when the eating of such food was an act of worship to Odin.[8]

This constant polemical reference to Canaanite worship and Canaanite morality gives to the element of ritual and forms of worship a much larger place in Deuteronomy than these things hold in the First Legislation. In points of civil order the new law still moves on the old lines. Its object is not legislative innovation, but to bring the old consuetudinary law into relation to the fundamental principle that Jehovah is Israel's Lawgiver, and that all social order exists under His sanction.

Thus we still find some details which bear the stamp of primeval Semitic culture. In chap. xxi. 10 *seq.* we have marriage by capture as it was practised by the Arabs before Mohammed, and even the detail as to the paring of the nails of the captive before marriage is identical with one of the old Arabic methods of breaking widowhood.

But in general we see that the civil laws of Deuteronomy belong to a later stage of society than the First Legislation. For example, the law of retaliation, which has so large a range in the First Legislation, is limited in Deut. xix. 16 *seq.* to the case of false witness. And with this goes the introduction of a new punishment, which, in the old law, was confined to slaves. A man who injures another may be brought before the judge and sentenced to the bastinado (xxv. 1 *seq.*). The introduction of this degrading punishment in the case of freemen indicates a change in social feeling. Among the Bedouins no sheikh would dare to flog a man, for he would thereby bring himself under the law of retaliation; and so it was in Israel in the old time. But Eastern kingship breaks down this sense of personal independence, while, at the same time, it modifies the strict law of revenge. In general, the executive system of Deuteronomy is more advanced. The sanctuary is still the highest seat of law, but the priest is now associated with a supreme civil judge (xvii. 9, 12), who seems to be identical with the king; and even the subordinate judges are not merely the natural sheikhs, or elders of the local communities, but include officers appointed with national authority (xvi. 18). Again, the law of manumission undergoes an important modification. On the old law a father could sell his daughter as a slave, and the bondwoman was absolute property; the master could wed her to one of his servants, and retain her when the servant left. In Deuteronomy all this has disappeared, and a Hebrew woman has a right to manumission after seven years, like a man (xv. 12, 17). A similar advance in woman's rights appears in the change on the law of seduction. By the old law this case was

treated as one of pecuniary loss to the father, who mus
be compensated by the seducer purchasing the damsel as
wife for the full price (*móhar*) of a virgin. In Deuteronomy the law is removed from among the laws of property to laws of moral purity, and the payment of full
móhar is changed to a fixed fine (Exod. xxii. 16, 17;
Deut. xxii. 28 *seq.*).

In other cases the new code softens the rudeness of
ancient custom. In Arabic warfare the destruction of
an enemy's palm-groves is a favourite exploit, and fertile
lands are thus often reduced to desert. In 2 Kings
iii. 19 we find that the same practice was enjoined on
Israel by the prophet Elisha in war with Moab; every
good tree was to be cut down. But Deut. xx. 19 *seq.*
forbids this barbarous destruction of fruit-trees. Still
more remarkable is the law of Deut. xxii. 30. It was a
custom among many of the ancient Arabs that a man
took possession of his father's wives along with the property (his own mother, of course, excepted). The only
law of forbidden degrees in the Deuteronomic Code is
directed against this practice, which Ezekiel xxii. 10
mentions as still current in Jerusalem. But in early
times such marriages were made without offence. The
Israelites understood Absalom's appropriation of David's
secondary wives as a formal way of declaring that his
father was dead to him, and that he served himself his
heir (2 Sam. xvi.); and when Adonijah asked the hand
of Abishag, Solomon understood him as claiming the
inheritance (1 Kings ii.). The same custom explains

the anger of Ishbosheth at Abner (2 Sam. iii. 7). The new code, you perceive, marks a growth in morality and refinement; it is still no ideal law fit for all time, but a practical code largely incorporating elements of actual custom. But the growth of custom and usage is on the whole upward, and ancient social usages which survived for many centuries after the age of Josiah among the heathen of Arabia and Syria already lie behind the Deuteronomic Code. With all the hardness of Israel's heart, the religion of Jehovah had proved itself in its influence on the nation a better religion than that of the Baalim.[4]

From Josiah's covenant to the fall of the Jewish state the Code of Deuteronomy had but a generation to run. Even in this short time it appeared that the reformation had not accomplished its task, and that the introduction of the written law was not enough to avert the judgment which the prophets had declared inevitable for the purification of the nation. The crusade against the high places was most permanent in its results. In the time of Jeremiah popular superstition clung to the Temple as it had formerly clung to the high places, and in the Temple the populace and the false prophets found the pledge that Jehovah could never forsake His nation. This fact is easily understood. The prophetic ideas of Isaiah, which were the real spring of the Deuteronomic reformation, had never been spiritually grasped by the mass of the people, though the *éclat* attending the overthrow of Sennacherib had given them a certain currency. The conception of Jehovah's throne on Zion was materialised in the Temple, and the moral conditions of acceptance with the King of Zion, on which Isaiah laid so much weight, were forgotten. Jehovah received ritual homage in lieu of moral obedience; and Jeremiah has again occasion to declare that the latter alone is the positive content of the divine Torah, and that a law of sacrifice is no part of the original covenant with Israel. In speaking thus the prophet does not separate himself from the Deuteronomic law; for the moral precepts of that code —as, for example, the Deuteronomic form of the law of manumission (Jer. xxxiv. 13-16)—he accepts as part of the covenant of the Exodus. To Jeremiah therefore the Code of Deuteronomy does not appear in the light of a positive law of sacrifice; and this judgment is undoubtedly correct. The ritual details of Deuteronomy are directed against heathen worship; they are negative, not positive. In the matter of sacrifice and festal observances the new code simply diverts the old homage of Israel from the local sanctuaries to the central shrine, and all material offerings are summed up under the principles of gladness before Jehovah at the great agricultural feasts, and of homage paid to Him in acknowledgment that the good things of the land of Canaan are His gift (xxvi. 10). The firstlings and the first-fruits and tithes remain on their old footing as natural expressions of devotion, which did not begin with the Exodus and are not peculiar to Israel. Even the festal sacrifices retain the character of "a voluntary tribute" (Deut. xvi. 10), and the paschal victim itself may be chosen indifferently from the flock or the herd (xvi. 2), and is still, according to the Hebrew of xvi. 7, presumed to be boiled, not roasted, as is the case in all old sacrifices of which the history speaks. Deuteronomy knows nothing of a sacrificial priestly Torah, though it refers the people to the Torah of the priests on the subject of leprosy (xxiv. 8), and acknowledges their authority as judges in lawsuits. In the Deuteronomic Code the idea of sin is never connected with matters of ritual. A sin means a crime, an offence to law and justice (xix. 15, xxi. 22, xxii. 26, xxiv. 16), an act of heathenism (xx. 18), a breach of faith towards Jehovah (xxiii. 21, 22), or a lack of kindliness to the poor (xxiv. 15). And such offences are expiated, not by sacrifice, but by punishment at the hand of man or God. This moral side of the law, which exactly corresponds to prophetic teaching, continued to be neglected in Judah. Oppression, bloodshed, impurity, idolatry, filled the land; and for these things Jeremiah threatens a judgment, which the Temple and its ritual can do nothing to avert (Jer. vii.).

In all this Deuteronomy and Jeremiah alike still stand outside the priestly Torah. As far as Deuteronomy goes, this is usually explained by saying that it is a law for the people, and does not take up points of ritual which specially belonged to the priests. But the code, which refers to the priestly law of leprosy, says nothing of ordinances of ritual atonement and stated sacrifice, and Jeremiah denies in express terms that a law of sacrifice forms any part of the divine commands to Israel. The priestly and prophetic Torahs are not yet absorbed into one divine system.

Nevertheless there can be no doubt that there was at this time a ritual Torah in the hands of the priests, containing elements which the prophets and the old codes pass by. In the time of Ahaz there was a daily burnt offering in the morning, a stated meat offering in the evening (2 Kings xvi. 15). There was also an atoning ritual. In the time of Jehoash the atonements paid to the priests were pecuniary—a common enough thing in ancient times. But atoning sacrifice was also of ancient standing. It occurs in 1 Sam. iii. 14,—" The guilt of the house of Eli shall not be wiped out by sacrifice or oblation for ever." The idea of atonement in the sacrificial blood must be very ancient, and a trace of it is found even in the book of Deuteronomy in the curious ordinance which provides for the atonement (wiping out) of the blood of untraced homicide by the slaughter of a heifer. Along with these things we find ancient ordinances of ceremonial holiness in the sanctuary at Nob (1 Sam. xxi. 4), and all this necessarily supposes a ritual law, the property of the priests. Only, we have already seen that the details still preserved to us of the temple ritual are not identical with the full Levitical system. They contained many germs of that system, but they also contained much that was radically different. And in particular the Temple worship itself was not stringently differentiated from everything heathenish, as appears with the utmost clearness in the admission of uncircumcised foreigners to certain ministerial functions, in the easy way in which Isaiah's friend Urijah accepted the foreign innovations of King Ahaz, and in the fact that prophets whom Jeremiah regards as heathen diviners still continued to be attached to the Temple up to the last days of the state, while worshippers from Samaria made pilgrimages to Jerusalem with heathenish ceremonies expressly forbidden in Deuteronomy as well as in Leviticus (Jer. xli. 5 ; Lev. xix. 27, 28; Deut. xiv. i; Isa. xv. 2). We see, then, that even Josiah's reformation left many things in the Temple which savoured of heathenism, and the presence of the priests of the high places was little calculated to improve the spirituality of the observances of Jehovah's house. In all this there was a manifest danger to true religion. If ritual and sacrifice were to continue at all, it was highly desirable that some order should be taken with the priestly ritual, and an attempt made to reorganise it in conformity with the prophetic conception of Jehovah's moral holiness. But no effort to complete Josiah's work in this direction seems to have been made in the last troublous years of Jerusalem. On the contrary, Ezekiel describes the grossest heathenism as practised at the Temple, doubtless not without the countenance of the priests (Ezek. viii.).

The Temple and its worship fell with the destruction of the city. Fourteen years later, Ezekiel, dwelling in captivity, had a vision of a new Temple, a place of worship for repentant Israel, and heard a voice commanding him to lay before the people a pattern of remodelled worship. "If they be ashamed of all that they have done, show them the form of the house . . . and all its ordinances, and all the Torahs thereof: and write them before them that they may keep all the form thereof, and all the ordinances thereof, and do them" (Ezek. xliii. 10, 11).

A great mystery has been made of this law of Ezekiel, but the prophet himself makes none. He says in the clearest words that the revelation is a sketch of ritual for the period of restoration, and again and again he places his new ordinances in contrast with the actual corrupt usage of the First Temple (xliii. 7, xliv. 5, *seq.*, xlv. 8, 9). He makes no appeal to a previous law of ritual. The whole scheme of a written law of the house is new, and so Ezekiel only confirms Jeremiah, who knew no divine law of sacrifice under the First Temple. It is needless to rehearse more than the chief points of Ezekiel's legislation. The first that strikes us is the degradation of the Levites. The ministers of the old Temple, he tells us, were uncircumcised foreigners, whose presence was an insult to Jehovah's sanctuary. Such men shall no more enter the house, but in their place shall come the Levites not of the house of Zadok, who are to be degraded from the priesthood because they officiated in old Israel before the idolatrous shrines (xliv. 5 *seq.*). This one point is sufficient to fix the date of the Levitical law as later than Ezekiel. In all the earlier history, and in the Code of Deuteronomy, a Levite is a priest, or at least qualified to assume priestly functions; and even in Josiah's reformation the Levite priests of the high places received a modified priestly status at Jerusalem. Ezekiel knows that it has been so in the past; but he declares that it shall be otherwise in the future, as a punishment for the offence of ministering at the idolatrous altars. He knows nothing of an earlier law, in which priests and Levites are already distinguished, in which the office of Levite is itself a high privilege (Num. xvi. 9).

A second point in Ezekiel's law is a provision for stated and regular sacrifices. These sacrifices are to be provided by the prince, who in turn is to receive from the people no arbitrary tax, but a fixed tribute in kind upon all agricultural produce and flocks. Here again we see a reference to pre-Exilic practice, when the Temple was essentially the king's sanctuary, and the stated offerings were his gift. In the old codes the people at large are under no obligation to do stated sacrifice. That was the king's voluntary offering, and so it was at first after the Exile. The early decrees of Persian monarchs in favour of the Jews provide for regular sacrifice at the king's expense (Ezra vi. 9, vii. 17); and only at the convocation of Nehemiah do the people agree to defray the stated offering by a voluntary charge of a third of a shekel (Neh. x. 32). It is disputed whether, in Exod. xxx. 16, "the service of the tabernacle," defrayed by the fixed tribute of half a shekel, refers to the continual sacrifices. If it does so, this law was still unknown to Nehemiah, and must be a late addition to the Pentateuch. If it does not, it is still impossible that the Levitical ordinance of stated offerings could have preceded the existence of a provision for supplying them. Again we are brought back to Jeremiah's words. The stated sacrifices were not prescribed in the wilderness.

A third point in Ezekiel's law is the prominence given to the sin offering and atoning ritual. The altar must be purged with sin offerings for seven consecutive days before burnt sacrifices are acceptably offered on it (xliii. 18 *seq.*). The Levitical law (Exod. xxix. 36, 37) prescribes a similar ceremony, but with more costly victims. At the dedication of Solomon's Temple, on the contrary (1 Kings viii. 62), the altar is at once assumed to be fit for use, in accordance with Exod. xx. 24, and with all the early cases of altar building outside the Pentateuch. But, besides this first expiatory ceremonial, Ezekiel appoints two atoning services yearly, at the beginning of the first and the seventh month (xlv. 19, 20, LXX.), to purge the house. This is the first appearance, outside of the Levitical code, of anything corresponding to the great day of atonement in the seventh month, and it is plain that the simple service in Ezekiel is still far short of that solemn ceremony.

The day of atonement was also a fast day. Now, in Zech. vii. 5, viii. 19, the fast of the seventh month is alluded to as one of the four fasts commemorating the destruction of Jerusalem, which had been practised for the last seventy years. The fast of the seventh month was not yet united with the "purging of the house" ordained by Ezekiel. Even in the great convocation of Neh. viii.-x., where we have a record of proceedings from the first day of the seventh month onwards to the twenty-fourth, there is no mention of the day of expiation on the tenth, which thus appears as the very last stone in the ritual edifice.

I pass over other features of Ezekiel's legislation. The detailed proof that in every point Ezekiel's Torah prepares the way for the Levitical law but represents a more elementary ritual may be read in the text itself with the aid of Smend's Commentary. The whole scheme presents itself with absolute clearness as a first sketch of a written priestly Torah, resting not on the law of Moses but on old priestly usage, and reshaped so as to bring the ordinances of the house into due conformity with the holiness of Jehovah in the sense of the prophets and the Deuteronomic Code. The thought that underlies Ezekiel's code is clearly brought out in xliii. 7 *seq*. To Ezekiel, who is himself a priest, the whoredom of Israel, their foul departure from Jehovah after filthy idols, appears in a peculiarly painful light in connection with the service of the sanctuary, the throne of Jehovah, the place of the soles of His feet, where He dwells in the midst of Israel for ever. In time past the people of Israel have defiled Jehovah's name by their abominations, and for this they have suffered His wrath. The new law is a gift to the people on their repentance —a scheme to protect them from again falling into like sins. The spontaneous unregulated character of the old service gave room for the introduction of heathen abominations. The new service shall be reduced to a divine rule, leaving no door for what is unholy. But so long as worship takes place with material ceremonies in an earthly sanctuary, the idea of holiness cannot be divested of a material element. From the earliest times the holiness of God's worship had regard to provisions of physical purity, especially to lustrations and principles of cleanness and uncleanness, which in their origin sprang from natural feelings of propriety, but gradually became more complex, as we find them in Deuteronomy, from the desire to exclude all that savoured of heathen grossness. From the priestly point of view, material and moral observances of sanctity run into one. Ezekiel finds equal fault with idolatry in the Temple and with the profanation of its plateau by the sepulchres of the kings (xliii. 7). And so his ritual, though its fundamental idea is moral, branches out into a variety of ordinances which, from our modern point of view, seem merely formal, but which were yet inevitable unless the principle of sacrifice and an earthly sanctuary was to be altogether superseded. If the material sanctuary was to be preserved at all, the symbolic observances of its holiness must be made stringent, and to this end the new ordinance of the Levites and Ezekiel's other provisions were altogether suitable.[1]

In proportion, now, as the whole theory of worship is remodelled and reduced to rule on the scheme of an exclusive sanctity, which presents, so to speak, an armed front to every abomination of impure heathenism, the ritual becomes abstract, and the services remote from ordinary life. In the old worship all was spontaneous. It was as natural for an Israelite to worship Jehovah, as for a Moabite to worship Chemosh. To worship God was a holiday, an occasion of feasting. Religion, in its sacrificial form, was a part of common life, which no one deemed it necessary to reduce to rule. Even in Deuteronomy this view predominates. The sacrificial feasts are still the consecration of natural occasions of joy; men eat, drink, and make merry before God. The sense of God's favour, not the sense of sin, is what rules at the sanctuary. But the unification of the sanctuary already tended to break up this old type of religion. Worship ceased to be an everyday thing, and so it ceased to be the expression of everyday religion. In Ezekiel this change has produced its natural result in a change of the whole standpoint from which he views the service of the Temple. The offerings of individuals are no longer the chief reason for which the Temple exists. All weight lies on the stated service, which the prince provides out of national funds, and which is, as it were, the representative service of

Israel. The individual Israelite who, in the old law, stood at the altar himself and brought his own victim, is now separated from it, not only by the double cordon of priests and Levites, but by the fact that his personal offering is thrown into the background by the stated national sacrifice.

The whole tendency of this is to make personal religion more and more independent of offerings. The emotion with which the worshipper approaches the Second Temple, as recorded in the Psalter, has little to do with sacrifice, but rests rather on the fact that the whole wondrous history of Jehovah's grace to Israel is vividly and personally realised as he stands amidst the festal crowd at the ancient seat of God's throne, and adds his voice to the swelling song of praise. The daily religion of the Restoration found new forms. The Scriptures, the synagogue, the practice of prayer elsewhere than before the altar, were all independent of the old idea of worship, and naturally prepared the way for the New Testament. The narrowing of the privilege of access to God at the altar would have been a retrograde step if altar-worship had still remained the form of all religion. But this was not so, and therefore the new ritual was a practical means of separating personal religion from forms destined soon to pass away. The very features of the Levitical ordinances which seem most inconsistent with spirituality, if we place them in the days of Moses, when all religion took shape before the altar, appear in a very different light in the age after the Exile, when the non-ritual religion of the prophets went side by side with the Law, and supplied daily nourishment to the spiritual life of those who were far from the sanctuary.

With all this there went another change not less important in the way of preparation for the work of our Lord. In the old ritual, sacrifice and offering were essentially an expression of homage, and the element of atonement held a very subsidiary place. But the idea of sacrificial homage lost great part of its force when the sacrifices of the sanctuary were so much divorced from individual life, and became a sort of abstract representative worship. In Ezekiel, and still more in the Levitical legislation, the element of atonement takes a foremost place. The sense of sin had grown deeper under the teaching of the prophets, and amidst the proofs of Jehovah's anger that darkened the last days of the Jewish state. Sin and forgiveness were the main themes of prophetic discourse. The problem of acceptance with God exercised every thoughtful mind, as we see not only from the Psalms and the prophets of the Exile and Restoration, but above all from the book of Job, which is certainly later than the time of Jeremiah. The acceptance of the worship of the sanctuary had always been regarded as the visible sacrament of Jehovah's acceptance of the worshipper, " when He came to him and blessed him." And now more than in any former time, the first point in acceptance was felt to be the forgiveness of sin, and the weightiest element in the ritual was that which symbolised the atonement or "wiping out" of iniquity. The details of this symbolism cannot occupy us here. It is enough to indicate in one word that the ritual of atoning sacrifice was so shaped by Divine wisdom that it supplied to the New Testament a basis intelligible to the Hebrew believers for the explanation of the atoning work of Christ. Not indeed that the blood of bulls and goats ever took away sin. The true basis of forgiveness, in the Old Testament as in the New, lies, not in man's offering, but in a work of sovereign love. It is Jehovah, for His own name's sake, who blots out Israel's transgressions and will not remember his sin. But the atoning ritual ever held before the people's eyes the mysterious connection of forgiving love with awful justice, and pointed by its very inadequacy to the need, for a better atonement of Jehovah's own providing.[5]

The Levitical legislation in our present Pentateuch is the practical adaptation of these principles to the circumstances of the Second Temple, when Jerusalem was no longer the seat of a free state, but only the centre of a religious community possessing certain municipal privileges of self-government. Its distinctive features are all found in Ezekiel's Torah—the care with which the Temple and its vicinity are preserved from the approach of unclean things and persons, the corresponding institution of a class of holy ministers in the person of the Levites, the greater distance thus interposed between the people and the altar, the concentration of sacrifice in the two forms of stated representative offerings (the *tamîd*) and atoning sacrifices. In all these points, as we have seen, the usage of the Law is in distinct contrast to that of the First Temple, where the temple plateau was polluted by the royal sepulchres, where the servants of the sanctuary were uncircumcised foreigners, the stated service the affair of the king, regulated at will by him (2 Kings xvi.), and the atoning offerings essentially fines paid to the priests of the sanctuary (2 Kings xii. 16). That Ezekiel in these matters speaks, not merely as a priest recording old usage, but as a prophet ordaining new Torah with Divine authority, is his own express claim, and appears in the clearest way in the degradation of the non - Zadokite priests, which is actually carried out in the Levitical legislation, with the natural consequence that, on the return from captivity, very few Levites in comparison with the full priests cared to attach themselves to the temple (Neh. vii. 39, *seq.*).[6]

The development of the details of the system falls therefore between the time of Ezekiel and the work of Ezra; and the circumstance already referred to, that the culminating and most solemn ceremony of the great day of expiation was not observed in the year of Ezra's covenant, shows that the last touches were not added to the ritual until, through Ezra's agency, it was put into practical operation. But, while the historical student is thus compelled to speak of the ritual code as the law of the Second Temple, it would be a great mistake to think of it as altogether new. Ezekiel's ordinances are nothing else than a reshaping of the old priestly Torah, and a close study of the Levitical laws, especially in Lev. xvii.-xxvi., shows that many ancient Torahs were worked up, by successive processes, into the complete system as we now possess it. In Lev. xxiv. 19 *seq.*, for example, we find the old law of retaliation for injuries not mortal, which is already obsolete in the Deuteronomic Code. The preservation of such a Torah shows that the priests did not give up their old traditional law for the written Code of Deuteronomy. They doubtless continued till the time of Ezra to give oral Torahs, as we see from Haggai i. 11. The analogy of all early law makes this procedure quite intelligible to us. Nothing is more common than to find an antique legislation handed down in the mouth of a priestly or legal guild in certain set forms of words.

To trace out in detail how much of the Levitical legislation consists of such old Torahs handed down from time immemorial in the priestly families, and how much is new, is a task which we cannot now attempt, and which indeed has not yet been finally accomplished by scholars. The chief interest of this inquiry lies in its bearing on the early history of Israel. It is for the historian to determine how far the Levitical law is mere law, of which we can say no more than that it was law for the Second Temple, and how far it is also history which can be used in describing the original sanctuary of the ark in the days of Moses. But in following out this inquiry we cannot assume that every law which is called a law of Moses was meant to be understood as literally given in the wilderness. For it is a familiar fact that in the early law of all nations necessary modifications on old law are habitually carried out by means of what lawyers call *legal fictions*. This name is somewhat misleading; for a legal fiction is no deceit, but a convention which all parties understand. But it is found more convenient to present the new law in a form which enables it to be treated as an integral part of the old legislation. Thus in Roman jurisprudence all law was supposed to be derived from the Laws of the Twelve Tables (Maine, *Ancient Law*, p. 33 *seq.*), just as in Israel all law was held to be derived from the teaching of Moses. In neither case was any falsehood meant or conveyed. The whole object of this way of treating the law was to maintain the continuity of the legal system. But *legal fiction* has much more curious developments. In old English law many writs give a quite imaginary history of the case, alleging, for example, that the plaintiff is the king's debtor, and cannot pay his debts by reason of the default of the defendant. This instance is not directly parallel to anything in the Old Testament; but it shows how impossible it would be to explain any system of ancient law on the assumption that every statement which seems to be plain narrative of fact is actually meant to be so taken. It would be the highest presumption to affirm that what is found in all other ancient laws cannot occur in the Old

Testament. The very universality of these conventions shows that in certain stages of society they form the easiest and most intelligible way of introducing necessary modifications of law; and the Israelites had the same habits of thought with other primitive nations, and doubtless required to be taught and to think things out on the same lines. In our state of society legal fictions are out of date; in English law they have long been mere antiquarian lumber. But Israel's law was given for the practical use of an ancient people, and required to take the forms which we know as a matter of fact to be those which primitive nations best understand.

If we find, then, by actual comparison of different parts of Scripture, that some points of law and ceremony are related in historical form, as if based on Mosaic precedent, but that there is other evidence, as in the case of the march from Sinai (*supra*, p. 319), that the thing did not happen so in Moses's own time, we have not hit on a self-contradiction in the Bible, but only on a case of legal convention; for one well-known type of this is to relate a new law in the form of an ancient precedent. Let me illustrate this by an example from Sir H. Maine's *Village Communities*, p. 110. In India, when the Government brings a new water supply into a village, the village authorities make rules for its use and distribution; but "these rules do not purport to emanate from the personal authority of their author or authors; there is always a sort of fiction under which some customs as to the distribution of water are supposed to have existed from all antiquity, although, in fact, no artificial supply had been even so much as thought of." In the same way the new laws of the Levitical code are presented as ordinances of Moses, though, when they were first promulgated, every one knew that they were not so,—though Ezra himself speaks of some of them as ordinances of the prophets.

A peculiarly clear case of this occurs in the law of war. According to 1 Sam. xxx. 24, 25, the standing law of Israel as to the distribution of booty was enacted by David, and goes back only to a precedent in his war with the Amalekites who burned Ziklag. In the priestly legislation the same law is given as a Mosaic precedent from the war with Midian (Num. xxxi. 27).[7]

To the indolent theologian the necessity of distinguishing between these quasi-historical precedents, which were meant to be taken only as laws, and the actual history, which was meant to be taken literally, is naturally unwelcome; but to the diligent and reverent student it affords the key for the solution of many difficulties, and the natural removal of contradictions, which, on the current exegesis, present a constant stumblingblock to faith.

NOTES AND ILLUSTRATIONS.

LECTURE I.

NOTE 1, p. 7.—According to Origen, *Princip.*, Bk. iv. p. 173, the literal sense of Scripture is often impossible, absurd, or immoral,—and this designedly, lest, cleaving to the letter alone, men should remain at a distance from the *dogmata*, and learn nothing worthy of God. Augustine in his hermeneutical treatise, *De Doctrina Christiana* (Bk. iii. c. 10), teaches that "Whatever has no proper bearing on the rule of life or the verity of faith must be recognised as figurative." A good example of the practical application of these principles will be found in the preface to Jerome's Commentary on Hosea.

NOTE 2, p. 13.—See, in particular, the first part of the *Freiheit eines Christenmenschen*, and the preface to Luther's German Bible. On Tetzel see *Freiheit des Sermons vom Ablass* (*Werke*, ed. Irmischer, vol. xxvii. p. 13). Compare Calvin's *Institutio*, Bk. iii. chap. 2—" The Word itself, however it be conveyed to us, is like a mirror in which faith beholds God."

NOTE 3, p. 17.—The Old Testament writers possessed Hebrew sources now lost, such as the Book of the Wars of the Lord, the Book of Jashar, and the Annals of the Kings of Israel and Judah. But Josephus, and other profane historians whose writings are still extant, had no authentic Hebrew sources for the canonical history, except those preserved in the Bible.

Within the last few years the decipherment of the monuments of Assyria and Babylonia has supplied contemporary evidence as to the relations of the Hebrews with Eastern powers; not merely elucidating perplexed points in the historical books, such as the chronology of the Books of Kings and the political relations of the Northern Kingdom under the dynasty of Jehu, but throwing most important light on the historical basis of the new prophecy of the eighth century B.C. The recently published Inscriptions of Cyrus (*Journal of Royal Asiatic Soc.*, 1880, pp. 70-97 ; *Trans. Soc. Bib. Arch.*, vol. vii. pp. 139-176) seem to be not less instructive. Compare Professor Sayce in the *Academy*, Oct. 16, 1880 ; M. Halévy in the *Revue des Études Juives*, No. 1, pp. 9-31 ; and Mr. Cheyne's *Isaiah*, vol. ii. pp. 264-270 (London, 1881).

Not second in importance to the cuneiform inscriptions is the stone of King Mesha of Moab, now in the Louvre. The Egyptian monuments have helped us little. When the external aids for the study of the period of revelation are so scanty, and of such recent discovery, we must recognise a supreme wisdom in the Providence which prevented the formation of the Old Testament Canon from being limited by those narrow dogmatic principles by which the Bible is still often measured.

LECTURE II.

NOTE 1, p. 34.—See, especially, the Arabic catena on Genesis published by Professor Lagarde in his *Materialien zur Kritik und Geschichte des Pentateuchs* (Leipzig, 1867) from a Carshunic MS. of the sixteenth century. This compilation of a Syriac scribe is full of Jewish traditions, and even in form, as the editor observes, is quite of the character of a Jewish *Midrash*.

NOTE 2, p. 35.—On the *Regula Fidei*, and its connection with the ambiguity of the allegorical interpretation, so keenly felt in controversy with heretics, compare Diestel, *Geschichte des alten Testaments in der Christlichen Kirche*, p. 38 (Irenæus, Tertullian), p. 85 (Augustine). The principle is clearly laid down by Origen: "Many think that they have the mind of Christ, and not a few differ from the opinions of the earlier Christians ; but the preaching of the Church, handed down in regular succession from the Apostles, still abides, and is present in the Church. Therefore, the only truth to be believed is that which in no point departs from ecclesiastical and apostolical tradition." (*Princip., Praef.*, § 2.)

NOTE 3, p. 40.—*Prologus Galeatus.*—"This prologue may fit all the books which we have translated from the Hebrew. Books outside of these are apocryphal. Therefore the so-called Wisdom of Solomon, the book of Jesus son of Sirach, Judith,

LECT. II.   *APOCRYPHA.*   391

Tobit, and The Shepherd are not canonical. The first book of Maccabees I found in Hebrew, the second is Greek, as may be proved from its very idiom."

Praef. in Jeremiam.—" We have passed by the book of Baruch, Jeremiah's amanuensis, which the Hebrews neither read nor possess."

Praef. in Esdram et Nehemiam.—" Let no one be offended that we have given but one book, nor let him delight in the dreams of the apocryphal third and fourth books [that is, First and Second Esdras of the English Apocrypha]; for among the Hebrews the words of Ezra and Nehemiah are united in a single volume, and what is not found with them is to be rejected."

Praef. in Librum Esther.—" The Book of Esther has unquestionably been vitiated by various translators. I have translated it word for word as it stands in the Hebrew archives."

Praef. in Danielem.—" The story of Susanna, the Song of the Three Children, and the fables of Bel and the Dragon are not found in the Hebrew Daniel; but as they are current throughout the world we have added them at the end, marking them with an obelus, lest the ignorant should fancy us to have excised a great part of the volume." Jerome adds an interesting account of arguments against the additions to Daniel, which he had heard from a Jewish doctor, leaving the decision to his readers.

NOTE 4, p. 40.—The quotation is from the *Prologus Galeatus*. Compare the preface to Chronicles addressed to Domnio and Rogatianus : " Let him who would challenge aught in this version ask the Jews, consult his own consciousness, examine the text and context of the passage ; then let him find fault with my work if he can. So wherever you find an asterisk in this volume, you are to recognise an addition from the Hebrew not found in Latin copies. Conversely, an obelus or transverse line prefixed to a passage denotes an addition made by the Septuagint interpreters, either for the improvement of the style, or by the authority of the Holy Spirit, though it is not read in the Hebrew."

NOTE 5, p. 41.—The version of Aquila, a Jewish proselyte and disciple of the famous Rabbi Akiba, was made expressly in the interests of Jewish exegesis, and reproduced with scrupulous accuracy the received text of the second Christian century. Sym-

machus and Theodotion followed later, but still in the second
century. The former, according to Eusebius and Jerome, was
an Ebionite, one of the sect of Jewish Christians who still held
to the observance of the law, like the opponents of Paul. It is
uncertain whether Theodotion was an Ebionite (Jerome), or a
proselyte (Irenæus). Aquila, says Jerome, sought to reproduce
the Hebrew word for word; Symmachus aimed at a clear expression of the sense; while Theodotion rather sought to give a
revised edition not very divergent from the Greek of the Septuagint. These versions were arranged in parallel columns in the
Hexapla of Origen, composed in the first half of the third century.
The fragments of them which remain in Greek MSS. of the
Septuagint, in the Patristic literature, or in the Syriac translation of the fifth column of the Hexapla made by Paul of Tela,
in Alexandria, A.D. 618, are collected in Dr. Field's edition,
Origenis Hexaplorum quae supersunt (Oxford, 1867-1875). All
that is known about these versions is put together in the prolegomena to Dr. Field's work.

NOTE 6, p. 41.—*Praef. in Librum Job.*—"To understand
this book I procured, at no small cost, a doctor from Lydda, who
was deemed to hold the first place among the Hebrews."

Praef. in Chron. ad D. et R.—"When your letters reached
me, asking a Latin version of Chronicles, I got a doctor of
Tiberias, in high esteem among the Hebrews, and with him collated everything, as the proverb goes, from the crown of the
head to the tip of the nails. Thus confirmed, I have ventured
to comply with your request." Bar Anina is named in *Epist.*
84. Jerome never gained such a knowledge of Hebrew as gave
him confidence to dispense with the aid of the Jews.

NOTE 7, p. 41.—The passage quoted in Art. VI. is from
Praef. in libros Salomonis.—"As the Church reads Judith, Tobit,
and the books of Maccabees, but does not receive them among
the canonical Scriptures, so let her read these two books
[Ecclesiasticus and the Wisdom of Solomon] for the edification
of the laity, but not to confirm the authority of ecclesiastical
doctrines."

NOTE 8, p. 42.—"On their promiscuous acceptance of all
books into the Canon, I will say no more than that herein
they depart from the consensus of the early Church. For it is
known what Jerome reports as the common judgment of the
ancients. . . . I am not unaware, however, that the decree

of Trent agrees with the third Œcumenical Council, which Augustine follows in his book *De Doctr. Christiana*. But as Augustine testifies that all were not agreed upon the matter in his time, let this point be left open. But if arguments are to be drawn from the books themselves, there are many proofs, besides their idiom, that they ought to take a lower place than the fathers of Trent award to them, etc." Compare the statement, *Institut.*, iv. 9, § 14.

NOTE 9, p. 48.—See the evidence of this from the Rabbinical literature in Zunz's *Gottesdienstliche Vorträge der Juden*, p. 7 (Berlin, 1832). Our Lord upon the cross quoted Ps. xxii. in a Targum.

NOTE 10, p. 48.—Mishna, *Megilla*, iv. 4.—" He who reads in the Pentateuch must not read to the Meturgeman more than one verse, and in the prophets three verses. If each verse is a paragraph, they are read one by one. The reader may skip in the prophets, but not in the law. How long may he spend in searching for another passage? So long as the Meturgeman goes on speaking." The practice of oral translation into Aramaic led ultimately to the formation of written Targums or Aramaic paraphrases; but these were long discouraged by the Scribes.

NOTE 11, p. 49.—The structure of the Semitic languages makes it much easier to dispense with the vowels than an English reader might suppose. The chief difficulty lay with vowels, or still more with diphthongs, at the end of a word, and was met at a very early date by the use of weak consonants to indicate cognate vowel-sounds (*e.g.* W = au, u ; Y = ai, i). This use of the vowel-consonants is found even on the stone of Mesha, and has been adopted in various measure, not only in Hebrew, but in Syriac and Arabic. But in all these languages the plan of marking every vowel-sound by points above or below the line came in comparatively late, was developed slowly, and never extended to all books. In Arabic, the vowel-points are hardly ever used except for the Koran, or in difficult poetry, and in philological books. The testimonies of the Talmudists and of Jerome are quite express to show that at their time the true vocalisation of ambiguous words was known only by oral teaching. Jerome, for example, says that in Hab. iii. 5 the Hebrew has only D, B, and R, without any vowel, which may be read either as *dabar*, "word," or *deber*, "plague." A supposed interest of orthodoxy long led good scholars like the Buxtorfs to fight for the antiquity and authority of the points. There is now no question on the subject; for MSS. brought from Southern Russia and Arabia, containing a different notation for the vowels, prove that our present system is not only comparatively recent, but is the outcome of a gradual process, in which several methods were tried in different parts of the Jewish world. The rolls read in the synagogue are still unpointed, a relic of the old condition of all MSS.

Lecture III.

Note 1, p. 55.—On the history of the period covered by this Lecture the English reader may consult with advantage Ewald's *History of Israel*, Bd. iv. (Eng. Trans., vol. v. London, 1874), and the later chapters of Kuenen's *Religion of Israel* (Eng. Trans., vol. iii. London, 1875). In French the most important recent work, and the best contribution of Jewish scholarship to the history of the period of the Second Temple, is Derenbourg's *Essai sur l'histoire et la géographie de la Palestine: Première Partie* (Paris, 1867). The most recent state of research, not fully represented in any English book, is to be found in Schürer's *Lehrbuch der neutestamentlichen Zeitgeschichte*, Leipzig, 1874, and Wellhausen's admirable monograph, *Die Pharisäer und die Sadducäer*, Greifswald, 1874. For the theology of the Scribes see Weber's *System der altsynagogalen palästinischen Theologie*, Leipzig, 1880. The oldest and most important traditions about the early Scribes are collected in the treatise of the Mishna called *Pirké Aboth*, edited in Hebrew and English in Mr. C. Taylor's *Sayings of the Jewish Fathers*, Cambridge, 1877.

Note 2, p. 57.—From the genealogy of the descendants of Zerubbabel, in 1 Chron. iii. 19 *seq.*, it seems to follow that the Chronicler lived at least two generations after Ezra. See the article "Chronicles" in the ninth edition of the *Encyclopædia Britannica*, and Bertheau's Commentary. But the Chronicles were originally one book with Ezra and Nehemiah, and therefore cannot have been written till the very close of the Persian period. *Supra*, p. 140, p. 170 and note.

Note 3, p. 62.—Josephus, *Antiquities*, xiii. 10, § 6: "The Sadducees had only the well-to-do classes on their side. The populace would not follow them; but the Pharisees had the multitude as their auxiliaries." *Ibid.* xviii. 1, § 4 : "The Sadducees are the men of highest rank, but they effect as good as nothing, for in affairs of government they are compelled against their will to follow the dicta of the Pharisees, as the masses would otherwise refuse to tolerate them."

The best account of the relative position of the Scribes and the governing class at different periods is given in Wellhausen's monograph on the Pharisees and Sadducees cited above. In addition to the works named in the first note to this Lecture, Geiger's *Urschrift und Uebersetzungen* (Breslau, 1857) deserves special notice ; but this book must be read with great caution, and has been too closely followed by several recent writers. On the position of the two parties in the Sanhedrin, Kuenen's essay *Over de samenstelling van het Sanhedrin*, in the Proceedings of the Royal Society of Amsterdam, 1866, is conclusive. On this topic, and on the whole meaning of the antithesis of the Pharisees and Sadducees, older scholars went astray by following too closely the unhistorical views of later Jewish tradition. When Judaism had ceased to have a national existence, and was merely a religious sect, the Schoolmen naturally became its heads ; and the tradition assumed that it had always been so, and that the whole history of the nation was made up of such theological and legal controversies as engrossed the attention of later times. (See Taylor's *Sayings of the Fathers*, Excursus III.). This view bears its condemnation on its face. Before the fall of the state the party of the Scribes was opposed, not to another theological sect, but to the aristocracy, which had its centre in the high priesthood, and pursued practical objects of political and social aggrandisement on very different lines from those of scholastic controversy. That the Sadducees are the party headed by the chief priests, and the Pharisees the party of the Scribes, is plain from the New Testament, especially from Acts v. 17. The higher priesthood was in spirit a very secular nobility, more interested in war and diplomacy than in the service of the Temple. The theological tenets of the Sadducees, as they appear in the New Testament and Josephus, had a purely political basis. They detested the doctrine of the Resurrection and the fatalism of the Pharisees, because these opinions were employed by their adversaries to thwart their political aims. The aristocracy suffered a great loss of position by the subjection to a foreign power of the nation which they had ruled in the early

Hasmonean period when the high priest was a great prince. But the Pharisees discouraged all rebellion. Israel's business was only to seek after the righteousness of the law. The redemption of the nation would follow in due time, without man's interference. The resurrection would compensate those who had suffered in this life, and the hope of this reward made it superfluous for them to seek a present deliverance.

NOTE 4, p. 63.—The word *Mishna* means instruction, literally repetition, inculcation. From the same root in Aramaic form the doctors of the Mishna bear the name of Tanna, teacher (repeater). After the close of the Mishna the collection and interpretation of tradition was carried on by a new succession of scholars whose contributions make up the Gemara (decision, doctrine), a vast and desultory commentary on the Mishna. There are two Gemaras, one Palestinian, the other Babylonian. The name for a doctor of the Gemara is Amôra, speaker. Mishna and Gemara together make up the Talmud. The Babylonian Gemara was not completed till the sixth century of our era.

The whole Mishna was published, with a Latin translation and notes, by G. Surenhusius, in 6 vols. folio (Amsterdam, 1698-1703). There is a German translation by Rabe (1760-1763), and another printed in Hebrew letters by Jost (Berlin, 1832-1834). There is no complete English version, but eighteen treatises, still important for the daily life of the Jews, were translated by Raphall and De Sola (London, 1845). Another selection is given by Dr. Barclay, now Bishop of Jerusalem, in his work, *The Talmud* (London, 1878).

NOTE 5, p. 65.—Mishna, *Maaser Sheni*, v. 15 (ed. Surenh., vol. i. p. 287). On the change in the law of redemption, introduced by Hillel, which is another example in point, see Derenbourg, *lib. cit.*, p. 188. Compare also Zunz, *Gottesdienstliche Vorträge der Juden*, pp. 11, 45 (Berlin, 1832).

NOTE 6, p. 67.—The point in which the grammatical exegesis of the Mediæval Jews was most defective was that they always assumed it to be possible to translate what lay before them, and would not recognise that many difficulties arise from corruption of the text. In a book of profane antiquity, a passage that cannot be construed grammatically is at once assumed to be corrupt, and a remedy is sought from MSS. or conjecture. The Jews, and until recently the great majority of Christian scholars, refused to admit this principle for the Hebrew Scriptures. The

Septuagint proves the existence of corruptions in the Hebrew text, and often supplies the correction. Yet in such cases the translators of 1611, and many of their successors, prefer to cling to the Hebrew text, and force a sense out of it in defiance of the laws of grammar. This method has filled Hebrew grammars with false rules, or exceptions to rules, and has caused the Hebrew prophets and poets to be charged with many confused and enigmatic utterances, nay, with much absolute nonsense, which is really due to corruptions of text.

Till commentators on the Old Testament frankly accept the principles undisputed among other interpreters, and are content to confess that there are passages and phrases in the Hebrew Bible which cannot be understood without emendation from the versions, or from conjecture where the corruption is older than the LXX., it cannot be said that the evil influence of Talmudic exegesis has been thoroughly overcome. An English Bible marking the places where no good sense can be got out of the text is much wanted. Messrs. Cheyne and Driver's notes in the *Variorum* and *Centenary* Bibles, published by Messrs. Eyre and Spottiswoode, supply the want in part ; but their plan does not embrace all that is required. Compare on this subject the remarks of J. Olshausen in the preface to his German Commentary on the Psalms (Leipzig, 1853), a book far too little known in our country. Examples of the few cases where the Authorised Version has been misled by dogmatical or historical prepossessions will be found *supra*, pp. 258, 265. See also Ezra ix. 4, 5, " sacrifice " for " meat-offering," *infra*, p. 421.

NOTE 7, p. 70.—In last century great hopes were entertained of the results to be derived from a collation of Hebrew MSS. The collections of Kennicott (1776-1780) and De Rossi (1784-1788) showed that all MSS. substantially represent one text, and, so far as the consonants are concerned, recent discoveries have not led to any new result. On the text that lay before the Talmudic doctors compare Strack, *Prolegomena Critica in Vetus Testamentum Hebraicum* (Leipzig, 1873). On Aquila see Lecture II., note 5. On the Targums consult Deutsch's article in Smith's *Dictionary of the Bible,* Schürer, *op. cit.*, p. 475 *seq.*, and *infra*, note 12.

NOTE 8, p. 71.—The proof that all copies of the Hebrew text go back to one archetype, and the explanation of the so-called " extraordinary points," were given independently by

Olshausen in his commentary on the Psalms (1853), and Lagarde in his *Anmerkungen zur Griechischen Uebersetzung der Proverbien* (1863). The result has been accepted by Nöldeke (whose remarks in Hilgenfeld's *Zeitschrift*, 1873, pp. 444 *seq.*, are worthy of notice), and by other scholars. I know of no attempt to refute the argument.

NOTE 9, p. 73.—Up to the time of Nehemiah's second visit to Jerusalem, there was still a party, even among the priests, which entertained friendly relations with the Samaritans, cemented by marriages. Nehemiah broke up this party; and an unnamed priest, who was Sanballat's son-in-law, was driven into exile. This priest, who would naturally flee to his father-in-law, is plainly identical with the priest Manasseh, son-in-law of Sanballat, of whom Josephus (*Antiq.* xi. 8) relates that he fled from Jerusalem to Samaria, and founded the schismatic temple on Mount Gerizim, with a rival hierarchy and ritual. The account of Josephus is confused in chronology and untrustworthy in detail; but the main fact agrees with the Biblical narrative, and it is clear that the establishment of the rival temple was a natural consequence of the final defeat of the Samaritans in their persistent efforts to establish relations with the Jewish priesthood and secure admission to the temple at Jerusalem. This determines the age of the Samaritan Pentateuch. The Samaritans cannot have got the law before the Exile through the priest of the high place at Samaria mentioned in 2 Kings xvii. 28. For the worship of Jehovah, as practised at Samaria before the fall of the Northern Kingdom, was remote from the ordinances of the law, and up to the time when the books of Kings were written the Samaritans worshipped images, and did not observe the laws of the Pentateuch (2 Kings xvii. 34, 41). The Pentateuch, therefore, was introduced as their religious code at a later date; and it could not be accepted except in connection with the ritual and priesthood which they received from Jerusalem through the fugitive priest banished by Nehemiah.

NOTE 10, p. 74.—On the *Book of Jubilees*, see especially H. Rönsch, *Das Buch der Jubiläen* (Leipzig, 1874), and Schürer, *op. cit.*, p. 459 *seq.* On the various readings of the book, Rönsch, pp. 196, 514.

NOTE 11, p. 75.—On Hillel and his school, see especially Derenbourg, *op. cit.* chap. xi; and on the development of his system by

R. Ishmael and R. Akiba, *ibid.*, chap. xxiii. "Akiba adopted, not only the seven rules of Hillel, but the thirteen of Ishmael; even the latter did not suffice him in placing all the *halachoth* or decisions of the Rabbins under the shield of the word of the Pentateuch. His system of interpretation does not recognise the limits established by the usage of the language, and respected by Ishmael; every word which is not absolutely indispensable to express the intention of the legislator, or the logical relations of the sentences of a law and their parts, is designed to enlarge or restrict the sphere of the law, to introduce into it the additions of tradition, or exclude what tradition excludes. No particle or conjunction, be it augmentative or restrictive, escapes this singular method of exegesis." Thus the Hebrew prefix *eth*, which marks the definite accusative, agrees in form with the preposition *with*. Hence, when Deut. x. 20 says, "Thou shalt fear *eth*-Jehovah thy God," Akiba interprets, "Thou shalt fear *the doctors of the law* along with Jehovah." So Aquila, the disciple of Akiba, translates the mark of the accusative by σύν. See Field, *Proleg.*, p. xxii.

NOTE 12, p. 76.—The progress of the stricter exegesis, and its influence on the treatment of the text, may also be traced in the history of the Targums or Aramaic paraphrases. Targum means originally the oral interpretation of the Meturgeman in the synagogue (*supra*, p. 48). The Meturgemanim did not keep close to their text, but added paraphrastic expositions, practical applications, poetical and romantic embellishments. But there was a restraint on individual liberty of exegesis. The translators formed a guild of scholars, and their interpretations gradually assumed a fixed type. By and by the current form of the Targum was committed to writing; but there was no fixed edition, and those Palestinian Targums which have come down to us belong to various recensions, and contain elements added late in the Middle Ages.

This style of interpretation, in which the text was freely handled, and the exposition of the law did not stand on the level of the new science of Akiba and his associates, fell into disfavour with the dominant schools, just as the Septuagint did. The Targum is severely censured in the Rabbinical writings; and at length the orthodox party took the matter into their own hands, and framed a literal Targum, which, however, did not reach its final shape till the third century A.D., when the chief seat of Jewish learning had been moved to Babylon. The Babylonian Targum to the Pentateuch is called the Targum of Onkelos, *i.e.* the Targum in the style of Aquila (Akylas). The corresponding Targum to the prophets bears the name of Jonathan. As Jonathan is the Hebrew equivalent of Theodotion, this perhaps means only the Targum in the style of Theodotion. At any rate, these Targums are not the private enterprise of individual scholars, but express the official exegesis of their age. The Targums to the Hagiographa have not an official character. Comp. Geiger, *op. cit.*, p. 163 *seq.*, 451 *seq.* Latin translations of the Targums (not quite complete) in Walton's Polyglott. English translations of the Targums to the Pentateuch, by J. W. Etheridge (London, 1862-64).

NOTE 13, p. 77.—Geiger, *op. cit.*, p. 232. *Massechet Sôpherîm*, vi. 4. A copy of the law was carried away by Titus among the spoils of the Temple; Joseph., *B. J.*, Book vii. cap. 5, § 5.

NOTE 14, p. 78.—The oldest list of the *Tikkûnê Sopherîm* is in the Mechilta, a work of the second century, which gives only eleven passages. Other lists in Geiger, p. 309 *seq.;* the full list in *Ochla w'ochla*, ed. Frensdorff, No. 168 (Han., 1864). In some cases the so-called old reading is certainly wrong, *e.g.* 2 Sam. xx. 1, "gods" for "tents." Nöldeke, in *Gött. Gel. Anz.*, 1869, p. 2001 *seq.*, advances the plausible hypothesis that the tradition merely expresses, in no very accurate form, the recollection that old copies sometimes varied from the later official text.

NOTE 15, p. 82.—A convenient conspectus of the forms of the Semitic alphabet at different times is given in Euting's Table, attached to the English translation of Bickell's *Hebrew Grammar* (1877). See also the plates from an Egyptian Aramaic Papyrus (Br. Mus. Papyrus CVI*), in the Oriental Series of the Palæographic Society, Pt. ii. (1877), pl. xxv. xxvi. which is probably of Jewish origin, and late Ptolemaic or early Roman. The most instructive monument for the old orthography is the stone of Mesha as compared with later Jewish inscriptions. Compare Wellhausen, in Bleek's *Einleitung*, § 296 (4th Edn., 1878); Lagarde, *Proverbien*, p. 4; Wellhausen, *Bücher Samuelis*, pp. 17 *seq.* (Göttingen, 1871).

NOTE 16, p. 82.—That the old Hebrew ink could be washed off appears from Numb. v. 23, Exod. xxxii. 33, etc. From the former passage is derived the Rabbinic objection to the use of a mordant in ink. See *Sôpherîm*, i. 5, 6, and the notes in Müller's edition (Leipz., 1878); Mishna *Sota*, ii. 4, and Wagenseil's Commentary (Surenh., iii. p. 206 *seq.*). The Jews laid no value on old copies, but in later times prized certain MSS. as specially correct. A copy in which a line had become obliterated, or which was otherwise considerably defective, was cast aside into the *Genîza* or lumber-room (*Sôpherîm*, iii. 9). There was a difference of opinion as to touching-up faded letters (*Ibid.* 8, and Müller's note). Compare Harkavy in *Mém. de l'Acad. de S. Petersbourg*, xxiv. p. 57, etc.

LECTURE IV.

NOTE 1, p. 84.—On the subject of this lecture compare, in general, Lagarde, *Anmerkungen zur Griechischen Uebersetzung der Proverbien* (Leipz., 1863); Wellhausen, *Der Text der Bücher Samuelis* (Gött., 1871). To these two books, the most important recent contributions to a sound use of the LXX. for the criticism of the Hebrew text, may be added the excellent *brochure* of J. Hollenberg, *Der Character der Alexandrinischen Uebersetzung des Buches Josua* (Moers, 1876). Less satisfactory in method and execution, though valuable in many respects, are the works of Scholz, Merx, Sinker (Cambridge, 1879), and others. On the relation of the Septuagint to the Palestinian tradition compare Geiger, *op. cit.*, and Frankel, *Ueber den Einfluss der palästinischen Exegese auf die Alexandrinische Hermeneutik* (Leipzig, 1851).

NOTE 2, p. 99.—Critical edition of the text of the letter of Aristeas to Philocrates, by M. Schmidt, in Merx's *Archiv*, i. 241 *seq.* (Halle, 1870). It is unnecessary to sketch its contents, for which the English reader may turn to the translations of Eusebius and Josephus. What basis of truth underlies the fables depends mainly on the genuineness of the fragments of Aristobulus. See on the one side Wellhausen-Bleek, § 279, on the other Kuenen's *Religion of Israel*, note 1 to chap. xi.

NOTE 3, p. 103.—Compare Morinus, *Exercitatio* viii. In Mishna, *Megilla*, i. 8, we read, "The Scriptures may be written in every tongue. R. Simeon b. Gamaliel says they did not suffer the Scriptures to be written except in Greek." On this the Gemara observes, "R. Judah said, that when our Rabbins permitted writing in Greek, they did so only for the Torah, and hence arose the translation made for King Ptolemy, etc." So

Josephus, though an orthodox Pharisee, makes use of the LXX., even where it depends from the Hebrew (1 Esdras). The thirteen variations are given in the Gemara, *ut supra*, and in *Sôpherîm*, i. 9. In both places God is said to have guided the seventy-two translators, so that, writing separately, all gave one sense. Side by side with this favourable estimate, *Soph.*, i. 8, following the glosses on *Megillath Ta'anith*, gives the later hostile tradition, which it supposes to refer to a different version. "That day was a hard day for Israel—like the day when they made the golden calf," because the Torah could not be adequately translated. See further on the gradual growth of the prejudice against the Greek translation, Müller's note, *op. cit.*, p. 11. Jerome, following the text supplied by Jewish tradition, will have it that the LXX. translators purposely concealed from Ptolemy the mysteries of faith, especially the prophecies referring to the advent of Christ. See *Quaest. in Gen.*, p. 2 (ed. Lagarde, 1868), and *Praef. in Pent.*

NOTE 4, p. 110.—Delitzsch, the ablest modern advocate of the Jesaianic authorship, says that "Isaiah left this deep and rich bequest to the church of the Exile and the church of the subsequent future, till the time of the New Jerusalem and the new earth. . . . It is a thoroughly esoteric book, left to be understood by the church in the future."

NOTE 5, p. 112.—It is argued by those who ascribe chaps. l.-li. to Jeremiah, that the expression "all these words" in chap. li. 60 necessarily refers to the context immediately preceding. But the order of Jeremiah's prophecies is greatly disturbed (*supra*, p. 120). No one will argue that "these words" in chap. xlv. 1 refer to chap. xliv.; yet the argument is as good in the one case as in the other. Compare Budde, *Ueber die Capitel L. und LI. des Buches Jeremia* in *Jahrb. f. D. Theol.*, vol. xxiii. pp. 428 *seq.*, 529 *seq.*

NOTE 6, p. 117.—There is one passage in Jeremiah, as we read it, which appears inconsistent with the view I have ventured to take of the prophet's attitude to the temporary elements of the Old Testament ritual. In Jer. xxxiii. 14-26 it is predicted that the Levitical priesthood and its sacrifices shall be perpetual as the succession of day and night. This passage is also wanting in the Septuagint. No reason can be suggested for its omission; for we know from Philo that even those Jews of Alexandria who sat most loosely to the ceremonial law regarded the Temple and its service as an essential element in religion (*De Migr. Abra.*, cap. xvi.). If taken literally, the eternity of Levitical sacrifices, as expressed in xxxiii. 18, seems quite inconsistent with all else in Jeremiah's prophecies. Taken typically the verse only fits the sacrifice of the mass, to which Roman Catholic expositors refer it; for the sacrifices are to be offered continually in all time.

LECTURE V.

NOTE 1, p. 123.—The earlier part of the book of Proverbs also falls into several sections :—(1) chap. i. 1-6, general title; (2) chap. i. 7-ix. 18, poetical admonitions in praise of wisdom, morality, and religion, not proverbial in form; (3) chap. x. 1 - xxii. 16, "Proverbs of Solomon;" (4) chap. xxii. 17 - xxiv. 22, —a collection of "Words of the Wise," as appears from the special title to this section, xxii. 17-21. Thus the book contains two collections of Salomonic proverbs, of which the second was copied out in the reign of Hezekiah, two anonymous collections of words of the wise, and several minor pieces, the whole prefaced by a poetical or rhetorical introduction. That the two Salomonic collections were formed independently, and not by the same hand, appears most clearly from the many cases in which the same proverb appears in both (see the Introduction to Delitzsch's *Commentary*, § 3). Even these parts of the book then were not collected by Solomon himself, and the title in chap. i. 1 is not from his hand, but was added by some collector or editor. Hence there is no reason to suppose that Solomon is the author of chaps. i.-ix. any more than of the "Words of the Wise." The whole book bears the name of Solomon's Proverbs, because the two great Salomonic collections are the leading element in it. There are close analogies between the composition of the Book of Proverbs and that of the Psalter. See Lecture VII.

NOTE 2, p. 130.—The insertion of the Septuagint in 1 Kings viii. 53 deserves special notice for its intrinsic interest. In 1 Kings viii. 12, 13, the Hebrew text reads, "Jehovah hath determined (said) to dwell in darkness. I have built a house of habitation for thee, a place for thee to dwell in eternally." These verses are omitted in LXX., but at ver. 53 we find instead a fuller form of the same words of Solomon. In the common editions of the LXX. the words run thus :—" The sun he made known in heaven: the Lord hath said that he will dwell in darkness. Build my house, a comely house for thyself to dwell in newness. Behold, is it not written in the book of song?" The variations from the Hebrew text are partly mistakes. The word "comely" is a rendering elsewhere used in the LXX. for the Hebrew word *naweh*, which in this connection must rather be rendered "house of habitation," giving the same sense as the Hebrew of ver. 13, with a variation in the expression. Then the phrase "in newness" at once exhibits itself to the Hebrew scholar as a mistaken reading of the Hebrew word "eternally." Again, "build my house" differs in the Hebrew from "I have built" only by the omission of a single letter. We may correct the LXX. accordingly, getting exactly the sense of the Massoretic text of ver. 12; or conversely, we may correct the Hebrew by the aid of the Septuagint, in which case one other letter must be changed, so that the verse runs, "Build my house, an house of habitation for me; a place to dwell eternally." We now come to the additions of the LXX. "The sun he made known in heaven" gives no good sense. But many MSS. read, "The sun he set in heaven." These two readings, ἐγνώρισεν and ἔστησεν have no resemblance in Greek. But the corresponding Hebrew words are הבן and הכין respectively, which are so like that they could easily be mistaken. There can be no doubt that the latter is right; and the error in the common Septuagint text shows that the addition really was found by the translators in Hebrew, not inserted out of their own head. We can now restore the whole original, divide it into lines as poetry, and render—

> Jehovah created the sun in the heavens,
> But he hath determined to dwell in darkness.
> Build my house, an house of habitation for me,
> A place to dwell in eternally.

Or on the other reading :—

> I have built an house of habitation for thee,
> A place to dwell in eternally.

The character of the expression in these lines, taken with the circumstance of their transposition to another place in the LXX., would of itself prove that this is a fragment from an ancient source, not part of the context of the narrative of the chapter. But the LXX. expressly says that the words are taken from "The

Book of Song." There might perhaps be an ancient book of that name, as we have in Arabic the great historical and poetical collection of El Isfahâny, called "The Book of Songs." But the transposition of a single letter in the Hebrew converts the unknown Book of Song into the well-known Book of Jashar. This correction seems certain. The slip of the Septuagint translator was not unnatural; indeed, the same change is made by the Syriac in Josh. x. 13.

NOTE 3, p. 131.—The scheme of the Hebrew Canon may be put thus :—

I. The five fifths of the Law	5
II. The Prophets—	
Earlier Prophets: Joshua, Jud., Sam., Kings . .	4
Later Prophets: Isaiah, Jer., Ezek., The Twelve . .	4
III. Hagiographa or Ketûbîm—	
Poetical Books: Psalms, Proverbs, Job . . .	3
The Megilloth: Canticles, Ruth, Lamen., Eccles., Esther	5
Daniel, Ezra-Nehemiah, Chronicles	3
	24

The fundamental passage in the Babylonian Gemara, *Baba Bathra*, ff. 14, 15, says, "The order of the prophets is Joshua and Judges, Samuel and Kings, Jeremiah and Ezekiel, Isaiah and the Twelve. Hosea is the first because it is written, 'the beginning of the word of the Lord by Hosea' (Hos. i. 2). . . . But, because his prophecy is written along with the latest prophets, Haggai, Zechariah, and Malachi, he is counted with them. Isaiah is earlier than Jeremiah and Ezekiel. . . . But because Kings ends with destruction and Jeremiah is all destruction, while Ezekiel beginning with destruction ends in consolation and Isaiah is all consolation, destruction is joined to destruction and consolation to consolation. The order of the Hagiographa is Ruth and Psalms and Job and Proverbs, Ecclesiastes, Canticles, and Lamentations, Daniel and Esther, Ezra and Chronicles." Compare Müller's note on *Sopherim*, iii. 5. Isaiah follows Ezekiel in some MSS. (Lagarde, *Symmicta*, i. 142, Göttingen, 1877) and the order of the Hagiographa varies considerably. On 2 Esdras xiv. 44, 46, see Lect. VI. p. 149 and note.

NOTE 4, p. 132.—See the three enumerations in Jerome, *Prol. Galeat*. His order for the Hagiographa is Job, David, Proverbs, Eccles., Canticles, Daniel, Chron., Ezra, Esther. On the Canon of Josephus see Lect. VI. p. 150 and note. Twenty-two books are reckoned by Origen in Eusebius, *H. E.* vi. 25, and by Epiphanius *De Mens. et Pond.* c. 4 (ed. Lagarde, p. 156).

NOTE 5, p. 136.—Two Greek recensions of Esther and Tobit exist, and are printed in O. F. Fritzsche's *Libri Apocryphi V. T. Græce* (Leipzig, 1871). Compare the commentaries of the same author on these books in *Kurzgef. Handbuch z. d. Apoc.* (Leipzig, 1851, 1853).

NOTE 6, p. 141.—The line between the old literature and the new cannot be drawn with chronological precision. The characteristic mark of canonical literature is that it is the record of the progress of fresh truths of revelation, and of the immediate reflection of these truths in the believing heart. The Psalms are, in part, considerably later than Ezra, but they record the inner side of the history of his work of reformation, and show us the nature of the faith with which Israel apprehended the Law and its institutes. This is a necessary and most precious element of the Old Testament record, and it would be arbitrary to attempt to fix a point of time at which this part of Old Testament Scripture must necessarily have closed. But the direct language of faith held by the psalmists is intrinsically different from such artificial reflection on the law, in the manner of the schools, as is found in Ecclesiasticus. The difference can be felt rather than defined, and a certain margin of uncertainty must attach to every determination of the limits of what is canonical. But, on the whole, the instinct that guided the formation of the Hebrew Canon was sound, because the theories of the schools affected only certain outlying books, while the mass of the collection established itself in the hearts of all the faithful in successive generations, under historical circumstances of a sifting kind. The religious struggle under the Maccabees, which threw the people of God upon the Scriptures for comfort when the outward order of the theocracy was broken, doubtless was for the later books of the Canon a period of proof such as the Captivity was for the older literature. Compare Lecture VI.

NOTE 7, p. 145.—*Midrash Rabba*, p. 529 (Leipz., 1864). For the law as everlasting, see Baruch, iv. 1. The pre-existence of the law (Ecclus. xxiv. 9) follows from its being identified with wisdom as described in Prov. viii. Compare further Weber *op. cit.* p. 18 *seq.*

NOTE 8, p. 146.—On the term *Kabbala* see Zunz, *op. cit.* p. 44, where the evidence from Jewish authorities is carefully collected. Compare Weber, *op. cit.* p. 79 *seq.* Mishna, *Megilla*, iii. 1.—" If the men of a town sell a Torah they may not buy with its price the other books of Scripture; if they sell Scriptures they may not buy a cloth to wrap round the Torah; if they sell such a cloth they may not buy an ark for synagogue rolls; if they sell an ark they may not buy a synagogue; nor if they sell a synagogue may they buy a street (an open ground for devotion, Matt. vi. 5)."

LECTURE VI.

NOTE 1, p. 149.—The Latin text of Fourth Esdras xiv. 44, 46 does not state the number of canonical books, which, however, ought to be got by subtracting the 70 esoteric books of ver. 46 from the whole number in ver. 44. The latter number, however, is hopelessly corrupt. It has been proved by Professor Gildemeister and Mr. Bensly (*The Missing Fragment of 4 Ezra*, Camb., 1875) that, with the exception of the Amiens MS. (A), unearthed by the latter scholar, all copies hitherto known are derived from the Cod. Sangermanensis (S) and have no critical value. Through the kindness of Mr. Bensly I am able to give the following readings. A has DCCCCLXXIIII. $\overset{\text{ñgenti septuaginta quatuor}}{}$; S. C. 1. 3. 5. 8. 9. 11. 12. C. 15 (= Add. 1848 Univ. Libr. Camb.) D. T. read DCCCCIIII. Other readings are XCIIII. (C. 4), octingenti IIII^{or} (C. 10), ducenti quatuor (C. 2). The Edinburgh MS., the only one which I have been able to consult personally, agrees with S. In this ambiguity of the Latin we must rely on the Eastern versions; some of which give 94 in ver. 44, and also add in ver. 45 the express statement that there were 24 books published. But even here there is great variation.

	Total books.	Canonical books	Esoteric books.
Ceriani's Syriac (1867)	94	24	70
Ewald's Arabic (1863)	94	24	70
Gildemeister's Arabic (1877)	Gives no numbers.		
The Aethiopic	94 (with variations)	not stated	not stated
The Armenian	94	not stated	not stated

Further, though the fragment of an Arabic translation from

the Syriac given by Professor Gildemeister (p. 41) agrees with the published Syriac, Jacob of Edessa, in his thirteenth epistle, published by Professor W. Wright (*Journ. Sac. Lit.*, 1867, p. 439), says that Ezra wrote 90 books. One cannot therefore feel confident that 94 is original any more than the explicit 24 of Syr. and Ar. Ew. The early Syriac church at least was too much influenced by Jewish tradition not to know the Talmudic enumeration. Besides, if 94 is original, it is still possible that 70 = 72 (as in the case of the LXX. translators), leaving 22 canonical books. More evidence is required to give a sure result.

On the supposed enumeration of 22 books in the *Jubilees*, as read by Syncellus and Cedrenus, see Rönsch, *op. cit.*, p. 527 *seq.*

NOTE 2, p. 150.—Josephus, *Contra Apion.*, Lib. I. cap. vii. § 5.—" Not every one was permitted to write the national records, nor is there any discrepancy in the things written; but the prophets alone learned the earliest and most ancient events by inspiration from God, and wrote down the events of their own times plainly as they occurred.

" (viii. 1).—For we have not myriads of discordant and contradictory books, but only two and twenty, containing the record of all time, and rightly believed to be divine. (2) And of these five are the books of Moses, comprising the laws, and the tradition of the early history of mankind down to his death. . . . But from the death of Moses till the reign of Artaxerxes, king of Persia, who succeeded Xerxes, the prophets compiled the history of their own times in thirteen books. The other four contain hymns to God and precepts of life for men. (3) But from Artaxerxes to our times all events have indeed been written down; but these later books are not deemed worthy of the same credit, because there has been no exact succession of prophets."

The allegorical interpretation of Canticles, Israel being identified with the spouse, first appears in 2 (4) Esdras, v. 24, 26; vii. 26.

NOTE 3, p. 157.—On the legend of the Great Synagogue, Kuenen's essay *Over de Mannen der Groote Synagoge*, in the proceedings of the Royal Society of Amsterdam, 1876, is conclusive. An abstract of the results in Wellhausen-Bleek, § 274. Kuenen follows the arguments of scholars of last century, and especially Rau's *Diatribe de Synagoga Magna* (Utrecht, 1725); but he completes their refutation of the Rabbinical fables by utilising and placing in its true light the important observations of Krochmal, as to the connection between the Great Synagogue and the Convocation of Neh. viii.-x., which, in the hands of Jewish scholars, had only led to fresh confusion. See, for example, Graetz (*Kohelet*, Anh. i. Leipz., 1871) for a model of confused reasoning on the Great Synagogue and the Canon. Krochmal's discovery that the Great Synagogue and the Great Convocation are identical rests on the clearest evidence. See especially the Midrash to Ruth. "What did the men of the Great Synagogue do? They wrote a book and spread it out in the court of the temple. And at dawn of day they rose and found it sealed. This is what is written in Neh. ix. 38" (Leipzig ed. of 1865, p. 77). According to the tradition of the Talmud, *Baba Bathra, ut supra*, the men of the Great Synagogue wrote Ezekiel, the Minor Prophets, Daniel, and Esther; and Ezra wrote his own book and continued the genealogies of Chronicles. This has nothing to do with the Canon; it merely expresses an opinion as to the date of these books. Further, the *Aboth of Rabbi Nathan* (a post-Talmudic book) says that the Great Synagogue arose and explained Proverbs, Canticles, and Ecclesiastes, which had previously been thought apocryphal. Such is the traditional basis for the famous conjecture of Elias Levita in his *Massoreth hammassoreth* (Venice, 1538), which took such a hold of public opinion that Hottinger, in the middle of the seventeenth century, could say: "Hitherto it has been an unquestioned axiom among Jews and Christians alike, that the Canon of the Old Testament was fixed, once and for all, with Divine authority, by Ezra and the men of the Great Synagogue" (*Thes. Phil.*, Zürich, 1649, p. 112). At p. 110 he says that this is only doubted by those *quibus pro cerebro fungus est*.

NOTE 4, p. 160.—In the Talmudic times it was matter of controversy whether it was legitimate to write the Law, the Prophets, and the Hagiographa in a single book. Some went so far as to say that each book of Scripture must form a separate volume. See *Sopherim*, iii. 1, and Müller's note. It appears that the old and predominant custom was in favour of separation. Boethos, whose copy of the eight prophets in one volume is referred to in *Baba Bathra* and *Sopherim*, iii. 5, lived about the close of the second Christian century. Some doctors denied that his copy contained all the books "joined into one." *Sopherim*, iii. 6, allows all the books to be united in inferior copies written on the material called diphthera, but not in synagogue rolls ; a compromise pointing to the gradual introduction in post-Talmudic times of the plan of treating the Bible as one volume.

NOTE 5, p. 160.—For the want of system in the public lessons from the Prophets in early times, see Luke iv. 17, and Lect. II., Note 10. According to *Sopherim*, xiv. 18, Esther was read at the feast of Purim, Canticles at the Passover, Ruth at Pentecost. The reading of Lamentations is mentioned, *ibid.* xviii. 4. It is noteworthy that there is still no mention of the use of Ecclesiastes in the Synagogue. Compare further Zunz, *op. cit.* p. 6.

NOTE 6, p. 163.—The only book as to which any dispute seems to have occurred was Ezekiel. The beginning of this book — the picture of the *Merkaba*, or chariot of Jehovah's glory (1 Chron. xxviii. 18)—has always been viewed as a great mystery in Jewish theology, and is the basis of the *Kabbala* or esoteric theosophy of the Rabbins. The closing chapters were equally puzzling, because they give a system of law and ritual divergent in many points from the Pentateuch. Compare Jerome's *Ep. to Paulinus* :—" The beginning and end of Ezekiel are involved in obscurities, and among the Hebrews these parts, and the exordium of Genesis, must not be read by a man under thirty." Hence, in the apostolic age, a question was raised as to the value of the book ; for, of course, nothing could be accepted that contradicted the Torah. We read in the Talmud (*Hagiga*, 13a) that "but for Hananiah, son of Hezekiah, they would have suppressed the Book of Ezekiel, because its words contradict those of the Torah. What did he do ? They brought up to him three hundred measures of oil, and he sat down and explained it." Derenbourg, *op. cit.* p. 296, with Graetz, *Geschichte*, vol. iii. p. 561, is disposed to hold that the scholar who reconciled Ezekiel with the Pentateuch at such an expenditure of midnight oil was really Eleazar son of Hananiah.

NOTE 7, p. 169.—It is sometimes said that the Haggada had no sacred authority. So Zunz, *op. cit.* p. 42 ; Deutsch's *Remains*, p. 17 ; but compare, on the other hand, Weber, *op. cit.* p. 94 *seq.* Certain Haggadoth share with the Halacha the name of *Midda*, rule of faith and life.

Note 8, p. 170.—*Aboth of R. Nathan,* c. 1.—" At first they said that Proverbs, Canticles, and Ecclesiastes are apocryphal. They said that they are parabolic writings, and not of the Hagiographa. So they prepared to suppress them, till the men of the Great Synagogue came and explained them."

Note 9, p. 170.—The most palpable argument for the original unity of Chronicles, Ezra, and Nehemiah is that mentioned in the text. But the parts of Ezra-Nehemiah which are not extracts from documents in the hands of the editor display all the characteristic peculiarities of the Chronicles in style, language, and manner of thought. See De Wette-Schrader, *Einleitung,* §§ 235-237. The identity of the author of Ezra and Chronicles is admitted by Keil, but it is impossible to accept his theory that Ezra wrote both books; for the genealogies, and, indeed, the whole character of the work, bring us down to a much later time. In Neh. xii. 22 Darius the Persian is Darius Codomannus.

Note 10, p. 172.—Eusebius, *Hist. Eccles.* Lib. iv. cap. 26. It is certainly very hard to understand what Jewish authorities could omit Esther at so late a date, but the statement of Eusebius is precise. In the fourth century Athanasius and Gregory of Nazianzus still omit Esther from the Canon. There is no doubt that the feast of Purim was first observed, not in Palestine, but in the far East. Lagarde has advanced a very powerful argument to connect both name and thing with the Persian feast Fûrdigan (*Gesammelte Abhandlungen,* p. 161 *seq.*). The ordinance of the fast of Purim (Esther ix. 31), which we see not to have been observed in Palestine in the time of Christ, is lacking in the Greek text of Esther.—On the *Megillath Ta'anith,* or list of days on which the Jews are forbidden to fast, consult Derenbourg, p. 439 *seq.*

Note 11, p. 172.—Mishna, *Sanhedrin,* xi. 1 (ed. Suren., vol. iv. p. 259). " All Israelites have a share in the world to come, except those who deny the resurrection of the dead, those who say that the Torah is not from God, and the Epicureans. R. Akiba adds those who read in outside books, and him who whispers over a wound the words of Exod. xv. 26,"—a kind of charm, the sin of which, according to the commentators, lay in the fact that these sacred words were pronounced after spitting over the sore. Compare on the " outside books " Geiger, p. 200 *seq.*

NOTE 12, p. 173.—Mishna, *Iadaim*, iii. 5.—" All the Holy Scriptures defile the hands : the Song of Solomon and Ecclesiastes defile the hands. R. Judah says, The Song of Solomon defiles the hands, and Ecclesiastes is disputed. R. Jose says, Ecclesiastes does not defile the hands, and the Song of Solomon is disputed. R. Simeon says, Ecclesiastes belongs to the light things of the school of Shammai, and the heavy things of the school of Hillel [*i.e.*, on this point the school of Shammai is less strict]. R. Simeon, son of Azzai, says, I received it as a tradition from the seventy-two elders on the day when they enthroned R. Eliezer, son of Azariah [as President of the Beth Dîn at Iamnia, which became the seat of the heads of the Scribes after the fall of Jerusalem], that the Song of Solomon and Ecclesiastes defile the hands. R. Akiba said, God forbid ! No one in Israel has ever doubted that the Song of Solomon defiles the hands. For no day in the history of the world is worth the day when the Song of Solomon was given to Israel. For all the Hagiographa are holy, but the Song of Solomon is a holy of the holies. If there has been any dispute, it referred only to Ecclesiastes. . . . So they disputed, and so they decided."

Eduiot, v. 3.—"Ecclesiastes does not defile the hands according to the school of Shammai, but does so according to the school of Hillel."

For the disputes as to Ecclesiastes, compare also Jerome on chap. xii. 13, 14. "The Hebrews say that this book, which calls all God's creatures vain, and prefers meat, drink, and passing delights to all else, might seem worthy to disappear with other lost works of Solomon ; but that it merits canonical authority, because it sums up the whole argument in the precept to fear God and do His commandment."

NOTE 13, p. 174.—Akiba's anathema in *Tosef. Sanhedrin*, c. 12 ; R. Simeon's utterance in Talmud Jer. *Megilla*, i. 5 (Krotoschin ed. of 1866, f. 70b).

LECTURE VII.

NOTE 1, p. 176.—On the Psalter in general, the most instructive discussion is still that in Ewald's *Dichter des alten Bundes* (vol. i., 2d ed., Göttingen, 1866 ; Eng. Transl. London, 1881). Ewald admits Davidic Psalms, and denies that there are any as late as the Maccabees. Against the existence of

Davidic Psalms see especially Kuenen, *Historisch-kritisch Onderzoek*, vol. iii. (Leiden 1865); for the existence of Maccabee Psalms see Olshausen in his *Commentar*, which certainly goes too far, and Kuenen, who is much more guarded; against them Ehrt, *Abfassungszeit und Abschluss des Psalters* (Leipzig, 1869). The strongest current argument against placing any Psalms so late is supposed to follow from the history of the Canon, and hardly possesses force. Older writers did not feel this difficulty, and were not insensible to the internal evidence which refers some poems to the Maccabee period. See, for example, Calvin on Psalms xliv. and lxxiv. Of commentaries essentially conservative on the subject of the titles, the best is that of Delitzsch; but it is not unfair to say that his exegesis, based on acceptance of the titles, often appears precarious to himself, as in Pss. lii., lv.

NOTE 2, p. 179.—On the *hallel* see especially Lagarde, *Orientalia*, ii. p. 13 *seq.* Lagarde makes the interesting observation that after the fall of the Temple worship, when the Psalms passed over to the use of the synagogues, they ceased to be *Tehillîm* and became *Mazâmîr, Mazmûrê*, as the Arabs and Syrians call them, after the Heb. *Mizmôr*, found in the titles of many Psalms.

NOTE 3, p. 183.—Another case where one Psalm has been made two is xlii.-xliii., where, by taking the words "O my God" from the beginning of xlii. 6 to the end of the previous verse, and making a single change on the division of the words, we get a poem of three stanzas, with an identical refrain to each.

NOTE 4, p. 183.—The five books of Psalms are mentioned by Epiphanius, *De Mens. et Pond.* cap. v. (ed. Lagarde, p. 157), and by Jerome in the *Prologus Galeatus*. The scheme is no doubt, as Epiphanius suggests, an artificial imitation of the Pentateuch. But this does not prove that the doxologies were added and the division made by the collector, for Books IV. and V. are originally one book.

NOTE 5, p. 185.—SOURCES OF PSALM LXXXVI.

1. Incline, O Lord, thine ear, answer me: for I am poor and needy.	1. *a.* Usual invocation, Is. xxxvii. 17; Ps. xvii. 6, etc. *b.* Ps. xl. 17.—"I am poor and needy;" Ps. xxv. 16.

2. Preserve my soul for I am holy : O thou, my God, save thy servant that trusteth in thee.
3. Be gracious to me, O Lord : for unto thee I cry continually.
4. Make glad the soul of thy servant : for to thee, O Lord, do I lift up my soul.

5. For thou, Lord, art good and forgiving : and abundant in mercy unto all that call upon thee.
6. Give ear, O Lord, unto my prayer : and hearken to the voice of my supplications.
7. In the day of my distress I call on thee : for thou wilt answer me.

8. There is none like thee among the gods, O Lord : and there is nought like thy works.
9. All nations whom thou hast made shall come and worship before thee, O Lord : and shall glorify thy name.
10. For thou art great and doest wonders : thou, O God, alone.
11. Teach me thy way, O Jehovah ; let me walk in thy truth : unite my heart to fear thy name.

12. I will praise thee, O Lord my God, with all my heart : and I will glorify thy name for ever.
13. For great is thy mercy towards me : and thou hast delivered my soul from deep Sheol (the place of the dead).
14. O God, proud men are risen against me, and an assembly of tyrants seek my

2. Ps. xxv. 20.—"Preserve my soul and deliver me : let me not be ashamed, for I take refuge with thee."

3. Current phrases ; *e.g.* Ps. xxx. 8.— "To thee, O Jehovah, I cry ;" ver. 10— "Hear, O Jehovah, and be gracious to me."
4. *a.* Ps. xc. 15.—"Make us glad ;" li. 8.—"Make me hear joy and gladness," etc.
b. Ps. xxv. 1.—"Unto thee, Jehovah, I lift up my soul."
5. Modification of Exod. xxxiv. 6, 7.— "Abundant in mercy . . . forgiving iniquity."

6. Ps. v. 1, 2.—"Give ear to my words, Jehovah . . . hearken to the voice of my cry."

7. Ps. cxx. 1.—"I called to Jehovah in my distress, and he answered me ; lxxvii. 2.—"In the day of my distress I sought the Lord."
8. Ex. xv. 11.—"Who is like thee among the gods, O Jehovah ?" Deut. iii. 24.—"Who is a God that can do like thy works ?"
9. Ps. xxii. 27.—"All ends of the earth shall . . . return unto Jehovah, and before thee shall all families of the nations worship."
10. Ex. xv. 11.—"Doing wonders."

11. *a.* Ps. xxvii. 11.—"Teach me thy way, O Jehovah ;" xxv. 5.—"Guide me in thy truth."
b. Jer. xxxii. 39.—"I will give them one heart, and one way to fear me continually."
12. Ps. ix. 1.—"I will praise thee, Jehovah, with all my heart," etc.

13. *a.* Ps. lvii. 10.—"For thy mercy is great unto the heavens."
b. Ps. lvi. 13.—"For thou hast delivered my soul from death."
14. Ps. liv. 3. — "For strangers are risen against me, and tyrants seek my life who have not set God before them. [In

life: and have not set thee before them.	Hebrew, "proud men" ZēDIM and strangers ZāRIM, differ by a single letter, and D and R in the old character are often not to be distinguished.]
15. But thou, Lord, art a God merciful and gracious, long-suffering, and plenteous in mercy and truth.	15. Quotation from Ex. xxxiv. 6, word for word.
16. Turn unto me and be gracious to me : give thy strength unto thy servant, and save the son of thy handmaid.	16. *a.* Ps. xxv. 16.—"Turn unto me, and be gracious to me." *b.* God the strength (protection) of his people, as Ps. xxviii. 8, and often; Ps. cxvi. 16.—"I am thy servant, the son of thy handmaid."
17. Work with me a token (miracle) for good : that they which hate me may see it and be ashamed : because thou, O Lord, hast holpen me and comforted me.	17. Ps. xl. 3.—"Many shall see it and fear;" Ps. vi. 10.—"Let all mine enemies be ashamed and sore vexed," etc. etc.

NOTE 6, p. 190.—No one can doubt that Psalm cxlix. is a late piece. But can verses 6 *seq.* suit any situation between the Exile and the Maccabee wars?

NOTE 7, p. 191.—The Hebrew *Shîr ham-ma'alôth* cannot have been originally prefixed to each psalm, for it does not mean " a song of ascents " but " the song of ascents." Grammatically the title can only be explained as a singular, not very correctly formed, from a previous collective title Shîrê hamma'alôth. Of this again the proper translation is not " the songs of ascents " (pl.), but " the songs of ascent " (sing.). It is important to observe in this instance how individual titles are derived from an earlier collective title. The same thing, no doubt, applies to the Davidic collections.—See p. 198.

NOTE 8, p. 199.—Keil has the courage to assert that the genuineness of the titles is confirmed by the practice of Arabian poets to prefix their names to their songs; *Introduction*, Eng. Tr., vol. i. p. 457. But let us hear Ahlwardt, the recognised master of this branch of Arabic literature, in his *Bemerkungen über die Aechtheit der alten Arabischen Gedichte*, p. 1 *seq.* (Greifswald, 1872). " Every one who opens the collections of old poems, or looks through books dealing with the oldest Arabic literature, will find that a great many ancient poems are ascribed now to this author now to that. It is undeniable that in this respect great uncertainty prevails, and this is easily understood when we consider, in general, that the use of writing for larger poems was certainly not yet current in those days; that the distance between the time of the poets and the time when their works were collected and written down may be 150 years or more. . . . Even in later times, when writing was fully developed and literature sedulously practised, there were doubts as to the authorship of many poems." The whole discussion is worth notice in its bearing on the Psalter.

NOTE 9, p. 202.—In connection with this acrostic and the similar case of Psalm xxxiv., Professor de Lagarde suggests that, as in later Jewish acrostics, the supernumerary verses may indicate the names of the authors, Phadael and Phadaiah (*Academy*, January 1, 1872. *Symmicta*, p. 107 ; Göttingen, 1877).

NOTE 10, p. 204.—Many would be glad to rescue the authority of the titles in the second Davidic collection for the sake of Psalm li. Yet the last two verses of the Psalm, with the prayer that God will build the walls of Jerusalem, refer so manifestly to the period of the Captivity, that recent supporters of the Davidic authorship are usually inclined to view them as a later addition (Perowne, Delitzsch). But every one can see that the omission of these verses makes the Psalm end abruptly, and a closer examination reveals a connection of thought between vv. 16, 17 (Heb. 18, 19) and vv. 18, 19 (Heb. 20, 21). At present, says the Psalmist, God desires no material sacrifice, but will not despise a contrite heart. How does the Psalmist know that God takes no pleasure in sacrifice ? Not on the principle that the sacrifice of the wicked is sin, for the sacrifice of the contrite whose person God accepts must be acceptable if any sacrifice is so. But does the Psalmist then mean to say, absolutely and in general, that sacrifice is a superseded thing ? No ; for he adds that when Jerusalem is rebuilt the sacrifice of Israel (not merely his own sacrifice) will be pleasing to God. He lives therefore in a time when the fall of Jerusalem has temporarily suspended the sacrificial ordinances, but—and this is the great lesson of the Psalm—has not closed the door of forgiveness to the penitent heart.

Let us now turn to the main thought of the Psalm, and see whether it does not suit this situation as well as the supposed reference to the life of David. The two special points in the Psalm on which the historical reference may be held to turn are ver. 14, "Deliver me from blood-guiltiness," and ver. 11, "Take

not thy Holy Spirit from me." Under the Old Testament the
Holy Spirit is not given to every believer, but to Israel as a
nation (Isa. lxiii. 10, 11), residing in chosen organs, especially in
the prophets, who are *par excellence* " men of the Spirit " (Hos. ix.
7). But the Spirit of Jehovah was also given to David (1 Sam.
xvi. 13 ; 2 Sam. xxiii. 2). The Psalm then, so far as this phrase
goes, may be a Psalm of Israel collectively, of a prophet, or of
David. Again, the phrase " Deliver me from blood-guiltiness,"
is to be understood after Psalm xxxix. 8, " Deliver me from all
my transgressions, make me not the reproach of the foolish."
In the Old Testament the experience of forgiveness is no mere
subjective feeling ; it rests on facts. In the New Testament the
assurance of forgiveness lays hold of the work and victory of
Christ, it lies in the actual realisation of victory over the world
in Him. In the Old Testament, in like manner, some saving
act of God is the evidence of forgiveness. The sense of forgiveness is the joy of God's salvation (verse 12), and the word " salvation " (ישע) is, I believe, always used of some visible delivery
and enlargement from distress. God's wrath is felt in His chastisement, His forgiveness in the removal of affliction, when His
people cease to be the reproach of the foolish. Hence the expression " deliver me." But blood-guiltiness (דמים) does not
necessarily mean the guilt of murder. It means mortal sin
(Ezek. xviii. 13), such sin as, if it remains unatoned, withdraws
God's favour from His land and people (Deut. xxi. 8 *seq.;* Isa. i.
15). Bloodshed is the typical offence among those which under
the ancient law of the First Legislation are not to be atoned for
by a pecuniary compensation, but demand the death of the
sinner. The situation of the Psalm therefore does not necessarily presuppose such a case as David's. It is equally applicable
to the prophet, labouring under a deep sense that he has discharged his calling inadequately and may have the guilt of lost
lives on his head (Ezek. xxxiii.), or to collective Israel in the
Captivity, when, according to the prophets, it was the guilt of
blood equally with the guilt of idolatry that removed God's
favour from His land (Jer. vii. 6 ; Hosea iv. 2, vi. 8 ; Isa. iv. 4).
Nay, from the Old Testament point of view, in which the experience of wrath and forgiveness stands generally in such ,im-
mediate relation to Jehovah's actual dealings with the nation,
the whole thought of the Psalm is most simply understood as a
prayer for the restoration and sanctification of Israel in the

mouth of a prophet of the Exile. For the immediate fruit of forgiveness is that the singer will resume the prophetic function of teaching sinners Jehovah's ways (ver. 13). This is little appropriate to David, whose natural and right feeling in connection with his great sin must rather have been that of silent humiliation than of an instant desire to preach his forgiveness to other sinners. The whole experience of David with Nathan moves in another plane. The Psalmist writes out of the midst of present judgments of God (the Captivity). To David, the pain of death, remitted on his repentance, lay in the future (2 Sam. xii. 13) as an anticipated judgment of God, the remission of which would hardly produce the exultant joy of ver. 12. On the other hand, the whole thought of the Psalm, as Hitzig points out and Delitzsch acknowledges, moves in exact parallel with the spiritual experience of Israel in the Exile as conceived in connection with the personal experience of a prophet in Isa. xl.-lxvi. The Psalm is a psalm of the true Israel of the Exile in the mouth of a prophet, perhaps of the very prophet who wrote the last chapters of the book of Isaiah.

LECTURE VIII.

NOTE 1, p. 208.—On the subject of this and the following Lectures the most important book is Wellhausen's *Geschichte Israels* (Erster Band, Berlin, 1878). Among older works Vatke's *Religion des alten Testaments* (Erster Theil, Berlin, 1835) is of the greatest value, but, being encumbered with a mass of Hegelian terminology of a repulsive kind, it practically remained unnoticed till inquiry was redirected into similar channels by the writings of Graf (*De Templo Silonensi*, Meissen, 1855 ; *Die geschichtlichen Bücher des alten Testaments*, 1866 ; *Zur Geschichte des Stammes Levi* in Merx's *Archiv*, 1870). Graf was also neglected in Germany, under the dominant influence of the Göttingen and Halle schools, but his point of view was taken up by Kuenen in Holland, and was for a time supposed to be necessarily connected with ultra-rationalism. Since the appearance of Wellhausen's book there are many signs that critics of every school are rapidly coming to be at one on the main facts of the religious history of Israel. In the interpretation of the facts, differences of theological standpoint will no doubt continue to assert themselves, as they did to an equal or greater extent when no one doubted that Moses wrote the whole Pentateuch.

NOTE 2, p. 219.—Mohammed boasts of his fabulous version of the history of Joseph that he has it by direct revelation, not having known it before; *Koran*, Sura xii. 3. The Biblical historians never make such a claim, which to a thinking mind is one of the clearest proofs of Mohammed's imposture. It is worth while to see how Astruc speaks on this topic more than a century ago. Many theologians do not think so clearly now. " Moyse parle toujours, dans la Genese, comme un simple historien, il ne dit nulle part que ce qu'il raconte, lui ait esté inspiré. On ne doit donc point supposer cette révelation sans aucun fondement. Quand les Prophetes ont parlé de choses, qui leur avoient esté révelées, ils n'ont point manqué d'avertir qu'ils parloient au nom de Dieu, et de sa part ; et c'est ainsi que Moyse en a usé lui mesme, dans les autres Livres du Pentateuque, quand il a eu quelque révelation a communiquer au peuple Hebreu, ou quelque ordre de Dieu a lui intimer. Auroit-il negligé la mesme précaution, en composant le Livre de la Genese, s'il s'etoit trouvé dans les mesmes circonstances ?" (*Conjectures sur la Genese*, p. 5, Bruxelles, 1753). When it is admitted that the Bible history is based upon written sources, oral testimony, and personal observation, no theory of inspiration can alter the principle that the knowledge of the writers was limited by their sources. Whatever they say which they did not find in their sources is not evidence, but commentary. On the question of fact, what the actual social and religious observances of Israel before the Exile were, the Chronicler can tell us nothing which he had not read in earlier authentic history. Anything which he adds to his sources is historical evidence for the state of things in his own time—which he may use to fill up his picture and give it colour—but not for the state of things before the Exile. Now, that the author of Chronicles does use the ritual and standing ordinances of his own time to give copiousness of detail to his pictures of ancient events, and bring them more vividly before the minds of his readers, is quite certain from comparison of his narrative with that of Kings. In doing so he does no more than is habitually done without offence in the pulpit. The Bible history, as paraphrased by a graphic modern preacher, is always coloured with the nationality of the speaker, and assimilated in greater or less degree to the life of his own time. What is innocent, and indeed inevitable, in an uninspired preacher may surely have happened in Bible times. And that the Chronicler is not so much a historian as a Levitical preacher on the old history, is plain from the whole manner of his book, and from the fact that he actually quotes among his sources a *Midrash* (E.V. *story*), or perhaps two books of this character. The word *Midrash* is not found in earlier parts of the Old Testament; and when we consider the date of the Chronicles, there can be no hesitation in giving to the word its ordinary meaning—viz., that of a *sermonising exposition*, such as was familiar in the preaching of the synagogue in the age of the Scribes. *Midrash* is a thing so unfamiliar to us that we are apt to think it impossible that anything of the kind should be found in the Bible. But we are not entitled to say *a priori* that any style of literature that was freely practised and perfectly understood in those days must have been excluded by Divine providence from the Canon as it was ultimately shaped. But in proportion as the Chronicles have the complexion of a *Midrash* they are improper to be directly used in a purely historical investigation into the ritual and usages of pre-Exilic times.

Without professing to offer a positive solution of the questions which these remarks suggest, I shall close this note with some illustrations of the relation of Chronicles to Kings, which seem sufficient to prove that the former books cannot safely be used in the way common to recent defenders of the traditional view of the Pentateuch :—

1°. 1 Kings viii. 3: "The priests took up the ark." 2 Chron. v. 4: "The Levites took up the ark." In this whole passage the Chronicles have no other source than the narrative of Kings, which, for the most part, is verbally followed. That the ark was carried by the priests is in accordance with Deut. xxxi. and the whole pre-Exilic history (Josh. iii. 3, vi. 6, viii. 33; 1 Sam. vi. 15 (compared with Josh. xxi. 16); 2 Sam. xv. 24, 29). The statement in Chronicles is a correction in accordance with the Levitical law.

2°. In 2 Kings xxiii. Josiah's action against the high places is represented as taking place in his eighteenth year, as the immediate result of his repentance on hearing the words of the law found in the Temple, and in pursuance of the covenant of reformation. In 2 Chron. xxxiv. the reformation begins in his eighth year, and the land is purged before the book of the law is found (ver. 8).

3°. In 2 Kings xi. Jehoiada's assistants in the revolution which cost Athaliah her life, are the foreign bodyguard which we know to have been employed in the sanctuary up to the time of Ezekiel (see p. 249). In 2 Chron. xxiii., the Carians and the footguards are replaced by Levites. No doubt the guard were the Levites of the First Temple. They did those services which the Levites did in the Second Temple. But they were not Levites in the sense of the Pentateuch, but, in part at least, uncircumcised foreigners.

4°. According to 2 Kings xii., the support of the Temple fabric in the early years of Jehoash was a burden on the priestly revenues brought into the house by worshippers. In 2 Chron. xxiv., it appears as defrayed by a special collection made through all Judah (see p. 252, and Wellhausen, *Gesch.*, p. 206 *seq.*).

5°. The speeches in Chronicles are not literal reports. They are freely composed without strict reference to the exact historical situation. Compare, for example, the correspondence between Solomon and Hiram (1 Kings v. 3-9; 2 Chron. ii. 3-16). Thus in Abijah's speech on the field of battle (2 Chron. xiii. 4 *seq.*), the king is made to say that Jeroboam's rebellion took place when Rehoboam was a mere lad and tender-hearted, and had not courage to withstand the rebels. The mere lad (נער), according to 1 Kings xiv. 21, was forty-one years old. Abijah then proceeds to boast of the regular temple service conducted according to Levitical law. But the service described is that of the Second Temple, for the king speaks of the golden candlestick as one of its elements. In Solomon's Temple there stood not one golden candlestick in the holy place in front of the *adyton* (דביר, oracle, *i.e.* Holy of Holies) but ten (1 Kings vii. 49). Again, the morning and evening burnt offerings are mentioned. But there is a great concurrence of evidence that the evening offering was purely cereal in the First Temple, or indeed in the time of Ezra and Nehemiah (1 Kings xviii. 36, *Hebrew;* 2 Kings xvi. 15 ; Ezra ix. 4, *Hebrew*). Compare Kuenen's *Religion of Israel*, chap. ix., note 1. This speech is one of the clearest proofs that the Chronicler's descriptions of ordinances are taken from the usage of his own time.

6°. Under the reign of David, the Chronicles insert a very full and valuable account of the order of the Levitical service of song, etc. But the order is that of the Second Temple. The gates and the like described in 1 Chron. xxvi. could not have existed in David's time, before the temple was built, and one of them has a Persian name. A very curious point remarked by Ewald (*Lehrbuch*, § 274 b), and more clearly elucidated by Wellhausen, is that six heads of choirs of the guild of Heman bear the names (1) I have given great (2) and lofty help (3) to him that sat in distress ; (4) I have spoken (5) a superabundance of (6) prophecies (1 Chron. xxv. 4). As the names of literal individuals in the time of David, these names are incredible. But the words seem to be an anthem in which six choirs of singers may well have had parts, and received names from their parts. In like manner Jeduthun, which, if the description of the temple music is literal history of David's time, must be the name of a man, head of a choir, is really, as we see from the titles of the Psalms, a musical term. The complete identification of the Levites with the temple singers which the order of Chronicles supposes was not yet actual in the time of Ezra and Nehemiah.

7°. The Kings say expressly that the high places were not removed by Asa and Jehoshaphat though their hearts were perfect with Jehovah (1 Kings xv. 14 ; xxii. 43). The Chronicler, on the contrary, says that both Asa and Jehoshaphat abolished the local high places (2 Chron. xiv. 5, xvii. 6), which, however, does not prevent him from copying the opposite statements of 1 Kings in connection with some other particulars which he has occasion to transfer from that book (2 Chron. xv. 17 ; xx. 33).

People may shake their heads at all this and say, You are touching the historicity of the book. But our first duty is to facts ; and the only question I raise is whether we can use the Chronicles to correct or modify unambiguous statements of the earlier books, or whether, in order to get real instruction from the later history, we must not frankly admit that its descriptions of ritual often belong to the Chronicler's own time. The proofs of this might be greatly multiplied. See especially De Wette's *Beiträge*, Bd. 1 (Halle, 1806), and Wellhausen's *Geschichte*, p. 177 *seq.*

NOTE 3, p. 226.—The English version of Hosea iii. does not clearly express the prophet's thought. Hosea's wife had deserted him for a stranger. But though she is thus "in love with a paramour, and unfaithful," his love follows her, and he buys her back out of the servile condition into which she appears to have fallen. She is brought back from shame and servitude, but not

LECT. VIII.   *IAHWÈ: SHADDAI.*   423

to the privileges of a wife. She must sit alone by her husband, reserved for him, but not yet restored to the relations of wedlock. So Jehovah will deal with Israel, when by destroying the state and the ordinances of worship He breaks off all intercourse, not only between Israel and the Baalim, but between Israel and Himself. See on the whole allegory the article HOSEA in the *Encyc. Brit.* (ninth edition).

NOTE 4, p. 227.—On the ephod, see Vatke, *op. cit.* p. 267 *seq.*; Studer on Judges viii. 27. The passages where teraphim are mentioned in the Hebrew but not in the English version are, Gen. xxxi. 19, 34, 35; 1 Sam. xv. 23, xix. 13, 16; 2 Kings xxiii. 24; Zech. x. 2. Compare, as to their nature, Spencer, *De Legibus Ritualibus Hebræorum*, Lib. iii., c. 3, § 2 *seq.*

NOTE 5, p. 231.—Colenso (*Pentateuch*, Part V.), Lenormant (*Lettres Assyriologiques*, vol. ii.), Tiele, Land, and others have sought to prove that Jehovah (Iahwè) is a name borrowed from Semitic heathenism, while Brugsch and others will have it that the Mosaic conception of God is borrowed from the Egyptians. The latter view is totally untenable, and the evidence for the former breaks down upon close examination. See especially the elaborate discussion in Baudissin's *Studien*, vol. i. No. 3 (1876). That the name Iahwè existed in a narrower circle before it became through Moses the recognised name of Israel's national God (Exod. vi. 3) is probable; and at that time the word may have had a much less lofty interpretation than it received in Exod. iii. 14. The physical meaning can hardly be other than *he who causes* rain or lightning *to fall* upon the earth. Compare Gen. xix. 24, where the brimstone and fire that destroyed Sodom are said to fall from (*lit.* from beside) Iahwè from heaven; and see Lagarde, *Orientalia* II. 29.

I take this opportunity to explain more fully than I have formerly done my view of the other old name Shaddai, recently cited by Mr. Cheyne in his commentary on Isaiah. It can be shown from the Greek versions, and even from Jerome's note, *robustus et sufficiens ad omnia perpetranda,* that the oldest form of the traditional interpretation of the name is not "almighty," but "sufficient," ἱκανός, which is again derived from the Jewish traditional etymology from the relative שׁ and די. Now, if this etymology is so ancient, it can hardly be doubted that the punctuation with *pathach* under the second radical is derived from it. But it is this punctuation which has misled many scholars to find in the word a derivative from שׁדד with a nominal formative affix. Such a form is highly improbable in an old divine name, which in the most ancient use is a substantive, not an adjective to *El;* and the punctuation loses all authority when we learn that it expresses an impossible etymology. (Compare cases like צלמות.) We are thus entitled to regard the word as an intensive from שׁדה, Aram. שׁדא, *eshad,* Arab. *thada,* to pour forth, and the name, which from its form is probably of Aramaic origin, will mean the god who gives rain. Compare the familiar fact that even under the Mohammedan empire land watered by rain from heaven is named *baʻl.*

NOTE 6, p. 235.—In some of these cases, evidence that the place was a sanctuary may be demanded. Kadesh is proved to be so by its very name, with which it agrees that it was a Levitical city and a consecrated asylum. Accordingly it formed the *rendezvous* of Zebulon and Naphtali under Barak and Deborah. Mahanaim was the place of a theophany, from which it had its name. It was also a Levitical city, and Cant. vi. 13 alludes to the "dance of Mahanaim," which was probably such a festal dance as took place at Shiloh (Jud. xxi. 21). As a holy place the town was the seat of Ishbosheth's kingdom, and the headquarters of David's host during the revolt of Absalom. Tabor, on the frontiers of Zebulon and Issachar, seems to be the mountain alluded to in Deut. xxxiii. 18, 19, as the sanctuary of these tribes, and it appears along with Mizpah, as a seat of degenerate priests, in Hos. v. 1. The northern Mizpah is identical with Ramoth Gilead and with the sanctuary of Jacob (Gen. xxxi. 45 *seq.*).

NOTE 7, p. 236.—Except at a feast, or to entertain a guest, or in sacrifice before a local shrine, the Bedouin tastes no meat but the flesh of the gazelle or other game. This throws light on Deut. xii. 22, which shows that in old Israel game was the only meat not eaten sacrificially. That flesh was not eaten every day even by wealthy people appears very clearly from Nathan's parable and from the book of Ruth. The wealthy man, like the Arab sheikh, ate the same fare as his workmen. According to *MI Noctes* (Calcutta edition, ii. 276), eating flesh is one of the three elements of high enjoyment.

LECTURE IX.

NOTE 1, p. 246.—Critics distinguish in Deuteronomy the legislative code (chaps. xii.-xxvi.) and the framework, which appears to be by a different hand or hands. In all probability the code once stood, along with an introduction, in a separate book corresponding to Deut. iv. 44-xxvi. 19. There is no evidence that Josiah had more than this book, and even the Fathers identify the book found in the Temple with Deuteronomy. So Jerome, *Adv. Jovin.*, i. 5 ; Chrysostom, *Hom. in Mat.* ix. p. 135 B. The relation of his reformation to Deuteronomy may be shown thus :—

2 Kings xxiii. 5	.	.	Deut. xii. 2.
,, ,, 7	.	.	,, xxiii. 17, 18.
,, ,, 9	.	.	,, xviii. 8.
,, ,, 10	.	.	,, xviii. 10.
,, ,, 11	.	.	,, xvii. 3.
,, ,, 14	.	.	,, xvi. 21, 22.
,, ,, 21	.	.	,, xvi. 5.
,, ,, 24	.	.	,, xviii. 11.

Compare further Wellhausen, *Composition des Hexateuchs*, III., in *Jahrbb. f. Deut. Theol.*, 1877, pp. 458 *seq.*

NOTE 2, p. 248.—The Pillars of Hercules are identical with the two steles or *maççeboth* of the Tyrian Melkart, described by Herodotus, Bk. ii. chap. 44, and were carried westward by the Phœnician navigators and colonists. Two huge pillars similar to those of Solomon stood in the *propylæa* of the temple of Hierapolis. See Lucian, *De Syria Dea*, chap. 16, 28.

NOTE 3, p. 248.—This passage is so important that I give it in a translation, slightly corrected after the versions in vv. 7, 8, as already printed in my *Answer to the Amended Libel* (1878). The corrections are obvious, and have been made also by Smend (*Der Prophet Ezechiel erklärt*, Leipz., 1880).

Ezek. xliv. 6. O house of Israel ! Have done with all your abominations, (7) in that ye bring in foreigners uncircumcised in heart and flesh to be in my sanctuary, polluting my house, when ye offer my bread, the fat, and the blood ; and so ye break my covenant in addition to all your abominations, (8) and keep not the charge of my holy things, but appoint them as keepers of my charge in my sanctuary. Therefore, (9) thus saith the

Lord, No foreigner uncircumcised in heart and flesh shall enter
my sanctuary—no foreigner whatever, who is among the children of Israel. (10) But the Levites, because they departed
from me when Israel went astray, when they went astray from
me after their idols, even they shall bear their guilt, (11) and
be ministers in my sanctuary, officers at the gates of the house,
and ministers of the house; it is they who shall kill the burnt-
offering and the sacrifice for the people, and it is they who shall
stand before them to minister unto them. (12) Because they
ministered unto them before their idols, and were a stumbling-
block of guilt to the house of Israel, therefore I swear concerning
them, saith the Lord God, that they shall bear their guilt, (13)
and shall not draw near to me to do the office of a priest to me,
or to touch any of my holy things—the most holy things; but
they shall bear their shame and their abominations which they
have done. (14) And I will make them keepers of the charge
of the house for all the service thereof, and for all that is to be
done about it. (15) But the Levite priests, the sons of Zadok,
who kept the charge of my sanctuary when the children of
Israel went astray from me—they shall come near unto me to
minister unto me, and they shall stand before me to offer unto
me the fat and the blood, saith the Lord God. They shall enter
into my sanctuary and approach my table, ministering unto me,
and keep my charge.

NOTE 4, p. 250.—There is, I think, good ground for supposing that the slaughtering of sacrifices, which Ezekiel expressly
assigns in future to the Levites, was formerly the work of the
guards. It was the king who provided the ordinary temple
sacrifices (2 Chron. viii. 13, xxxi. 3; Ezek. xlv. 17), and there
can be little doubt that the animals killed for the royal table
were usually offered as peace offerings at the temple (Deut xii.
21). In Saul's time, at least, an unclean person could not sit at
the royal table, which implies that the food was sacrificial (1
Sam. xx. 26; Lev. vii. 20; Deut. xii. 22). Now the Hebrew
name for "captain of the guard" is "chief slaughterer" (*rab
hattabbâchîm*)—an expression which, so far as one can judge
from Syriac and Arabic as well as Hebrew, can only mean
slaughterer of cattle (comp. מטבח, Euting, *Pun. Steine*, p. 16).
So the bodyguard were also the royal butchers, an occupation
not deemed unworthy of warriors in early times. Eurip. *Electra*,
815. *Odys.* A. 108. In Lev. i. 5, 6 it is assumed that every

man kills his own sacrifice, and so still in the Arabian desert every person knows how to kill and dress a sheep.

NOTE 5, p. 254.—According to 1 Sam. ii. 27-36 the whole clan or "father's house" of Eli, the family which received God's revelation in Egypt with a promise of everlasting priesthood, is to lose its prerogative and sink to an inferior position, in which its survivors shall be glad to crouch before the new high priest for a place in one of the inferior priestly guilds which may yield them a livelihood. As 1 Kings ii. 27 regards this prophecy as fulfilled in the substitution of Zadok for Abiathar, it is plain that the former did not belong to the high-priestly family chosen in the wilderness. That his genealogy is traced to Aaron and Eleazar in 1 Chron. vi. 50 *seq.* does not disprove this, for among all Semites membership of a guild is figured as sonship. Thus in the time of the Chronicles sons of Eleazar and Ithamar respectively would mean no more than the higher and lower guilds of priests. The common theory that the house of Eli was not in the original line of Eleazar and Phinehas is inconsistent with Num. xxv. 13 compared with 1 Sam. ii. 30. The Chronicler places Ahimelech son of Abiathar in the lower priesthood of Ithamar (1 Chron. xxiv. 3, 6), but Abiathar himself is not connected with Ithamar by a genealogical line. The deposition of the father reduces the son to the lower guild.

NOTE 6, p. 257.—1 Sam. i. 20, 21. "When the new year came round, Hannah conceived and bare a son, and named him . . . and Elkanah went up with his whole household to sacrifice to Jehovah the yearly sacrifice and his vow." The date of the new year belongs to the last of this series of events. Compare Wellhausen, *Text Samuelis*, p. 39 ; *Geschichte Israels*, p. 97 *seq.*, 111, note. The autumn feast was also the great feast at Jerusalem (1 Kings viii. 2), and in the Northern Kingdom (1 Kings xii. 32).

In Judges ix. 27 read, "They trode the grapes and made *hillûlîm* (a sacred offering in praise of God from the fruits of the earth, Lev. xix. 24), and went into the house of their god and feasted," etc.

NOTE 7, p. 266.—Some other examples of irregularities in the ritual of Israel before the Captivity may be here appended. (1) According to the Levitical law it is the function of the Levites to carry the ark. In the history, the ark is either borne by the priests (Josh. iii. 3, vi. 6, viii. 33 ; 1 Kings viii. 3) or conveyed in a cart (2 Sam. vi. 3). In 2 Sam. xv. 24, 29, the Levites aid the chief priests in carrying the ark, but it must be remembered that before Ezekiel priests and Levites are not two separate classes. The Levites in the early history are the priestly guild and family (see p. 359 *seq.*). (2) On the use of sacred symbols prohibited in the Law, see p. 353 *seq.* (3) Under the Law the Levites and priests had a right of common round their cities, but this pasture ground was inalienable (Lev. xxv. 34), so that 1 Kings ii. 26, Jer. xxxii. 7, where priests own and sell fields, are irregular.

LECTURE X.

NOTE 1, p. 268.—Compare especially Duhm, *Theologie der Propheten* (Bonn, 1875), and Wellhausen's *Geschichte Israels*, Kap. 10.

NOTE 2, p. 270.—For the subject here touched on I refer in general to the arguments and authorities adduced in my essay on *Animal-worship*, etc., in the *Journal of Philology*, ix. 75 *seq.* In Psalm xlv. 12 render, "And, O daughter of Tyre, with a gift shall the rich among the people entreat thy favour."

NOTE 3, p. 278.—Plato, *Timæus*, cap. xxxii. p. 71 D. The mantic faculty belongs to the part of the soul settled in the liver, because that part has no share in reason and thought. "For inspired and true divination is not attained to by any one when in his full senses, but only when the power of thought is fettered by sleep or disease or some paroxysm of frenzy."

This view of inspiration is diametrically opposite to that of S. Paul (1 Cor. xiv. 32), and the complete self-consciousness and self-control of the prophets taught in that passage belong equally to the spiritual prophecy of the Old Testament. Plato's theory, however, was applied to the prophets by Philo, the Jewish Platonist, who describes the prophetic state as an ecstasy in which the human νοῦς disappears to make way for the divine Spirit (*Quis rerum div. haeres*, § 53, Mang. i. p. 511). Something similar has been taught in recent times by Hengstenberg and others,—substituting, as we observe, the pagan for the Biblical conception of revelation.

NOTE 4, p. 285.—In ancient times the priestly oracle of Urim and Thummim was a sacred lot; for in 1 Sam. xiv. 41 the true text, as we can still restore it from the LXX., makes Saul pray, If the iniquity be in me or Jonathan, give Urim; but if in Israel, give Thummim. This sacred lot was connected with the ephod, which in the time of the Judges was something very like an idol (p. 227 and note). Spencer therefore seems to be right in assuming a resemblance in point of form between the priestly lot of the Urim and Thummim and divination by Teraphim (*De Leg. Rit.*, lib. iii. c. 3). The latter again appears as practised by drawing lots by arrows before the idol (Ezek. xxi. 21, "he shook the arrows"), which was also a familiar form of divination among the heathen Arabs (Ibn Hishâm, 97 ; C. de Perceval, *Essai sur l'histoire des Arabes*, 1847, ii. 310). The very name of Thummim seems to reappear in the Arabic *tamâ'im* (Imraulkais, *Moal.*, 14 ; Lagarde, *Proph. Chald.*, xlvii.). Under the Levitical law the priestly lot exists in theory in a very modified form, confined to the high priest, but in reality it was obsolete (Neh. vii. 65).

NOTE 5, p. 287.—The argument of Amos v. 25 is obscured in the English translation by the rendering of the following verse. The verbs in that verse are not perfects, and the idea is not that in the wilderness Israel sacrificed to Moloch and Saturn (Keiwan) in place of Jehovah. Verse 26 commences the prophecy of judgment, "Ye shall take up your idols, and (not as E.V. "therefore") I will send you into captivity."

NOTE 6, p. 291.—The Greek doctrine of the inspiration of the poet never led to the recognition of certain poems as sacred Scriptures. But the Indian Vedas were regarded in later times as infallible, eternal, divine. In the priestly bards, therefore (the *Rishis*), the first authors of the Vedic hymns, we may expect to find, if anywhere, a consciousness analogous to that of the prophets. Their accounts of themselves have been collected by Dr. John Muir in his *Sanscrit Texts*, vol. iii., and some recent writers have laid great stress on this supposed parallel to prophetic inspiration. But what are the facts ? The Rishis frequently speak of their hymns as their own works, but also sometimes entertain the idea that their prayers, praises, and ceremonies generally were supernaturally inspired. The gods are said to "generate" prayer ; the prayer is god-given. The poet, like a Grecian singer, calls on the gods to help his prayer. "May prayer, brilliant and divine, proceed from us." But in all this there is no stricter conception of inspiration than in the Greek poets. It is not the word of God that we hear, but the poet's word aided by the gods (compare Muir, p. 275). How different is this from the language of the prophets ! "Where do the prophets," asks Merx (*Jenaer Lit. Zeit.*, 1876, p. 19) "pray for illumination of spirit, force of poetic expression, glowing power of composition?" In truth, as Merx concludes, Kuenen still owes us the proof of his statement that other ancient nations share the prophetic consciousness of inspiration. That consciousness is as clearly separated from the inspiration of the heathen μάντις as from the afflatus of the Indian or Grecian bard.

On Mohammed's inspiration see Nöldeke, *Geschichte des Qorâns*, p. 4. "He not only gave out his later revelations, composed with conscious deliberation and the use of foreign materials, as being, equally with the first glowing productions of his enthusiasm, angelic messages and proofs of the prophetic spirit, but made direct use of pious fraud to gain adherents, and employed the authority of the Koran to decide and adjust things that had nothing to do with religion."

NOTE 7, p. 304.—Properly to understand the prophetic doctrine of forgiveness, we must remember that the problem of the acceptance of the individual with God was never fully solved in the Old Testament. The prophets always deal with the nation in its unity as the object of wrath and forgiveness. The religious life of the individual is still included in that of the nation. When we, by analogy, apply what the prophets say of the nation to the forgiveness of the individual, we must always remember that Israel's history starts with a work of redemption—deliverance from Egypt. To this objective proof of Jehovah's love the prophets look back, just as we look to the finished work of Christ. In it is contained the pledge of Divine love, giving confidence to approach God and seek His forgiveness. But while the Old Testament believer had no difficulty in assuring himself of Jehovah's love to Israel, it was not so easy to find a pledge of His grace to the individual, and especially not easy to apprehend God as a forgiving God under personal affliction. Here especially the defect of the dispensation came out, and the problem of individual acceptance with God, which was acutely realised in and after the fall of the nation, when the righteous so often suffered with the wicked, is that most closely bound up with the interpretation of the atoning sacrifices of the Levitical ritual.

LECTURE XI.

NOTE 1, p. 310.—*Berachoth Bab.*, 5a (p. 234 in Schwab's French translation, Paris, 1871). *Megilla Jer.*, cited in Lect. VI. p. 174. Compare Weber, *op. cit.* p. 89 *seq.*, and Dr. M. Wise in the *Hebrew Review*, vol. i. p. 12 *seq.* (Cincinnati, 1880).

NOTE 2, p. 317.—It is of some importance to realise how completely Deuteronomy covers the same ground with the First Legislation. The following table exhibits the facts of the case:—

Exod. xxi. 1-11 (Hebrew slaves)—Deut. xv. 12-18.
,, ,, 12-14 (Murder and asylum)—Deut. xix. 1-13.
,, ,, 15, 17 (Offences against parents)—Deut. xxi. 18-21.
,, ,, 16 (Manstealing)—Deut. xxiv. 7.
,, ,, 18—xxii. 15. Compensations to be paid for various injuries. This section is not repeated in Deuteronomy, except as regards the law of retaliation, Exod. xxi. 23-25, which in Deut. xix. 16-21 is applied to false witnesses.
Exod. xxii. 16, 17 (Seduction)—Deut. xxii. 28, 29.
,, ,, 18 (Witch)—Deut. xviii. 10-12.
,, ,, 19—Deut. xxvii. 21.
,, ,, 20 (Worship of other gods)—Deut. xiii., xvii. 2-7.
,, ,, 21-24 (Humanity to stranger, widow, and orphan)—Deut. xxiv. 17-22.
,, ,, 25 (Usury)—Deut. xxiii. 19.
,, ,, 26, 27 (Pledge of raiment)—Deut. xxiv. 10-13.
,, ,, 28 (Treason)—Not in Deuteronomy.
,, ,, 29, 30 (First fruits and firstlings)—Deut. xxvi. 1-11, xv. 19-23.
,, ,, 31 (Unclean food)—Deut. xiv. 2-21. The particular precept of Exodus occupies only ver. 21; but the principle of avoiding food inconsistent with holiness is expanded.
Exod. xxiii. 1 (False witness)—Deut. xix. 16-21.
,, ,, 2, 3, 6, 7, 8, } (Just judgment)—Deut. xvi. 18-20.
,, ,, 4, 5 (Animals strayed or fallen)—Deut. xxii. 1-4.
,, ,, 9-11 (Sabbatical year)—Deut. xv. 1-11.
,, ,, 12 (Sabbath as a provision of humanity)—Deut. v. 14, 15.
,, ,, 13 (Names of other gods)—Deut. vi. 13.
,, ,, 14-19a (Annual feasts)—Deut. xvi. 1-17.
,, ,, 19b (Kid in mother's milk)—Deut. xiv. 21.

The parallel becomes still more complete when we observe that to the Code of Deuteronomy is prefixed an introduction, iv. 44—xi. 32, containing the ten commandments, and so answering to Exod. xx.

NOTE 3, p. 319.—According to Exod. xxxiii. 7; Num. x. 33, the sanctuary is outside the camp and at some considerable distance from it, both when the people are at rest and when they are on the march. That the ark precedes the host is implied in Exod. xxiii. 20, xxxii. 34; Deut. i. 33. The same order of march is found in Joshua iii. 3, 4, where the distance between the ark and the host is 2000 cubits, and the reason of this arrangement, as in Num. *l. c.*, is that the ark is Israel's guide. (Comp. Isa. lxiii. 11 *seq.*) That the ark when at rest stood outside the camp is implied also in Num. xi. 24 *seq.*, xii. 4. This corresponds with the usage of the early sanctuaries in Canaan, which stood on high points outside the cities (1 Sam. ix. 14). So the Temple at Jerusalem originally stood outside the city of David, which occupied the lower slope of the Temple hill (comp. Micah iv. 8, which, on the correct rendering, places the original seat of the kingdom on Ophel). But, as the city grew, ordinary buildings encroached on the Temple plateau (Ezek. xliii. 8). This appears to Ezekiel to be derogatory to the sanctity of the house (comp. Deut. xxiii. 14), and is the reason for the ordinance set forth in symbolic form in Ezek. xlv. 1 *seq.*, xlviii., where the sanctuary stands in the middle of Israel, but isolated, the priests and the Levites lodging between it and the laity, as in the Levitical law, Num. i.-iii. Here, as in other cases, the Levitical law appears as the latest stage of the historical development.

NOTE 4, p. 320.—Of the immense literature dealing with the linguistic and other marks by which the Levitical document may be separated out, it is enough to refer particularly to Nöldeke, *Untersuchungen zur Kritik des A. T.*, Kiel, 1869; Wellhausen, *Composition des Hexateuchs*, in the *Jahrb. f. D. T.* 1876, p. 392 *seq.* 531 *seq.*; 1877, p. 407 *seq.*, and many important articles by Kuenen in the *Theologisch Tijdschrift*. The document contains also a brief sketch of the history from the creation, and includes most of the statistical matter of Joshua. Nöldeke gives the following determination of the Levitical parts of the middle books. (An asterisk means that only part of the verse is Levitical.)

Exod. i. 1-5, 7, 13, 14; ii. 23*, 24, 25; vi. 2-13, 16-30; vii. 1-13, 19, 20*, 22; viii. 1-3, 11*, 12-15; ix. 8-12; xi. 9, 10; xii. 1-23, 28, 37a, 40-51; xiii. 1, 2, 20; xiv. 1-4, 8, 9, 10*, 15-18, 21*, 22, 23, 26, 27*, 28, 29; xv. 22, 23*, 27;

xvi. ; xvii. ; xix. 2a ; xxiv. 15-18a ; xxv. 1—xxxi. 17 ; xxxv.—xl.

Leviticus i. 1—xxvi. 2 ; xxv. 19-22 ; xxvi. 46 ; xxvii.

Numbers i. 1—viii. 22 ; ix. 1—x. 28 ; xiii. 1-17a, 21, 25, 26*, 32*; xiv. 1-10, 26-38 ; xv. ; xvi. 1a, 2*, 3-11, 16-22, 23, 24*, 26*, 27*, 35 ; xvii.—xix ; xx. 1*, 2-13, 22-29 ; xxi. 4*, 10, 11 ; xxii. 1 ; xxv. 1-19 ; xxvi. 1-9a, 12-58, 59*, 60-66 ; xxvii.; (xxx. 2-17 ?); xxxii ; xxxii. 2 (3 ?), 4-6, 16-32, 33*, 40 ; xxxiii. 1-39, 41-51, 54 ; xxxiv. ; xxxv. ; xxxvi.

Some passages in this list have undergone changes, and all the Levitical laws are not of one hand and date, though they form a well-marked class. Other recent inquirers have been chiefly occupied with this further analysis of the Levitical legislation. So far as Nöldeke goes, his table is generally accepted as careful and correct in essentials. On the language of this part of the Pentateuch compare Ryssel, *De Elohistae Pentateuchi sermone* (Leipzig, 1878), whose grammatical material is, however, better than his historical conclusion.

A good example of the fundamental difference in legal style between the Levitical laws and the Deuteronomic Code is found in Num. xxxv. compared with Deut. xix. In Numbers, the technical expression city of refuge is repeated at every turn. In Deuteronomy the word *refuge* does not occur, and the cities are always described by a periphrasis. In Numbers the phrase for "accidentally" is *bish'gaga*, in Deut. *bib'li da'at*. The judges in the one are "the congregation," in the other "the elders of his city." The verb for *hate* is different. The one account says again and again "to kill any person," the other "to kill his neighbour." The detailed description of the difference between murder and accidental homicide is entirely diverse in language and detail. The structure of the sentences is distinct, and in addition to all this there is a substantial difference in the laws themselves, inasmuch as Deuteronomy says nothing about remaining in the city of refuge till the death of the high priest. On a rough calculation, omitting auxiliary verbs, particles, etc., Num. xxxv. 11-34 contains 19 nouns and verbs which also occur in Deut. xix. 2-13, and 45 which do not occur in the parallel passage ; while the law, as given in Deuteronomy, has 50 such words not in the law of Numbers.

NOTE 5, p. 328.—Jehovistic narrative—Gen. vi. 5-8 ; vii. 1-5, 10, 12, 16b, 17, 23 ; viii. 26, 3a, 6-12, 13b, 20-22.

Elohistic narrative—vi. 9-22; vii. 6, 11, 13-16a, 18-22, 24; viii. 1, 2a, 3b-5, 13a, 14-19; ix. 1-17. A few words and clauses are added by the redactor.

NOTE 6, p. 337.—The protected stranger is still known in Arabia. Among the Hodheil at Zeimeh I found in 1880 an Indian boy, the orphan child of a wandering Suleimâny or travelling smith, who was under the protection of the community, every member of which would have made the lad's quarrel his own. The *dakhîl*, as he is called, is, as it were, adopted into the tribe, and his lack of relations to help him is supplemented by the whole community. So, no doubt, in early Hebrew times the Gêr is in process of conversion into an Israelite. In Deuteronomy the relation is somewhat looser, or rather the distinctive position of an Israelite is more sharply defined. In Deut. xiv. 21, unclean food which the First Legislation commands to be thrown to the dogs may be given to the Gêr. In the Levitical Legislation the word Gêr is already on the way to assume its later technical sense of proselyte. It is noteworthy that in the Levitical law the opposite of Gêr is אזרח, αὐτόχθων, that is, one who belongs to the old inhabitants of Canaan. In the earlier times the autochthonous population were not the Israelites but the Canaanites; and so still in 1 Kings iv. 31 [v. 11], Ezrahite seems to be the name of a non-Israelite family. See Lagarde, *Orientalia* II., p. 25 *seq.*

NOTE 7, p. 341.—In Amos iv. 5, the general thought is that the people's ritual zeal pleases themselves but not Jehovah. But when the prophet draws particular attention to the fact that they "burn a thank-offering of leaven," he plainly does so in an unfavourable sense. Now according to Lev. ii. 11 the leaven forbidden in fire-offerings includes not only yeast but grape-honey (*debásh*, the modern *dibs*). We are therefore justified in connecting the expression with the grape-cakes (אשׁישׁי ענבים) in Hosea iii. 1, which the prophet sarcastically says that the false gods love, implying that they were offered to them on the altar. For the *ashîshîm* are pressed cakes, and so plainly identical with the Syriac *ḥ'bîçê* (Bernstein, *Chrest.*, p. 2), composed of meal, oil, and *dibs*. These sweet cakes appear in connection with a sacrificial feast in 2 Sam. vi. 19, Heb., but the presentation of them on the altar appears to have been regarded as one of the Dionysiac features of the Baal-worship with which in the eighth century the religion of Jehovah had been mixed. An anti-Dionysiac element appears also in the vow of the Nazarites, to whom Amos attaches weight as representatives of true religion (Amos ii. 11 ; comp. ii. 8 ; Hos. iv. 11). The point is interesting as an early indication of the line of thought which underlies the ritual observances of holiness in the Deuteronomic Code.

LECTURE XII.

NOTE 1, p. 358.—Exod. xx. 26 is addressed not to the priests but to Israel at large, and implies that any Israelite may approach the altar. Comp. Exod. xxi. 14, and contrast Num. iv. 15, xviii. 3. That the old law allows any Israelite to approach the altar appears most clearly from the prohibition of an altar with steps, lest the worshipper should expose his person to the holy structure. In the case of the Levitical priests this danger was provided against in another way, by the use of linen breeches (Exod. xxviii. 43). In the case of the brazen altar, which was five feet high, or of Solomon's huge altar, ten cubits in height, there must have been steps of some kind (Lev. ix. 22), and for Ezekiel's altar (xliii. 17) this is expressly stated. The important distinction between the altars of Exod. xx., which are approached by laymen in their ordinary dress, and the brazen altar approached by priests protected against exposure by their special costume, was not understood by the later Jews, and consequently it was held that the prohibition of steps (*ma'alôt*) did not prevent the use of an ascent of some other kind—as for example a sloping bridge or mound (see the Targum of Jonathan on our passage, and also Rashi's Commentary). In the second Temple, the altar was a vast platform of unhewn stone approached by a sloping ascent (Joseph., *B. J.*, Lib. v., cap. 5, § 6 ; Mishna, *Zebachim* v., *Tamid* i. 4). But the expression *ma'alôt* seems to cover all kinds of ascent, and the risk of exposing the person *to the altar* would be unaffected by the nature of the ascent. In fact with a large altar the priest could not put the blood of a victim on the four horns without standing and walking on the altar (*Zebachim*, l. c.), which is clearly against the spirit of Exod. xx., except on the understanding that that law does not apply to priests appropriately clad for the office.

NOTE 2, p. 360.—I give here some fuller details of the evidence on this important topic.

1°. Except in the Levitical legislation and in Chronicles, Ezra,

and Nehemiah, where the *usus loquendi* is conformed to the final
form of the Pentateuchal ordinance, Levite never means a sacred
minister who is not a priest, and has not the right to offer
sacrifice. On the contrary, Levite is regularly used as a priestly
title. See the list of texts in Wellhausen, *Geschichte*, p. 150. The
only passage to the contrary is 1 Kings viii. 4, where "the priests
and the Levites" appear instead of "the Levite priests." But
here the particle "and"—a single letter in Hebrew—appears to
be an insertion in accordance with the later law. The Chronicler
still reads the verse without the "and" (2 Chron. v. 5). The
older books know a distinction between the high priest and lower
priests (*e.g.* 1 Sam. ii. 35, 36), but all alike are priests, that is,
do sacrifice, wear the ephod, etc. The priesthood is God's gift
to Levi (Deut. x. 8, xviii. 1, xxi. 5, xxxiii. 8 *seq.*), and Jeroboam's
fault, according to 1 Kings xii. 31, was that he chose priests who
were not Levites. From the first, no doubt, there must have been
a difference between the chief priest of the ark (Aaron, Eli,
Abiathar, Zadok) and his subordinate brethren, but there is no
trace of such a distinction as is made in the Levitical law.

2°. Ezekiel knows nothing of Levites who were not priests in
time past; he knows only the Zadokite Levites, the priests of the
Temple, and other Levites who had formerly been priests, but
are to be degraded under the new temple, because they had
ministered in the idolatrous shrines of the local high places.
The usual explanation that these Levites were the sons of
Ithamar is impossible. For the guild of Ithamar appears only
after the Exile as the name of a subordinate family of priests who
were never degraded as the prophet prescribes. Moreover, Ezek.
xlviii. 11-13 clearly declares that all Levites but the Zadokites
shall be degraded. Ezekiel's Levites are the priests of the local
high places whom Josiah brought to Jerusalem, and who were
supported there on offerings which the non-priestly Levites under
the Levitical law had no right to eat.

3°. In Deuteronomy all Levitical functions are priestly, and to
these functions the whole tribe was chosen (x. 8, xxi. 5). The
summary of Levitical functions in x. 1 is (1) *to carry the ark*,
which in old Israel was a priestly function (Lect. IX. note 7); (2)
to stand before Jehovah and minister to Him. This expression invariably denotes priesthood proper; see especially Ezek. xliv. 13,
15; Jer. xxxiii. 18, 21, 22. The Levites of the later law minister
not to God but to Aaron, Num. iii. 6; (3) *to bless in Jehovah's*

name. This in the Levitical law is the office of Aaron and his sons (Num. vi.). Accordingly in Deut. xviii. 1 *seq.,* the whole tribe of Levi has a claim on the altar gifts, the first-fruits and other priestly offerings, and any Levite can actually gain a share in these by going to Jerusalem and doing priestly service. In the Levitical law common Levites have no share in these revenues, but are nourished by the tithes and live in Levitical cities. There were no Levitical cities in this sense in the time of the Deuteronomist, for all those mentioned in Joshua—in passages which are really part of the Levitical law—lay outside the kingdom of Judah. And Deuteronomy knows nothing of a Levitical tithe, though it could not have failed to be mentioned in chap. xviii. if it had existed. The Levite who is not in service at the sanctuary is always represented as a needy sojourner, without visible means of support, and this agrees with Judges xvii. 7, 8 ; 1 Sam. ii. 36.

That the priesthood of Dan was a Levitical priesthood descended from Moses is generally admitted. In Judges xviii. 30, the N which changes Moses to Manasseh is inserted above the line thus : משה, Moses ; מנשה, Manasseh. The reading of our English Bible was therefore a correction in the archetype (*supra,* p. 70). On the whole subject of the Levites before the Exile, see especially Graf in Merx's *Archiv,* i. ; Kuenen, *Theol. Tijdschr.,* 1872 ; and Wellhausen, *Gesch.,* Kap. iv.

NOTE 3, p. 366.—For the detailed proof of these statements see my article in the *Journal of Philology,* vol. ix. p. 97 *seq.* If the אחד of Isa. lxvi. 17 is Adonis (Lagarde, *Hieron. Qu. Heb.,* p. 72 ; Leipz., 1868), the eating of swine's flesh is the well-known custom of devouring the hostile totem. But see against this Cheyne, *Isaiah* (ii. 124). In other cases the rite consisted in the sacramental use of one's own totem. To the animal gods mentioned in my essay add the quail-god Eshmûn (Lagarde, *Proverbien,* p. 81), from whom Delos takes the name Ortygia.

No doubt some of the laws of abstinence simply expressed natural feelings of disgust at vile things, and became sacred on the principle explained at p. 378. Compare in the Arabic field, the disgust at locusts, *Div. Hodh.* 116, 1, in Nöldeke's transl. of Tabary, p. 203. The lizard was not eaten in Mecca ; Bokhâry, vi. 190 (Bûlâq ed.). The law against eating blood may be compared with the objection of some Arabs to eat a heart, Wüstenfeld, *Register,* 407. The most curious law of food is the prohibition of seething a kid in its mother's milk, common to the first code and Deuteronomy. As early sacrifices were boiled, the ordinance means that the sacrifice must not be boiled in milk, which from the fermenting quality of the latter may be a variety of the law against leaven in ritual. Milk, no doubt, was generally eaten in a sour form (Arabic *aqit*, Bokhâry, vi. 193). "Its mother's milk," as the Jewish tradition recognises, means simply goat's milk, which was that in general use (Prov. xxvii. 27).

NOTE 4, p. 369. See *Journal of Philology, ut supra*, pp. 86, 94; Pococke, *Specimen* (ed. White), p. 325; Abu'l Sa'ûd, *Tafsîr*, i. 284; Shahrastâny, *Milal wa-niḥal*, p. 440. Examples in *Kitâb el Agh.* i. 9, 10; Sprenger, *Leb. Moh.*, i. 86, 133. I reserve for future publication extracts from Tabary's Com. on the Koran (MS. of the Vice-regal library in Cairo) and from the *Asbâb* of El Wâḥidy (MS. of A.H. 627, *penes me*). The advance in the laws of forbidden degrees from the Deuteronomic Code through the " Framework " (Deut. xxvii.) and Ezekiel (xxii. 10, 11) to the full Levitical law is one of the clearest proofs of the true order of succession in the Pentateuchal laws. Marriage with a half-sister was known among the Phœnicians in the time of Achilles Tatius, and indeed forbidden marriages, including that with a father's wife, seem to have been practised pretty openly in Roman Syria down to the fifth Christian century. See Bruns and Sachau, *Syrisch-Römisches Rechtsbuch*, p. 30 (Leipz., 1880).

NOTE 5, p. 382.—The original meaning of *kapper*, to atone, is still disputed. Wellhausen, in his important note on the subject (*Geschichte*, p. 66), starts from Gen. xxxii. 20 [21], "I will *kapper* his face with the present," and compares Gen. xx. 16, Job. ix. 24. But the sense "cover" will not explain Isa. xxviii. 18, where, on the contrary, the verb has its well-known Syriac sense, ἐκμάσσειν; Harkl. John xi. 2, xii. 3, xiii. 5; Syro-Hex., Ep. Jer. xiii. 24; Hoffmann's Bar Ali, 5924. Thus חלה פנים=כפר פנים, to smooth (wipe) the face, blackened or contracted with displeasure. The religious sense, as Wellhausens admits, does not start from the idea of covering the face. Except in the Levitical Law, it is God who *kipper* (wipes out) sin, so that מחה=כפר (I note in passing that מחה strike, has nothing to do with מחה, wipe, but is Aramaic מחא for מחיץ=מחע, with softening of ע after ח). This notion of God

LECT. XII.   *ATONEMENT.*   439

wiping out sin is the pure religious idea of atonement, as we find it in the Prophets, without any relation to sacrifice. But in common life an offence was blotted out by payment of compensation, as we see in the First Legislation, and this payment, which made the score between the two men a *tabula rasa*, was called *kôpher*. For certain offences, apparently, the payment was made to the judge at the sanctuary (2 Kings xii. 16, Amos ii. 8); or a sacrifice was offered (1 Sam. iii. 14) which, on the oldest way of thought, was a gift to appease the Divine anger (1 Sam. xxvi. 19, compare with Psalm xlv. 12 [13]). Illegitimate payment to a judge to make him ignore an offence is equally *kôpher*, and in the then state of justice was perhaps the commonest application of the word; but this does not lie in the original idea—*kôpher* is simply the compensation which, in a primitive form of the law, is the equivalent of an offence. The conception that sin demands a compensation paid to the Divine judge at the sanctuary is then combined, in bloody atoning sacrifices, with the notion of presenting a life to God. This idea, again, has a simpler and a more complicated form. In the simpler form the life of the sacrifice is simply returned to God, because it belongs to Him. But in other forms of ritual the blood, which is assumed to be living blood, is applied not only to the altar, but to the worshipper. So we find it in the covenant sacrifice, Exod. xxiv. 8, and in forms of consecration, Lev. viii. 23, xiv. 6, 14. The parallel to this is the Arabic ceremony, in which contracting parties dip their hands in a pan of blood, and are called "blood-lickers" (Ibn Hishâm, 125). Here, as in many similar ceremonies among early peoples, the bond of blood is a living bond of brotherhood. So consecration by blood is consecration in a living union to Jehovah. In the ordinary atoning sacrifices the blood is not applied to the people; but in the higher forms, as in the sacrifice for the whole congregation (Lev. iv. 13 *seq.*), the priest at least dips his hand in it, and so puts the bond of blood between himself, as the people's representative, and the altar, as the point of contact with God. Another form of atoning ceremony, in which a live goat or bird is charged to bear away sin or leprous impurity (Lev. xvi. 22, xiv. 7), is a natural symbolic action similar to that in which in old Arabia a live bird was made to fly away with the impurity of a woman's widowhood. The bird, it is added, died. See Lane, s.v. *faḍḍa* VIII., and an Assyrian analogy, *Records of the Past*, ix. 151. We see then that the ultimate form of the atoning ritual, as it is found in the day of atonement, is a combination of many different points of view—satisfaction to the Judge at the sanctuary, the renovation of a covenant of life with God, the banishment of sin from His presence and land (comp. Micah vii. 19).

NOTE 6, p. 383.—One of the chief innovations of the ritual law is the increased provision for the priesthood. This occurs in two ways. In the first place they receive a larger share in the gifts which on the old usage were the material of feasts at the sanctuary. In Deuteronomy the firtslings are eaten by the worshipper at the annual feasts, the priest of course receiving the usual share of each victim. But in Num. xviii. 18 they belong entirely and absolutely to the priest. This difference cannot be explained away, for according to Deut. xiv. 24 the firstlings might be turned into money, and materials of a feast bought with them. But in Num. xviii. 17 it is forbidden to redeem any firstling fit for sacrifice. Again, in Deuteronomy the produce of the soil, but not of the herd, was tithed for the religious use of the owner, who ate the tithes at the feasts. But in the Levitical law the tithe includes the herd and the flock (Lev. xxvii. 32), and is a tribute paid to the Levites, who in turn pay a tithe to the priests (Num. xviii.). This is quite distinct from the Deuteronomic poor-rate or tithe of the third year, which was stored in each township and eaten by dependents where it was stored (Deut. xxvi. 12, 13, where for *brought away* read *consumed*: the tithe was consumed where it lay; see ver. 14 Heb.). The Levitical tithe might be eaten by the Levites where they pleased, and in later times was stored in the Temple. It appears to take the place under the hierarchy of the old tithe paid to the king (1 Sam. viii. 15, 17). Once more, the priest's share of a sacrifice in Deuteronomy consists of inferior parts, the head and maw, which in Arabia are still the butcher's fee, and the shoulder, which is not the choicest joint (Pseudo-Wâkidy, p. 15, and Hamaker's note). In fact Exod. xii. 9 requires to make special provision that the head and inwards be not left uneaten in the paschal lamb, which proves that they were not esteemed. But in the Levitical law the priests' part is the breast and the leg (not as E. V. the shoulder), which is the best part (1 Sam. ix. 24).

In the second place, the Levitical law, following a hint of Ezekiel (xlv. 4, 5), assigns towns and pasture grounds to the priests and Levites. The list of such towns in Josh. xxi. is part of the

Levitical law and not of the old history. In ancient times many of these towns certainly did not belong either to priests or Levites. Gezer was not conquered till the time of Solomon (1 Kings ix. 16). Shechem, Gibeon, and Hebron had quite a different population in the time of the Judges. Anathoth was a priestly city, but its priests held land on terms quite different from those of the later law (Lect. IX. note 7).

On the Levitical modifications of the festivals, see Hupfeld, *De primitiva et vera festorum ratione*, Partic. I., II., Halle, 1852; Partic. III., 1858; Appendix, 1865; and Wellhausen, *Geschichte*, Kap. iii.

NOTE 7, p. 387.—The application of this principle may be extended to the Levitical parts of the book of Joshua, *e.g.*, as we saw in last note, to the list of Levitical cities. In recent controversy in Scotland it has often been affirmed that Josh. xxii. proves that the Deuteronomic law was known to Joshua. If that narrative does assume the later law, this, in face of the evidence already adduced, would only prove that the chapter, or part of it, is one of those interpolations which have been shown above to exist in several parts of the Old Testament. Hollenberg has proved with the aid of the LXX. that there are such interpolations in Joshua, *e.g.* one from Neh. xi. in chap. xv., and another, mainly borrowed from Deuteronomy, in xx. 3-6. But in fact the altar was not a local altar under Exod. xx., for it lay on the west of the Jordan and was of huge size, whereas the old law only allows small altars without steps. The whole narrative is puzzling, but the speeches in their present form must be late, for at ver. 28 the altar is said to be constructed on the תבנית, manner of building, of the altar before the *mishkan*. *Mishkan*, which means the divine dwelling, is a word of the Levitical law and the second Temple, and the altar in the author's mind is not the small brazen altar of the tabernacle, which was not built, but the huge stone altar of the second Temple.

INDEX.

AKIBA, 75, 174, 399.
Al-taschith, 190.
Altar, early importance of the, 224; as asylum, 336, 341, 353; of Ahaz, 253; of second Temple, 435; with steps, *ib.*; law of one altar, 233, 352; consecration of the, 376.
Amos, 274, 280, 341.
Ancient poetry, transmission of, 198.
Anonymous books, 107.
Antilegomena in the O. T., 153, 170 *seq.*
Antiochus Epiphanes, 82.
Apocrypha, 40, 42, 134 *seq.*, 172; value of, 138.
Aquila, 76, 391, 399.
Arabic customs, retaliation, 336; firstlings, 340; marriage law, 368; warfare, *ib.*; sacred lot, 429; widowhood, 368, 439; Dakhîl, 434; use of animal food, 424.
Aramaic, 48, 193.
Archetype of Old Testament, 74.
Ark, 117; at Shiloh, 258; not mentioned in Deuteronomic Code, 357; precedes the host, 319, 432; borne by priests, 427.
Asaph and Korah, Psalms of, 194.
Ashēra, 226, 353.
Astruc, 325, 419.
Atonement, note on, 438; great day of, 376, 377.

BAAL, 79; Tyrian, 222; local Baalim, 229.
Bensly, Mr., 407.
Bible, Hebrew, arrangement of, 130, 131; Protestant translations of, 30 *seq.*

Biblical books, often anonymous, 107 *seq.*; titles of, 107.
Blood not to be eaten, 236, 341.

CANON, ecclesiastical, 35 *seq.*; the, 132 *seq.*; left open by Calvin, 42; history of, 149; and tradition, 168, 169.
Canticles, 173.
Cappellus, Ludovicus, 86.
Carians, 249.
Chronicles, 168, 219, 266; compared with Kings, 420 *seq.*
Copyists, early, 106.
Covenant, Mosaic, 299, 331; Josiah's, 245; Ezra's, 55 *seq.*
Criminal laws, 336, 367.

DAN, Sanctuary of, 227; priesthood in, 359, 437.
David and Goliath, 125; Saul's hostility to, 128.
Davidic Psalms, 192, 200.
Daniel, Book of, 168, 171.
Decadence of Israel, 344 *seq.*; causes of, 347.
Deuteronomic code, 317; basis of Josiah's reformation, 246; relation to Isaiah, 354, 365; not forged by Hilkiah, 362; laws of sanctity, 365; civil laws of, 367.
Divination, 277 *seq.*; and prophecy, 281.

Ecclesiastes, 172 *seq.*
Ecclesiasticus, 132, 144.
Eli, House of, 256, 359.
Ephod, 220, 226, 423.
2 Esdras, 131, 149, 155, 407.
Esther, 171, 172.

Exegesis, Protestant and Catholic, 31, 32.
Exodus xxi.-xxiii., 316, 336 seq.
Ezekiel xliv., 249, 425; His Torah, 374 seq.; controversy as to his book, 410.
Ezra, the Scribe, 55, 158; book of, 131, 170.

FEASTS, annual, 257, 338, 341, 371.
First Legislation, the, 316, 336 seq.
Flood, the, 327 seq.
Forgeries of books, 25, 157 seq.

GÊR, 337, 434.
Great Synagogue, 156, 408.

HAGGADA, 58, 168, 410.
Hagiographa, 130, 160, 166.
Halacha, 58, 64, 168, 174.
Hasmonean dynasty, 63.
Hebrew, so called in the New Testament, 47, 48; vowel points and accents, 50; Bible, MSS. of, represent the same text, 69.
Hercules, pillars of, 248.
Hezekiah, 351, 354, 357.
Higher Criticism, 104, 105.
High places, 221, 225, 227, 235, 265; abolished by Josiah, 245, 351 seq.; in Deuteronomy, 352 seq.; priests of, 245, 360, 375, 476.
Hillel, 75, 172.
Historians, method of Eastern, 325.
Holiness, in Pentateuch, 209 seq.; in Deuteronomy, 365 seq.; in Ezekiel, 378 seq.; Isaiah's doctrine of, 364.
Hyrcanus, John, 65, 144.

IDOLATRY, 228, 230, 355.
Isaiah, attacks the idols, 355; sanctity of Zion, 355 seq.; his doctrine of holiness, 364.
Isaiah, Book of, 109.
Ishbosheth or Eshbaal, 78, 79.

JASHAR, Book of, 403.
Jehoiada, 247.
Jehovah (Iahwè), 186, 231, 423.
Jeremiah, Chaps. l., li., 112, 402;
Chap. xxvii., 113 seq.; prophecies of, against the nations, 118.
Jerome, 36, 40, 41, 69, 132, 392.
Josephus and the Canon, 149, 408.
Jubilees, Book of, 73, 74, 98, 132, 149.
Judges, Age of the, 220, 255.

KABBALA, 146, 160.
Kadhi of the Arabs, 300, 319.
Kemarîm, 246.
Kerethim and Pelethim, 249.
Keri and Kethib, 71.
Kid in mother's milk, 438.
Kimhi, Rabbi David, 43, 44.
Kings, Books of, 123 seq.

LAW, function of the, 269, 312 seq.; Pauline view of, 314.
Law, Oral, 60 seq., 146.
Law, Prophets, and Psalms, The, 164.
Leaven in sacrifice, 341, 434.
Legal Fictions, 385 seq.
Levites, 358 seq.
Levitical law, its system, 209 seq., 231 seq.; unknown to Josiah, 246; in Solomon's temple, 248 seq.; at Shiloh, 257 seq.; to Samuel, 261 seq.; to the prophets, 287 seq.
Levitical law-book, 317 seq.; later than Ezekiel, 375 seq.; origin of, 383 seq.

MACCABEE PSALMS, 196, 413.
Maççēba, 226, 353 seq.
Maine, Sir H., 385, 386.
Marriages, mixed, 254, 269; ancient marriage laws, 270, 368, 438.
Massorets, 72.
Meturgeman, 48, 135, 393.
Midrash, 135, 420.
Mishna, 63, 396.
Morinus, John, 86.
Moses, Judge and Lawgiver, 300, 334; his writings, 320, 331; Law of, meaning of the phrase, 309 seq., 385 seq.

NEHEMIAH, 56, 157; his book, 107, 140.

INDEX.   445

OLD TESTAMENT, standard text of, 74-76, 80, 81.
Origen and his Hexapla, 103, 392.

PENTATEUCH, contains several distinct codes, 316; not written by Moses, 320 *seq.;* sources of, 324; composite structure of, 325 *seq.;* Samaritan, 73; in the Synagogue, 96, 160.
Pharisees, 59, 61 *seq.*, 395.
Philo, 136, 402, 428.
Pirkè Aboth, 151, 394.
Poll tax, 64, 376.
Precedents, legal, 300, 318.
Priests, 358; revenues of, 252, 440.
Prophecy, cessation of, 142.
Prophets, their work, 271; mark of true prophets, 274; Canaanite, 279; professional, 280; consecration of, 282; prophets and priests, 285; their inspiration, 289 *seq.;* writings of, 296; their doctrine of forgiveness, 301; not politicians, 349; their ideal, 283, 294, 350; canon of the, 161.
Proverbs, Book of, 121, 122, 403.
Psalms, titles of, 110, 111, 190; text of, 182; five books of, 184; Davidic, 185, 192, 199 *seq.*, 202 *seq.;* Elohistic, 186; Levitical, 188; age of, 189; typology of, 206; imprecatory, 207.
Psalm li., 416; lxxxvi., 413.
Psalter, the, 163, 176 *seq.*
Psalmody, early, in Israel, 204 *seq.*
Puncta Extraordinaria, 70 *seq.*

RASHI, Rabbi Solomon of Troyes, 44.
Redaction, editorial, 112, 113.
Reformation, the, 11 *seq.*
Reformers, scholarship of, 44, 45.
Religion, tribal or national, 271; popular, of Israel, 222, 272 *seq.;* prophetic, 273, 282.
Reuchlin, John, 43.
Retaliation, law of, 336, 367.
Revelation, the record of, 16, 139; close of the age of, 140 *seq.;* Jewish theory of, 144, 145.

SACRED DUES, 338, 370, 440.
Sacrifice, Pentateuchal law of, unknown to Amos, 238, 287; to Jeremiah, 287 *seq.;* atoning, 210, 372, 376, 381; by laymen, 248, 264, 358; stated sacrifice, 234, 375, 383.
Sacrificial feasts, 236, 338.
Sadducees, 395.
Samaritans, 73, 398.
Samuel, 259 *seq.; Books of*, 94-96.
Sanctuary as seat of judgment, 334, 358, 367; plurality of sanctuaries in the old law, 338; abolished in Deuteronomy, 352 *seq.*
Sanhedrin, 62.
Scribes, and Pharisees, 54, 55 *seq.;* work of, 57; guilds of, 57; altered Pentateuchal laws, 65; the, as critics, 67 *seq.*, 77.
Septuagint, 33, 84 *seq.*, 99; an independent witness as to the text, 85; value of, 88; its variations from the Hebrew, 88-90, 103-130; Jewish estimate of, 101, 102.
Shaddai, 423.
Shiloh, Temple of, 256 *seq.*
Sin and trespass money, 251, 372.
Songs of degrees, or pilgrimage songs, 191.
Square characters not introduced by Ezra, 81.
Syncretism, 228, 353.

TABERNACLE or Tent of Meeting, 232.
Targums, 70, 399.
Temple of Solomon, 248 *seq.*, 373.
Teraphim, 227, 423.
Tikkunê Sôpherîm, 78, 400.
Torah, meaning of, 292 *seq.;* prophetic, 293 *seq.;* Divine, 334 *seq.;* Mosaic, 297; priestly, 293, 372, 384; Ezekiel's, 374 *seq.;* Jewish estimate of, 145 *seq.*
Tradition of the Scribes, 52, 53.
Traditional Law, growth of, 60, 61.

Traditional theory of O. T. history, 208 *seq.*
Trent, Council of, 37, 38.

UNCLEAN animals, 365.
Unpointed text, 49 *seq.*
Urijah, 253.
Urim and Thummim, 428.

VOWEL points and accents, 72.

WORSHIP, notion of, 223; popular in Israel, 225 *seq.*, 241 *seq.*; under the Second Temple, 239, 380.

ZADOKITES, 254, 359, 374, 427.

THE END.

www.ingramcontent.com/pod-product-compliance
Lightning Source LLC
Chambersburg PA
CBHW071234300426
44116CB00008B/1027